How Nations Behave

COUNCIL ON FOREIGN RELATIONS BOOKS

The Council on Foreign Relations, Inc. is a non-profit and non-partisan organization devoted to promoting improved understanding of international affairs through the free exchange of ideas. Its membership of about 1,700 persons throughout the United States is made up of individuals with special interest and experience in international affairs. The Council has no affiliation with, and receives no funding from, the United States government. The Council does not take any position on questions of foreign policy.

The Council publishes the quarterly journal, *Foreign Affairs*. In addition, from time to time, books and monographs written by members of the council's research staff or visiting fellows, or commissioned by the Council, or (like this book) written by an independent author with critical review contributed by a Council study group, are published with the designation "Council on Foreign Relations Book" or "Council Paper on International Affairs." Any book or monograph bearing that designation is, in the judgment of the Committee on Studies of the Council's board of directors, a responsible treatment of a significant international topic worthy of presentation to the public. All statements of fact and expressions of opinion contained in Council books, monographs, and *Foreign Affairs* articles are, however, the sole responsibility of their authors.

HOW NATIONS BEHAVE

BEHAVE

Law and Foreign Policy

second
edition

LOUIS HENKIN

Published for the
COUNCIL ON FOREIGN RELATIONS
by COLUMBIA UNIVERSITY PRESS
New York 1979

Library of Congress Cataloging in Publication Data

Henkin, Louis.
    How nations behave.

    Includes bibliographical references and index.
        1. International law.   2. International relations.
    I. Title.
JX1395.H45   1979   341   79-1015
ISBN 0-231-04756-8
ISBN 0-231-04757-6 pbk.

To My Father, 1881–1973
Who All His Days Loved Law,
Sought Peace And Pursued It*

Psalms 34: 12–14

contents

Law has suffered many definitions and all of them proclaim the law's many lives. International law, on the other hand, has not been unduly troubled in definition, but it must still constantly defend its existence. Even more earnestly must it defend its relevance to world events.

Open any volume, scholarly or lay, on foreign policy or international relations: the probabilities are high that the index will contain no reference to international law and that the text itself will give to law only passing mention at most. If the volume contains substantial treatment of any important international event or institution—say, the United Nations—it will hardly be noted that the event or the institution may rest on a legal document and may have produced an extensive field of law. Books on international law, in their turn, usually say little about the international society in which that law operates, about the nations and the relations between nations which that law orders, about the national interests and policies which that law furthers.

There have been studies of Law in Diplomacy,* of Theory and Reality in International Law,† of the Political Foundations of International Law.‡ Others, indeed, have seen the law wholly as part of the political process.§ There has been no attempt, so far as I know, to focus on the influence of law on how nations behave, on their national policies and their international actions.

How nations behave, in regard to international law, is the principal focus of this book. Jurisprudential discussion and other suggestions about the character of law are incidental to the key question: in what ways does international law determine, or govern, or modify, the policies of governments and how nations behave toward each other? The reader with general interest in law or in foreign relations will, I expect, move quickly past the occasional paragraphs addressed particularly to those with scholarly or professional preoccupations. I hope that the latter, in turn, will forgive me for catering to the general reader who tends to be distracted by the *impedimenta* of scholarship: I have limited explicit cross-reference and have placed at the back of the book notes containing supporting authorities and specialized information or comment. "Footnotes"—at the bottom of the page—are generally substantive in character and parenthetical to the text.

I have learned and profited much from the volumes I have mentioned, and from others cited in the footnotes and backnotes of this volume, even from those with which I do not agree. I have also had the benefit of advice and criticism from several who have read the manuscript, in particular from members of the staff of the Council on Foreign Relations, and from a group of friends generously convoked by the Council for my guidance. The reader will be thankful, as I am, to my editors, Elisabeth Sifton and Robert Valkenier, who have done much to make this book more readable.

Very valuable has been the support—financial, moral, and intel-

---

* By P. Corbett (1959).
† C. de Visscher, *Théories et Réalités en Droit International Public* (2d ed., 1955).
‡ By M. Kaplan and N. Katzenbach (1961).
§ See M. McDougal, "International Law, Power and Policy: A Contemporary Conception," cited below, Chapter 3, n. 2.

lectual—of my friend and colleague Professor William T. R. Fox, Director of the Institute of War and Peace Studies at Columbia University. I am grateful also to Paul Sherman, class of 1968 at the Columbia University Law School and the School of International Affairs, who assisted me in research. (At various times I was also assisted by other students at the Columbia Law School: Wayne Gehring, Rena Gordon, and Gerald Secundy.)

Many of the chapters of this volume, in a previous version, were delivered in July 1965 before the Hague Academy of International Law, where I was "Carnegie Lecturer," designated by the Carnegie Endowment for International Peace. The text of the original lectures appears in the *Recueil des Cours* of the Academy.* I am grateful to the Academy's Curatorium for permission to adapt them for this volume.†

June, 1967   LOUIS HENKIN

*"International Law and The Behavior of Nations," 114 *Recueil des Cours* 167 (1965).

† With the permission of the copyright owners, I have also drawn on two published articles: "Force, Intervention and Neutrality in Contemporary International Law," *Proceedings of the American Society of International Law* 147–62, 165–69 (1963); "The United Nations and Its Supporters: A Self-Examination," 78 *Pol. Sci. Q.* 504 (December 1963).

In introducing this study I note (p. 7): "Any inquiry into the role of law must take into account the state of 'the system'—the character of international society and of the law at a given time."

The decade since the first edition has seen transforming changes in international society and its institutions, and some in international law. There are ever new, ever more awesome developments in strategic weapons, and small efforts to control them. Nuclear proliferation is upon us, and competition to sell and buy sophisticated arms is acute and widespread. The confrontation between the United States and the Soviet Union (and their allies) that dominated international politics after the Second World War has been reshaped into an irregular triangle with the People's Republic of China, with other countries in modified relations to them. Nuclear "balance" and big-power competition and other political deterrents have rendered military force by the big powers largely unusable or ineffective and have liberated and enhanced other influences and other actors—geographic advantage, monopoly of scarce resources (e.g., oil), the numbers and solidarity of "the Third World" and its abilities to attract big-power support.

In the final quarter of the twentieth century the character and significance of international law, I believe, will be importantly influenced by the Third World. That includes more than 100 states, a large majority of the units of the system, with voices, and votes, and national practices that can effectively reject old law and build new law. The aspirations, the ideas and the rhetoric of the new majority—"self-determination," "the elimination of all forms of racial discrimination," "the common heritage of mankind" (in the seabed), "the new economic order"—have become political currency and are shaping and reshaping the effective law. The solidarity of the Third World, and the divisions between North and South that have become the new ideological conflict cutting across that earlier one between East and West, have complicated the political forces that shape international law and determine how nations behave in respect of law.

Important events have both reflected and contributed to these changes, and have had their own direct impact on international law and politics: the birth of Bangladesh attended by a Pakistan-India War, a third war in the Middle-East, another Cyprus crisis in 1974, the extrication of the United States from Vietnam, civil war and foreign intervention in Lebanon and in Angola, the intensifying struggle against white rule in Rhodesia and Namibia and against *apartheid* in South Africa, modified relations regionally and with big powers in the Middle East and about the Horn of Africa, international changes of international import in Portugal and Spain, in Chile, in Ethiopia, new hostilities in Vietnam-Cambodia-China.

With the changing complexion of the system came a drive by the new majority to re-examine the legal system, to make new law outlawing colonialism and racism, to transform or modify other law of interest to them, particularly that relating to economic relations. The enlarged number of states in the system, and the redistribution of effective influence in it, also complicated efforts to make new law of universal interest, and brought various challenges to the commitment to law. For years, states struggled to develop a new law which would accommodate the exclusive and the common interests of states in the sea. The effort to control hijacking and other forms of terrorism by international agreements was seriously weakened by the refusal of some states to adhere to them. Politicization of legal issues in the United Nations has weakened the organization's effectiveness for enforcing the law of the Charter outlawing force and the special law of human rights.

The changes in the character, condition and prospects of international society have required important modifications in this volume, and further reflection and the criticism of friends have suggested others.* I have restructured and updated, provided new examples. How nations behave in economic relations is given more attention and prominence. A few sentences have been expanded into a new chapter on the politics of law-making, and several new chapters consider the politics of trying to make new law in the world of the last quarter of the century, notably the long, complex, effort to achieve a new law of the sea and the Third World's demand for a New Economic Charter. I single out for emphasis the special character of the international law of human rights and of the politics of inducing adherence to and compliance with that law. Part Four, "The Law in Operation," now includes the case of Vietnam. My reflections on the tension between lawyer and diplomat, my perspectives on the prospects for order and law in international relations, are of more recent date and about a changed world.†

---

* Between the first and the revised editions there have appeared several volumes addressing the questions in the field in different ways, *e.g.*, *The Relevance of International Law*, K. Deutsch and S. Hoffman, eds., (1968); *The Effectiveness of International Decisions*, S. Schwebel, ed., (1971).

The American Society of International Law has sponsored three studies on International Crises and the Role of Law: R. Bowie, *Suez 1956* (1974); A. Chayes, *The Cuban Missile Crisis* (1974); T. Ehrlich, *Cyprus 1958–1967* (1974). A "covering" essay by R. Fisher is anticipated.

† For this edition, I have drawn also on articles published in the interim, *i.e.*, "The Politics of Law Making: Changing Law for the Changing Seas," *Political Science Quarterly*, March 1974; "The United States and the Crisis in Human Rights," 14 *Va. J. Int'l L.* 653 (1974); "Human Rights and 'Domestic Jurisdiction',"

In preparing this edition I have again had the editorial assistance of Robert Valkenier, which I gratefully acknowledge.

LOUIS HENKIN

in *Human Rights, International Law and the Helsinki Accord*, T. Buergenthal, ed., (1977); "Human Rights: Reappraisal and Readjustment," in *Essays on Human Rights, Contemporary Issues and Jewish Perspectives*, D. Sidorsky, ed. (1979); also a book, *The Rights of Man Today* (1978). I am grateful to the copyright owners for permission to do so.

introduction

In relations between nations, the progress of civilization may be seen as movement from force to diplomacy, from diplomacy to law.* The hope of civilized men has long been that nations would cease to pursue their interests by force, and attempt instead to negotiate in quest of agreement. Some have hoped, too, that sufficient consensus might grow to support norms of wide acceptability; in time, consensus might achieve that sense of obligation and habit of compliance, that confident expectation and reliance on the part of others, perhaps even those institutions for inducing or compelling conformity, which we associate with law and which promote—and reflect—stability and order.

> *Throughout I frequently refer to "nations" even where, strictly, the lawyer and the political scientist would insist on "states." I borrow this convenience from them for both use "international" (instead of "interstate") to modify both "law" and "relations." (This is common usage, and avoids confusion between the states of international society and the states of the United States.)

Faith in the suggested progression persists; but to date, one must admit, the history of international relations hardly presents an encouraging "progress report." As the daily press proclaims, we are not yet out of the age of force—witness the conflicts, since the last world war, in the Middle East, Korea, the Asian subcontinent, Indochina, and increasingly in Africa; surely there is yet no general rule of law in international society. The end of the Second World War did indeed promise a new birth of law, epitomized in the United Nations Charter. But intervening years have brought disillusionment and skepticism; the drive toward law appears spent or even reversed. New law has been hard to come by; old law has been unmade. Some questions that once seemed governed by law are now decided unilaterally as matters of national policy. International adjudication has not become an important force in international life. Nations today promote their interests principally by *ad hoc* negotiation, influence, compromise, political accommodation. Relations between nations are primarily the responsibility neither of generals nor of judges; they remain the domain of diplomacy between representatives of nations promoting national policies.

Of course, force, diplomacy, and law do not represent discrete stages in international history. They have long coexisted, waxing and waning, in different "proportions" at different times, among different nations in different contexts. Force and diplomacy have both been with us from the beginning of "nations," peoples, tribes. For several hundred years—in some senses much longer—there has also been international law. Today, international law is taught in the universities, practiced by lawyers, weighed by foreign offices, invoked by governments in relations with other governments. About the scope of international law, however, about its role in international relations, about its influence in the foreign policies of nations, there is little agreement and, I dare say, little learning and much misunderstanding.

In general, the student of foreign affairs is skeptical about international law, and fulsome claims in its behalf tend to make him cynical. When he thinks of law at all, he sees it in the main as an esoteric subject for academic speculation by wishful professors, with little relevance to affairs between nations. He is aware that governments frequently talk about international law and sometimes invoke it to justify themselves or to attack others; that appears to him as formal incantation and tactical rhetoric. Even friends of international order whisper that there *really* is no international law. As for the diplomat and the maker of foreign policy, they do not appear to consider international law important.[1] International law is convenient for formalizing routine diplomatic practices so as to give free rein to the art of diplomacy; it is often an acceptable minor obstacle in the pursuit of policy; it is not a significant restraint on a nation's freedom to pursue important national interests as it sees them. Indeed, if those who conduct foreign policy appear to give law a significant role, they are likely to be contemned for—the words are George Kennan's—their "legalistic-moralistic approach to international problems."[2] The United States, we shall see, was criticized for invoking law against its allies during the Suez crisis of 1956 (Chapter 13). Law, it was suggested, had little place in the resolution of the Cuban missile crisis (Chapter 15), or in Israel's magnificent dénoument of the hijacking at Entebbe in 1976. It was force, not law, that was prominent in Korea and in Vietnam, repeatedly in the Middle East, in Bangladesh, Cyprus, Angola. These strictures are commonly seen as representing the diplomat's view that international law is a good thing if only it is not taken too seriously.

Students of international law, on the other hand, tend to begin with international law, and often they end there: law is law; all of it should be observed, and respectable governments observe it; there is also a need for more law and nations should agree to create that law and abide by it. The lawyer is concerned with law, not with "politics"—not, for example, with why law is made and why particular law emerges, why nations will or will not agree to some new law, whether law really matters in international relations, how and how much law influences a nation's foreign policy, to what extent law is observed or violated, why nations behave as they do in the

face of international law. That is "applied international law," he
might say with faint disdain like that which some "pure" mathe-
maticians reserve for the engineer.

The diplomat and the international lawyer, the student of law
and the student of politics whom I have described, may be carica-
tures; they are not, I believe, straw men, or "sports." Lawyer and
diplomat are engaged in a *dialogue de sourds*. Indeed, they are not
even attempting to talk to each other, turning away in silent disregard. Yet both purport to be looking at the same world from the
vantage point of important disciplines. It seems unfortunate, indeed destructive, that they should not, at the least, hear each other.

To facilitate such a dialogue is a principal purpose of this volume. Obviously, I believe that the dialogue will be mutually en-
lightening. In my opinion, the two attitudes toward international
law which I have described, with some exaggeration for emphasis,
are starkly inadequate. If the view rejecting international law reflected the realities of international relations and the attitudes and
practices of governments, international law would be frivolous;
universities that teach it would be perpetrating fraud; international
lawyers might well be dismissed, as often they are, as "technical,"
visionary, sentimental, and irrelevant. The lawyer, in turn, would
be right to condemn governments as hypocritical, cynical, reaction-
ary, and subversive of international order. In fact, however, international law does far better than its reputation. I wish to move the
diplomat and the student of foreign affairs toward a more sophisticated view of what international law is, how much of it there is,
where it lies. I wish to show that cynical "realism" about international law *is* unrealistic, that it does not reflect the facts of international life: law *is* a major force in international affairs; nations rely
on it, invoke it, observe and are influenced by it in every aspect of
their foreign relations.

I should like, also, to interest the lawyer* to think beyond the

* Throughout, when I speak of the lawyer, I refer to the international lawyer.
The lawyer generally, at least in the United States, also tends to think of international law as not being "hard law," and his attitude is often not substantially different from that of the diplomat.

substantive rules of law to the function of law, the nature of its influence, the opportunities it offers, the limitations it imposes—as well as to understand the limits of its influence in a society of sovereign nations. The lawyer may recall that "the law," Mr. Justice Holmes said, "is not a brooding omnipresence in the sky."[3] International law in particular is not a self-contained abstraction, or even a distant star for nations to steer by. It affords a framework, a pattern, a fabric for international society, grown out of relations in turn. The law that is made or left unmade reflects the political forces effective in the system. Law that is made is a force in international affairs, but its influence can be understood only in the context of other forces governing the behavior of nations and their governments.

In brief, I wish to attempt to dispel misconceptions, of "too much" as of "too little," about the place of law in foreign policy. To that end, I shall begin by suggesting why the lawyer thinks of law as fundamental, while the diplomat might dismiss it as hardly relevant to the politics of nations. I look at the purposes law serves, why nations act together to make law, and what determines the law that emerges, especially when national interests do not coincide. I shall then look at law as it is reflected in the behavior of governments,* attempting a kind of "psychological" study of the "criminal" behavior of states. Do nations comply with international law? When do they comply? Why do they observe law? Why do they violate it? Compliance apart, has international law any other significance in shaping their conduct? And is it "law," or is it "politics"? I consider, too, the impact of the major influences in contemporary international society on national behavior under law. Several chapters are devoted to the politics of new law: to transform the law of the sea, establish a new economic order, promote human

---

*Throughout, my focus is on how nations (or states, or governments) behave in regard to law. Even to speak of "behavior" smacks of anthropomorphism. In fact, as will appear, for me governments "are aware" or "ignore," "think" and "feel," "consider" and "decide," "expect" and "rely." Obviously, these are linguistic conveniences which, I hope, do not obscure the multifaceted complexities of the processes of governmental decision.

rights. Finally, I suggest the different influences of law, or why law failed to have any influence, on some major events in contemporary history.

The undertaking is ambitious and, I believe, important. Answers to some of the questions raised here would, at the least, help us to appreciate the place of law in international life and to understand the "pathology" of national behavior with respect to law. Answers might even help us find ways to extend the domain of law and improve law observance, for greater order and stability in international relations. Unfortunately, what may properly be called "answers" are not possible to come by. The processes by which decisions in foreign policy are made are mysterious altogether. Sometimes foreign policy is not made; it happens, and can only later be sorted out of the confusion of many actions and inactions. Adequate records of the processes of deciding on national policy do not exist, and many that exist, as concerns contemporary events at least, are likely to be classified. Those who make policy in different countries are not available for cross-examination. Indeed, if records were available, if political leaders told all, we might still not be able to assay with any precision the significance of law. The motivations of governmental behavior are complex and often unclear to the actors themselves. If we can sometimes identify various factors that contribute to a national policy, and find law among them, there are no scales to determine the weight of each of them. If in an occasional decision the influence of law can be shown and measured, any generalizations would still be deficient, given the inevitable inadequacy of sampling. One cannot examine all the violations, or indeed all observances, of law by all nations. When a nation violates the law, why did law fail to deter violation? When a nation acts consistently with international law, to what degree did the law motivate the action? And the extreme difficulty of assaying the influence of international law in decisions to act becomes much greater when we attempt to examine what nations do not do, and why they refrain from doing.

In substantial measure, then, the exploration must be *a priori* and speculative, less scientific than impressionistic. I shall assert propo-

sitions about how nations behave, based on what appears reasonable, on what international actors have done and said, on the opinions of observers, on impressions gained from some experience in a
foreign office. These suggestions may perhaps be only "education
in the obvious." The examples cited are few, and many of them
come from the United States. I am better acquainted with how international law is dealt with and how national policy is made there
than elsewhere; the United States, also, is so open a society that
one frequently learns even when the government is eager to conceal. The cases examined are not typical of international conduct,
nor do they even represent random sampling. Those which best
lend themselves to study involve alleged violations rather than observances of law, deal with special norms and particular nations,
and reflect the distortions of drama and passion. Still, at the least,
one may learn whether the behavior of nations in regard to international law is susceptible of meaningful study, and what additional
knowledge might make such study more fruitful. My propositions,
I hope, may promote hard study of particular governmental decisions and suggest other inquiries which might support more confident assertions about the role of law in international relations.[4]

Any inquiry into the role of law must take into account the state
of "the system"—the character of international society and of the
law at a given time. At different times the actors, the problems, the
law and its influence are all different. Both law and society would
look different, to cite several examples, after the Peace of Westphalia established the modern secular state and the society of such
nations; after the birth of international institutions, mostly since
1918; after the United Nations Charter and the advent of nuclear
weapons; after the end of colonialism and the proliferation of nation-states. The post-Napoleonic period, as a specific instance,
found European powers asserting a right to intervene in other
countries to support "legitimacy," *i.e.*, monarchic institutions, and
to suppress republican revolution. Obviously, if such intervention
was deemed permissible under the law of that time, the behavior of
states would reflect that law, instead of the different law of a later
period. In the last third of the twentieth century, national behavior

would reflect instead the principle of "self-determination" and national sovereignty over natural resources.

What I shall say about the influence of law and how nations behave under law is in focus on the contemporary scene. For familiarity and better understanding, the examples will be largely from the period since the Second World War. For my purposes, then, I assume a system which includes proliferating international organizations, the United Nations Charter, the outlawing of war, the advent of atomic weapons, ideological competition, and, more recently, the proliferation of states and the emergence of the Third World.

Much apparent disagreement about the role of law in foreign affairs reflects differences in perspective. The lawyer may see what law there is and what law does; the critic may see only what law there is not and what law has not achieved. The lawyer may be talking about law broadly conceived, ubiquitous, essential, inherent in society, therefore also in international society. He is not differentiating among various forms and roles of law; he is not thinking of the desirability or effectiveness of any particular law; he is not concentrating on the ultimate purposes of law or asking how far law succeeds in meeting them. The critic of law may begin with the larger purposes, noticing primarily where they are not achieved, blaming the law for these failures. The law he sees is only the "spectacular," dramatic law, and he may blame abiding disorder on its ineffectiveness. He may especially object to attempts to deal with particular political problems by particular

forms of law which he considers undependable, even undesirable. Inevitably, perhaps, the respective preoccupations
of lawyer and diplomat may bring them into some disagreement when each is compelled to look up to consider what interests the other.

The lawyer's perspective is more perceptive as regards the
character, the content, the varieties of law; it is sometimes
defective as to the uses of law, the purposes it serves, and
whether, to what extent, how and why it achieves those purposes. Why do nations make law and conclude international
agreements? What is the content and substance of the law
which they make? How much order does law bring, how
much freedom (anarchy?) does it leave? To what extent do
nations observe the law and agreements they make? In what
other ways might the law influence how governments behave? When nations observe law, why do they? And why, at
other times, do they disregard their obligations? Where, at
bottom, does law stand in relation to a nation's foreign policy?

One frequently encounters the view that international law
is made by the powerful few to support their particular interests. Paradoxically, it is a common view also that the norms
of international law are so widely disregarded as to be largely
irrelevant to the behavior of nations. Some have even elevated
this impression to a doctrine, questioning whether one may
meaningfully speak of international norms, of their observance or violation. When nations do behave consistently with
law, it is commonly seen as fortuitous: the law happened to
coincide with what nations wished to do. But this coincidence
is too frequent to be mere concidence. There are reasons why
nations make law and conclude agreements, and why they
make particular law; like law in many national societies, international law results from the complex interplay of varied
forces in international politics. There are reasons why nations
act in accordance with these undertakings. One can explain,
too, why law is sometimes disregarded. Not unlike law in a

national society—and for reasons that are not dissimilar—international law is observed by nations as national policy, shared with other nations, in support of an orderly society.

THE ROLE OF LAW
AND

one

ITS LIMITATIONS

Those whose concern is law may not understand how others can question its significance for diplomacy. They conclude that the common criticisms of international law reflect a limited view of both international law and foreign policy, in which both are distorted—indeed, most law and most policy are overlooked.

Not surprisingly, when most of us think of American foreign policy since World War II, we tend to think of "containment of communism," cold war or détente, support for the United Nations, the Marshall Plan, NATO, intervention in Korea, Vietnam or the Dominican Republic, and near-intervention in Angola, the Cuban missile crisis, the Two-Chinas Policy, Secretary Kissinger's shuttle diplomacy in the Middle East and something similar and less successful in southern Africa and Cyprus. Earlier, we might have thought of the Good Neighbor Policy, the Monroe Doctrine, "manifest destiny," "no foreign entanglements." But the diplomat knows that, even in our tension-ridden times, foreign policy and foreign relations are not all, or principally, drama and grand design. Foreign policy is the sum of all the attitudes reflected in myriads of relationships and numberless points of contact that one nation has with others, large and small. For a country like the United States it is the sum of all the attitudes revealed in thousands of telegrams daily between the Department of State (and other departments) and more than a hundred foreign missions, mostly about small subjects: a citizen claims an inheritance in a foreign land; a company wishes to do business abroad; an extradition treaty is negotiated; there is a request for economic aid or a research reactor; a head of state will come to visit; a public statement is explained, or explained away. Foreign policy also includes the attitudes enshrined in the Constitution, in legislative enactments, executive orders and regulations, judicial decisions, that have import for relations with other nations or their nationals. It includes even unofficial attitudes of peoples and individuals, of domestic companies, trade unions and institutions, their actions and reactions which affect relations with others. In largest part, then, foreign policy is routine, undramatic, uncontroversial, "uninteresting"—I do not say unimportant—aimed at achieving national ends usually through stability, order, good relations. Like good health, or a good marriage, it is mostly unnoted and taken for granted—unless the routine is interrupted.

THE VARIETIES OF INTERNATIONAL LAW

As for international law, much misunderstanding is due to a failure to recognize law where it exists. That failure may be due to a narrow conception of law generally. The layman tends to think of domestic law in terms of the traffic policeman, or judicial trials for the thief or murderer. But law is much more and quite different. I do not invoke any esoteric or eccentric definition of law when I say that in domestic society law includes the scheme and structure of government, and the institutions, forms, and procedures whereby a society carries on its daily activities; the concepts that underlie relations between government and individual and between individuals;

the status, rights, responsibilities, and obligations of individuals and incorporated and non-incorporated associations and other groups, the relations into which they enter and the consequences of these relations. Men establish families, employ one another, acquire possessions and trade them, make arrangements, join in groups for ill or good, help or hurt each other, with little thought to law and little awareness that there is law that is relevant. By law, society formalizes these relationships, creates new ones, legitimates some and forbids others, determines the content and consequences of relationships. The individual remains hardly or hazily aware that he is enmeshed and governed by "law"—laws of property, tort, contract, crimes, laws of marriage, divorce, family, inheritance, laws of employment, commerce, association; and that there are procedures and institutions and formalities which are ever there and maintain an order in society, although they may assert themselves only at critical points, when relations are established, or change, or break down.

In relations between nations, too, one tends to think of law as consisting of a few prohibitory rules (for instance, that a government may not arrest another's diplomats) or the law of the U.N. Charter prohibiting war. Readers may think of law as including major treaties, such as those of Utrecht, Vienna, Paris, or Versailles. But international law, too, is much more and quite different. Although there is no international "government," there is an international "society"; law includes the structure of that society, its institutions, forms, and procedures for daily activity, the assumptions on which the society is founded and the concepts which permeate it, the status, rights, responsibilities, obligations of the nations which comprise that society, the various relations between them, and the effects of those relations.* Through what we call

* I do not include here that which nations do merely from habit, custom, "convention." I refer to *law*, to behavior as to which there is—on the part of the actor, the victim, and others—a sense of obligation, and a sense of violation when it fails. Between law and non-law the line is, of course, sometimes uncertain. Compare, however, non-legally-binding but important political-moral undertakings like those in the Final Act of the Conference on Security and Cooperation in Europe (Helsinki, 1 August 1975), pp. 16–17, 237, below.

foreign policy, nations establish, maintain, change, or terminate myriads of relations; law—more or less primitive, more or less sophisticated—has developed to formalize these relationships, to regulate them, to determine their consequences. A major purpose of foreign policy for most nations at most times is to maintain international order so that they can pursue their national interests, foreign and domestic. That order depends on an "infrastructure" of agreed assumptions, practices, commitments, expectations, reliances. These too are international law, and they are reflected in all that governments do.

To move from the abstract, consider some of the "givens" of international relations. First, they are relations between nations (states).* The nation is the principal unit. All the forms of intercourse, all the institutions, all the terms even, depend on the existence of "nations." (One can conceive of a different society: in a centralized world government there would be no nations, no international relations, no "transnational law." [1]) That political society is based on the nation is not commonly seen as involving either policy or law; ordinarily, nationhood is the unspoken assumption of political life. But the nation ("state") is not only a political conception; it is also a fundamental legal construct with important consequences. Statehood—who is and shall be a state—has been one of the major political issues of our day. The legal concept of statehood is crucial, of course, when the character of an entity as a state is itself in issue. It figured in Soviet insistence on U.N. membership for Outer Mongolia, as well as in continued recognition by the United States of governments-in-exile for the Baltic republics incorporated

---

* While international society today recognizes other entities—intergovernmental and other international organizations (the United Nations, the International Committee of the Red Cross), national and multinational companies with major transnational activities, even individual human beings—these are normally of concern only when, and because, their actions and the effects of their actions spill over national boundaries. Even to the extent that the individual has become a "subject" of international law, it is *international law* he is a subject of. Even the new concern for the human rights of individuals finds expression to date only through treaties and practice between nations, or through organizations of nations or bodies created by nations. See Chapter 12.

by the U.S.S.R. It was raised when Palestine was partitioned and Israel created and underlies the recent claims of Palestinians to a state of their own. It was entangled in the question of Chinese representation in the United Nations and still bedevils the future of Taiwan. The "nation" has been in issue in differences over recognition of divided countries and their membership in international organizations—China, Korea, Vietnam, Germany. The legal concept and consequences of nationhood underlie the explosion of "self-determination" which ended Western colonialism and transformed the map of the world, and have troubled even the new nations, *e.g.*, Biafra, Bangladesh. It still deeply troubles Cyprus, and also Kashmir. It has given new significance to the problem of the "micro-state" or "mini-state."

Relations between nations generally begin with "housekeeping arrangements," including recognition and establishment of diplomatic relations. That these involve law (*e.g.*, in regard to recognition, sovereign and diplomatic immunities) is commonly known, but the importance of this law for foreign policy is commonly depreciated. In fact, this law is basic and indispensable, and taken for granted because it rarely breaks down. The newest of nations promptly adopts it and the most radical scrupulously observes it. The occasional exception confirms the obvious, that there would be no relations with a nation that regularly violated embassies and abused diplomats. There are also the special cases when "housekeeping" becomes important policy: whether to recognize Communist China and seat its representatives in the United Nations were major questions for many nations, and the United States did not resolve them for many troubling years. The importance of these questions depends on legal concepts of recognition (or U.N. representation), on legal definitions of "state" and "government"; it reflects, too, the failure of law to develop clear distinctions between accepting the effective existence of a government, "recognizing" a government, and maintaining relations with it. Law does not determine the policy of governments on these issues, but it directs whatever actions might be taken and limits the choices available to governments. The United States could not meaningfully recognize the Queen of England as the government of China; it could not even continue indefinitely to insist that the government of China was Chiang Kai-shek; it could not recognize both the regime at Peking and that at Taipei as the government of China.

The relations of one nation with another, as soon as they begin, are permeated by basic legal concepts: nationality, national territory, property, torts, contracts, the rights and duties and responsibilities of states. These do not commonly figure in major policy doctrines, nor do they commonly occupy the attentions of diplomats. They too are taken for granted because they are rarely in issue. The concept of territory and territorial sovereignty is not prominent in foreign policy; but every foreign policy assumes the integrity and inviolability of the national territory, and any intentional violation would probably lead to major crisis. Territorial disputes are still with us, on several frontiers in Latin America and Africa, in Kashmir, between China and India, and China and Russia, over Gibraltar, in the Sahara, between Israel and its neighbors. Contemporary international relations were long troubled by other "territorial" issues turning on law: for example, the reach of the territorial sea, the continental shelf and coastal state authority for other purposes; innocent and less-than-innocent passage, and free transit through international straits; the right to broadcast inland, to dig for oil and gas, or to fish for food or pearls in coastal waters. Foreign policy takes for granted that nations observe the territorial airspace of others, but planes have been shot down in incidents leading to diplomatic tensions, to United Nations debates, to judicial proceedings.[2] The implications for foreign policy of the U-2 incident with the Soviet Union, in 1960, and of continued overflights of Cuba, are not yet exhausted.

Related to territoriality is the concept of internal sovereignty. Except as limited by international law or treaty, a nation is master in its own territory. That principle is fundamental, and commonly observed. Yet it is in issue whenever there is a claim that internal action violates international law. It figures in disputes about nationalization of alien properties and about violations of human rights. It is proclaimed by South Africa, and challenged by many nations, in regard to *apartheid*.

The concepts of property lie deep in international relations.

Property rights are taken for granted in all international trade and finance. When a vessel plies the seas, the assumption is that others will observe the international law prohibiting interference with free navigation, recognizing rights of ownership in property, forbidding torts against persons and property. The United States went to war in 1917, in part because it thought this law was being violated to its detriment.

Contemporary international relations have seen recurrent issues as to the law of the responsibility of states, particularly in regard to the treatment of aliens and their property. But even in times when nationalizations are not everyday occurrences, even when there are no accusations that governments are denying "justice" to aliens, the law on the treatment of foreign nationals pervades relations between nations. Because there is this law (and because it is largely observed), there is tourism and foreign investment; and consular activity and "diplomatic protection" are a common, friendly, continuous part of international intercourse.

Not least, by far, are particular prohibitions of the law deriving from the basic concepts, such as those designed to protect the independence of nations against various forms of intervention. Accusations of intervention are common fare; to refrain from "intervention" is a tenet of foreign policy for many nations.*

Law is also essential to foreign policy and to diplomacy in that it provides mechanisms, forms, and procedures by which nations maintain their relations, carry on trade and other forms of intercourse, resolve differences and disputes. There is international law in the establishment and operation of missions and in communications between governments, in the writing of contracts and other commercial paper, in oil concessions, in tariffs and customs practices, in the registry of vessels, the shipment of goods, the

---

* Intervention is an effort to bring influence to bear on other governments by particular means. Strictly, intervention is unlawful interference; what by definition constitutes intervention is unlawful. Strictly, too, intervention means dictatorial interference by force or threat of force, but the term is often used loosely for any impermissible interference or attempt to influence.

forms of payment, in all the intricacies of international trade and finance. There is law in and about the variety of international conferences. International organization—from the United Nations to the Universal Postal Union—involves legal concepts, and different organizations have contributed substantial law. For settling disputes, the law provides diplomats with claims commissions, arbitration bodies, mediators and conciliators, even courts.

For foreign policy, perhaps the most important legal mechanism is the international agreement, and the most important principle of international law is *pacta sunt servanda:* agreements shall be observed. This principle makes international relations possible. The mass of a nation's foreign relations involve innumerable agreements of different degrees of formality. The diplomat promotes, develops, negotiates, implements various understandings for various ends, from establishing diplomatic relations to trade, aid, allocation of resources, cultural exchange, common standards of weights and measures, to formal alliances affecting national security, cease-fire and disengagement, arms control, and a regime for outer space. The diplomat hardly thinks of these arrangements and understandings as involving law. He does assume that, if agreement is reached, it will probably be observed; if he did not, he would not bother to seek agreement. No doubt, he thinks that nations generally observe their undertakings because that is "done" in international society and because it is generally in the interest of nations to do so. That is law, the lawyer would say.

Some international agreements have particular political significance because they shape the character of international society; those from an earlier day—bearing names like Utrecht, Westphalia, Vienna, Versailles—determined nations and defined territories of today. Such arrangements involve international peace and stability, or the identity, security, integrity, and independence of nations: *e.g.*, treaties that confirmed the achievement of independence (say, by the United States from Great Britain, or by Indonesia from the Netherlands); the arrangements deriving from the Congress of Vienna, the Treaty of Versailles, the Yalta and Potsdam agreements; the agreement establishing French protection for Morocco, and the agreement terminating that relation; the United Nations Charter, the North Atlantic Treaty; the Treaty of Constantinople establishing the regime of the Suez Canal; the agreements of the European Community. As we shall see, the legal character of these agreements may differ from that of other treaties, and surely they are treated differently in the foreign policies of nations. But nations have usually insisted on putting these arrangements in solemn legal form;* in maintaining them, they have invoked the principle of international law that agreements shall be observed. Even nations that wish to escape from such arrangements are usually compelled to invoke legal principles of escape—whether by reinterpreting the agreement, by attacking its original validity, or by invoking some principle of law to claim that it permits escape or is no longer valid or binding.

In our times, there flourishes a type of international agreement that has added new dimensions to foreign policy and international law.[3] Much of contemporary international law consists of new arrangements, often among large numbers of nations, to promote cooperation for some common aim. In this category one might place the various intergovernmental organizations and institutions, universal or regional—the United Nations, the World Bank and the Monetary Fund, the FAO, UPU, ITU and the IAEA, OECD, GATT, the International Coffee Agreement and UNCTAD, NATO and the European Economic Community, the OAS and OAU or the anticipated International Sea-bed Authority[4]—as well as bilateral aid agreements.† One might include, too, arrangements, not exclusively governmental, like the International Telecommunications Satellite Consortium (INTELSAT) or oil concessions.

---

*Sometimes they insisted on not putting them into formal legally-binding agreements in order to avoid legal consequences, as in the Final Act of the Conference on Security and Cooperation in Europe (Helsinki).

†Such "law of cooperation" is sometimes distinguished from the traditional international law of "abstention" that prescribes limits on the freedom of action of governments. The lawyer at least finds that he is struggling less with ordinary questions of treaty law but often with a new kind of international constitutional and administrative law.

These programs for cooperation figure prominently in the foreign policy of many nations. The political officers who develop and maintain these policies may not think of them as creating or involving law—until issues arise involving alleged violations or differences in the interpretation of agreements. But the law supports these arrangements even—or especially—when there are no issues, when they run as intended. The foreign policy involved in these arrangements depends on assumptions, habits, practices, and institutions that derive their vitality from their quality as law and international legal obligation.

Law reflected in the assumptions, concepts, institutions, and procedures of international society is not the kind of international law one commonly thinks about because it does not, on its face, direct governments how to behave. But, in fact, all law is intimately related to national behavior. Even that "submerged" law molds the policies of governments. The concept of the nation determines that the United States has relations with Canada, not with Quebec. The concept of territoriality means that the United States can do largely as it likes within the United States, but is sharply restricted in what it can do outside. There are clear prohibitions in the basic legal concepts, in the rights and duties they imply: territoriality, property, tort imply that the United States cannot, at will, invade or violate the territory or seize the property of another nation. Freedom of the seas means that one nation cannot prevent the vessels of others from going their way. Contracts and agreements are not to be broken. Even organizations for cooperative welfare, though commonly distinguished from traditional law of "abstention," impose obligations on members which they must "abstain" from violating: they may not interfere with the international mails; they must pay budget assessments to the FAO. These organizations have also promoted common procedures and minimum standards of national behavior, e.g., in regard to labor, or the treatment of refugees, or basic human rights even for a nation's own citizens.

There is also the law which aims directly at controlling behavior. Governments may not arrest accredited diplomats or deny basic justice to foreign nationals. I have mentioned, and shall discuss, the law forbidding intervention in the internal affairs of other nations. Extended consideration will be given to the provision in the Charter of the United Nations which outlaws war and the use of force.

International relations and foreign policy, then, depend on a legal order, operate in a legal framework, assume a host of legal principles and concepts which shape the policies of nations and limit national behavior. If one doubts the significance of this law, one need only imagine a world from which it were absent—approximately a situation in which all nations were perpetually in a state of war with each other. There would be no security of nations or stability of governments; territory and airspace would not be respected; vessels could navigate only at their constant peril; property—within or without any given territory—would be subject to arbitrary seizure; persons would have no protection of law or of diplomacy; agreements would not be made or observed; diplomatic relations would end; international trade would cease; international organizations and arrangements would disappear.

Those who would dismiss international law from foreign policy, the lawyer concludes, tend to misconceive both law and foreign policy. Those who do not see much role for law in foreign policy do not know where to look. Those who do not sense the law's significance are merely taking it for granted. Not unlike *le bourgeois gentilhomme*, who learned that he had been speaking prose all his life, the diplomat—says the lawyer—may be surprised to know that international law permeates his universe, that he uses it every day, that his life depends on it, that attention to the law, in Justice Holmes's phrase, may not be a duty but only a necessity.[5]

THE LIMITATIONS OF
INTERNATIONAL LAW

The student of foreign affairs may grant, if the lawyer insists, that the law implied in international society gives some direction to national policies and places some limitations on how nations behave. But he remains skeptical of the influence of law as it is commonly and more narrowly conceived, of that law which seeks to control the conduct of nations within the framework of the society of nations. In particular, he questions whether nations really observe the important prohibitory norms of international law or really keep their important agreements. Governments may sometimes act consistently with norms or obligations, but, he insists, only when it is in their interest to do so; and it is their interest, not the law, which governs their behavior. Such skepticism in the diplomat and the policy-maker is sometimes reflected in the foreign policies they promulgate and carry out.

The tendency to dismiss international law reflects impressions sometimes summed up in the conclusion that it is not really law because international society is not really a society: the world of nations is a collection of sovereign states, not an effective body politic which can support effective law. In this judgment are subsumed a number of alleged weaknesses and inadequacies.

The society of nations has no effective law-making body or process. General law depends on consensus: in principle, new law, at least, cannot be imposed on any state; even old law cannot survive if enough states, or a few powerful and influential ones, reject it. New universal law, then, can come about only through long, gradual, uncertain "accretion" by practice and acquiescence, or through multilateral treaties difficult to negotiate and more difficult to get accepted. Law is also slow and difficult to clarify, or amend, or repeal. The law is therefore haphazard and static. As concerns customary law in particular, there is often uncertainty and little confidence as to what it is. The law is also inadequate, for many important actions and relations remain unregulated. There are important disorders—for example, the arms race or the oil embargo— which are not subject to law.[6] In the absence of special undertakings, nations may engage in economic warfare, may boycott, even starve each other. And law has not achieved a welfare society: there is no law requiring social and economic assistance by the very rich to the very poor, or providing community relief even to the starving.

Also lacking is an effective judiciary to clarify and develop the law, to resolve disputes impartially, and to impel nations to observe the law. The International Court of Justice does not satisfy these needs. Its jurisdiction and procedures are starkly insufficient: jurisdiction requires the consent of the parties, and few consent to it; only a minority of nations have accepted the Court's compulsory jurisdiction, some of these with important reservations, the notorious "Connolly reservation" continues to make U.S. acceptance essentially illusory.[7] The Court's justice is slow, expensive, uncertain: even nations which can invoke the Court's compulsory jurisdiction are reluctant to do so. Nations still prefer the flexibility of diplomacy to the risks of third-party judgment. In the result, few issues of substantial significance to international order ever get to the Court. No one would claim that the Court has a major influence in international affairs.

The greatest deficiency, as many see it, is that international society lacks an executive authority with power to enforce the law. There is no police system whose pervasive presence might deter violation. The society does not consider violations to be crimes or violators criminals, and attaches no stigma which might itself discourage violation. Since nations cannot be made to observe rules and keep promises, they will not do so when they deem it in their interest not to do so.

To some, indeed, the realities of international society imply even more devastating limitations for international law.* In a society of sovereign states, in the absence of an effective legislature representing all the competing interests and able to accommodate them, nations must be free to pursue their interests, to work out reasonable accommodations with others. What is called for is the flexibility of diplomacy, not the strait jacket of law. In particular, there is no place for law where important political interests are at stake. Nations will not—and should not be expected to—submit important disputes to third-party decision in accordance with fixed law. To these critics there cannot be effective law against war or other uses of force, and nations should not be expected to observe any such

---

* I summarize here criticisms set forth and examined at length in the conclusion.

law when they desire change hard enough to fight for it. And other nations will not effectively enforce such "violations."

In sum, to many an observer, governments seem largely free to decide whether to agree to new law, whether to accept another nation's view of existing law, whether to comply with agreed law. International law, then, is voluntary and only hortatory. It must always yield to national interest. Surely, no nation will submit to law any questions involving its security or independence, even its power, prestige, influence. Inevitably, a diplomat holding these views will be reluctant to build policy on law he deems ineffective. He will think it unrealistic and dangerous to enact laws which will not be observed, to build institutions which will not be used, to base his government's policy on the expectation that other governments will observe law or agreement. Since other nations do not attend to law except when it is in their interest, the diplomat might not see why his government should do so at the sacrifice of important interests. He might be impatient with his lawyers who tell him that the government may not do what he would like to see done.

These depreciations of international law challenge much of what the international lawyer does. Indeed, some lawyers seem to despair for international law until there is world government or at least effective international organization. But most international lawyers are not dismayed. Unable to deny the limitations of international law, they insist that these are not critical, and they deny many of the alleged implications of these limitations. If they must admit that the cup of law is half-empty, they stress that it is half-full. They point to similar deficiencies in many domestic legal systems. They reject definitions (commonly associated with the legal philosopher John Austin) that deny the title of law to any but the command of a sovereign, enforceable and enforced as such.[8] They insist that despite inadequacies in legislative method, international law has grown and developed and changed. If international law is difficult to make, yet it is made; if its growth is slow, yet it grows. If there is no judiciary as effective as in some developed national systems, there is an International Court of Justice whose judgments and opinions, while few, are respected.[9] The inadequacies of the judicial system are in some measure supplied by other bodies: international disputes are resolved and law is developed through a network of arbitrations by continuing or *ad hoc* tribunals. National courts help importantly to determine, clarify, develop international law.[10] Political bodies like the Security Council and the General Assembly of the United Nations also apply law, their actions and resolutions interpret and develop the law, their judgments help to deter violations in some measure. If there is no international executive to enforce international law, the United Nations has some enforcement powers and there is "horizontal enforcement" in the reactions of other nations. The gaps in substantive law are real and many and require continuing effort to fill them, but they do not vitiate the force and effect of the law that exists, in the international society that is.

Above all, the lawyer will insist, critics of international law ask and answer the wrong questions. What matters is not whether the international system has legislative, judicial, or executive branches, corresponding to those we have become accustomed to seek in a domestic society; what matters is whether international law is reflected in the policies of nations and in relations between nations. The question is not whether there is an effective legislature; it is whether there is law that responds and corresponds to the changing needs of a changing society. The question is not whether there is an effective judiciary, but whether disputes are resolved in an orderly fashion in accordance with international law. Most important, the question is not whether law is enforceable or even effectively enforced; rather, whether law is observed, whether it governs or influences behavior, whether international behavior reflects stability and order. The fact is, lawyers insist, that nations have accepted important limitations on their sovereignty, that they have observed these norms and undertakings, that the result has been substantial order in international relations.

In the end, the issues do not turn on theoretical answers to theoretical questions, or on unexamined impressions or assertions about the fate and influence of law in the chancelleries of nations. We must examine as well as we can the role that law, in fact, plays in daily diplomacy, the extent to which law, in fact, affects the behavior of nations, the contribution which law, in fact, makes to order and welfare.

THE POLITICS OF
two
LAW-MAKING

To understand why international society has produced the law we have, and how nations behave with respect to that law, one might begin by considering why nations make law and enter into international agreement.

WHY NATIONS MAKE LAW

Much international law was there "from the beginning." From "natural law," from widespread influences of Roman and Canon law, from laws common to all "civilized" countries and legal systems reaching back before history, early relations between communities reflected notions of property, contract, and tort that are basic to international as to domestic law. Even notions of territorial and ethnic identity, and an individual's links to a territory or a "people," long antedated the modern nation-state and the concepts of territorial sovereignty and nationality in modern international law.

The use of "ambassadors" and the practice of granting them extraordinary respect also have ancient roots and came nearly fullblown into modern international law.[1]

Some principles of customary international law are centuries old, among them the principle that international agreements shall be observed. On entering international society, new nations find these obligations (and corresponding rights) upon them, and few purport to reject them or even to seek jurisprudential answers as to why they are subject to them. Especially at times of great flux, like those that have followed the Second World War and the proliferation of states resulting from the end of colonialism, new nations (and some old ones) may find a common interest to challenge a particular norm or standard—e.g., the obligation to compensate for nationalized alien properties (see Chapter 6). But there has not been a major challenge to the system of international law as a whole, to the bulk of its content, to its major norms. Nations old and new also accept or help to develop new law and enter into new international agreements.

Every nation derives some benefits from international law and international agreements. Law keeps international society running, contributes to order and stability, provides a basis and a framework for common enterprise and mutual intercourse. Because it limits the actions of other governments, law enhances each nation's independence and security; in other ways, too, by general law or particular agreement, one nation gets others to behave as it desires. General law establishes common standards where they seem desirable. Both general law and particular agreement avoid the need for negotiating anew in every new instance; both create justified expectation and warrant confidence as to how others will behave.

All these advantages of law and agreement have their price. Law limits freedom of action: nations are "bound" to do (or not to do) other than they might like when the time to act comes. Political arrangements legitimized by law are more difficult to undo or modify. Stability and order mean that a particular nation is not free to be disorderly or readily to promote external change. To promote its own independence and security and the inviolability of its territory, to control the behavior of other governments, a nation may have to accept corresponding limitations on its own behavior. For the confidence bred by law, one pays the price of not being free to frustrate the expectations of others.

More or less consciously, more or less willingly, all governments give up some autonomy and freedom and accept international law in principle as the price of "membership" in international society and of having relations with other nations. For that reason, too, they accept basic traditional international law, undertaking to do (or not to do) unto others what they would have done (or not done) unto them. Since much of its foreign policy is reflected in international agreements, bilateral or multilateral, every nation accepts the legal principle that agreements shall be observed. For the rest, whether a nation desires more law or less and whether it will desire some new law or agreement are also questions of foreign policy, and nations accept or refuse new law—universal, multilateral, or bilateral—in terms of their national interest, as they see it. Nations may have "attitudes" in regard to the desirability of extending the domain of law. At different times they see greater or less interest in self-limitation and cooperation than in the freedom of "no law" and the flexibility of negotiation and improvisation. Nations differ in regard to how much "freedom" they are prepared to sacrifice for some common enterprise or to some supranational institution. They differ too as to how much confidence they have in law as a means to achieve peace, security, order, justice, welfare. The amount and kind of law which international society will achieve will depend, of course, on the degree of homogeneity of the political system and the degree of common or reciprocal interest.

Periodically—particularly after major disorder, like a world war—nations dedicate themselves anew to increased order, make an extraordinary sacrifice of their freedom, and accept law in the common interest (e.g., the United Nations Charter). At any time a nation's foreign policy may include a desire for some particular law: a revised definition of the coastal states' jurisdiction out to sea, a treaty against proliferation of nuclear weapons, a prohibition against racial discrimination, or a new regime for international trade. While willingness to accept a law or agreement will depend on what it provides, powerful nations often see less interest in curtailing their own freedom. Even the rich and the mighty, however, cannot commonly obtain what they want by force or dictation and must be prepared to pay the price of reciprocal or compensating obligation. Even they, moreover, seek legitimacy and acceptance for their policies, desire order and dependability in their relations and the conservative influence of law. Sometimes, even, they seek protection in the law from the will of majorities and the "tyranny of the weak." And they may agree to limit themselves in order to achieve corresponding limitations on competing powerful nations, as, for example, in the Nuclear Test-Ban Treaty of 1963, or the later Strategic Arms Limitations Talks (SALT).

Other nations, too, see advantage in law. They adhere to old law as a mark of their acceptance in international society; or because they approve of its objectives; or because they desire its advantages; or because they would assert their adherence to laudable principles. In new law they may seek codification or clarification to eliminate uncertainties. Governments feel freer, of course, to accept law which may in fact not hinder them seriously, in order to see such law accepted by others (*e.g.*, the non-proliferation treaty, for states that can have little hope of becoming nuclear powers), perhaps also to satisfy world or domestic opinion (*e.g.*, international human rights covenants).

A foreign-policy decision whether to accept new law involves considerations very different from those which determine whether a nation will observe existing law. Refusal to accept new law does not usually bring "sanctions" or other undesirable consequences.* Nations which are reluctant to undertake new obligations may be

---

* There are exceptions in special cases: the founding nations were determined that all nations had to abide by the law of the United Nations Charter outlawing the use of force [Article 2(6)]; the foreign relations of France have suffered because it failed to honor the limitations of the nuclear test ban of 1963; there would be sharp reaction if wealthy nations refused to contribute to development and other assistance programs; the Federal Republic of Germany would not dream of abstaining from the Genocide Convention.

scrupulous about honoring those which they accepted. In fact, a nation particularly concerned to observe law may be more hesitant about accepting new law in the first instance. Occasionally, however, a government will agree to a law with little intention of observing it, in order to gain some kudos and perhaps the advantage of observance by others, especially if it believes that its violations might not be detected. Hitler accepted the Munich Pact, probably without intention to observe it, perhaps to lull the Allies into a false sense of security; the United States has feared that the Soviet Union might enter into disarmament agreements it had no intention to keep, unless its compliance could be verified. Some believe that a number of states have adhered to international covenants on human rights because it is "the thing to do," because there are pressures to do so, without seriously expecting to honor them fully. But these are exceptional cases in exceptional situations for exceptional kinds of international law. Generally, nations seek law they wish others to observe and are prepared to observe it themselves.

HOW LAW IS MADE

The character, shape, and content of international law—as of national law—are determined by prevailing political forces within the political system,* as refracted through the way law is made.

*The scope and the content of international law are commonly credited to (or blamed upon) lawyers. That is error. For international as for national law, law-making is a political act, the work of politicians; lawyers, *qua lawyers*, contribute to that process only peripherally and interstitially—when they advise and provide technical assistance to policy-makers engaged in law-making; when they interpret and apply the law in advising political actors, or in handling claims between their government and others.

International judges get few opportunities to make law by adjudication, and on those infrequent occasions they tend to be restrained. Even national judges with "activist" traditions (*e.g.*, those of the United States) are restrained in developing international law by its international character and by deference to the political branches of their government. Compare *Banco Nacional de Cuba* v. *Sabbatino*, 376 U.S. 398 (1964).

"Publicists" made important contributions to customary international law in past centuries and are still recognized as a "subsidiary means for the determination of

The core of traditional international law and its principal assumptions and foundations have been unwritten "customary law," made over time by widespread practice of governments acting from a sense of legal obligation. Increasingly, however, customary law is being codified and modified, and new universal and regional law is also made by formal international agreement negotiated at international conferences. In some measure, law is made also by resolutions or declarations of international organizations, notably the U.N. General Assembly, and some, too, by the actions of such organizations interpreting existing law.

International law has been built on the "principle of unanimity": no state is bound by any proposed norm or regulation without its consent, though consent once given is binding and cannot be withdrawn at will.[2] The principle of unanimity has been justified on the ground of the sovereign equality of states.* But the equality of states in constitutional theory does not imply that all states are equal in their influence in the making of law. While the law that emerges, moreover, may apply equally to all, it will often not be even-handed in fact: a norm requiring "justice" for aliens and their property, for example, applies equally everywhere; but, obviously, it has favored states that export people and capital, and has been an obstacle to governments seeking to divest foreign holdings as a basis for social revolution. (See Chapters 6 and 10.)

Emerging law will depend on the interest of influential states to

---

rules of law." Statute of the International Court of Justice, Article 38(1)d. Their influence in law-making has decreased, especially as new law is increasingly made and customary law is being codified and developed by treaty, but they contribute indirectly through the codification and development activities of the International Law Commission and other bodies.

* In domestic societies, even where the principle of the equality of individuals was accepted, it did not lead to the principle of unanimity, but to equal vote and majority rule—perhaps from the ancient lineage of majority vote, perhaps because the individual did not acquire the aura and trappings of "sovereignty," perhaps from the practical difficulty of governing growing numbers by unanimity, or of allowing dissenters not to participate.

Unanimity does not imply veto, the ability to prevent others from taking a decision. The consenting states can make law for themselves, but it is not binding on the dissenters.

espouse it, a common interest in developing it, and the inability, or lack of interest, of others to resist it. Political influence in law-making, however, does not lie exclusively, or even primarily, where it is commonly assumed to be—that is, with militarily or economically powerful states. Even when war and threats of force were not unlawful, military power did not necessarily determine the law, for force could not be used or threatened lightly or frequently for less-than-compelling purposes.* Economic pressure or persuasion, too, was not always available and effective to obtain the consent of a resisting state. In our day, "power" (*i.e.*, influence, both in law-making and elsewhere in international relations) belongs also to small developing states, joined in blocs, adroit at exploiting the competition of the powerful, and armed with ideas claiming their time has come. (See Chapter 6.)

Because the process of making customary law is informal, haphazard, not deliberate, even partly unintentional and fortuitous, the resulting law may also suffer these qualities. While influence in the formation of customary law is of the same stuff as elsewhere, here it is not readily focused. Some principle, norm, or standard may result from the fortuitous initiative of a statesman, the coincidence of need and opportunity, and acquiescence or lack of care by others. Consent or acquiescence can be "bought," or compelled by political pressure from other states, or by the press of circumstances; it may go on in one corner while others are unaware, unconcerned, or not mobilized to act.

The process being unstructured and slow, there is opportunity for modifying the law and adjusting to it. Over centuries, of course, customary norms have responded to changed circumstances and interests and new configurations of influence. Whether in the same or in a modified form, moreover, norms that are originally imposed or one-sided, may become widely acceptable. For ex-

---

* Traditional international law did not question a state's consent on the ground that it was coerced, and for special reasons international law accepted even the wholly fictitious consent of a state to a peace treaty imposed on it upon defeat in war and unconditional surrender. See p. 80, below.

ample, one can surmise that some particular powerful prince early asserted sovereign or diplomatic immunity, and his lawyers provided conceptual underpinning for it. But the example and precedent thus provided doubtless prompted similar claims even by the less-powerful. In time the norms of immunity found appeal with officials of all governments as being important to effective and smooth international relations.[3] Similarly, that freedom of the sea for navigation became the governing principle reflected the prevailing balance of naval power and the inability of any one nation to assert and maintain hegemony over the large seas against all others during the years when the law was being formed. In fact, freedom of the seas proved generally acceptable in time of peace as the basis of intercourse, and of competition in discovery and commerce. The growth of an exception to freedom of the seas in a narrow band of "territorial sea" reflected a common concern of coastal states for their security against military enemies, marauders, or smugglers. Powerful maritime states, while chafing at such limitations on their freedom, did not challenge the authority even of weaker coastal states, or were unwilling to bear the cost of challenging it by force. In time the maritime states, themselves also coastal states and concerned to protect their coasts, came to appreciate the "territorial sea" and were generally content with the "trade-off." (See Chapter 11.)

The politics of law-making is less dis-orderly and more comprehensible when general law is made by formal multilateral agreement,* the dominant method of law-making in our time.[4] Nego-

---

* A treaty between two states also makes law, for the parties, and will be the result of what each desires from the other, and their comparative bargaining power; it will not be impervious to other interests of the parties, or to their relations with other nations. A traditional treaty of friendship, commerce and navigation may be reciprocal in form, granting each other the same privileges; in fact, of course, a provision, say, in a treaty between the United States and a small undeveloped country that guarantees the investment of each against expropriation by the other is only speciously reciprocal. But even a powerful state cannot impose its will, at will, in peaceful negotiation: it cannot take all and give little; it cannot lightly discriminate in its relations with different states; it cannot disregard standards that prevail between other states.

tiated at a particular time, with virtually all states participating, any emerging treaty will reflect what the participants perceived as their interests as regards the matter at issue, in the context of the system at large. But with ever more governments participating, with their interests often varied and complex, the process is confused and the result often not only impossible to predict but even difficult to explain when it appears. It may help to perceive both process and result with mathematical analogy or metaphor: when vectors of different magnitude and direction are brought to bear at one point, a vector of particular force and direction results. To be sure, political influence cannot be measured, and neither its magnitude nor direction is firm; both respond to other forces, to the bargaining situation, to conference procedures, strategy, personalities, to other issues in negotiation, to political interests and forces beyond the conference and the subject. In the large, however, the law that comes out of a conference can be seen as the result of the various directions in which different participants pulled and the magnitude of the influence they were able to bring to bear in support of their preferences. (I study the process and the result in the major contemporary effort to remake the law of the sea in Chapter 11.)

The emphasis on international law-making as a process of interaction among national policies of particular influence, as well as the metaphor that sees them as forces producing a resultant vector, both risk giving the impression that every nation's policy on law-making is monolithic, firm, and straightforward. The process of developing national policy itself, in fact, often brings to bear a complex of forces with the resultant policy also inviting the vector metaphor.

A government's policy as to whether some activity of international interest should remain unregulated, or what form regulation should take, is a political decision like others made by policymakers in the light of national interest as they see it. But national interest is not a single or simple thing; and often various national interests are implicated, and policy-makers must attempt to balance, compromise, or choose among them.

The process of deciding, and the difficulty of decision, will be different for different governments on different issues. For the United States, for example, a single issue may involve competing political, military, economic, and other public interests, as well as the interests of particular citizens or national companies. The process of developing policy will often reflect the size and complexity of the executive branch; the constitutional dependence of the executive on the Senate for consent to treaties, and on Congress as a whole for implementing them; the influence of private interests and public opinion on the executive branch and on Congress; and, inevitably, the bureaucratic and personal interests of a host of individual participants. Smaller, oligarchic governments can decidce more simply, but they too will often suffer internal differences, as well as the difficulty of deciding what their national interest requires, and which of competing national interests they should prefer or how these should be accommodated.

FAILURES TO MAKE LAW

An international political system of sovereign states is inherently "laissez-faire," resisting regulation by law. Surely, norms curtailing national autonomy in any important respect are not likely to be adopted unless the need for them is commonly seen as compelling and the result promises compensating advantage. Often, the absence of control by international law is purposeful, and many would say desirable: for states, too, there is an area of "privacy," *i.e.*, autonomy, that is not the law's business.[5] Even law commonly seen as desirable, however, is prevented or delayed by the diffuse law-making process.

No doubt, law-making in the international system is seriously hampered by "the principle of unanimity," which prevents a majority from making law binding on dissenters. Efforts to circumvent that principle, particularly in international organizations which use majority vote for other purposes, occasionally have small successes, as majorities devise means to make law in other guises while pretending not to. (See Chapters 6, 7, 9.) But surely in a world of unequal and diverse states, law-making by majority vote will not be accepted by the big and the powerful, and indeed is usually resisted even by the small and the weak. Law-making will have to be by agreed compromise or by various forms of consensus, or will be limited to those who can agree:* nothing prevents the like-minded from making law for themselves when less-than-universal agreements serve some purpose.

* The international system, of course, is not alone in failing to achieve desirable law. Even the most enlightened society, surely democratic societies, suffer the difficulties of law-making due to conflicting interests, disagreements about the desirability of regulation by law, or about what law is desirable, failures of will, perception and understanding, or inadequate legislative process. Indeed, even the most totalitarian of societies, governed effectively by a single powerful legislator, is often hampered in law-making by competing values and interests, by the need to accommodate conflicting "constituencies," by external pressures.

THE POLITICS
OF

three

LAW OBSERVANCE

That states have made international law for hundreds of years, that all governments devote considerable effort to law-making every day, surely testifies that in their view international law matters, governing in meaningful measure how governments behave. For professors and practitioners of international law the reality and importance of what they profess and practice is beyond question. The lay newspaper reader, by contrast, and many a practitioner of diplomacy commonly carry the impression that governments pay little attention to law. Why the stark difference in impression, and which corresponds more accurately to fact?

DO NATIONS
OBSERVE INTERNATIONAL LAW?

For this inquiry, I largely avoid special perspectives on international law which are the subject of contemporary jurisprudential controversy. That nations are the actors, the legislators, the executives, the judges of international law has led some international lawyers to see law not in terms of norms, standards, and obligations, but as a "policy-oriented," "comprehensive process of authoritative decision" made largely by the nations themselves.[1] Law, as they see it, is part of the political process; law is made and agreements are given meaning by the total political process—when governments act and other governments react, when courts (national or international) decide cases, when political bodies debate and pass resolutions and nations act in their light. The process is always going on, and the law which it is continuously creating is instinct with ambiguity. International law, then, has even less certainty than does law in domestic society, and there can be no confident assertion of what it is. It is not meaningful to ask simply what the law is or whether it has been observed or violated. That judgment, if it has to be made, can be made only after carefully weighing all the factors in a case, in the light of some basic value and dominant purpose, which ought to be the promotion of human welfare, dignity, and freedom.

This way of looking at the law provides important insights into the jurisprudence of international law, indeed of all law. But it is less relevant to an examination of how nations behave in regard to law. It seems to see the law *sub specie aeternitatis*, ever-changing, reflecting every action of every government. It seems to see law not as is but always as becoming, and to ask not what the law is but what it ought to be. For that inquiry, too, it seems to see the law from on high and in retrospect: the law is what God, or the United Nations, or History, or the Judge, or the Wise Man will say— later—in judging what nations had done in the light of context and consequences.[2]

This is not, however, the way nations commonly look at the law in deciding their own policy or in reacting to the behavior of others. Governments may be more or less aware that law is created, grows, changes, or withers within a political process that reflects, among other things, the policies and interests of individual nations. But the government formulating a policy or contemplating an action is not an eternal, retrospective judge or observer of either the legal or the political process. It is, and acts, within these processes, and it sees the law at a moment within them. It regards the law as having its own existence and validity within the political process. To say that—even to say that law is "policy-oriented"—is not to say that law depends on the policy of any particular nation [3] or that any nation is free to do as it likes, regardless of law.* Once law or agreement is made, the obligation to abide by it is independent of the wishes of any particular nation. A government contemplating action usually asks what the law has been, independently of what it proposes to do. It knows that ordinarily nations will judge and react to its action in the light of the law as it is deemed to be now. A government may sometimes seek escape from the law as it is, but it recognizes that in most instances there is no escape, and it, in turn, will usually deny escape to others. From its perspective, uncertainties of law are occasional and peripheral, change is small and slow and often to be resisted.

Admittedly, there are areas of international relations for which there are no relevant norms; there are issues on which the law is so uncertain that to speak of a "norm" is at least exaggeration; there are cases—including, alas, some that are very important for international order—where the law's uncertainties render it difficult to decide whether there has been compliance or violation.† Nations sometimes have to determine law for themselves from ambiguous precedents, in circumstances rendering objectivity difficult and where the area of permissible conduct is not obviously defined. These cases, however, are exceptional. In general, I assume what all nations assume in their foreign relations: that there are norms and that nations either observe or violate them. However disputed some of them are, others are generally accepted; however uncertain

---

* A nation ordinarily can decide that it will not observe a particular norm or understanding, but it will have to face the consequences of violation, much as an individual is ordinarily free to commit a crime and take the consequences. See p. 91.

† For example, the law on external "intervention" in civil wars (see Chapter 7), or the width of the continental shelf (Chapter 11); compare the consequences of uncertainties, both of fact and of characterizations, in Vietnam (Chapter 16).

many may be at the periphery, they have an established core; however ambiguous is language—say, in a treaty—it usually has a substantial area of clear meaning. However difficult it may be, in some instances, to determine what the law is and whether it has been violated, generally one may speak confidently of observance or violation. And, usually, what nations mean when they consider the lawfulness of an action (their own or that of another state) is not too far from the traditional determinant: whether a hypothetical impartial international tribunal would conclude that particular behavior violated some international rule, standard, or undertaking. That the action will never in fact be passed upon by such a tribunal, that some may question the very concept of impartiality of an international tribunal, that lawfulness is in fact determined for their own purposes by governments inevitably more-or-less partial, may modify but does not vitiate the basic conception of lawfulness or unlawfulness in the behavior of nations.

Nor is that conception fundamentally affected by the fact that in international affairs the action of a government may itself have substantial legislative impact.[4] In some cases, a government contemplating action inconsistent with what had theretofore been deemed the rule may be hoping to change the law. And sometimes—if the norm has been uncertain or has ceased to correspond to prevailing forces and concepts, if the acting government is influential, if other governments share its interest in changing the norm—the actor may succeed:* the new action does not evoke reactions as to a violation, and eventually our hypothetical international tribunal would also assert that the new action has come to represent the norm. Even in such cases, however, the actor took the risk that its "proposed norm" would not be accepted and its action would be treated as a violation. In any event, this is hardly a prevalent complication. It has particular relevance to major political issues (usually involving major political actors), some relevance in regard to some norms that are challenged or in flux, and almost no

* Consider the effect of unilateral extensions of their jurisdiction by coastal states, Chapter 11.

relevance to many established norms or to the mass of treaty obligations.

Usually it is meaningful to speak of violation or compliance. There are many instances where a state is admittedly in violation, as, for example, when the Congress of the United States purposefully imposes a tariff, discriminates against foreigners of a particular nationality, or subjects some aliens to military service, in derogation of earlier treaty undertakings;[5] or flouts a resolution of the U.N. Security Council to boycott Rhodesia, contrary to our commitment in the U.N. Charter.[6] The United States also virtually pleaded guilty to overflights in the U-2 incident.[7] While nations, generally, still deny that they are violating international law, often the denial merely falsifies the facts—as in 1950 when North Korea alleged that the South Koreans had initiated hostilities. At times, when a nation seeks to justify its action by asserting that international law is or ought to be something else, the justification in effect admits violation, especially when the nation cannot reasonably expect that its "proposed norm" would be acceptable. Sometimes, indeed, it might be quite unhappy if its action became a general norm.* Occasionally the justification for violating a treaty is a polite confession—for example, some clearly implausible reading of the agreement, or some far-fetched invocation of *rebus sic stantibus* (the principle that agreements are binding only so long as circumstances remain as they were, or as they were contemplated at the time of the treaty). The difficulty of judging compliance with law in exceptional cases does not prevent us from studying compliance or violation in the abundance of instances.

Of course, one should not deal with the influence of law in misleading simplicity. The whole body of the law, including the legal framework of international society, shapes and limits the behavior of nations and determines the alternatives available to them. Even as to the norms of the law, their influence on diplomacy is more subtle and more complex than merely to deter violation or induce

---

*One wonders, for example, whether France and Great Britain would accept the "norm" they asserted at Suez in 1956. See Chapter 13.

compliance. He contributed an important insight who first suggested a spectrum of compliance or violation. While international law does not divide neatly into degrees of crime with graduated penalties, or into felonies, misdemeanors and petty offenses, or even into crimes and torts, there are nevertheless norms and norms, obligations and obligations, and also violations and violations. Some may shake the foundations of international society— for example, a nuclear aggression. Some may seem minor on the world scene but loom very important in the eyes of the acting government (e.g., the abduction of Adolf Eichmann by Israel in 1960), or of the "victim" (e.g., the unlawful detention of a diplomatic officer). Some violations, say, in breach of a contract, may involve "only money." Some minor violations of an old treaty may raise objections "only in principle." Some violations are unintentional or technical, as when a friendly plane strays over foreign territory. Sometimes the law is more or less clear, the obligations more or less debatable. Some law or agreement is purposefully "loose," because states cannot or will not regulate by firm prescription, and the observance of such law is correspondingly loose, as in the General Agreement on Tariffs and Trade (GATT). In the various cases there would be important differences in the consequences of the violation, in the temptations to commit it, and in the influence of law to deter it.

The ways in which international norms affect governmental behavior are also less than simple. International law obviously influences behavior when it helps to deter violations. It may keep nations from doing what they may otherwise deem to be in their interests, say, from overflying foreign territory in search of intelligence or seizing valuable foreign property. Or obligations may impel nations to do what they might otherwise not do—say, come to the assistance of an ally or adopt sanctions at the behest of an international organization.* If an international norm does not com-

---

*E.g., Bolivia, Chile, and Uruguay complied with the resolution of the Organization of American States calling for severance of relations with Castro's Cuba, although they had voted against the resolution. 51 Dep't State Bull. 174 et seq., 579 (1964);

pletely deter, it may at least delay violative action until the needs are clear, until other alternatives are explored and rejected, or exhausted.

International norms will also determine choice among alternatives. With more than one way of achieving a desired policy, nations will not readily choose the one that violates, or more clearly or deeply violates, an international norm or obligation. They will tend to choose the lesser violation, sometimes at substantial sacrifice.

If international law affects what nations do, it will influence also what they say. We may be cynical about the rhetoric of nations and their proclamations of respect for law.[8] Even Hitler pretended that he was acting consistently with Germany's international obligations at the time of his most terrible violations. Still, we need not wholly dismiss rhetoric or justification. When a nation claims to observe international law to create an image of itself, either in its own eyes or in its neighbors' eyes, it is significant that this is the image which nations value. Even when a nation hypocritically invokes international law as a cover for self-interested diplomacy-as-usual, it is significant that it feels the need to pay this homage to virtue.[9] The rhetoric may still be the aspiration, the reach that exceeds the grasp. Rhetoric, moreover, is often employed in the hope that it will be believed; this can only be if, to an extent at least, it is consistent with the nation's behavior. The fact that nations feel obliged to justify their actions under international law, that justifications must have plausibility, that plausible justifications are often unavailable or limited, inevitably affects how nations will act. The choice of justification may also have important legal and political consequences, as I shall suggest in relation to the Cuban missile crisis.

---

only Mexico, which claimed that the resolution contravened Article 96 of the U.N. Charter, refused to act upon it. *N.Y. Times*, Aug. 4, 1964, § 1, p. 9. (The OAS ended the Cuban embargo in 1975.) Compare the alternating compliance and violation by the United States of sanctions against Rhodesia.

HOW MUCH LAW IS OBSERVED?

To most of us, the world we read about in our journals is tense, troubled, and disorderly, and we assume that relevant law is being disregarded. In fact, some of the disorder we observe is wholly within states—massacres in Burundi or ruthlessness resulting in a million deaths in Cambodia, civil war in Angola or Lebanon, rioting in South Africa, terrorism in Argentina or Northern Ireland, political disorder in Portugal or Spain, crime in urban United States—and at least some of these disorders are not the concern of international law. Even in transnational matters, we know, there are serious lacunae in the domain of international law: the state of international law is still primitive, the relations and actions to which international law speaks are limited, and many deplorable acts are not violations because there is no relevant law—*e.g.*, the arms race or granting haven to hijackers.[10] Its adequacies are a weakness in the international order but, while intimately related, they differ in cause and in consequence from deficiencies in the observance of existing law. Sometimes, although there is relevant law, disorder reflects not clear violation but only different views about an uncertain law, or different versions of confused facts on which the law depends—as in regard to intervention in Vietnam, or the rights and wrongs of Kashmir. Sometimes we see violations because we wish to, in the actions of our non-friends. Sometimes, although there may be violations, they are not the cause of disorder or even its principal manifestation. In the ideological conflict after the Second World War, for example, any violations of law or agreement were incidental to the basic breakdown of cooperation between the world's dominant powers, the sharp divergence in their interests, their hard pursuit of antagonistic policies.

Even those who are aware of the law's limited reach often share the common impression that the field of international law is sown with violated norms and broken treaties. Although there are reasons for this impression, it is grossly mistaken. There is a tendency to judge law observance by counting the violations, or, without counting them, from a general sense that they are common. But the influence of international law can hardly be assessed by the number of violations alone, even by the number of violations which are not suppressed, or rectified, or punished. Also relevant is the record of law observance—decisions not to commit violations, failures to do so, and decades of diplomacy in which a nation does not even consider violating some norm or obligation.

To judge the effectiveness of law one would have to examine not only the considered decisions of governments but, especially, the operation of law on the working levels of foreign ministries. Every day, legal counsel suppress or modify proposals that are deemed illegal before they reach the level of decision; political officers themselves stifle or fail even to think of measures which they know would probably be unlawful. In the life of a foreign office it is not uncommon that officers responsible for relations with Country X wish particularly that those relations remain friendly and untroubled; "desk officers" are even known to acquire special sympathies for their "clients." They would hardly propose policy that would violate law and roil relations, and would resist any such proposal by others. If a political officer were tempted to propose a violation of a norm or treaty, it is highly probable that the proposal would be sent to the office of the legal adviser for clearance, and it would be stopped or modified there. It would be the highly unusual case in which a decision were taken in the face of the lawyers' opinion that the proposed action would constitute a violation.

Violations of law attract attention and the occasional important violation is dramatic; the daily, sober loyalty of nations to the law and their obligations is hardly noted. It is probably the case that *almost all nations observe almost all principles of international law and almost all of their obligations almost all of the time.* Every day nations respect the borders of other nations, treat foreign diplomats and citizens and property as required by law, observe thousands of treaties with more than a hundred countries.* Of course, violations are not fungible; they must be weighed as well as counted: one

---

*The number of agreements registered at the United Nations is more than ten thousand. There are thousands of agreements in effect which are not registered at the United Nations.

nuclear aggression by a major power might render meaningless all the observances of all norms and obligations by all the nations of the world. It is relevant, perhaps critical too, to ask why particular violations have not occurred. Obviously, non-violation is significant only if there is capacity to commit the violation, the interest to do so, perhaps even the temptation or provocation. The failure, say, of the United States to commit aggression against Canada "take place" every day of the year: I would not claim 365 observances of the U.N. Charter—any more than, as an individual, one would claim credit for being law-abiding every day that one does not steal or commit murder. Surely, to press the point, distant Yemen, without a major air force or missiles and without interest or interests in Canada, cannot meaningfully be said to be respecting the territorial integrity of Canada when it does not violate Canadian airspace. But where the capacity and the temptation exist, where in another day or another context armed attack or some other violation might have taken place, self-restraint surely owes something to international law. Law is involved, for example, when, especially during periods of hostility between them, the United States refrained from attacking Cuba, or the Soviet Union respected the borders of Iran. In less dramatic contexts it is relevant that, despite the continuing temptations in daily intercourse, unnumbered principles of customary law and thousands of treaties are regularly observed.

To assert that nations generally observe law, or even that they refrain from violating law, may imply an exaggerated and unproven claim of the law's influence. One can say that the behavior of nations, generally, is not inconsistent with law or obligation. That has at least negative significance; were this not so, it would be a self-deluding mockery to speak of international "law" at all. Affirmatively, it suggests at least that international law does not pretend too much, is not unviable, and bears substantial relation to the facts of international life. It suggests, too, that international law achieves—and reflects—a measure of order in the life of nations. One may still ask how much of this consistency of national behavior with law measures true observance of law. One must still consider the violations—what kind, between which nations, and with what effect on order. Again, evidence is difficult to obtain and to evaluate, but one may gain insights into the influence of law when one considers why nations observe law, and when and why they flout it.

WHY DO NATIONS OBSERVE LAW?

The impression that nations commonly violate international norms and undertakings may be due not only to incomplete observation, but also to erroneous *a priori* assumptions about how nations behave. Much is made, in particular, of the lack of executive authority to enforce international law and the lack of effective "sanctions" against the violator. The assumption seems to be that since laws and agreements limit the freedom of nations, governments will not observe these obligations, unless they are compelled by external authority and power. In fact, we know—although effective "sanctions," as that term is commonly used, are indeed lacking—that nations do generally observe laws and obligations. The preoccupation with "sanctions," then, seems largely misplaced. The threat of such sanctions is not the principal inducement to observe international obligations. At least, the absence of sanctions does not necessarily make it likely that nations will violate law. There are other forces which induce nations to observe law.[11]

A more sophisticated suggestion has it that since there is no body to enforce the law, nations will comply with international law only if it is in their interest to do so; they will disregard law or obligation if the advantages of violation outweigh the advantages of observance. Of course, if national interest and advantage are defined broadly enough, this formula may be true and may indeed be a truism. The cynic's formula, if I may call it that, is, however, out of focus. The fact is that law observance, not violation, is the common way of nations. It usually requires an expectation of important countervailing advantage to tempt a nation to violate law. Observance, one may conclude, appears to be generally "more advantageous" than violation; indeed, nations seem to see advantage in law observance "in principle." At least, then, one would have to revise the judgment to state that barring an infrequent non-rational act, nations will observe international obligations unless violation promises an important balance of advantage over cost. Moreover, there are domestic as well as external costs of violation, and observance will be importantly affected also by internal forces and impulsions not strictly related to national cost or advantage.

To adopt some formula like that suggested is, of course, the beginning of inquiry, not the end of it. We must attempt to discover what are the costs and advantages nations consider in their international relations, what weights they might assign to different advantages and costs at different times. We may ask which norms or agreements, in what circumstances, are particularly observed; which are more likely to be violated. And we may ask how these considerations of international advantage or disadvantage are modified by domestic facts and forces.

Foreign Policy Reasons for Observing Law

That nations act on the basis of cost and advantage may seem obvious, but the notions of cost and advantage are not simple and their calculation hardly precise.* To explore any such accounting we must assume that nations act deliberately and rationally, after mustering carefully and weighing precisely all the relevant facts and factors. But foreign policy often "happens" or "grows." Governments may act out of pique, caprice, and other irrationality, as well as thoughtlessness and bad judgment. When they would act

---

* My concern in this chapter is with the cases where a government might see some advantage and be tempted to commit a violation. In the abundance of relations between nations, although there is law or agreement and violating them is theoretically possible, nations have no interest in doing so. In many instances the lack of interest to commit a violation may reflect acceptance of law and habits of law observance; or it may be due to the fact that the law reflects the mores of a society (see Chapter 4). But nations ordinarily have no benefit to gain from molesting an alien or interfering with consular activities. In such cases it is difficult to speak of the cost and advantage of law observance. Perhaps one can say that the advantages of violation are negligible because the cost of observance is negligible.

rationally, they may yet not have the time or the facilities or the data for careful policy-planning, and any "accounting" is wholly impressionistic and instinctive. Even in large, organized, and developed foreign offices, where the "policy paper" is common, it may not be read by those who actually make decisions. The best and most careful policy paper, moreover, may have to compare incomparables and weigh imponderables in attempting to reach a conclusion, giving due weight to conflicting interests, tangible and intangible, direct and indirect, immediate and long term. Still, some calculation of advantage and cost, more or less deliberate, more or less conscious, is no doubt determinative in the abundance of cases; and, without claiming precision about forces that can only be suggested, not measured, we can indicate the principal elements that go into the accounting.

For any nation, the cost and advantage of law observance or violation must be seen largely in the context of its foreign policy as a whole. This is obvious in regard to some laws, like the law against unilateral force, and in regard to some obligations, like those of the United Nations Charter or the North Atlantic Treaty or the European Community agreements. Although less obvious, it is no less true, say, in regard to laws pertaining to the treatment of aliens or agreements on consular activities. (Indeed, we can learn much about a nation's foreign policy by observing its behavior under traditional law in routine matters, by examining the pattern of its undramatic agreements—treaties of friendship, commerce and navigation, arrangements about trade, or aid, or cooperation.) At bottom, all norms and obligations are "political"; their observance or deliberate violation are political acts, considered as part of a nation's foreign policy and registering cost and advantage within that policy.

Nations observe law in part for reasons that are rarely articulated and of which government officials are often only faintly aware. That international law will be generally observed is an assumption built into international relations. Nations have a common interest in keeping the society running and keeping international relations orderly. They observe laws they do not care about to maintain others which they value, and to keep "the system" intact; a state observes law when it "hurts" so that others will observe laws to its benefit.

Every nation's foreign policy depends substantially on its "credit" —on maintaining the expectation that it will live up to international mores and obligations. Considerations of "honor," "prestige," "leadership," "influence," "reputation," which figure prominently in governmental decisions, often weigh in favor of observing law.[12] Nations generally desire a reputation for principled behavior, for propriety and respectability.

Governments do not like to be accused or criticized. They know that violation will bring protest, will require reply, explanation, and justification. In our time, at least certain kinds of violations are likely to be brought to the United Nations (or the OAS, or OAU) and few governments would face that prospect with equanimity.

Law is commonly observed because nations desire their relations with other countries to be friendly. Any violation between two countries will disturb relations, in degree depending on the cordiality of relations and the nature of the violation.* Even when rela-

---

* Of course, "friendly relations" is not a single state of cordiality; every nation has special friends (and sometimes special "enemies"), and something of a spectrum of friendliness with other nations. Friendship or coolness, however, is not always decisive. Friendly nations, even close allies, have some adverse interests that can lead to violations or charges of violation. E.g., at the height of their "special relationship" the United Kingdom charged that the United States was unlawfully applying its laws, and its administrative bodies were unlawfully issuing orders, to British companies. See *In re Investigation of World Arrangements with Relation to the Production, Transportation, Refining and Distribution of Petroleum*, 13 F.R.D. 280 288–91 (D.D.C. 1952). Compare *British Nylon Spinners, Ltd.* v. *Imperial Chemical Industries, Ltd.* [1953] 1 Ch. 19 (C.A. 1952). More recently, the United Kingdom charged that U.S. exclusion of the Concorde airplane violates international agreements. On the other hand, enemies, even during actual war, have common or reciprocal interests causing them to observe many obligations toward each other, e.g., the Geneva Conventions on the Treatment of Prisoners of War. During the Cold War, the United States and the U.S.S.R. continued to carry out numerous agreements; the U.S. and Cuba even made and implemented a new agreement on hijacking. One may assume that between friends the violation will usually not be important enough to destroy the friendship; between enemies the compliance will not be in a matter important enough to be of major usefulness to the other side.

tions are not cordial and there is no interest in improving them, nations will refrain from violations that might create major dispute.

Law observance will have a different importance in the foreign policy of different nations and even of the same nation at different times. Since international law was developed largely by the nations of Western Europe and their offspring in the Americas, these nations learned to attend to this law in their foreign relations; they have also been more satisfied with their creation. Since law is generally a conservative force, it is more likely to be observed by those more content with their lot. Nations that believe they have a particular stake in world order will themselves attend to law, and their compliance will establish a comfortable position from which to insist that others do the same.* The United States—and the U.S.S.R. and the People's Republic of China—deeply engaged in competition for influence and leadership, for the good will of governments and peoples, would weigh carefully the cost of certain violations, say, the invasion of a neighbor's air-space. A nation's foreign policy may depend heavily on its reliability for living up to a particular obligation.[13] The United States labored for decades to gain credibility for its undertakings not to intervene in the internal affairs of Latin American countries. American policy to deter a Soviet attack on Western Europe has depended on persuading the Soviet Union that the United States will live up to its obligations to come to the assistance of NATO allies, even at risk of nuclear destruction in the United States. A nation may have particular concern to behave properly—e.g., Germany, after Hitler left it with much to live down. A small nation, especially insecure and vulnerable, may be particularly cautious—e.g., Greece, or Israel in its relations outside the Arab world. In special political contexts—say, for nations reluctant to take sides in the Cold War, or between Israel and the Arab states—scrupulous adherence to international law affords protection from pressure by either side.

---

*In turn, the climate of international order will influence law observance; an atmosphere of disorder will encourage violations, but they are less likely in stable times and areas.

Costs of Particular Violations

The forces for law observance mentioned are general, intangible, imponderable; they are not the less significant, and they are often determinative. Usually, the accounting includes also, perhaps principally, particular costs and advantages arising from the specific case. These, too, tend to favor observance. A main deterrent to violation is the realization that the anticipated cost is too high. The principal cost is usually the response of the victim, and such response may be anticipated for almost every breach, whether from a wish to punish, or to deter further violations, or to recoup what was lost, or from considerations of prestige, or "on principle," or because of domestic pressures.

The victim's response will vary with the violation and may range from mild protest to war; it will tend to be proportional, to "fit the crime," and will often be directly related to the violation. For that reason, in large measure, laws or obligations that operate symmetrically between nations—and as long as they continue so to operate—are rarely violated. A government may wish to arrest a diplomat who has flouted its laws, but it knows that, if it does so, its own diplomats may be arrested.[14] It will not confiscate the property of another government or of its nationals when it has property in that country and is not prepared to risk retaliatory confiscation.[15] Of course, the response of the victim is not limited to direct retaliation. For failure to protect an embassy there will be a claim for compensation. Planes that violate the territorial airspace of another nation may be shot down. From a myriad of arrangements and relations between two nations, a victim can always find some form of retaliation, even one more or less related to the violation. In 1952, when it was persuaded that Hungary had denied justice to the crew of an American airplane forced down in its territory, the United States forbade American tourists to travel to Hungary and closed two Hungarian consulates in the United States.[16] A would-be violator will also consider costs deriving from any special dependence on the victim. Nationalizations of American properties which the United States considered unlawful led to cancellations of economic aid, as in Ceylon in 1965.[17] Apart from how the victim government may respond, some violations bring undesirable consequences in the world marketplace: nations will not violate the rights of aliens if they do not wish to discourage tourism and foreign investment.

Like customary law, treaty violations also have their spectrum of possible responses that tend to deter violation.* Even minor breaches of particular provisions may bring protest, and substantial breach of a treaty will generally result in its termination by the other party. A government generally observes the common treaty—of friendship, commerce and navigation, on extradition, or on avoidance of double taxation—because a breach would deprive it of the treaty's benefits. Breach of important treaties may bring other unwelcome consequences. Violation of the nuclear test ban or the agreements against nuclear weapons in outer-space or on the seabed, by either the Soviet Union or the United States, would mean that the other power would feel free to do likewise. It would mean an end to détente and a return to the Cold War; each side would accelerate the arms race, increase its military budget, step up research and development of new weapons, tighten its alliances. Obviously, only a major advantage from such a violation would seem worth the price. The breach of some new major disarmament agreement might cost even more—perhaps war.†

International agreements sometimes include special provision to deter violation. They may provide for inspection and procedures

---

*Some treaties are easier to observe than other because they demand less. Nations are less likely to violate "functional" or "technical" agreements than political ones, agreements that require a nation to follow certain procedures (arbitration, resort to the United Nations) than those that impose substantive limitations on conduct. International agreements also sometimes include imprecise, hopeful, hortatory undertakings (to "cooperate with," to "look with favor on"), which are easy to comply with, and the violation of which it is difficult to prove.

†The Nuclear Non-Proliferation Treaty is of sufficient importance to many states to engage their concern if it is violated. Although a multilateral treaty it is also an agreement among the few nuclear powers, and particularly between the U.S. and the U.S.S.R., not to export this weaponry. As such, it may be that there is so much concern to avoid or retard the proliferation of weapons, so much reluctance to see any additional nations in the "Nuclear Club," that, if one nation "violated" the understanding, another might still be reluctant to "respond" in kind. On the other hand, if one nuclear state should begin to give weapons to its allies or assist them in

for determining and dealing with violations. Some may make explicit the cost or consequences of a violation, sometimes providing an especially high price.* In olden days a breach of obligation might mean death to hostages. It has been suggested that hostages in various forms might be used today as an inducement to comply with important undertakings, but to give hostages in the ancient way would surely be deemed uncivilized. Still, hostages have in fact induced compliance with important arrangements, as when Greek minorities lived in Turkey and Turkish minorities in Greece.[18] In a different sense, American troops in Berlin serve as hostages to guarantee compliance by the United States with its undertakings to defend the city.†

Tacit Agreements

Some of the reasons inducing nations to perform their international agreements operate even as to "tacit agreements"[19] which, while not strictly "law," are not unlike law in their effects on national behavior.‡

The tacit agreement is not a new phenomenon; what is new

----

developing such weapons, there might be irresistible pressures on another major state to do likewise for its allies. "Third nations" might then also prove adroit at engendering a competition between the United States and the U.S.S.R. to sell them nuclear weapons. Compare the competition between exporters of nuclear reactors and materials.

*While usually the principal purpose of such provisions is to render response more nearly certain and violation therefore prohibitive, definition in advance may also serve to limit the response and thus avoid excessive reaction, counter-retaliation, and the breakdown of the treaty system.

† The United States "nailed itself" to its commitments to NATO and Berlin by solemn, repeated pledges and by various guarantees and "hostages," so that friends and enemies alike will recognize how costly it would be for the United States to fail to carry out its undertakings. United States troops are in Berlin principally to make it very difficult for the United States not to respond to Soviet aggression, and thus to make it likely that the Soviet Union would be deterred from any attack. See T. Schelling, "Deterrence: Military Diplomacy in the Nuclear Age," 39 *Virginia Quarterly Review* 531, 539 (1963).

‡ Compare also non-legally binding agreements like the Final Act at Helsinki, 1975, which are not too different from binding agreements in the consequences of violation and in their deterrent effect. See Chapter 12.

perhaps is the recognition that it exists and that it has some of the characteristics of an expressed agreement. Nations have always recognized that their acts influence those of others. If one nation built up its armies, its neighbors might do likewise; if one raised tariffs, it could expect responding or corresponding barriers from others. In many circumstances it might be said that there were tacit agreements between particular nations not to enlarge armies or raise tariffs. Specifically, there was in effect a tacit agreement between the United States and Great Britain (later with Canada) not to fortify the frontiers between the United States and Canada. There was perhaps a tacit agreement during the Second World War that neither side would use chemical warfare. It is not unrealistic to say that there was a tacit agreement during the Korean War that the United Nations Command would not bomb across the Yalu River, and the Communist Chinese would not bomb United States bases outside Korea. For some years there was a tacit agreement between the United States and the Soviet Union not to aggravate tensions in Berlin and not to accelerate the arms race by major increases in military budgets. There are complex tacit understandings in operation about developing or deploying weapons during the extended SALT negotiations. Before the Nuclear Non-Proliferation Treaty, many believed there was a tacit agreement between the United States and the Soviet Union not to give nuclear weapons to other nations, including their respective allies.

New sophistication about tacit agreements may impel nations to rely on them more frequently. A tacit agreement does not entail difficult negotiation or drafting, needs no ratification or proclamation. Its very existence can be denied if that proves desirable for political reasons, foreign or domestic. It can be terminated by either side at will, without legal liability, political onus or sanction, or stigma in world opinion.* Even more than with formal agreements,

---

* In important instances, especially where a tacit agreement may represent a temporary substitute for a formal one, the differences between these and formal agreements may be less. The unilateral moratoria in 1958 on testing nuclear weapons while negotiations went on, which, while not wholly tacit, did not represent a "legal" agreement, were "violated" at the cost of considerable criticism.

then, the principal inducement to compliance is the desire to have
the agreement continue.

Multinational Agreements
and Multinational Response

Domestic law is often observed from fear not of what the victim
will himself do but of the "response" of the community. For most
international norms or obligations there is no judgment or reaction
by the community to deter violation. The ordinary violation of law
or treaty is not yet a "crime" against the society to be vindicated by
the society. It is unusual for nations not directly involved to respond to a violation even of a widely accepted norm—say, Egypt's
alleged violation of the immunities of French diplomats in 1961.[20]
With important international agreements that are multilateral in
character, however, violation may infringe on the rights and invite
the response of many or all the participating states. For a few major
norms and agreements, moreover, there may be communal reaction, especially through the United Nations, e.g., for *apartheid* and
other gross forms of racial discrimination.[21] Its adverse judgment
and other possible response would have to be anticipated by any
would-be violator of the law of the U.N. Charter outlawing war.

But the U.N. and regional and other organizations have sometimes cast their net wide and responded to what were basically
violations between two states—e.g., when Chile complained, in
1949, that Russia refused to permit the wives of Chileans to leave
the country,[22] or when Israel was charged with abducting Eichmann from Argentina (Chapter 14). Where available, suit in the International Court of Justice or other third-party adjudication is a
kind of international response that might deter a would-be violator.[23]

International "sanctions" and other multilateral inducements to observance may be particularly effective in the organs for cooperation
for common welfare. This law, too, of course, is not all of a kind:
there are differences in the institutional patterns and relations established—for example, between the World Health Organization
and the European Economic Community—as well as in the nature

and onerousness of the undertakings involved. In some instances, undertakings are reciprocal and mutual, as in the Universal Postal Union; but the advantages of the arrangement may still be different for different nations. (The International Labor Organization, for example, has differing significance for the Soviet Union, for the United States, and for other countries with their diverse domestic institutions and economic structures.) There are arrangements that, while nominally equal and mutual, operate primarily for the benefit of the disadvantaged, as in the World Health Organization and the Food and Agriculture Organization. Others are explicitly designed to channel assistance from some nations to others, as in the International Atomic Energy Agency or the International Development Bank.

The special international law which these programs represent is also subject to an accounting of the cost and advantage of participation or non-participation, violation or compliance. But the accounting differs from that in regard to other international law; it is different too in the various cooperative arrangements described. Many involve interdependent programs, and a violation will involve other nations and evoke communal reactions—e.g., in GATT, in the International Civil Aviation Organization, in the World Bank. Such organizations and their members are often particularly vigilant to detect violations and ready to respond effectively. It is difficult to conceive that any modern nation would find advantage in withdrawing from the Postal Union or in violating any of the undertakings involved and risking stern reactions from other members.

In another way, the members of the European Community have established patterns and institutions, which suggest interest in their continued existence and which could not be easily disentangled. The parties are closely interdependent, ever vigilant to preserve their rights; there is machinery for determining obligations and enforcing them; there is sure to be a strong response to violations.[24] With these and other forces to induce compliance, even individual violations of the undertakings involved are unlikely. Important violations could not be indulged without full appreciation of the consequences, far beyond the immediate issue, for the institutions and for what they represent in the life of these nations and of Europe. On the other hand, while the costs to the United States or the Soviet Union of abandoning its commitments to the IAEA are indirect and subtle (and open to question by national "budgeteers," isolationists, and others), they too help deter violation.

The calculus that might determine compliance or violation of the special international law of human rights is considered in Chapter 12.

Domestic Influences in Law Observance

Although the principal reasons for observing international law are reasons of foreign policy, there are also internal forces, general and particular, which influence every government to observe international norms and the nation's undertakings.

Nations observe law, in part, for what may be called "psychological" reasons. There is an influence for law observance in the very quality of law, in the sense of obligation which it implies. Nations observe law from habit and in imitation of others. That a nation consented to an obligation inevitably generates some influence for its observance; that it caused others to rely on its undertaking sets in motion a sense of estoppel which helps to deter violation; that a nation has itself invoked a rule builds commitment to that rule when it is, in turn, invoked by others. Unlike an individual, whose "conscience" about law observance may be dissipated when he is anonymous, when he acts "in a crowd," nations generally have relations with all the other units in the society, cannot be anonymous, do not act in a crowd.

A major influence for observance of international law is the effective acceptance of the law into national life and institutions.[25] When international law or some particular norm or obligation is accepted, national law will reflect it, the institutions and personnel of government will take account of it, and the life of the people will absorb it. With acceptance comes observance, then the habit and inertia of continued observance. That the United States and Canada have accepted the border between them, and the principle that it shall not be violated, is built into border arrangements, the regulations of immigration agencies, passport practices, and the expectations of the citizens of both countries. Violations of the border, or denunciation of international agreements about border control, would require uprooting these arrangements, changing laws and regulations and practices and habits. When, in the Headquarters Agreement with the United Nations, the United States agreed that members of foreign delegations to the United Nations should enjoy diplomatic immunity from arrest,[26] that agreement was built into the life of New York. The laws of New York reflect the agreement, police regulations provide for it, the individual policeman is taught it, the citizen—grumbling perhaps—acquiesces.[27] Systematic violations of this agreement could not take place without top-level decisions and deliberate, coordinated, and extensive modifications.

In more complicated ways, accepted international arrangements—whether of the Universal Postal Union, or NATO, or a fisheries convention—launch their own dynamism, their own inertia, their own bureaucracy with vested interests in compliance, their own resistances to violation and to interference and frustration. The European Community agreements are observed, in part, because they have been accepted in member countries and enmeshed in national institutions; there are national bureaucrats whose job it is to assure that the agreements are carried out; powerful domestic groups have strong interests in maintaining these agreements.

Attitudes toward international law reflect a nation's constitution, its laws and institutions, its history and traditions, its values and "style." Indeed, allowing for the dangers of metaphor and the particular inadequacies of analogy from individual to national behavior, it seems permissible to suggest that some nations are more law-abiding than others by reason of their national "morality" and "character."[28] Some governments seem especially sensitive to the stigma—the "guilt"—of violating international law.* Some have a

---

* Perhaps, even, governments that are concerned for their internal order may hesitate to set their citizens an example of an international violation.

stronger sense that national "honor" or "duty" requires the observance of law and of agreement. Whether or not one deems such attitudes appropriate, government officials are also human beings and cannot lightly do as officials what they would be reluctant to do as men or women, nor in a representative government can they lightly do what the people would deplore.

Through much of its history the conduct of the United States, I believe, has reflected internal forces impelling observance of international law. Conceived in "decent respect for the opinions of mankind," born in the heyday of the "law of nature," fathered and raised by men who respected law, the United States was the first modern "new nation" and sought protection for its independence in the law of nations. Geographic isolation, natural wealth, and the desire to be let alone to develop in its own way enhanced its respect for the conservative influence of law in support of international order. Federalism, separated branches of government, a written constitution, all helped to develop a respect for law, legalism even, which has pervaded national life. Whether it be virtue or vice, the people of the United States have had moral, perhaps moralistic, attitudes toward their relations with other nations, and respect for international law has been included in that morality.[29]

As a powerful and affluent nation, the United States may sometimes be restive under restraints; it may sometimes be reluctant to submit to new law (say, human rights covenants) or to international adjudication;[30] it may seek to transform legal questions into political ones to be determined in the light of its own foreign policy;[31] but it does not lightly violate accepted norms, customary or conventional. Major violations by the United States have been rare. It did not threaten the political independence or territorial integrity of others even while it had a monopoly of atomic power. Only under pressure of ideological conflict, for example, during the Cold War did the United States behave in ways that have been seriously challenged: it is accepted that the United States had some role in the deposition of President Arbenz of Guatemala in 1954 and assumed that it had some in the overthrow of Allende in Chile in 1973; it apparently committed some violation at the Bay of Pigs in

Cuba in 1961; many have condemned as unlawful the intervention in the Dominican Republic in April 1965; some question the lawfulness of various of its actions in Vietnam and Cambodia.[32] Even in such instances, however, the concern for law is not wholly absent. In the Bay of Pigs, United States ambivalence and restraint, induced in substantial measure by concern for law and obligation, limited its involvement;[33] later, the reaction to the enterprise, in and out of government, was one of guilt and penitence. In the Dominican Republic, the United States eagerly strove to extricate itself and sought legitimation of its actions by the OAS.

Particular national values and traditions will also mold attitudes toward law or toward a particular law or obligation. In general, Western-style democracies have tended to observe international law more than do others.* Free institutions make it more difficult for a government to risk violation in the hope that it will not be detected—say, mistreatment of an alien, or conducting a nuclear test in violation of an agreement not to do so. The United States in particular may be deterred by the recognition that it seems unable to do anything clandestine, to keep a secret (especially from its own people), or to deny a true accusation, as in the 1960 U-2 incident in Russia. Open societies are also less likely to be tempted into certain violations by any compulsion to maintain a curtain of secrecy. And a society in which individuals are valued is likely to treat aliens, too, at least as well as customary international law requires and to observe any human rights undertakings; and, such obligations apart, it will also wish to avoid possible retaliation against its citizens by other governments.

International law will also enjoy the support of those forces in a democracy that check the abuses of government. Separated branches of governments—as in the United States—may also prevent violations of international law. The President may veto a statute that contravenes international obligations;[34] Congress, or its

---

* In part, this may reflect that Western democracies are principally the Western European powers (and their colonial offspring), which created international law in their image and their interest.

committees, may resist or deter executive violations.[35] An opposition party, an independent and ubiquitous press, a scholarly community, various pressure groups—all vigilant to criticize the government—will also seize on violations of international law, particularly those of political import, for example, the unlawful use of force.[36] (Sometimes indeed, officials act from concern for "public opinion" although in fact the public may have no opinion on the issue.) Some international arrangements also enjoy the support of a special "constituency" that seeks to assure that the government will observe them; for example, the international trade community is concerned for good relations generally and for compliance with international law, particularly for the observance of commercial treaties and trade arrangements.

National constitutions and institutions will contribute to observance of international law. In the United States, for example, international law is part of the law of the land, without need for legislative or executive intervention to make it so. International law can be invoked in an appropriate case in the courts and the courts will give it effect.[37] Treaties too are, by the express terms of the Constitution, law of the land and, if self-executing, will be enforced by the courts on their own initiative.[38] Thus, the Supreme Court annulled a state's discrimination against a Japanese alien which violated a treaty provision.[39] Some principles of international law—for example, minimum rights for aliens and their property—coincide with guarantees of the Constitution, and the alien receives in the courts of the United States, even against the President and Congress, far more protection than international law requires.[40]

Political personalities, and their personal power and tenure, may exert an important influence for law observance in the degree of their commitment to international order.* Special commitment to a particular rule or agreement (by President Kennedy to the Nuclear

---

* They differ, of course, in their commitment to international order. President Johnson's handling of the U.S. intervention in the Dominican Republic in 1965 may reflect, in part, attitudes toward international law and obligation different from those evinced by President Kennedy in the Cuban missile crisis in 1962.

Test-Ban Treaty, for example) makes it to that extent less likely that the nation would breach it during that official's tenure or perhaps while his party continues in power. That important congressional leaders initiated, sponsored, and fought for NATO or the United Nations will help to assure their continued support for the obligations undertaken at least for some years.*

In the United States an important influence for compliance with international law is the role of lawyers in the life of the country. The spiritual fathers of the United States were principally lawyers, as were many of its leading presidents, and lawyers have usually dominated both houses of Congress. Many of the secretaries of state—the best and the worst of them—were trained in the law, and the Department of State has a legal adviser with a substantial staff. Major issues of foreign affairs come for discussion to the President's Cabinet, of which the Attorney General is a member and which usually has other lawyers as well. That principal participants in the policy-making process were trained in the law does not assure that they will cast their votes for law observance; it does mean that some knowledge of the law, some appreciation of its significance, and some attitudes and habits of respect for law find a place in the process of decision. Outside the government, particularly through professional associations, lawyers exercise important influence on their government and that influence tends to support international law.

The law officer, particularly the legal adviser to a foreign office, may be a potent influence for law observance.[41] All governments have legal counsel to advise them in their foreign affairs, obviously because their opinions are deemed relevant to the process of making national decisions. A skeptic might suggest that they are used merely to justify what the political officers wish to do, but even in that role lawyers help shape the policy so that it lends itself to plausible justification. Since the early days of the Republic the At-

---

*It has been suggested that the likelihood of compliance with important agreements can purposefully be enhanced by requiring heads of state personally to commit their prestige to the agreement.

torney General of the United States has rendered a substantial number of opinions on matters involving international law, and some of these opinions have told the Executive that he was not permitted to act as he wished.[42] The advice has usually been heeded. More numerous even are such opinions by the Legal Adviser of the State Department. In Great Britain there are volumes of opinions of the law officers of the Crown which include numerous instances in which the advice given was that the government could not take the proposed action, or had no grievance against the action of another government.[43]

The role and influence of the legal adviser are not, of course, the same in the various foreign offices. They may even differ importantly from time to time in the same office, principally with the personality and attitudes of the foreign minister and of the legal adviser himself. His significance for law observance is probably greatest in the United States, where organization, procedures, and practice give the Legal Adviser of the State Department an active and varied role. He regularly attends the staff meetings of the Secretary of State and takes full part in their deliberations. His staff of seventy lawyers daily advises and guides the political officers in the light of international law. A member of the Legal Adviser's office often participates in working-level meetings from which proposed policy may emerge. Lawyers see almost every outgoing instruction to diplomatic missions which might conceivably have legal implications. It is rare that policy-makers reach a decision without consulting the Legal Adviser, or at least giving him the opportunity to be heard. Rarely is a decision made against strong views by the Legal Adviser that it would constitute a violation of law or agreement.*

---

* The exceptions are principally in the realm of "intelligence activities," or the secret decision to take sudden action by force for "national security." Intelligence and some other covert activities are commonly treated as beyond the law. The Legal Adviser, I am guessing, did not participate in the decisions of the United States to send U-2 planes over Russia in 1960, or to dispatch Marines to the Dominican Republic in April 1965 or engage in some of the "dirty tricks" charged to the Central Intelligence Agency. Neither, I guess, were their legal officers consulted when Great Britain and France used force at Suez, or the U.S.S.R. in Hungary in 1956 or

The influence of the legal adviser may depend on how he and the policy-makers see his role. In some foreign offices the lawyer is a "technician," available to give advice whenever the minister decides that he wishes to have it, and is expected only to pass judgment whether some proposed action would be legal or not. Other policy-makers recognize that law, not least international law, is not wholly technical, that there is room for creative cooperation between legal and political officers to use the concepts, techniques, and instrumentalities of the law to develop more desirable policy. Some legal advisers and political officers appreciate, too, that in the policy-making process the legal adviser sometimes appears as the "conscience" of the foreign office, as the spokesman for a national interest often unrepresented—his country's long-term interest in legal order and stability—as against the claims of some immediate advantage.

Sometimes the political officer's perspective is that epitomized in the much-bruited attitude: "Don't tell me that we may not do it; tell me why (or how) we can."[44] The policy-maker, feeling responsible to act in the national interest as he sees it, often does not see any national interest in heeding legal niceties. Impatient with restrictions on his government's freedom to act, he may wish to see the law as wholly flexible, especially since there is no judge to reject any position that the legal adviser might perpetrate. Most legal advisers and some policy-makers, however, know that the law is not so flexible, that the honest lawyer cannot play that role, that if he did he would not be serving his government's interest since his advice would not accurately reflect the law which operates in international society and which will determine the reactions of other nations. Rather, they believe, the legal adviser should tell the political officers whether proposed action conforms to international norms or treaty obligations, how deep an inroad into law and order it would make, whether there is indeed uncertainty or ambiguity in

---

in Czechoslovakia in 1968. In some of these cases, perhaps the governments were aware, without advice of counsel, that their actions were probably unlawful, knew that their lawyers would say so, but had decided to act nonetheless.

the law and how much, how plausible any available justification
would be, how other nations involved are likely to view the law
and the justification. He should consider alternatives and suggest
where each might lie in a spectrum of violation. And the wise poli-
tician listens, because he knows that violations bring consequences—immediate and eventual, potent and subtle—that may
not be worth the advantages to be gained.

I have been emphasizing forces for law observance in national
life, as distinguished from the demands of a nation's foreign policy.
This dichotomy, for emphasis and clarity, should not suggest that
domestic and foreign considerations are nicely separable. A nation's
foreign policy is intimately related to national qualities and domestic factors such as those considered. It would not be easy to determine how much it is due to national "character" and domestic influences, how much to foreign policy and the elements that
contribute to it, that the United States could not violate its solemn
unambiguous undertakings as easily, say, as could Stalin's Russia
or Mussolini's Italy. On the other hand, the internal forces which
impel a nation like the United States to comply with law may
themselves in some measure be the result of a long history during
which that nation learned to favor international law because the
law supported its foreign interests.

WHY NATIONS VIOLATE LAW

While nations generally observe both customary international
law and international agreements, all nations have violated them
and, no doubt, will violate them again. Law observance is usually
the rational policy, but nations do not always act rationally. Law
observance usually has dominant advantages, but governments do
not always act deliberately on the basis of a careful calculus of cost
and advantage.* When, as in regard to most decisions, there is

---

* Sometimes a violation is unintentional, or committed for a nation by others than
those principally responsible for its foreign policy; sometimes an important policy
may involve incidental violations which did not receive careful attention, or which
appeared only a minor consideration.

some rough, more or less explicit, weighing of all the considerations, there are cases when the cost of law observance seems too high, the cost of violation temptingly low. Occasionally there is uncertainty as to whether law will be enforced and whether there will be undesirable consequences. And there may be domestic forces that press for violation, and sometimes prevail.

Advantages of Violation

Usually a nation deliberately violates a norm or agreement because it expects that the advantages of violation will outweigh its costs. Faced with the temptation to act in disregard of law or obligation, the government will know what it hopes to gain.* By aggression it may hope to achieve prestige and power and wealth, to acquire territory, to improve its strategic position, to extend its political influence, or to change the political or economic policies of others. From unauthorized overflight of another country's territory it may obtain valuable intelligence. By unlawful seizure of the property of aliens it can obtain funds for important domestic programs. By breach of a treaty it seeks relief from a bargain that was bad or has turned bad. Sometimes a violation provides a special advantage—for example, the satisfaction or prestige that comes from slapping a bigger power, as when Castro nationalized American properties,[45] or Amin abused British subjects in Uganda.

Against such concrete and immediate advantages, the costs of violation are not always clear and decisive. The general advantages of law observance are unmeasurable and long-term, and their importance cannot be easily demonstrated. "Realists" in foreign offices sometimes do not see national advantage in maintaining law, especially when other countries seem to be flouting it.[46] Order and stability, they grant, are desirable, but some immediate, more tangible national interest should be preferred; besides, how much

---

*Sometimes, of course, a government may miscalculate the benefits anticipated from a violation, or prove unable to obtain or retain them; France and Great Britain had to withdraw their forces from Suez in 1956, retaining no advantage from their enterprise; Iran could not readily market the oil of the Anglo-Iranian company which it had nationalized in 1954 in alleged violation of law.

order is there anyhow, and will it be jeopardized by one violation? "Honor" and "duty" are unsophisticated considerations. "Morality" has no place in relations between nations, and national interest should not be sacrificed to a private ethic; violation of law, moreover, is not *per se* immoral. A particular violation may even appear just, because the norm or agreement broken was outdated or unfair. World opinion is largely myth. Credit, credibility, prestige, influence, leadership are real, but one cannot prove that they are seriously tarnished by ordinary violations of law; indeed, some violations, by displaying power and forcefulness, may enhance leadership and prestige. Violations may sometimes disturb relations with other countries, but most relations can readily survive them and some are not very cordial anyhow.

These arguments reflect common attitudes that help to explain why the general advantages of law observance do not always prevail. For some governments, in some cases, these advantages may be particularly weak or absent. While at the end of the Second World War, order seemed the principal concern of all nations, some now place it second to other values—for example, the end of colonialism, or radical economic and political transformations. The Communist nations in principle, and countries like the Soviet Union, Communist China, Castro's Cuba, Nkrumah's Ghana, Nasser's Egypt, at various times and by different means, actively sought instability as a prelude to a different international order, or sought to influence the shape of change in some country (*e.g.*, Angola). If some nations have a special interest in law observance, others may have very little—*e.g.*, Communist China during the time that it was content to be virtually outlawed. If the United States and the Soviet Union sometimes observe law from a special sensitivity to the opinion of other nations, others sometimes see their influence in actions that involve violation of law. The very competition for leadership which contributes to American and Soviet observance of law sometimes impels them to violate law, as in Hungary in 1956, and Czechoslovakia in 1968, or in the Dominican Republic in 1965. Fear of criticism in the foreign press or in the United Nations has meant little to Communist China in its isolation, to the Soviet Union during the time when it considered the United Nations a hostile bloc in the control of the United States, or to the Republic of South Africa after it had become inured to hostile world opinion. Even nations with special concern to obey law may find an issue where other interests seem more important—as Israel did when its agents abducted Eichmann from Argentina, as perhaps the United States did when it suspended convertibility of the dollar to gold in August 1971.

The specific, immediate costs of violation may also appear especially low and seem worth the price. The major cost in the response of the victim may not be very "costly," especially where violations are isolated and the victim wishes to continue friendly intercourse with the violator. Apart from the fact that the victim's responses are limited by law, nations do not go to war for minor infractions, or lightly rupture diplomatic relations, or treat the violator's citizens as hostages, or terminate commercial intercourse, or even denounce treaties unrelated to the violation. Since the principal response is usually retaliation to kind, obligations that do not operate reciprocally and do not lend themselves to simple retaliation may be violated without concern for this particular cost. That Communist countries, especially under "Stalinism," did not generally permit their citizens to travel abroad meant that their governments did not have to fear retaliation if they harassed Western visitors, or denied them justice or effective diplomatic protection. That in a country like the United States mob action against foreign embassies is unlikely meant that American embassies in some other countries did not enjoy the added protection that lies in the threat of retaliation. Concern for friendly relations will not deter violations when relations are not friendly, even nonexistent, as when North Korea seized the *Pueblo* in 1968, or Cambodia the *Mayaguez* in 1975. Again, human rights law gives rise to separate reasons for its violation.[47]

One kind of violation inherently enjoys enhanced advantage and limited cost—the action which is quickly done and presents a *fait accompli:* often, pressure cannot be applied to discontinue or undo the action, the purpose of the violation is achieved, its advantage cannot be taken away. Opprobrium, censure, or sanction may follow; but unless the violation is serious enough to lead to war, even the "responses" are helpless to undo what is done, and are likely to be lighter, especially if repetition is unlikely. The circumstances which led to the act are probably extraordinary, and the violator, whether he denies or admits, justifies or apologizes, usually implies good behavior for the future. Examples might include the assassination instigated by a foreign government, whether of a government leader or of a refugee enemy (Trotsky, Galindez, Delgado, Ben Barka).[48] In modern times a nation might be tempted to make a single bombing attack to destroy a dam, a canal, an oil refinery, a nuclear center or a missile site, or refuse to extradite a terrorist and allow him to escape to a country of haven (as in the Daoud affair in France), or to accomplish some other political, economic or psychological effect.[49]

There is further encouragement to violation if the cost of a violation is uncertain and might prove low. Cost might be nearly discounted, for example, if there were substantial likelihood that the violation could not be detected. Despite modern publicity and communication techniques, mistreatment of an alien behind an iron or bamboo curtain might never be discovered; a government can deny death or disappearance or claim not to know a person's whereabouts; or it might be difficult to pin responsibility for his fate on the government.[50] Important arms control agreements might be violated if there were not effective verification to discourage violation by making detection probable.[51] Espionage, though usually entailing various violations of law, is common practice and always denied by governments; "dirty tricks" by intelligence agencies are also never admitted, difficult to prove, and are regarded by some governments as "extra-legal" (rather than illegal).

Inevitably, there are also uncertainties as to the consequences of being caught in a violation. That the victim will respond can usually be expected, but the form that the response will take and its effectiveness may be conjectural. Sometimes there are uncertainties as to the response of the victim's friends or allies; at least General de Gaulle used to question whether the United States would respond to Soviet aggression against Western Europe at risk of destruction to itself.[52] Communal reactions are even more problematic. Action by the United Nations (or by other political organizations) depends on votes, and necessary majorities cannot always be counted on. (Compare the failure of the General Assembly to adopt major resolutions after Israel's victory over the Arab states in June 1967.) In Korea, the U.N. reaction to Communist aggression in 1950 probably came as a surprise; had it appeared more likely, the violation might not have occurred. With the changed complexion of the United Nations, indeed, some violators can assume with confidence that the majority will not condemn their actions, e.g., India's at Goa or Bangladesh, Uganda's expulsion of Asians, violations of human rights in Communist, Arab, or other Third World countries. When some community reaction is to be expected, its effectiveness is frequently uncertain; calls for economic sanctions, in particular, are often unheeded or unsuccessful because they hurt the nations imposing them as well as third countries.

At times whether there is a violation of law may depend on complex, ambiguous, or disputed issues about facts and how they may properly be characterized. (Compare Vietnam, Chapter 16.) In such circumstances, an acting government may genuinely believe one version of the facts although a court, upon careful investigation, would find the facts otherwise and conclude that there was a violation of law. Or, in less than good faith, the violator may take advantage of the factual ambiguities, knowing that it could deny the violation, that the uncertainties would infect and reduce the responses to the violation, even by allies of the victim, particularly responses that depend on decision in the United Nations or in a regional organization.

The uncertainties of "cost" and the likelihood of violation are increased when the norm or obligation itself is not wholly certain. An established rule is more likely to be observed than one in doubt, or in controversy, or in the process of change, or one outdated and different from what it "ought" to be. Where there are *bona fide* differences as to whether there was a violation, even a response by the victim is less likely or would be less strong—and the threat of it less of a deterrent. Even if the law appears clear enough, a nation might risk violation in the hope of modifying the law. Sometimes, if an influential nation sets a precedent of deviation, others may even better the instruction: the United States claimed the continental shelf only for the limited purpose of exploiting its resources, but the action precipitated claims by other nations of wide fishing zones and even complete territorial jurisdiction to wide areas of sea.[53] Greek officials on Cyprus in 1974 thought they saw an opportunity to modify an arrangement they had not liked and which had become even more distasteful, and gave Turkey a plausible basis for more radical change to its own advantage.

Domestic Influences for Violation

Even when considerations of international advantage and cost dictate observance, there are domestic forces and impulses that might make a nation violate law. As there are "psychological" inducements to law observance, there may also be countervailing pressures to violate. A nation's sovereignty, and the absence of obvious external restraints, may give it a heady sense of freedom and power to do as it likes, regardless of law. The high stakes and the inherent instabilities in international relations may frighten a state into taking "pre-emptive" precautions for its security, sometimes at the expense of law. Official habits of mind tend to set up "legalism" in contradistinction to "national interest" to which legal obligation must yield.

Where national passions are engaged, opposition parties, impending elections, a hostile press, pressure groups, organized and vocal segments of public opinion may all be forces for violation of international law rather than compliance. Such domestic pressures, it is believed, helped to persuade the Indian government to take Goa by force.[54] It is generally accepted that recurrently opinion within the Arab states has inveighed for action against Israel, regardless of the United Nations Charter or any armistice agreements. (Opinion in Israel may impel governments to take strong measures against terrorism.) In the United States there were pressures to act against "international communism" which might have impelled the government to be less than scrupulous about law, as at the Bay of Pigs. National predilections, even principles, are not limited to major issues. In the United States, for example, one has found a reluctance to afford aliens better tax treatment than is enjoyed by citizens or to allow resident aliens to avoid military service obligations borne by citizens—sometimes even in the face of an earlier treaty provision.[55] Pressures from special economic interests are often behind violations of tariff or trade provisions, as in the occasional violations of the European Community agreements.

If some national institutions further the cause of compliance, others hinder it. In the United States, international law sometimes suffers from the separation of branches in the national government; the executive and the legislature, in particular, were separated and balanced in order to prevent tyranny, at some price in efficiency.[56] Unlike parliamentary systems,[57] the American system does not assure a single government policy, does not guarantee that President and Congress will look in the same direction, whether in domestic or foreign affairs.[58] Congress can refuse to enable the United States to live up to its obligations under a treaty by failing to enact implementing legislation or to appropriate the necessary funds.[59] Or Congress can pass legislation inconsistent with the international obligations of the United States.[60] A court also can render a decision which an international tribunal might deem a violation of international law and which the makers of foreign policy helplessly regret. Although it has not yet happened, a court can even find that a treaty violates the Constitution and cannot be carried out in the United States despite the international undertaking.[61]

Federalism too has its price. In the United States, in theory, there are no "states' rights" in regard to foreign affairs. International law and treaties are the law of the land for the states as for the nation. But in practice, states may sometimes infringe such obligations, and there is not always an effective remedy, juridical or practical, to make them comply.[62]

Any country, moreover, may find itself liable for violations (intentional or negligent) committed by local authorities—say, failure to accord adequate protection or the requirements of justice to aliens.[63] Sometimes there are violations when governmental machinery is inadequate, when administration is ineffective, when departments responsible for carrying out undertakings are remiss in doing so. There have apparently been such violations even in the politically developed countries of the European Economic Community, despite all the forces making for observance of the Community agreements.[64]

Violations may also occur due to inadequacy of legal advice. Unlike the United States, even some established nations, whether from habit, shortage of personnel, organizational pattern, or methods of operation, do not subject all of their foreign policy to the scrutiny and counsel of legal advisers. (Where foreign policy is not developed in the foreign office but is made by an executive or his coterie, systematic legal consultation is even less likely.) The legal adviser may be only an *ad hoc* consultant, not a full-time officer of the government; he may not know of a proposed measure unless someone decides to consult him; consultation may be limited in time and form and hence in influence. His status or his personality may limit his intervention. Or the lawyer may not be consulted, owing to oversight, haste, or a desire to limit the number of persons knowing of a secret proposal.*

Violation of Treaties

Although the forces that lead to occasional violations apply generally to international agreements as well as to customary law, there are additional factors that may modify the calculation of cost and advantage in observing some treaties. Treaties are sometimes of indefinite duration or for a long term. An old treaty, though still technically in effect, may be outmoded; treaties of long duration, also, may no longer be reasonable or fair. If the advantaged nation

---

*Sometimes the policy-makers may decide to avoid counsel because they are determined to act regardless of legal considerations. There are reports that in a certain foreign office, when the policy-makers decided to act in a major instance in knowing contravention of law, the legal adviser was told to take a holiday.

will not renegotiate, the other may be tempted to terminate the treaty, even if our hypothetical court would not deem it a case in which a party could consider itself released from its obligation because of changed circumstances (the principle of *rebus sic stantibus*). An international agreement may represent a policy which a new regime, breaking with the past, may denounce (even when it cannot do so lawfully under the terms of the agreement).[65]

For many treaties one may anticipate that the response to a violation would be only termination of the agreement; sometimes that is not a sufficient deterrent. Often agreements involve a number of more-or-less interdependent provisions, some of greater interest to one party than to another. A government which does not highly value a particular provision may violate it in the belief that the response will be only termination of that clause. One party may not desire a particular provision in the first instance but acquiesces in order to obtain the rest of the agreement; that party is not likely to be deterred from violating that provision by any fear that the provision will not be maintained.

This is one of several lessons afforded by the Korean Armistice Agreement. In the armistice negotiations both sides sought an end to hostilities, and a provision to that effect is the heart of the Agreement.[66] If either side had reopened the fighting, the Agreement would of course have been destroyed. Because neither side wished to resume hostilities, the provisions ending the fighting continue in effect, having survived the failure of political negotiations,[67] breaches of the other provisions in the Agreement, and major political changes in the world around Korea.

The Armistice Agreement also provided for exchange of all prisoners that wished to be repatriated.[68] The Chinese Communists and the North Koreans (and presumably their "protector," the Soviet Union) long resisted the principle of voluntary repatriation but ultimately accepted it as the price of an armistice, and because it was a source of embarrassment to them.[69] Prisoners were repatriated immediately,[70] and there remained no question of continuing compliance. The United Nations Command later indeed accused the Communists of failing to account for many prisoners, particularly South Koreans.[71] But the U.N. Command knew at the time the armistice was signed how many prisoners the Communists were prepared to return. In entering into the agreement, ending hostilities, exchanging the prisoners listed, the U.N. Command knew that the Communists could continue to withhold any other prisoners they might have without fear of costly disadvantage. The U.N. Command would have difficulty proving that there were in fact other prisoners; it had no prisoners left which could be detained in retaliation; it would not on this ground resume hostilities.

Different again is the lesson of a third provision in the Agreement, an undertaking by both sides not to introduce into Korea new personnel or equipment except as replacements; the provision was to be monitored by the inspecting body established in the Agreement.[72] For geographic, military, and political reasons, this provision did not operate symmetrically for both sides. The U.N. Command had far greater interest than did the Communists in maintaining that provision, as well as the effectiveness of the inspection system, and was also subject to greater political restraints deterring violation. For the Communist powers, the expectation that if they built up their forces in violation of the Agreement, the U.N. Command might eventually do likewise was no deterrent at all.* That if they frustrated the inspection system it might eventu-

* Eventually, in response to Communist violations, the U.N. Command declared itself relieved of this obligation. See 12 U.N. GAOR, Annexes, Agenda Item No. 23, at 1, U.N. Doc. A / 3631 (1957).

The Korean experience teaches that an inspection system must not only be capable of detecting violations, but must also be "sabotage-proof." The Commission established in the Korean Armistice Agreement, by contrast, was "sabotage-prone," indeed, with hindsight, "sabotage-inevitable." (The Commission consisted of two Communist nations and two Western "neutrals." The former, it soon appeared, were fully prepared to cooperate with the North Koreans in frustrating the Commission's inspections behind Communist lines.) A verification system that can be readily sabotaged does not deter violations. Often, indeed, a nation can sabotage such a system without it even being clear that it is intentionally doing so and, therefore, without even the onus of having prevented verifications. See F. Iklé, D. Elliot, L. Henkin, H. Linde, R. B. von Mehren, C. Zoppo, report prepared for Advanced Research Projects Agency, *Alternative Approaches to the International Organization of Disarmament* 8–9 (The RAND Corporation, 1962).

ally cease to operate behind the U.N. lines as well was also no high "cost" to them.[73] The Communists might also have guessed, correctly, that for political reasons in the United States and within the United Nations, their breach of the provision against reinforcement would not lead to invalidation of the Armistice Agreement as a whole and resumption of hostilities. Nor did the Communist powers have reason to fear other sanctions; vis-à-vis most countries, both North Korea and Communist China were then already virtually outlaws, while they would surely continue to enjoy the assistance of the Soviet bloc. On the whole, then, there was little inducement to abide by this provision, and it soon appeared that they were not doing so.*

Some kinds of agreements are more susceptible to violation than others. Some agreements, for example, though cast as formal treaties, are primarily business arrangements, resemble private contracts, and suffer the special mores of the market place. While breach of agreement is not taken lightly in the market, some of the political reasons which compel law observance in other cases may be absent.†

Political Treaties

Forces that encourage violation are particularly telling where "political" law and agreements are concerned. The term should not

---

* Of course, U.N. negotiators might have desired such a provision even if they had realized that there were few inducements for the other side to honor it—in the hope that it might be observed nevertheless, or, at least, that its existence will slow up "violations" by the other side. Perhaps such provisions were included also from a need to appear "untrusting" of the Communist adversaries—to an ally (e.g., the Republic of Korea) or to congressional or public opinion in the United States.

It may be that U.S. negotiators accepted the Paris agreement ending Vietnam hostilities in 1973 with some hope but without any real confidence that it would be observed, because they wished to end the war at almost any cost.

† Occasional breach of contract does not carry opprobrium, is often considered legitimate, a sound business practice, and legal "penalties" for breach are often treated as a legitimate business expense. International society takes breach of treaty more seriously, because treaties usually deal with more than business transactions, have national and international consequences, and are often a vehicle for international legislation.

be misunderstood. All international law and agreements are political in that they are part of foreign policy and affect political relations between nations. There are, however, laws and agreements whose political character is paramount, in particular those which involve international peace and stability, or the security, integrity, and independence of nations. I refer to the law of the U.N. Charter outlawing war, to law (customary and by treaty) forbidding intervention in the affairs of other nations and particularly in their internal wars, and to various "political treaties," particularly treaties of peace, various treaties of "protection" and other special political relationships, and military alliances. This law is particularly vulnerable; often, the stakes—the cost of observance, the advantages of violation—are high; often there is uncertainty of law or obligation, and confusion and ambiguity of the facts and their evaluation. It is principally these laws and agreements, directly related to international order, that the student of foreign affairs may have in mind when he asserts that international law is widely disregarded.

The peace treaties at Vienna, Paris, Versailles, and those following the Second World War are treaties in form, and courts and lawyers have persisted in treating them as such. Political officers sense, however—and lawyers often forget—that at bottom many of them are not "agreements." The Treaty of Versailles, for example, was imposed by force and did not have those qualities of mutual consent and *quid pro quo* that characterize agreements and that support the principle that agreements should be observed. The terms of such treaties often reflect the emotions of victory and unexamined, even capricious, notions of "reparation." Although for lack of a better mold the treaty form is used, these arrangements are really an attempt by the victors to reap the fruits of victory and with other controlling powers to legislate rearrangement of international society.* As between victor and vanquished, though equally "parties"

---

*Peace treaties are often acceptable, even to the victims, because the alternative may be continued occupation by the victor to achieve the same ends. After World War II, for example, if the vanquished had not accepted and did not abide by to the treaty, the forces that make for observance of treaties generally are not here applicable.

Among the victors, too, while peace treaties do not suffer the defect of duress, they still have special qualities. These agreements may in large measure be hegemonial, as when they redistribute empires. They may be legislative, as when they seek to rearrange the government of territories, reorganize institutions, and impose an order in a region or in the world. They may be deeply political in that the arrangements determine relations and rights among the victors themselves, and define their future policies. They may be capricious in the disposition of spoils among the victors and the imposition of burdens on the vanquished. They usually reflect the glow of victorious alliance, the assumption of continued cooperation, the desire to "settle things" quickly and to avoid issues, rather than any true consensus based on careful anticpation of the individual interests of the victorious nations in the years after the peace.

Peace treaties that do not follow an unconditional surrender may also have political qualities that reflect on their legal character and affect their observance. Take the Geneva Conventions of 1954 on Indochina, deeply relevant to subsequent events in Vietnam. The parties solemnly agreed to a "provisional military demarcation line" in Vietnam, with elections throughout the country to follow in short course.[74] As is well known, the partition remained, elections never took place, and a terrible war rent the country, with full-scale American participation designed to keep partition permanent. Although there were mutual recriminations and accusations of breach of agreement, many readily saw, at least in hindsight, that much in the agreements was not viable and perhaps was not what the parties really desired. It was important in 1954 to end the fighting; the agreement was designed in large part to permit France to extricate itself with "face." It is not clear that either side thought there could be mutually acceptable elections in either North or South Vietnam. As in other such cases (like the Korean Armistice),

---

human rights provisions in a treaty, the victors might have felt obliged to continue in occupation to ensure that human rights would be respected.

an agreement is written to achieve an immediate purpose on which there is consensus—the end of hostilities. More is written into it, reflecting mood, hope, gamble, temporary pressures, the need to soften blows and to buy time, and much of this fails.*

I am not suggesting that peace treaties are not "good law" or that they need not be observed.[75] International society is built on them, and the nations of today, the territories they occupy, the peoples they encompass, reflect the "compelled" treaties and "hegemonial" arrangements of an earlier day. As to the long past, surely, the binding character of these treaties must be accepted, unless voluntarily reordered. With the passage of time forces of inertia and stability, rights based on reliance and investment and prescription, weigh heavily in favor of continued observance. In such instances, generally, it is important that political determinations be accepted as settled, without asking whether they were rightly settled 100 or 300 years ago. And, in fact, except for die-hard irredentist movements, or other interests artificially kept alive (like the claims of the Arab refugees to "return to Palestine"),† the settlements of a receding past are generally accepted and raise no problems of compliance or violation.

Some kinds of provisions, however, often begin to erode—particularly, occupation arrangements, reparations, limitations on the behavior of the vanquished inside their territory (for example, disarmament requirements or human rights guaranties applicable only to the defeated countries, as in the treaties following both world wars).[76] Of such provisions, too, one might say that would-be violators will compute cost and advantage. But particular considerations I have mentioned look quite different. The assumption of *pacta sunt servanda* rings differently and *rebus sic stantibus* also has special meaning.[77] As Hitler showed, the vanquished will not tolerate provisions they consider Draconian when they feel able to do

---

* Compare the fate of the Paris Agreements of 1973, ending hostilities in Vietnam.

† The drive for a Palestinian "homeland" that began in 1970s had plausibility and support only insofar as it might be realized in territories occupied in the 1967 war, not in Israeli territory by undoing the State of Israel.

something about them. Other nations and "world opinion" will not support imposed regimes indefinitely, and even those who imposed them will not continue to maintain them and to respond to their violation. Political stakes in the maintenance or dissolution of such arrangements are so high that the influence of law and legal obligation is inevitably secondary. Such arrangements are maintained by the political forces that created them; the legal principle that "agreements should be maintained" will not support them when there are new forces calling for new arrangements. There are many reasons for condemning Hitler, but that he failed to live up to Germany's "legal obligations" in the Treaty of Versailles seems among the least of them. Even among the victors themselves, say, after the Second World War, despite the clear requirements of law and politics that arrangements must be observed, the postwar arrangements could not survive the basic conflict of interest. One side or the other in the Cold War may indeed have been the first to "violate the agreements," but compliance and violation began to lose meaning when the agreement to maintain order in Europe proved to have no foundation in common interest.

In Indochina, too, there is no doubt that the 1954 agreements were and should have been treated as binding law. That must be said even of those provisions which, I have suggested, were never viable and perhaps never quite wholly intended. There is no way in law of distinguishing these provisions from those terminating hostilities, which surely were intended as binding; any doubt cast on the legal validity of any of the provisions would cast doubt on the whole. (For some of the participants, at least, the agreement to stop fighting may have depended on inclusion—and observance— of the other provisions.) But it should not be surprising that some of these provisions were not observed, just as ancillary clauses in the Korean Armistice were destroyed. In Vietnam, the political evolution in both parts, in the nearby countries, in China, and elsewhere made the "violation" of these provisions by one side or another inevitable, and led to new hostilities between new parties.

In the decades after World War II, another group of political treaties, colonial arrangements, also suggested a different calculus of compliance. These too have been less than mutual, in free consensus and in benefit, reflecting less than equal bargaining power and sometimes the use or threat of force. Treaties of protection and other quasi-colonial relationships (United Kingdom-Egypt, France-Tunisia) and treaties of capitulation and extraterritoriality (United States-Morocco) were agreements in which even the "ascendant" party has been compelled to recognize that these *pacta* were not *servanda*, whether because of a superseding principle of "self-determination," or some new doctrine denying enforceability to unequal treaties, or because *rebus* no longer *stantibus*. Among the things that are no longer so is an international opinion tolerant of colonial status. Even opinion in the metropolitan countries themselves rejected patent colonialism. Whatever our hypothetical court might say of the legal obligation to comply with these treaties, nations were unable to insist on compliance and have been compelled to abandon or renegotiate these agreements—in Morocco and Tunisia, in Egypt in 1954, in Panama in 1964-65 and again in 1977-78, and elsewhere in Asia and Africa.*

For different reasons, even in voluntary peacetime arrangements of political character, the influence of law tends to be subordinated and the forces for observance and violation have a special quality. Consider military alliances of the traditional kind, or even NATO, which is supported by impressive institutions long and carefully nurtured. They are created as responses to immediate danger, which causes nations to agree to arrangements that might otherwise be distasteful—for example, to commit themselves to war in defense of others, to subordinate national independence to collective judgment, to place national forces under foreign command, to permit foreign bases on home territory, to dedicate much national

---

* The end of colonialism also affected other laws as well. For example, the law of state succession—hardly agreed at best—was subjected to serious strains when new countries were asked to carry out obligations of their former colonial masters. See D. O'Connell, "Independence and Succession to Treaties," *British Yearbook of International Law, 1962*, at 84 (1964).

Colonial arrangements responded particularly to new forces in international relations in the postwar world. See Chapter 6.

wealth to extraordinary military expenditures. The agreements are often of indefinite duration or for a period deemed, conservatively, long enough to outlast the danger, as well as to make the political and financial investment worthwhile. Usually, as in the North Atlantic Treaty, these arrangements are in the form of a treaty to underscore the solemnity of the undertaking and to assure the parties as well as the potential enemy that the undertaking will be carried out.

For a period these agreements are scrupulously observed (although when the stakes are as high as those involved in NATO, the political reasons for maintaining the arrangements are so overwhelming as to render the additional influence of law almost supererogatory). Then, long before the term of the alliance expires, the original danger seems reduced, political forces begin to shift. The alliance itself, if it works, builds an effective deterrent and reduces the danger which created it. The need for the alliance then appears less; the cost of it—political as well as financial—begins to seem excessive. The sense of legal obligation is not sufficient to withstand the changes in a nation's political orientation, releasing political forces which replace those that supported the agreement and seek its dissolution or modification. One may suggest that despite a fixed long-term provision, there is in these cases an implied denunciation clause or a special application of *rebus sic stantibus*. In any event, even if a court might find that to do so would constitute a violation, a party might yet denounce the agreement or insist on its renegotiation under threat of denunciation. And erstwhile allies will not respond as to a violation. A new government bent on "nonalignment" took Iraq out of the Baghdad Pact in 1958. Changing roles and relationships in South Asia altered the character of Pakistan's participation in SEATO and in CENTO and led to their eventual demise. Although France continued to adhere to the North Atlantic Treaty, it left the Treaty Organization and denounced some agreements implementing the treaty. France, I note, was criticized for undependability as an ally, not for violating its treaty obligations.

Other peacetime arrangements, even those unrelated to security, may also be subject to special political forces affecting their observance as law. The merger of states—as when Syria and Egypt became the United Arab Republic, or when the Federation of Malaysia was created—may have been by binding agreement, but the force of law often proves insufficient to maintain them against explosive centrifugal forces. Arrangements for welfare cooperation, like the European Community agreements, may also be deeply political, involving fundamental rearrangements within societies and in relations among them. The international law they establish is different, operating more like constitutional law in a federated state. The European Community can readily command observance of the various agreements in detail, but it could hardly survive, or remain recognizable, if, say, the France of President de Gaulle had turned her back on its basic philosophy.*

Violations of international law or agreements happen for many of the reasons that cause violations within domestic legal systems: an important immediate advantage outweighing less-measurable, long-term interests; the hope of not getting "caught," of escaping an adverse legal judgment, of avoiding or minimizing adverse consequences. Occasionally national behavior may even reflect a kind of "sociopathic" element, as between the Arabs and Israel. There are also the special factors contributing to violations in international relations—greater uncertainty in the law, deficiencies in judicial and executive aspects of the system. Many of the violations are of "political agreements," where legal forms are used to confirm spe-

---

*Perhaps, however, the law of the Community had been so deeply incorporated into French life and institutions that, even had they wished, General de Gaulle or his successors could not eliminate it.

While there are no meaningful analogies to these political arrangements in domestic society, what I have said about observance and violation of colonial relationships and military alliance echoes comparable attitudes in regard to special personal relationships. The law in many societies, for example, has long ceased to penalize breaches of promise to marry. Desertion, separation, divorce, even if the other side resists them and insists on maintaining the "marriage contract," are not treated like other breaches of contract. Colonial arrangements might be viewed also as a kind of agreement which society ceased to tolerate, and declared to be against public policy, like contracts or indentures for servitude or slavery in domestic society.

cial relationships, and nations more readily abandon observance of these arrangements when their political foundations disappear. In total, the violations are few: are they frequent or weighty enough to negate the existence of an international order?

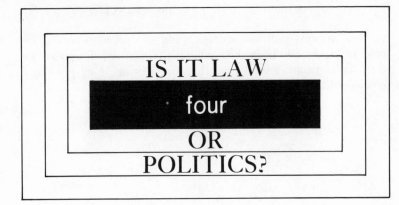

IS IT LAW

four

OR POLITICS?

The reasons why nations observe international law, in particular the emphasis I have put on cost and advantage, may only increase skepticism about the reality of the law and its influence in national policy. What I have said, it may be argued, only proves the voluntary, political character of international law. Nations decide whether to obey law or agreements as they decide questions of national policy not involving legal obligation—whether to recognize a new regime, or to give aid to Country X—on the basis of cost and advantage to the national interest. That nations generally decide to act in accordance with law does not change the voluntary character of these decisions. Nations act in conformity with law not from any concern for law but because they consider it in their interest to do so, and fear unpleasant consequences if they do not observe it. In fact, law may be largely irrelevant. Nations would probably behave about the same way if there were no law. The victim would respond to actions that adversely affect its interests and the threat of such reaction would be an effective deterrent, even if no law were involved.

This skepticism is sometimes supported by contrasting international law with domestic law in a developed, orderly society. Domestic law, it is argued, is binding and domestic society compels compliance with it. No one has a choice whether to obey or violate law, even if one were satisfied that observance was not in one's interest. In international society, the critics insist, nations decide whether or not they will abide by law. Violations are not punished by representatives of the legal order acting in the name of the society. Any undesirable consequences of violation are political, not legal; they are the actions of other nations vindicating their own interests, akin to extra-legal consequences in domestic society, like "social stigma." The violator may even be able to prevent or minimize adverse consequences. In any event, he will continue to be a full member of international society, not an outlaw.

The arguments I have strung together command consideration. Some of them are mistaken. Others do indeed reflect differences between international and domestic law, the significance of which must be explored.

Much of international law resembles the civil law of domestic society (torts, contracts, property); some of it is analogous to "white collar crimes" (violations of antitrust or other regulatory laws, tax evasion) sometimes committed by "respectable" elements. Like such domestic law, international law, too, has authority recognized by all. No nation considers international law as "voluntary." If the system is ultimately based on consensus, neither the system nor any particular norm or obligation rests on the present agreement of any nation: a nation cannot decide that it will not be subject to international law;* it cannot decide that it will not be subject to a

* I know of no satisfying jurisprudential explanation as to why a nation cannot totally reject international law. The most plausible reason is rooted in "consensus": ultimately, all nations desire "the system," whatever they may think of it or of any of its components at any particular time. And, in fact, no modern nation has rejected "the system," and governments (if not academics) have stopped asking why they are subject to international law.

particular norm, although it may choose to risk an attempt to have the norm modified; surely, it cannot decide to reject the norm that its international undertakings must be carried out. Like individuals, nations do not claim a right to disregard the law or their obligations, even though—like individuals—they may sometimes exercise the power to do so. International society does not recognize any right to violate the law, although it may not have the power (or desire) to prevent violation from happening, or generally to impose effective communal sanction for the violation after it happens.*

In arguments that international law is voluntary there lies also a common confusion about the relation of law to "policy." The two are often contrasted, suggesting that law is obligatory while policy is voluntary. In fact, law and policy are not in meaningful contrast, and their relation is not simple, whether in domestic or international society. All law is an instrument of policy, broadly conceived. Law is not an end in itself: even in the most enlightened domestic society it is a means—to order, stability, liberty, security, justice, welfare. The policies served by law are sometimes articulated—in a constitution, in statutory preambles, in legislative pronouncements, in the opinions of the courts; often these policies are tacit, and commonly assumed. International law, too, serves policy, and the policies are not too different from the domestic: order and stability, peace, independence, justice, welfare.

The policy that the law serves may be said to be the policy of the society; it is not the less the policy of its individual members. In

---

* Under its Charter and in the United Nations there is, in practice and in theory, some power to deter, prevent, undo, even penalize certain violations

International law generally is more like the domestic law of torts than like criminal law in that a violation is seen as an offense against the victim state, not one against the society as a whole, and the remedies provided are reparation to the victim rather than punishment by society. In recent years, however, there may have burgeoned a small international criminal law whereby certain serious offenses—perhaps aggression, colonialism, genocide, full-scale racial discrimination—are considered offenses against the community and may evoke community sanction. See Report of the International Law Commission, 28th session, 3 May–23 July 1976, GAOR 31st Sess. Supp. No. 1 (A/31/10), pp. 226 et seq.

developed domestic society, enlightened individuals are aware that
the law which governs their activities is ultimately in their own interest, although immediately it denies them the "right" to kill those
they do not like, take property they may covet, withhold from the
tax collector money they wish to keep. Governments are even more
likely to be aware that law, international law, serves a common policy which is also their policy.

The individual, of course, has conflicting interests. He desires
the protection of laws against trespass but may wish to invade
another's property. He may favor taxes and the civilization which
it buys for him[1] but prefer, himself, to keep his money rather than
to give it to the revenue service. The nation also has direct, immediate interests which sometimes conflict with its ultimate interest in
the policy of the law. The United States approves the law of territorial inviolability; it still saw interest in U-2 flights over Russia.

When, in the face of temptation, a person (or a nation) decides to
observe the law, to favor his ultimate interest rather than some immediate one, that too may be seen as a voluntary, policy decision.
In regard to most laws, the individual in domestic society has in
fact the policy option either to observe the law or to violate it to obtain some immediate advantage, at the risk of undesirable consequences. An individual in Anglo-American law is free to decide
whether to carry out his contract or to breach it and pay damages.*
(By contrast, nations indeed recognize a far stronger obligation to
perform most international agreements, constituting the bulk of international "law." Except, perhaps, in some commercial agreements, they do not consider it legitimate, sound international practice to break a treaty and abide the consequences.) Traffic laws are
frequently violated because detection is uncertain, and the cost is
low and does not include social opprobrium. Even where violation
brings criminal penalties, individuals may think of themselves as
free to violate law and pay the penalty. (Surely that is the view of

---

*Specific performance of a contract will be ordered only in special instances
where the law deems compensation for the breach in money damages an inadequate
remedy. See *Williston on Contracts* (3rd ed., 1957) §§ 1418–53.

those practicing civil disobedience.)* Consider tax evasion. Some individuals decide not to pay the taxes due, presumably weighing the money they save against the penalties they might incur, discounted by the likelihood of not getting caught or "beating the rap." Even as concerns the major crimes—say, murder—an individual is ordinarily not physically prevented from committing them, but is "free" to commit the crime, "as a policy matter," if he is willing to risk the consequences. In principle, is the nation that decides to violate or to observe the law making a different kind of "policy decision"?

Much is made of the fact that, in international society, there is no one to compel nations to obey the law. But physical coercion is not the sole or even principal force ensuring compliance with law. Important law is observed by the most powerful, even in domestic societies, although there is no one to compel them. In the United States, the President, Congress, and the mighty armed forces obey orders of a Supreme Court whose single marshal is unarmed.†

Too much is made of the fact that nations act not out of "respect for law" but from fear of the consequences of breaking it. And too much is made of the fact that the consequences are not "punishment" by "superior," legally constituted authority, but are the response of the victim and his friends and the unhappy results for friendly relations, prestige, credit, international stability, and other interests which in domestic society would be considered "extralegal." The fact is that, in domestic society, individuals observe law principally from fear of consequences, and there are "extra-legal" consequences that are often enough to deter violation, even were

* Civil disobedience is designed primarily to achieve not the immediate advantage of the violation but some ultimate purpose of protest, usually to bring about a change in the law. Such disobedience may have some rough analogy in international law, when a nation decides to violate law in the hope of changing it. But, unlike civil disobedience, that nation's purpose is usually to achieve the immediate advantage of violation, to avoid the consequences of a violation, *as well as* to change the law.

† In our day, again, by Richard Nixon. *United States* v. *Nixon*, 418 U.S. 683 (1974).

official punishment lacking. (Where law enforcement is deficient, such consequences may be particularly material.) In the mainstreams of domestic society an illegal action tends to bring social opprobrium and other extra-legal "costs" of violation.* This merely emphasizes that law often coincides so clearly with the interests of the society that its members react to antisocial behavior in ways additional to those prescribed by law. In international society, law observance must depend more heavily on these extra-legal sanctions, which means that law observance will depend more closely on the law's current acceptability and on the community's—especially the victim's—current interest in vindicating it. It does not mean that law is not law, or that its observance is less law observance.

There are several mistakes in the related impression that nations do pursuant to law only what they would do anyhow. In part, the criticism misconceives the purpose of law. Law is generally not designed to keep individuals from doing what they are eager to do. Much of law, and the most successful part, is a codification of existing mores, of how people behave and feel they ought to behave. To that extent law reflects, rather than imposes, existing order. If there were no law against homicide, most individuals in contemporary societies would still refrain from murder. Were that not so, the law could hardly survive and be effective. To say that nations act pursuant to law only as they would act anyhow may indicate not that the law is irrelevant, but rather that it is sound and viable, reflecting the true interests and attitudes of nations, and that it is likely to be maintained.

At the same time much law (particularly tort law and "white collar crimes") is observed because it is law and because its violation would have undesirable consequences. The effective legal system, it should be clear, is not the one which punishes the most violators, but rather that which has few violations to punish because the law deters potential violators. He who does violate is

---

* When violation of law carries no opprobrium, we get an unhappy story, like that of the American experiment with Prohibition.

punished, principally, to reaffirm the standard of behavior and to deter others. This suggests that the law does not address itself principally to "criminal elements" on the one hand or to "saints" on the other. The "criminal elements" are difficult to deter; the "saint" is not commonly tempted to commit violations, and it is not law or fear of punishment that deters him. The law is aimed principally at the mass in between—at those who, while generally law-abiding, may yet be tempted to some violations by immediate self-interest. In international society, too, law is not effective against the Hitlers, and is not needed for that nation which is content with its lot and has few temptations. International law aims at nations which are in principle law-abiding but which might be tempted to commit a violation if there were no threat of undesirable consequences. In international society, too, the reactions to a violation—as in Korea in 1950 or at Suez in 1956—reaffirm the law and strengthen its deterrent effect for the future.

In many respects, the suggestion that nations would act the same way if there were no law is a superficial impression. The deterrent influence of law is there, though it is not always apparent, even to the actor himself. The criticism overlooks also the educative roles of law, which causes persons and nations to feel that what is unlawful is wrong and should not be done. The government which does not even consider certain actions because they are "not done" or because they are not its "style" may be reflecting attitudes acquired because law has forbidden these actions.

In large part, however, the argument that nations do pursuant to law only what they would do anyhow is plain error. The fact that particular behavior is required by law brings into play those ultimate advantages in law observance that suppress temptations and override the apparent immediate advantages from acting otherwise. In many areas, the law at least achieves a common standard or rule and clarity as to what is agreed. The law of the territorial sea established a standard and made it universal. In the absence of law, a foreign vessel would not have thought of observing precisely a twelve-mile territorial sea (assuming that to be the rule), nor would it have respected the territorial sea of weaker nations which had no shore batteries.[2] In regard to treaties, surely, it is not the case that nations act pursuant to agreement as they would have acted if there were none, or if it were not established that agreements shall be observed. Nations do not give tariff concessions, or extradite persons, or give relief from double taxation, except for some *quid pro quo* pursuant to an agreement which they expect to be kept. Nations may do some things on the basis of tacit understanding or on a conditional, reciprocal basis: If you admit my goods, I will admit yours. But that too is a kind of agreement, and usually nations insist on the confidence and stability that come with an express undertaking.

The influence of law appears even in important political law or agreement. Had there been no applicable alliance agreements in 1914, Germany might nevertheless have come to the assistance of Austria, or Russia to the assistance of Serbia. It is less clear, however, that had there been no undertakings to do so, France would have joined Russia or that Great Britain would have followed France. The obligations of the agreements induced observance; the existence of the agreements had led to advance cooperative arrangements and made prompt assistance possible—which added further inducement to honor the alliance.

Or take the North Atlantic Treaty. One may accept that it was in the interest of all the parties in 1949 to recognize a common danger and to come to each other's assistance if the danger materialized. One may assume that there is considerable accuracy in the view that the United States would have come to the assistance of Western Europe even if there had been no treaty. A treaty, and numerous supplemental arrangements, might still have been necessary to create an organization and delegate various "assignments" and responsibilities. But clearly, all the parties believed, and almost all still believe, that it was important to have a formal treaty. All of them thought that the likelihood that all would come to each other's assistance would be enhanced by the legal undertaking; they believed that the possible enemy would be more likely to be deterred by a treaty entailing a solemn American commitment. And the Soviet Union has appeared persuaded that the United States would honor that commitment. In the United States, too, the President, the Congress, the people all recognized that they were assuming a legal obligation. And the political officer who does not care or talk about law and legal obligations will still recognize that failure to live up to the NATO obligation would cast doubt on the commitments of the United States everywhere, destroy its credit with friends and enemies, might-be friends and might-be enemies, and shake the foundations of American policy throughout the world.

Similarly mistaken is the impression that behavior contrary to law would evoke the same consequences, and be deterred by the threat of these consequences, even if there were no law. No doubt that is sometimes the case: Hitler violated many laws in invading Poland, and Britain and France were legally committed to come to Poland's aid; it may well be that Hitler's invasion would have brought England and France into the war even had there been no obligation. But that is the special case which shows, again, the coincidence between law and the interests of society or some of its members. In most cases a nation incurs consequences for a violation of law—consequences that would not occur otherwise—*because* it was a violation, because common standards were flouted, because advantage had been gained and the *quid pro quo* was not fulfilled, because expectations had been raised and were disappointed. The fact that these consequences do not follow a judicial proceeding obscures but does not negate that they are largely consequences of a violation of law. Indeed, nations feel obliged to respond to violation far beyond any substantive interest in doing so, just because there was a violation and to enhance future deterrence. That many nations joined the victim in opposing the use of force in Korea reflects the fact that by 1950, force had been rendered illegal. The victim too sometimes reacts more strongly than its practical interests would suggest, *e.g.*, Argentina, when Israel's agents abducted Adolf Eichmann from Argentine territory. Nations react strongly to unauthorized overflights because it is universally accepted that such intrusion is illegal, not because they are inherently damaging or "painful." That nations claim airspace "up to the sky" and resist overflight at any height but claim only a narrow territorial sea and accept "innocent passage" there without authorization is a reflection of the different rules that have developed—although we know that "out" is not different from "up," that one can inflict injury from the sea as well as from the sky.

The most common deprecation of international law, finally, insists that no government will observe international law "in the crunch, when it really hurts." If the implication is that nations observe law only when it does not matter, it is grossly mistaken. Indeed, one might as well urge the very opposite: violations in "small matters" sometimes occur because the actor knows that the victim's response will be slight; serious violations are avoided because they might bring serious reactions. The most serious violation—the resort to war—generally does not occur, although it is only when major interests are at stake that nations would even be tempted to this violation. On the other hand, if the suggestion is that when it costs too much to observe international law nations will violate it, the charge is no doubt true. But the implications are less devastating than might appear, since a nation's perception of "when it really hurts" to observe law must take into account its interests in law and in its observance, and the costs of violation. The criticism might as well be leveled at domestic law where persons generally law-abiding will violate laws, commit even crimes of violence, when it "really hurts" not to do so. Neither the domestic violations nor the international ones challenge the basic validity of the law or the basic effectiveness of the system.

The deficiencies of international law and the respects in which it differs from domestic law do not justify the conclusion that international law is not law, that it is voluntary, that its observance is "only policy." They may be relevant in judging claims for the law's success in achieving an orderly society. In many domestic societies, too, the influence of law is not always, everywhere, and in all respects certain and predominant; the special qualities of international society, different perhaps only in degree, may be especially conducive to disorder. Violations of international law, though infrequent, may have significance beyond their numbers: international society is a society of states, and states have power to commit violations that can be seriously disruptive; also, the fact that the units of international society are few may increase the relative significance of each violation. Still, violations of international law are not common enough to destroy the sense of law, of obligation to comply, of the right to ask for compliance and to react to violation. Rarely is even a single norm so widely violated as to lose its quality as law. Agreements are not violated with such frequency that nations cease to enter into them, or to expect performance or redress for violation. Colonialism apart, even political arrangements continue to thrive and to serve their purposes, although they may not run their intended course. Over-all, nations maintain their multivaried relations with rare interruptions. There is, without doubt, order in small, important things.

Whether, in the total, there is an effective "international order" is a question of perspective and definition. Order is not measurable, and no purpose is served by attempts to "grade" it in a rough impressionistic way. How much of that order is attributable to law is a question that cannot be answered in theory or in general, only in time and context. Law is one force—an important one among the forces that govern international relations at any time; the deficiencies of international society make law more dependent on other forces to render the advantages of observance high, the costs of violation prohibitive. In our times the influence of law must be seen in the light of the forces that have shaped international relations since the Second World War.

CONTEMPORARY
POLITICAL FORCES
PART TWO
AND
INTERNATIONAL LAW

In our age, law has worked its effect among the hopes and fears, actions and reactions, tensions and détentes of the turbulent years since 1945. I shall consider in Part Two the particular impact on the law, and on national behavior under law, of the major forces that have molded contemporary international relations:* the technological revolution of the nuclear age and the ideological struggle that for long divided the world in a cold war and is not dissipated yet; the "explosion" which in three decades virtually ended traditional colonialism and more than tripled the number of nation-states. The United Nations, as conceived and as it has grown (and perhaps declined), also has special relevance for national behavior and

---

*The political forces I consider, dramatic and immediate in their relevance, are themselves of course products of history and geography, of "natural," social, cultural, and other political forces, *e.g.*, religion and ideas, the population explosion, medical progress, climate.

national attitudes toward international law. I shall deal with these influences singly, although in reality they have interacted, added to or offset, even multiplied one another.

To understand the impact of contemporary forces on the influence of law, it seems necessary to consider first their impact on the law itself, on its condition and its changing content. How nations will act in regard to international law will be influenced by the state and status of the law; whether they will observe a particular norm will be influenced by the state and status of that norm. International law, deeply political in conception and operation, is particularly sensitive to political forces.

The survival and authority of international law depends on its capacity for necessary change. If there is change in the law in moderate times, surely the law will respond to revolutionary transformations in the lives of nations and to ideological conflict rending their society. If old nations seek and accept change, new nations, surely, will look critically at the old norms; former colonies will scrutinize what colonial nations established; poor nations come to independence and influence will suspect what richer, established nations have favored.

And yet—I stress what has not happened and what we take for granted—despite major political convolutions, international law did not go under or suffer major deterioration or transformation. *A priori*, this was not certain and inevitable. In different ways, international law was threatened by all the major phenomena of contemporary international relations that I have singled out: by the advent of the nuclear age, by ideological conflict, by the emergence of a Third World of more than a hundred states and billions of people. None of these threats has materialized.

But new forces, new actors and events have raised new problems or given to old problems a new appearance and a new urgency. New problems have brought some new law and pressed on old law for change and accommodation, eroding some, modifying others, giving to some a new importance. Contemporary forces have also affected the influence of accepted law, the reasons why nations observe or violate it, the calculus of cost and advantage of law observance.

It is commonplace to stress the profound significance for international relations of the technological revolution of our times. The terrible destructive power which it has produced has revolutionized the role of force in international relations, compelling international society to live in danger of annihilation. At the same time, technology has opened new cosmic vistas and holds promises of untold blessings.

Our society of nations and its law have now survived three decades of the nuclear age. Few may find that surprising or noteworthy: international society and law had successfully assimilated radical technological change on previous occasions. But thirty years ago it was commonly asked whether the atomic bomb had not rendered the nation obsolete and with it, of course, the old law of nations.* The original American plan for control of the atom by

---

*I do not consider whether mankind might have benefited had nations disappeared entirely and international law were replaced by some world government or

international development of atomic energy, conceived and promoted not by visionaries but by hard-headed men of vision, would have brought us much closer to world government than to a society of nations.[1] Since then, recurrent proposals for general and complete disarmament,[2] if they were to be taken seriously, might be feasible only if nations were prepared to accept powerful supranational institutions for the enforcement of disarmament and for the maintenance of peace, with other concomitant intrusions into national societies that would leave little of the traditional society and the traditional law among independent nations.

There are periodic warnings that even such independence as nations still have is an anachronism and that mankind will not survive unless weapons are eliminated or controlled, peace maintained, populations limited, the environment protected, food, energy and other basic human needs assured through supranational institutions. To date there has been little movement toward that end. More than thirty years of disarmament negotiations compel the conclusion that governments are not even looking in that direction. Largely because nations are not prepared to give up substantial national independence, the promises of disarmament are modest, and the agreements that have some hope of realization will not revolutionize international society.[3] Indeed, the strategic stability achieved by the new weapons—along with other forces, including the proliferation of nations—has given nationalism (and nationhood) new vigor, not only among those newly enjoying its heady flavor, but even where, one might have thought, its fruits had long ago been found bitter, as in the France of and since General de Gaulle.

If the nuclear age has brought no revolutionary transformations in international society, it has already affected the content of international law and its place in international affairs. Technology is modifying established law: for example, satellites and other me-

---

world law. I note merely that contemporary international law assumes the existence of nations and that if the nation disappeared, international law, as presently conceived, would disappear also.

chanical-electronic advances qualify the significance of traditional notions of territorial sovereignty. Satellites now "see" into national territory without violation of traditional airspace. Even the U-2, which can fly over territory without easy detection and without too-patent intrusion, has led to activities claimed to be lawful—as in United States overflights of Cuba since 1962—that international law would have clearly outlawed and probably deterred when planes had to fly lower and more visibly.

Contemporary technology has also already contributed some new law. There is new cooperative international law for the peaceful uses of atomic energy, in the International Atomic Energy Agency, in EURATOM, and in numerous bilateral agreements for assistance in atomic research. The communications satellite has brought new international law of cooperation in communication. There is law about outer space and the use of satellites.[4] The Nuclear Test-Ban Treaty, the first international law of arms control in the nuclear age,* has been followed by a seabed disarmament treaty, a nuclear non-proliferation treaty, a nuclear-free zone in Latin America, SALT agreements and more promised.

To date, the principal contribution of the new technology to international law is its influence on the law against war. Even before the advent of nuclear weapons, the destructiveness of the "primitive" weaponry of the Second World War impelled nations, in the United Nations Charter, to seek to end the scourge of war and to outlaw the unilateral use of force. Since this paramount development in international law, military technology has leaped to new levels of terror, underscoring—if indeed further emphasis were meaningful—the place of the norm against force at the heart of international law. It has also produced the view that any use of nuclear weapons, even in defensive war, would be illegal.[5] While this view has not been accepted by all those who have nuclear weapons,† it will, no doubt, reinforce the political arguments

* Unless one would so characterize the "hot line" between Moscow and Washington.

† The United States voted against General Assembly Resolution 1653. Although the U.S.S.R. voted for it, one may question Soviet motives in doing so. See p. 180, below.

against using them and increase the hesitation of nations to do so.

Having impelled the growth of new law against the use of force, the new technology has also had paramount influence in inducing compliance with this major norm of international law. I write of this at length in Chapter 7, but here it is sufficient to note that we may well owe more than thirty years without major war between major powers to the fact that technology has rendered the cost of such violation of law prohibitive. If so, technology may claim that it has built finally the fundament of a rule of law—the end of the supremacy of national force in the society of nations. Technology has other relevance for compliance with law. In regard to laws controlling armaments, for example, new devices may enable a nation to circumvent obligations or to keep violation secret; counter-developments may, of course, induce compliance by increasing the likelihood that a violation would be detected. The test-ban agreement and other arms control arrangements came into effect and are being observed because it is now possible to monitor compliance from afar with confidence that violations will be detected and without fear that the "inspection" could be sabotaged or frustrated.[6] The high probability of detectión, with a corresponding increase in the probability that a violation would bring costly response, makes it more likely that such agreements will continue to be observed.

More complex, more subtle, more gradual, but more radical changes in international life and law will result if the new technology brings to fruition some of the yearnings and expectations of nations old and new. Someday sea water will be desalinated, deserts will bloom, more nations will be "developed," population may be controlled, the food supply may be less inadequate, trade may be regularized, illiteracy eliminated, disease further reduced. Inevitably, these developments will require and in turn produce new forms of cooperation and new law, expanding greatly the cooperative welfare law that is already so significant a part of contemporary international law. It is too early to assert, but not too early to hope, that such developments will build an international community in which other kinds of international law can also flourish. New reaches for transportation and communication may make practical larger units of government and give impetus to new internal and limited supranational institutions. The law of a world in which living standards of nations are not starkly disparate will be quite different from our law, and nations more content with their lot will show a better record of compliance with the law.

"INTERNATIONAL LAW IN A DIVIDED WORLD"[7]

The nuclear revolution would have transformed international relations even in a society of nations generally similar in attitudes, like those, for instance, which dominated the scene at the turn of the last century. Its effect has been magnified by the political and ideological convolutions of our times. But the effects on law of technology and of ideology have been very different. The influence of the nuclear age reveals the dynamic quality of the law in responding to a new international environment; the changes which technology brings to the law generally reflect a new consensus and a new community of interest. The ideological conflict brought, for the most part, not new law but the disappearance of old law; not new community of interest but the erosion of old; not the achievement of new agreement but the falling away of old consensus. To date, and at least pending further proliferation of atomic weapons,* technology has been generally a stabilizing influence, in support of the norm of international law which forbids the unilateral use of force. Ideological conflict, on the other hand, increased instability, threatened the foundations of international law, reduced its content, and weakened its observance.

Fascination with the events of our own time should not be allowed to distort their significance in the historical perspective. The Cold War was not the first period of sharp conflict among nations below the threshold of war, not even the first where the conflict was ideological. The post-Napoleonic period, for example, was one of ideological conflict between advocates of republicanism and

---

*It remains to be seen whether and when there will be an increase in the "nuclear club" beyond the unhappy addition of India in 1974.

upholders of "legitimacy" and monarchical institutions, both in Europe and in rebelling colonies; and that conflict affected, in particular, the law against intervention.* But, monarchy versus republicanism apart, all nations of that time lived generally by the same rules and practices.[8] Communism, on the other hand, in early theory and practice, appeared to challenge all the foundations of international law and some of its principal tenets. The Cold War, while not unprecedented, was long lasting, intense, pervasive, widespread, and its influence is with us yet.

For some years it was common to characterize international society since World War II as "bipolar." As a description of a world in which there were two foci of major military power, the term cannot be faulted. That the existence of two military giants attracted all the others into their political orbits was frequently assumed but was always open to question. Surely for some years now it has been increasingly clear that despite the superpowers and their superweapons—perhaps, in the end, because of them, since they have largely neutralized each other—the world is not effectively divided in two.[9] Schism between the U.S.S.R. and the People's Republic of China, and some rapprochement between the latter and the United States, have established a lasting if irregular triangle. Other forms of influence—for example, that of OPEC, the oil cartel—further negated the implications of bipolarism; and the rise of the Third World and its economic aspirations created a "North-South" division that put developed states of East and West into the same camp for important purposes. (More recently, some spoke of polycentrism, but that too may have the misleading connotation that all nations cluster at one center or another and are subject to a measure of firm control.)

Still, there can be no doubt that ours has been a divided world. Major nations pursued sharply adverse interests, often with the dedicated effort characteristic of war. Continued war, even of Cold War, was hardly conducive to law between nations. Surely, law

---

* That law was never wholly meaningful so long as nations could lawfully wage war, whether to achieve political change in another country or for other purposes.

does not flourish when the conflict is ideological and one of the conflicting doctrines strikes at some of the law's basic tenets.* Ideology apart, a world divided between dynamic, aggressive Communist states and anti-Communist states could not be promising for international law. Modern international law, it is often said, arose only after the religious wars of the seventeenth century ended with the Peace of Westphalia, and a society of equal, sovereign, mutually-tolerating secular states was born.[10] One might expect, then, that this law would come into jeopardy in the new "religious wars" of our time. Surely, ours has not been that community of nations which, it is common to say, is indispensable to a rule of law. There has not even been that kind of community which in nineteenth-century Europe sought to maintain a balanced peace supported by a modest law of nations.

The ideological Cold War reversed the process of civilization in international society, reducing law to harsh diplomacy, to economic and political warfare, with only the terror of terrible weapons keeping the war cold. Even in the West, where forces favoring law were strong, the Cold War engendered the vocabulary and attitudes of war, discouraging efforts to achieve order and stability, breeding resistance to legal restraints on national policy, conducing to struggle for superiority and advantage rather than co-operation and consensus.

In retrospect, however, that international law has survived dynamic international communism and cold war is not surprising. In the beginning, Soviet Russia was alone, a single Communist state in the world of states; indeed, it soon had to adjust its theoretical

---

*Even before it acquired the support of military power, the ideology of communism did not live comfortably with a traditional law based on the nation—independent, equal, sovereign, its territory its own domain, its nationals professing a single loyalty. Communism began as a political creed which regarded neither nation nor territory. In theory at least, a strictly Communist world, with the millennial "withering away" of the state, might well dispense with both nations and a law of nations. Soviet theoreticians early entered strong reservations about "capitalist" international law, and asserted the Soviet Union's right to reject any of it which it did not approve.

foundations and pursue a policy of "communism in one country" only. Soviet theoreticians were soon constrained to subordinate the believed demands of Marxist theory to the national interests and policies of Russia.[11] When Soviet influence spread, Communist nations, even while they formed a single bloc, were a small minority among the nations, and they had to pursue their foreign intercourse in a context of nations and international law. In large part, international law survived because it is still primitive, because it is not a complete network of developed norms governing all relations among all nations. What law there is consists of fundamentals which Communist and other nations alike cherish: those norms which protect internal autonomy and minimal unavoidable relations of diplomacy, trade, and functional cooperation. Even during Cold War Communist Russia was most vigorous in asserting such customary principles of international law as territorial integrity and inviolability, sovereign and diplomatic immunities, the binding effect of treaties.[12] Even at the depth of the Stalinist repression, when the ideological war was coldest and the iron curtain most impenetrable, the Soviet Union could not survive without trade or be a world power without diplomacy. Stalin's Russia was ungenerous with respect even to traditional diplomatic immunities, but it could not dispense with them. Today, Russia seeks intercourse, not isolation, and influence, not mere independence; for these the observance of international law and agreements is indispensable. Growing interdependence has compelled Soviet participation in the new international law of cooperation and welfare.

Nor was international law threatened by the advent of Communist China, which, from its early days, accepted international law in principle.[13] For some years it was content with isolation and seemed to seek relations only within the Communist family. When China decided to emerge on the international scene and strive for influence with governments and with Communist parties, it had to be prepared to play largely by existing rules. It did not seek to destroy or remake international law. Indeed, it invoked international law and acquiesced in its authority, as in its territorial disputes with India.[14] Now, having broken with the Soviet Union, having normalized its relations with the United States, and competing with both for influence among the new nations, China will presumably increase its respect and support for agreed law of nations.

IDEOLOGICAL CONFLICT AND
THE CONTENT OF LAW

While international law survived, important changes in it have occurred. International Communist bodies early began to claim the right to "intervene" in capitalist societies in ways that affronted traditional standards, even before there was political and military intervention (on both sides) in the Spanish Civil War. The Soviet Union, with its distaste for private property, its expropriation program at home, and the nationalization of properties which its citizens had in other countries, threw its influence against traditional rules protecting the property of individual aliens.[15]

The Cold War brought wider and deeper effects. Between the Soviet Union and its satellites, despite observance of the external forms of international relations, it was not traditional international law that governed. (To a lesser extent, relations in the West also subordinated national "sovereignty," but they never went beyond unusual forms of cooperation.*) Between blocs, ideological conflict destroyed the old assumptions about a society of nations, all friendly though some friendlier than others. Discrimination among nations became the rule rather than the exception, as when the West barred shipment of certain materials to Communist countries or froze the assets of some of them.[16] The rights of diplomats were sharply limited, first by the Soviet Union, then in retaliation by the United States.[17] Ideology and conflict led to and maintained the division of states—Germany, Korea, Vietnam, China—with concomitant problems for the law of status, recognition, treaty formation and performance, state succession, and nationality. The

---

* While within its limited domain the law of the European Communities may also be said to have replaced traditional international law, that development was not closely related to the Cold War.

Cold War created new problems requiring modification of old norms, as when the Unified Command in Korea, under the United States, refused to repatriate thousands of prisoners of war unwilling to return, and the United Nations General Assembly affirmed the principle of voluntary repatriation.[18]

Sharp ideological cleavage affected even the growing forms of international cooperation. (The failure of the United Nations Security Council is only the best-known example.) The West often sought propaganda victories and begrudged benefits to Communist countries. Communist China was everywhere excluded. For the Communist nations, in turn, participation in various specialized agencies was, for many years, sporadic and grudging, often obstructive. If communism could not admit error, could not accept the concept of neutrality and the judgment of neutrals or other impartial arbiters, there was little room for third-party determination, whether by the International Court of Justice or in the framework of some new international disarmament agency.[19]

But ideological conflict, it should be clear, left intact the submerged mass of international law, the principal norms and concepts, as well as numerous multilateral and bilateral agreements. The Cold War also did not preclude the creation of new law. If there was no true "community," there were particular interests common to the Soviet Union and the West—in avoiding war, in limiting the spread of nuclear weapons, in trade. With some détente, the adversaries in the Cold War joined to create new law of outer space and a ban on testing nuclear weapons.[20] Despite new frost on U.S.-Soviet relations that followed the deposition of Khrushchev, the death of President Kennedy, and the growing American involvement in Vietnam, the two countries adopted a consular agreement and adhered to an outer-space treaty.[21] Since then, there have been further agreements not to proliferate nuclear weapons and to slow the missile race.* Common interests found ideological foes on the same side on many issues in the law of the

* Compare the anti-hijacking agreement between the United States and Cuba in 1975.

sea and elsewhere, where the interests of developed and developing states diverged, although the U.S.S.R. frequently masked that fact in its desire to appear to identify with the Third World.*

THE OBSERVANCE OF LAW
DURING IDEOLOGICAL CONFLICT

Inevitably, the rise and spread of communism and the consequent ideological conflict have affected also the observance of norms and obligations that remained unchallenged and unchanged. Some of the factors which make for compliance with international norms have been absent. Soviet Russia's slow and grudging acceptance of the "capitalist" law of nations did not promote eager observance of law. Born of revolution, Soviet Russia recognized no links to any traditions, nor did it quickly develop new institutions, that made for compliance with traditional international law. (The Soviet Union early refused to accept liability for the obligations of the Czarist government, insisting on the relevance of *rebus sic stantibus*![22]) There were few domestic forces inducing law observance. Much of the time, relations between the Soviet Union and other countries lacked that basic friendliness conducive to the observance of obligations between them. The Western powers had intervened in Russia in the vain hope of suppressing the revolution; thereafter, nonrecognition, general unfriendliness, and growing anti-communism weakened forces in international relations making for law observance.

On the other hand, the record hardly remained one of lawlessness. The Soviet Union began early to exhibit concern for conformity to law, at least in regard to its own treaty obligations and those customary norms which it particularly valued, at least where its actions were open to scrutiny and criticism.[23] In the West, the policy of law observance prevailed, and improved in the 1930s and during the wartime alliance. Even during the Cold War it was not

* The U.S.S.R. was particularly reluctant to leave to the People's Republic of China the mantle of Third World champion among the big powers.

true that *inter arma silent leges*. Between nations in the Cold War there were still common interests (avoidance of nuclear war), as well as reciprocal ones (trade).[24] There remained the interest in maintaining diplomatic relations. Reciprocity and mutual advantage, the fear of retaliatory response, still operated to induce compliance with agreements. It is not commonly noticed how much international law and obligation applied and were effectively observed between the United States and the Soviet Union even when their relations were most strained.

The Cold War nevertheless deeply affected the observance of international law by the Great Powers and members of the respective blocs *inter se*, within the blocs, or toward the "unaligned" nations. For the Great Powers, actions that were central to the Cold War and the ideological conflict were of an especially political character and not as readily deterred by legal considerations—witness the failure of agreements on the occupation of Germany, Soviet intervention to achieve a Communist regime in Czechoslovakia, Soviet troops in Hungary and the invasion of Czechoslovakia in 1968, or American intervention to assure a non-Communist government in Guatemala or the Dominican Republic, or to resist a Communist victory in Vietnam. In smaller matters, too, the absence, during Stalinism, of a desire for friendly relations removed a principal influence for observance of law. One could be confident of observance only as to norms or obligations of direct reciprocal advantage and subject to retaliation in the event of breach. Even there, asymmetrical situations and interest made for violations. Western properties were not secure in Communist countries which did not have corresponding properties in the West. Western embassies could be attacked by "spontaneous" mobs without fear of similar response in the West. Western aliens in Communist countries could not be confident of international standards of justice.[25] The iron curtain helped hide evidnce of violation; there were few citizens of Communist countries subject to retaliation in the West. If mistreatment of Western citizens discouraged others from traveling, so much the better for maintaining a closed society.

The record of the West was somewhat better; influences for law observance were stronger, and in regard to the treatment of aliens, in particular, the West could not retaliate, could not compete in lawlessness or cynicism. But the West also found reasons to disregard law or obligation under pressure of the Cold War: sometimes violation resulted from a desire to gain advantage in the conflict; fear of communism also created strong internal pressures, even before Senator Joseph McCarthy, to be "tough on communism," which were not conducive to scrupulous concern for international law. The United States terminated most-favored-nation commitments to Communist countries.[26] It pressed Denmark—without success—to bar shipment of a tanker, in violation of a trade agreement with the Soviet Union.[27] There was the notorious U-2 affair, and the Bay of Pigs.

Smaller members of the blocs were not deterred either, especially from violations of political importance, since they enjoyed the protection of ideological leaders, or may have represented them—for example, the North Korean invasion of South Korea. In the *Corfu Channel* case Albania even disregarded a judgment of the International Court of Justice. Of course, the expectation of protection from an ally sometimes proved illusory, as when the United States abandoned France and the United Kingdom at Suez.

The influence of the Cold War went beyond inducing clear violations. Laws and agreements have their ambiguities of interpretation and uncertainties of application. While nations generally assert their rights reasonably and in a spirit of accommodation, the Cold War engendered niggardliness and an uncompromising insistence on extreme constructions, especially where there were fears that reasonableness might be attacked as "softness" to the enemy.

Within the blocs, the Cold War had a different influence. Violations of important law or obligation were less likely. When the Cold War was intense, the Communist bloc had a meaningful unity, NATO was strong and members were constrained to get along. Greece and Turkey could be compelled to bury animus and accept a compromise Cyprus. On the other hand, a small nation might take advantage of its importance to the alliance to tweak a larger ally: some believe that little Iceland may have seized something of that mood when it began to challenge fishing by Great Britain in waters beyond Iceland's territorial sea.[28]

When East and West began to compete for influence with "neutrals," compliance with international law was affected. The opinions of Third World nations even influenced attitudes of East and West *inter se*, especially where those nations had a direct interest and their views could be focused, as in cases that came within the ken of the United Nations. Competition for world opinion constrained both the United States and the Soviet Union to observe for an extended period a moratorium on nuclear testing that had no formal status as law, although, as in other instances, the "neutral nations" seemed able to influence the West more effectively than the Soviet Union or Communist China. The opinion of third countries also constantly pressed the Big Powers at least to negotiate to achieve new law for the control of armaments. One may assume too, for example, that the acceptance by countries like India of the principle of voluntary repatriation of prisoners of war strengthened the hand of the United States to insist on the principle and influenced the Communists to concede.[29] The West, clearly, was compelled to concession and change on issues involving self-determination and racial discrimination. Competition between East and West enhanced the care that both sides took to observe international law in respects that concern all generally (*e.g.*, the test ban) or particular new nations directly. East and West were careful to respect those principles of international law that have been hallmarks of independence and prestigious equality to which new nations were particularly sensitive. For their part, on the other hand, third nations sometimes found encouragement for violation in the Cold War, relying on the protection of one side, or on the reluctance of both sides to antagonize the violator, to escape harsh response to the violation. (See Chapter 6.)

In time, the Cold War gave way to different phases in ideological controversy. Between the Soviet bloc and the West came a period of détente, followed by new uncertainties after the fall of Khrushchev and greater American involvement in Vietnam, and in the 1970s something like détente again. Détente brought not only some new law but also better observance of existing law between blocs: it is instructive to compare, for example, the treatment of Western citizens during the early 1950s and ten years later.[30] Within the blocs, in contrast, restraints relaxed. The Sino-Soviet divergence sharpened and, we know, led to violations of important agreements between them.[31] In the West, the NATO Alliance appeared less certain; France, in particular, asserted an eccentric independence, grew restless in NATO, even to some extent in its undertakings towards the European Community. Greece and Turkey were no longer influenced to comply with their own agreements or with the United Nations Charter, and engaged in hostilities in Cyprus. Vis-à-vis the new nations, the détente did not relax East-West competition for their friendship, with both sides compelled to respect the rights of new nations protected by law. Soviet competition with Communist China also tended to enhance Soviet attention to the forms and norms of international society; Communist China, in turn, competing with both Russia and the West, especially in Africa and Asia, appeared to moderate its attitudes toward other nations and to respect both the forms and the substance of traditional international law. Uncertainties in relations due principally to the war in Vietnam also created uncertainties as to the level of law observance that could be expected. The end of the Vietnam War removed a source of disturbance, but other areas—the Middle East, Angola, southern Africa—were a source of competition that affected law observance adversely.

The Conference on Security and Trade in Europe (Helsinki 1975) gave détente a new form and focus. It was not an East-West conference in theory or in form; some Communist states sought in it protection against Soviet aggression and other extreme interventions, like that in Czechoslovakia in 1968, which had been justified (and threatened for the future) in the "Brezhnev Doctrine." But in the large, the Final Act at Helsinki, although only a political-moral not a legal undertaking, constituted an East-West exchange. The West accepted the political and territorial *status quo* in Eastern Europe; the Soviet bloc undertook to respect human rights generally and to cooperate in promoting human contacts and exchange in information and culture. Both sides agreed to promote "inter-bloc" trade. A détente which included increased inter-bloc intercourse and respect for individual freedom promised new international law and improved respect for existing law, including human rights law. But in the early aftermath, at least, Helsinki (coinciding perhaps with uncertainty and impending change in Soviet leadership) produced its own tensions as domestic "dissidents" and external scrutiny focused on the human rights promises; they raised questions whether the Helsinki concept of détente was really accepted by all, and whether it would last.

In one basic respect, moreover, the ideological conflict has continued to trouble international order and law, regardless of tension or détente. Even when "peacefully coexisting," East and West are in fundamental opposition. The interest of the West is in stability: change should be peaceful and consistent with international order.* The West hopes for liberalization within most Communist countries, too, as a result of prosperity rather than of instability and revolution. The Communists, even a moderate Soviet Union, see an ultimate interest in instability within non-Communist countries which could lead ultimately to people's revolution and people's democracy. Since international law and law observance, inherently, are on the side of stability, the West has more incentive to comply, and the Communists are more tempted to violation. (The threat, real or imagined, of Communist violation may, however, sometimes induce Western violation.) In particular, in its support of "people's revolutions," whether by political or military action, the Soviet Union has frankly announced its disregard of traditional norms against intervention;[32] in some circumstances, at least, intervention may be subversion in probable violation of the U.N. Charter.[33] The United States has resorted to "counter-intervention" and even to "preventive intervention," as in the Dominican Republic, which is difficult to justify under law.

Perhaps this too will pass. Except for its continued relevance to

---

* To some observers, Western interest in stability too often appears to be opposed to any change.

stability, the abiding influence of ideological conflict on law is uncertain as both ideology and conflict change character, intensity, and direction. Perhaps, internal improvement and stability will give to Communist societies, even to Communist China someday, an interest in international stability as strong as that of Western countries. If so, despite the new, irreversible levels of military terror, contemporary tensions and ideological conflict may appear less different from those of an earlier day, and their significance for international law no greater or more enduring.

I have been discussing division and competition between East and West, between communism and more-or-less capitalism, between "people's democracy" and libertarian republican democracy, between NATO and Warsaw Pact. But that division has been modified, though not superseded, by a different division that is not without ideological undertones, a division between North and South, between developed and developing nations, between "free enterprise" and "new order." That division has resulted largely from the end of colonialism and the birth of many new nations, and their expanding influence in the international system, transforming its law as well as its politics.

THE
six
THIRD WORLD

"The Third World" was conceived largely as a rhetorical reaction to bipolarism. It denied that mankind was and had to be identified or aligned with either the First World of the West or the Second World of Communism. It implied "nonalignment," even, perhaps, "a plague on both your houses." Soon it asserted more. The Third World has its own identity and its own interests.It has its particular claims in and upon international society. And it has power, if not yet the power of wealth and weapons. Indeed, oil gave some members of the Third World enormous wealth, and their "oil-weapon" could bring many powerful and developed states to their knees. In Vietnam, a Third World country even stood up militarily to the world's greatest military power.

The Third World includes most of the globe's states, and most of its people. It includes the oldest countries in history, and the newest; very large and populous countries as well as "mini-states" in both size and population; incredibly rich and incredibly poor countries. (Some break off the very poor into a Fourth World, and a few have been assigned even to a Fifth World.) The Third World is not ideologically or politically monolithic. It includes authentic libertarian democracies and repressive autocracies. Some of its members are deeply sympathetic to the West: the United States retains important influence in Latin America, and Great Britain and France in their former colonies in Africa. Some Third World states have been virtually aligned with the U.S.S.R. and a few are quite in tune with the People's Republic of China. But that world also has much in common. In it a mass of new states are tied to older states in Latin America, the Middle East, Asia and Africa by a common history of former dependence, and by some continuing resentment against the Western, developed states which had long dominated the international scene. By the 1960s the nations that constitute the Third World came to recognize a substantial identity of condition, principally underdevelopment, and a substantial identity of interest. Beginning with "the group of 77" (now in fact numbering well over 100 states), they have succeeded in maintaining substantial unity of purpose and substantial solidarity in political action, at least on selected subjects. (That a few in the Third World have become very rich as a result of their petroleum resources, and have shown political power as an oil cartel, has, to date, not shaken the basic sense of identity and solidarity.) For many purposes the Third World is joined by the powerful, developed Communist countries, which aspire to identify with, "protect," even lead the Third World. And the United States and other Western powers, often the principal targets of revolutionary changes which the Third World proposes, have not always resisted wholeheartedly, perhaps from some guilt over past imperialism and present wealth, some sensitivity to "world opinion," some sympathy for the aspirations of the many, some reluctance to have these states identify their interests with those of the Communist powers.

With the military prowess of the superpowers largely neutralized; with these and the People's Republic of China competing for influence in the Third World; with the uncertain but not-to-be-dismissed crippling potentialities of the oil weapon, especially against the Western allies of the United States; with an ideology and rhetoric of justice and equality, concentrated in multilateral forums, widely and effectively disseminated, and striking sympathy even in developed states—the counters of influence in the international system are changed, and political weapons loom larger than in the past. Inevitably, the proliferation of nations and the emergence of the Third World have had important implications for the international political system and international relations, international law, and how all the nations behave under law.

NEW NATIONS: NEW SUBJECTS OF INTERNATIONAL LAW AND NEW MASTERS

The first Hague Conference in 1899 was attended by 26 states, the second in 1907 by 44. At its largest, the League of Nations had 60 members. The United Nations began life with 51; today, the headquarters of the United Nations accommodate 145 members and more are expected; more than 150 nations participated in the Third Law of the Sea Conference. The League had only 14 members from Asia and Africa; the original United Nations had 13; today it has more than 80 members from those continents. Most of these were recently in varying degrees of colonial subordination to some Western nation, and their territories and their peoples are defined by past accidents of competition between colonial powers. Most of these states are inhabited by non-whites. Most of them are on the low rungs of the climb to industrialization.

We are frequently reminded that international law was the product of European civilization, intended primarily for the guidance of European powers (later adopted by their erstwhile colonies in the Western Hemisphere), and reflecting their Christian, capitalistic, imperialistic interests. One might expect, then, that this law would not survive the decline of Europe's dominance, surely would not govern a society of nations most of which were not European, not Christian, not imperialist, not capitalist, which did not participate in the development of the law, and whose interests were different from those of the nations that shaped the law. In fact, however, international law has survived and would not be unrecognizable to our parents and teachers in the law and in diplomacy. The new nations raised the theoretical difficulties which have long troubled jurists as to why newborn nations should be bound by pre-existing law. Some of those nations spoke and speak suspiciously of white, colonial law and have proclaimed the need for revolutionary transformations. Many indeed have challenged particular principles. But all were eager to enter international society and to accept its law.*

The reasons why new nations accepted international law are not difficult to perceive.[1] They came into an established system accepted by all nations, including the revolutionary governments and the many small powers which had supported their struggle for self-determination. Acceptance into that society as an independent equal was the proof and crown of their successful struggle, and international law provided the indispensable framework for living in that society. They adopted traditional forms in international trade and the growing cooperation for welfare of which they have been the principal beneficiaries, and early in their young history they have had to invoke international law in their disputes, among themselves or with others—on the Indus River and in Kashmir, between India and Bangladesh, on the definition of the continental shelf.

NEW NATIONS AND CHANGING LAW

International law has survived the birth of many new nations but the law has hardly been unaffected by this, and eventually these new subjects of the law may prove to be masters of its content. The ways of the law have been importantly affected also by the fact that there are now more than 150 states, 150 makers of international law, 150 judges of each other's behavior, and all of them potentially responding to that behavior.

---

*Even the hostile reaction following the decision of the International Court of Justice in the South West Africa case did not represent any rejection of traditional law. It struck primarily at the Court rather than at international law. The Court was not high in favor before the decision, and increased hostility did not prove permanent and has not been the cause of continued skepticism about resort to the Court. See p. 186, below.

The proliferation of new states has not led to a proliferation of new international law. In general, new nations have not been eagerly seeking new law. In most respects new nations are not unlike old nations; they are not monochromatic; their interests, as they see them, differ widely. Some have radical leadership, some conservative; some cultivate their garden, some aspire to dramatic roles on the world scene. They are not equally concerned with international law; in general, they are hardly agreed whether to seek new or different law and what law they will seek. Surely, they do not share an eagerness to extend the domain of international law by norms and standards that would apply generally. Like many old nations, rather, they are not eager to undertake obligations and limitations. (For example, it remains to be seen how many will adhere to strong covenants on human rights without important reservations or resistance to external scrutiny of how they live up to them.)

The explosion of new states, moreover, has made it yet more difficult to make new law. It has been long established that law of universal applicability can be made only by universal agreement or acquiescence;* the likelihood of general agreement decreases, of course, as the number of nations who must agree increases. New universal customary law, then, may become a rarity. It was never easy to prove customary law among "civilized nations"; it will be far more difficult to show that some new practice is generally accepted, or even acquiesced in, among 150-odd states. The multilateral convention, then, has become the principal form of general law-making, but already experience suggests that universality (or general acceptance) will be hard to come by.† Regulation which depends for success on universal cooperation, e.g., denial of haven to terrorists, will not quickly flourish. General agreement may be possible only to codify accepted basic principles and practices, or

* On the legislative significance of General Assembly resolutions, see Chapter 8, pp. 181–85.

† After years of complex negotiations a new law of the sea has emerged, and one may hope that it will be widely accepted and observed. But the law of the sea governs areas which no one claimed, in which interests had not vested, and compromises were not unduly difficult. And major issues remain unresolved. See Chapter 11.

perhaps to adopt some general, imprecise, and ambiguous standards to which time and experience may give some agreed content. (One may wonder whether even the Charter of the United Nations, hardly an instrument of legal precision, could be universally adopted today.) Regional law and law for other, smaller groupings may be the new law of the future, with universality a distant hope that we must learn not to expect or even desire.

The reluctance to make new law and the difficulties of making it do not apply equally to unmaking or remaking old law. Whatever the theory, new nations can in fact have a sharp impact on the law by collective "massive resistance," especially where older states are reluctant to insist on the old law. Mass abstentions might render what were once universal agreements merely a regime for a minority of the world's states.* Customary law cannot long retain validity if a substantial number of states reject it. (This was the fate of the traditional limits of the territorial sea, long before Third World states led to a new consensus on wider limits.) New nations resisted claims upon them as "successor governnments" for the undertakings of their erstwhile masters, and generally succeeded in establishing for themselves an option as to which undertakings they would succeed to. New nations, following an earlier lead by the U.S.S.R. and Mexico, resisted claims for "prompt, adequate and effective" compensation for nationalized foreign properties with important consequences for the state of this law. (See pp. 128–30.)

But there has been no wide rejection of traditional norms. There have been calls for a complete re-examination of traditional interna-

---

*Some have feared that this might happen to the International Court of Justice. Of approximately 45 states that have accepted its compulsory jurisdiction, only about half have done so without substantive reservations, and few of these have used the Court. New nations in particular seem reluctant to do so. See Chapter 8, pp. 186–88. There has even been resistance to incorporating provisions for settlement of disputes by the International Court in new multilateral conventions. Compare, e.g., Colloquium on the Legal Aspects of Refugee Problems (Note by the High Commissioner), U.N. Doc. A/AC.96/INF.40 (1965); compare also the dispute- settlement provisions negotiated at the U.N. Law of the Sea Conference.

tional law, and one of the purposes of continuing codification and development of the law has been to give new states a voice in re-establishing the legal system, whether by reaffirming traditional law or modifying it. But re-examination has not meant and does not promise to mean wide rejection or radical revision. In most respects what traditional law has given to the old nations is what the new nations now desire. If some norms have in the past been supported by a now outdated "theology" or jurisprudence—*e.g.*, archaic theories for sovereign immunity or for national control of the claims of citizens—the same norms and practices may find modern pragmatic foundations in common interest or reciprocal advantage. As seen today, at least, there will be substantial agreement tomorrow on the content of international law, by old nations and new, and it is largely traditional international law on which they will agree. It will not be agreement reflecting a common theory of international law, or any theory at all. It will be in part the agreement of inertia, in part the agreement of common interest and practical compromise.

THIRD WORLD IMPACT ON LAW

In several particular respects, however, the new nations, especially as they joined with other developing states and emerged as the Third World, have created new law in their image and interest. The Third world has succeeded where it was united and determined, had the full support of the Communist world, and had some support or sympathy, at least not resistance, among Western powers. They have succeeded in making that new law in the face of the principle of unanimity, by reinterpreting universal agreements (*e.g.*, the U.N. Charter), by overwhelming or silencing or even disregarding remaining opposition, especially through the use of U.N. resolutions. To date, the changes they have achieved in international law have been limited and special, but some see more radical transformation ahead.

The Third World has been united and determined on matters on which a substantial group of them felt strongly. Many of them being recently independent, they united to have the principle of "self-determination" enshrined in high status in international law,[2] effectively outlawing white colonialism in Asia and Africa, and troubling hegemonial relations like that of the United States in the Panama Canal Zone. The particular animus against colonialism has made the Third World intolerant also of general law which they think stands in the way of ending the remnants of white colonialism (Namibia, Rhodesia), even the law against the use of force. (See Chapter 7.) Many of its states being "colored," the Third World has united against white racism (as in South Africa) and may have effectively achieved general agreement that *apartheid* is a violation of international law even for states that have not adhered to any covenant outlawing it.

The Third World has been united, too, in regard to law that would further their common qualities, needs, and attitudes. They are "have-nots,"* inevitably questioning laws which seem to favor the "haves" and seeking new laws that will accelerate change, bring them to industrial development and technological sophistication, afford them status and prestige, give them a greater share of the world's goods and a greater say in the world's affairs. The principal changes which new nations are seeking in the last decades of this century are packaged under the label "a new economic order," including economic and technological aid not by grace of a few wealthy donors but as of right, higher prices received for raw materials and lower prices paid for manufactured goods, easy credit, access to advanced technology. (See Chapter 10.) But the new economic order has deep political roots, and at bottom the new nations are seeking participation if not control in economic and political decisions that determine their future.†

---

* Even the oil-rich identify with the "have-nots"; they too are in fact "have-nots" in industrial, technological, social and political development.

† At the Third Law of the Sea Conference, for example, the Third World sought not merely revenue from the deep sea bed, but control of the processes of exploitation, and a controlling voice in all decisions about that exploitation. (Chapter 11.) Some saw their insistence on such authority as an aspect of a general desire for dominant political authority in the sea, even of general political authority in the international system.

The success of Third World countries in virtually ending colonialism and racism, their solidarity on economic issues and their ability to extend that solidarity to other issues, on which enough of them feel strongly, have stirred dreams or fears that they might try to eliminate or erode the principle of unanimity in favor of more lawmaking by majority. Increasingly, they have been encouraged to seek new institutions based essentially on "one state-one vote" and majority rule (e.g., the proposed International Sea-bed Authority); to eliminate special voting rights (like the veto in the U.N. Security Council); to increase the matters subject to majority vote, e.g., in U.N. General Assembly resolutions. They have effectively exploited other procedures, for example, decision by "consensus." The developed majority perhaps originally saw in that change protection against being overwhelmed by top-sided majority votes, but in time the drives for consensus, where the Third World largely agreed, began to weigh heavily on would-be dissenters not to dissent. And resolutions in the United Nations and other multilateral bodies have begun to weigh more heavily in the law-making process.*

The success to date and further prospects of the Third World are substantial but should not be exaggerated. The Third World is not in fact monolithic and has been divided on many issues. The Communist powers strive to identify with and support them but are not likely to do so at major expense to themselves, and the increasing reference to "North-South divisions" suggests essential identity of interest between Communist and Western developed states and essential diversity between the developed and the Third World. Insofar as the Third World demands are upon the West in particular (as in greater economic aid, better conditions of trade, and access to sophisticated technology), the West will doubtless continue to resist demands it considers extravagant. Neither the First nor the Second World (and not even some of the Third World) is likely to agree to sacrifice the principle of unanimity, or agree to major law-

---

* Some in the Third World seem to envisage also that the "oil-weapon" might be at the disposal of the Third World to bring about acquiescence by developed states in law which is of compelling interest to the Third World.

making by majority, or accede to equal voting and majority rule in bodies which have significant regulatory authority. (The United States has already withdrawn from or reduced participation in international bodies when it concluded that majorities were usurping or abusing authority. See Chapter 8.)

The story of the law of alien property and investment affords a lively example of change and continuity in the law, of the efforts of the Third World to make and unmake law, the resistance of the West, the realities of international life in promoting or resisting change. Early in its history, the first major new nation of the twentieth century, the new Russia of the Soviet Union, generally refused to pay the obligations of its predecessors and, with its extensive nationalization program, denied any international obligation to compensate aliens for expropriated properties.[3] Later, in the 1930s, there was a famous exchange between Secretary of State Cordell Hull and the Mexican government.[4] The United States insisted that regardless of how a nation treats the property of its own nationals, it has an obligation under international law to afford minimum protection to the properties of foreign nationals, including prompt, adequate, and effective compensation if the properties are nationalized. Mexico, expressing a view shared by other Latin American countries, insisted that international law was satisfied if an alien's property was treated equally with that of nationals.

In the postwar world, most nations have been importers of capital; they have not liked law that protects foreign investments against the host country. Since the Second World War, also, nationalization of alien properties has become a form of anticolonialism, even called "economic self-determination," and a major element in social reform and economic development;[5] host governments have not wished to be prevented from major programs by the insistence of aliens (and their governments) that law requires sophisticated evaluations and prompt payment in freely withdrawable hard currency. Nations that have not contemplated nationalization programs have still been reluctant to agree to major legal requirements that might prevent them from nationalizing in the future. New nations have been particularly reluctant to accept responsibility to tolerate, or to compensate fully, properties obtained by foreign nationals from earlier colonial governments. Inevitably, the traditional norm as invoked by Western exporters of capital has met strong resistance. States old and new (Iran, Indonesia, Cuba), particularly regimes born in revolution, have challenged it. Other nations have sympathized. Theoreticians have questioned the intellectual foundations of the traditional norm.[6]

Capital-exporting states fought back, challenged title to expropriated properties in Western courts, froze assets of expropriating states, denied aid, and engaged in other forms of economic reprisal. But the new states were determined, and the future of the old norm has not looked promising. And yet, despite wide rejection of the conceptual underpinning, despite the colonial antecedents, despite a lack of reciprocity of interest, the old norm has not died. It is instructive that in 1962 the United Nations Resolution on Permanent Sovereignty over Natural Resources,[7] the title of which clearly suggests its principal motivation, found an overwhelming majority accepting—however reluctantly—the principle that imported capital and earnings "shall be governed by the terms thereof, by the national legislation in force, and by international law." Expropriation, too, they agreed, should be compensated "in accordance with international law." Importing nations, then, felt compelled to agree that international law affords some protection for foreign property. On the other hand, as over-optimistic Westerners sometimes failed to note, these nations did not agree to any articulation of the degree of protection afforded by international law. They voted down attempts to write in the standard of compensation desired by the United States.[8]

The following years were years of stand-off and postponement. Where full, prompt and effective expropriation was not possible or politic, developing states began what foreign interests called "creeping expropriation," including new heavy taxes, renegotiated royalty arrangements (often under threat of expropriation if resisted), restrictions on withdrawal of profits or repatriation of capital, and counterclaims for back taxes, unjust enrichment, unconscionably high profits or low wages. When new regimes sought to improve relations and compensate for past expropriations (as in 1969 in Bolivia, Chile, Peru), they negotiated settlements at modest valuations, payable over long terms, at low interest. Steadily, developing states began to renegotiate old concessions into joint ventures with the government maintaining large control, the foreign entity sometimes reduced to operating functions pursuant to contract. But the issue of principle did not lie dormant long. In 1975 in the New Economic Charter,[9] the Third World, buoyed by increased numbers, solidarity, confidence and a sense of mission, adopted a new formula which rejected any international obligation to compensate for nationalization of foreign properties. The West voted against, continuing to insist on the international obligations. The outcome is yet to be seen, part of the story of the New International Economic Order (Chapter 10).

NEW NATIONS AND LAW OBSERVANCE

The attitude of new nations to the content of law, what they would keep and what they would change, has, of course, influenced their compliance with accepted law. In fact, as in regard to alien property, the sudden emergence of many new nations has given particular emphasis to the interrelation of observance and change in international law. Sometimes change and noncompliance are hopelessly tangled. Some changes begin as noncompliance, which is then widely practiced or accepted. Some noncompliance may be a purposeful invitation to others to join to make, unmake, or remake a norm. And the new nations are still developing their attitudes. The first time that the temptation not to comply had to be faced, a new nation wished to know how the norm stood, whether it had colonial roots and reasons, whether other new or poor countries accepted it, what support there might be for its rejection or modification, and, of course, what sanctions there might be against the violator or what protection it might find.

It is not possible to judge the record of law observance by new nations generally. As with older nations, the conduct of new nations is determined by considerations of foreign policy and by internal impulsions. Some of the forces encouraging compliance are still absent. Newly in control of their own foreign relations, some new states have regarded international law tentatively and not without suspicion. In some states there has been no time for norms of international law to be accepted and incorporated into their laws and institutions; there are as yet no traditions of law observance. Many new nations have few lawyers, and almost all of them are concentrating on the overwhelming legal tasks involved in building a nation. In most of these countries there are few pressures for law observance from opposition parties, or a critical press, or an enlightened public. There may indeed be domestic pressures to violate or reject some norms—say, to confiscate foreign properties or to promote or tolerate attacks on the embassy of some foreign government. Nor is general observance of international law integral to the foreign policy of the new nations. If, unlike Communist countries, they have no general interest in instability, they may care more about other matters than about stability: *e.g.*, the end of colonialism and of anti-black racism, and rapid economic development. New nations may even affirmatively favor disorder where colonialism or racism still prevails, as in South-West Africa and Rhodesia; some fostered disorder also in the special case of the Congo; some, like Nkrumah's Ghana, sought instability elsewhere in the region to achieve a new order to their liking. Instability at home or among one's neighbors may render uncertain the orientation of a nation's foreign policy and the pattern of its friendly relations that induce compliance with international law, for example, in the changing alignments in the Middle East or about the Horn of Africa in the late 1970s.

On the other hand, many new nations have a strong interest in friendly relations with most other nations, in an international atmosphere which would leave them free to concentrate on their awesome domestic problems and would encourage assistance and cooperation from others. Favoring compliance, too, are the general advantages of observance over violation, as well as *ad hoc* influences in regard to particular norms. New nations are concerned to maintain the framework of diplomatic intercourse and its reciprocal advantages. Diplomatic privileges and territorial integrity are generally observed. Cooperative welfare arrangements are maintained. Treaties which new nations make are usually also to their advantage to preserve. Even arrangements made earlier by their erstwhile colonial masters will often continue to be advantageous for the new nation—as, for example, favorable trade patterns, or concession agreements which bring in major revenues.[10] There are also the inducements to comply that come from fear of the consequences of violation. The usual responses apart, the new nations also seek respect and friendly relations; they seek trade, investment, tourism; they seek technical, economic, and military assistance. For example, the imminent loss of United States aid impelled Ceylon to arrange acceptable compensation for nationalized properties.[11] Some countries appeared to respond in some measure when the Carter administration threatened to cut off U.S. aid for gross violations of human rights.*

In regard to international obligations of a political character, the compliance of new nations has special patterns and is subject to special influences. The principal ones have been mentioned: "self-determination" has eliminated the question of compliance with colonial treaties; where issues are tinged with colonialism or race, treaty undertakings may not be recognized, territorial integrity may not be observed, even force may be used. Where colonial-white influence is seen—as in the Congo or Angola—some new nations even disregard their most earnestly proclaimed values such as nonintervention in the internal affairs and quarrels of other nations.

Especially when it was acute, the East-West conflict was not a happy influence on compliance by new nations. In the competition for their "affection," some new nations found protection for law violation. No doubt, the persistence of Egypt for many years in refusing to allow Israeli shipping through the Suez Canal, despite the Treaty of 1888, the Palestine Armistice Agreements, and a Se-

---

* The United States did not necessarily claim that these human rights infringements violated international obligations to the United States. See Chapter 12.

curity Council resolution, was supported in part by the expectation that East-West competition for Arab favor would preclude either side from using strong measures to frustrate the blockade, and that in any event it could obtain from the Soviet Union protection against any such efforts by the West.[12] The blockade of the Gulf of Aqaba in May 1967 probably resulted from similar expectations, and the Arab states counted on and received Soviet support in preparing and waging the 1973 war against Israel. Iran flouted an order of the International Court of Justice in the Anglo-Iranian oil case and received Soviet support in the Security Council.[13] African and Asian nations openly supported rebellion in Angola and Rhodesia and threatened force against South Africa, in part because they counted on Soviet support, and expected that the Western powers will be reluctant to appear as less of a friend of new nations, less of a foe of colonialism or racism, than the Communist states.

Other alignments and organizations also exert influence on law observance. The Organization for African Unity and "organizations" like those of Bandung and Casablanca may contribute to common attitudes on some issues of international law; they may also afford members protection for violations against other states. Regional groupings may also develop new norms for themselves, measures for enforcement and deterrence in support of these norms, and common attitudes favoring compliance with these norms. Latin America began to develop a regional international law long before there was formal regional organization.[14] The Organization of American States—the oldest regional grouping—wields substantial influence on compliance by its members, as Premier Castro learned.

The emergence of the Third World with its growing sense of power and common mission has also been a less-than-happy influence for compliance with law. Of course, the Third World has condoned its members when they rejected norms to which the Third World objected in principle, e.g., the nationalization of property without just compensation; or where the purpose ranked high in Third World values, e.g., the use of force against colonialism in

Goa (1954) or later (Rhodesia). But the demands of Third World solidarity and the desire to maintain it even at high cost has sometimes led the Third World to condone violations by its members even of laws that are not ideologically disputed and are generally favored, especially when "the victim" is a developed state. Compare the reaction, or lack of it, when Uganda expelled Asians bearing British passports.

The emergence of the Third World can be attributed directly to the U.N. Charter and the United Nations organization. These established the principle of self-determination and equality by outlawing the use of force in international relations. The influence of the Third World on law and law observance promises to be greatest in and through the United Nations organization in regard to those international obligations that have been the principal concern of that organization and the new law which they have tried to make there.

LAW AND FORCE:
seven
THE UNITED NATIONS CHARTER

The principal development in international law in our time is the law of the United Nations Charter outlawing the use of force in international relations.[1] That law, resulting from the political forces prevailing in the international system at the end of the Second World War, has influenced the struggle between East and West during the following decades and has contributed to the end of colonialism and the multiplication of states. In turn, ideological struggle and the emergence of the Third World have exerted pressures on, and changed the contents and influence of, that law.

THE LAW OF THE CHARTER

It was not a cynic who once suggested that international law establishes order in unimportant matters but not in important ones.[2] Doubtless, the comment referred in particular to the anomaly of international law before our times, which set up rules about international conduct in time of peace but did not forbid nations to commit the ultimate "aggression" against international order, the resort to war. That incongruity had its explanations, principally in the failure of early attempts to distinguish just wars (to be permitted, even encouraged) from unjust wars (to be outlawed). Third nations also wished to avoid becoming involved in the wars of others and wished to go their way in relation to both belligerent sides without having to decide which was in "the right." And, in fact, one cannot say that the anomaly nullified international law. Indeed, nations were more likely to observe the international law of peace, knowing that if their interests were too gravely jeopardized they could go to war to vindicate them and establish a new basis for new relations in a revised international order with different international obligations.

Still, the paradox troubled many, as did the increasing destructiveness of war, and there were recurrent attempts to make law to prevent or control the resort to war. The most earnest ones came after the First World War, in the Covenant of the League of Nations and the Kellogg-Briand Pact. Their fate is well known. After the terrible Second World War, peoples were determined to try again, and the stone which builders of international order had long rejected became the headstone of the corner. Article 2(4) of the United Nations Charter provides:*

---

*The Charter contains little else of a general normative character, as distinguished from obligations to obey or cooperate with U.N. organs. Even the provision forbidding the threat of force has had only limited significance: for example, expressed and constantly reiterated Arab threats to destroy Israel have not been treated as violations; surely, the mere possession and deployment of weapons with capacity to destroy has not been deemed a prohibited threat of force. The ancillary undertaking that members "settle their disputes by peaceful means" [U.N. Charter, Article 2(3)] has, in practice, seemed to mean only that members may not resort to force. (Compare, again, the relations between the Arab states and Israel.) Other undertakings—for example, "to take joint and separate action," in cooperation with the United Nations, to promote economic and social ends (Articles 55 and 56)—are too vague to be normative and, originally at least, seemed principally hortatory. But compare Chapter 12.

All members shall refrain in their international relations from the threat or use of force against the territorial integrity or political independence of any state, or in any other manner inconsistent with the purposes of the United Nations.

The only exception expressed was in Article 51:

Nothing in the present charter shall impair the inherent right of individual or collective self-defense if an armed attack occurs against a member of the Organization, until the Security Council has taken the measures necessary to maintain international peace and security.

Unlike the limited restraints in the Covenant of the League and the provisions of the Kellogg-Briand Pact, the Charter's prohibition on unilateral force was to apply universally: members were bound by it; they were to see to it that nonmembers also complied.[3] For the first time, nations tried to bring within the realm of law those ultimate political tensions and interests that had long been deemed beyond control by law. They determined that even sincere concern for national "security" or "vital interests" should no longer warrant any nation to initiate war.[4] They agreed, in effect, to forgo the use of external force to change the political status quo. Nations would be assured their fundamental independence, the enjoyment of their territory, their freedom—a kind of right to be let alone. With it, of course, came the corresponding obligation to let others alone, not to use force to resolve disputes, or even to vindicate one's "rights." Change—other than internal change through internal forces—would have to be achieved peacefully, by agreement. Henceforth there would be order, and international society could concentrate on meeting better the needs of justice and welfare.

This most political of norms has been the target of "realists" from the beginning. They have questioned whether it is viable, even whether it is clearly desirable. Some who approved the norm in 1945 began to ask later whether it was acceptable. A "realist" would suggest that the law could have worked only if the United States and the Soviet Union had been prepared to cooperate to enforce peace. A lawyer might ask whether the law remains law, according to the principle of *rebus sic stantibus*, when the assumptions on which it was based have failed, when the circumstances in which it was made and those for which it was contemplated have radically changed.

For me, the changing facts and faces of international law have not detracted from the validity of the law of the Charter and have only reinforced its desirability.[5] Consider, first, the argument based on the failure of the original conception of the United Nations: it has not established an effective international police system; it has not developed and maintained machinery for peaceful settlement of disputes (making self-help unnecessary and undesirable). But the draftsmen of the Charter were not seeking merely to replace "balance of power" by "collective security"; they were determined, according to the Preamble, to abolish "the scourge of war." All the evidence is persuasive that they sought to outlaw war, whether or not the U.N. organization succeeded in enforcing the law or in establishing peace and justice. And none of the original members, nor any one of the many new members, has ever claimed that the law against the use of force is undesirable now that the United Nations is not what had been intended.

The major transformations in international society also have not led to wide questioning of the law against use of force. That law is at least as necessary and as desirable in the age of nuclear weapons, of cold war or détente, of the U.S.-Sino-Soviet triangle, as it was in 1945. Neither established big powers nor new small nations have sought to throw over the restraints of this law, however much they have sometimes chafed under it (and sometimes violated it). The United States believes that it has abided by that law, and that even in Korea and Vietnam it acted consistently with that law, in collective self-defense. The Soviet Union has not claimed any right to use force against other nations and even its determination to maintain communism, by force if necessary (as in Czechoslovakia in 1968, justified by the Brezhnev Doctrine), may have been abandoned at Helsinki if not earlier.[6] The new states recognize that their own existence and their emergence into influence have resulted from that contemporary law and the new political morality it reflected, and that these continue to help protect them from big-power "take-over" and from latter-day manifestations of gun-boat diplomacy. In their relations with each other, too, the new states—although their national boundaries are irrational, the fortuitous result of the accident of colonial competition—are nonetheless reluctant to court the chaos that might result if change by force became acceptable. (Compare their support, for that reason, of Ethiopia's resistance to Somalia's effort in 1977–78 to "regain" the Ogaden area by force.) The law of the Charter, rather than questioned, has been repeatedly reaffirmed. It was reasserted in the Declaration on Principles Concerning Friendly Relations adopted overwhelmingly in 1970.[7] It was reaffirmed at Helsinki in the Final Act of the Conference on Security and Cooperation in Europe in 1975.[8] The Third World led also in promulgating the resolution reinforcing the Charter by declaring against the acquisition of territory by force.[9]

The law of the Charter, I conclude, remains "good law." Our hypothetical court, I am confident, would apply it much as originally written and intended. Governments generally treat it as law in determining their own policy and in reacting to the behavior of others. It is also, I am satisfied, desirable law, its desirability emphatically reinforced by the weapons and conflicts and transformations of contemporary society. There are questions however as to what that law means in some respects, and whether it has "worked," whether it has been generally observed, what its influence has been on the policies and behavior of governments.

WHAT DOES THE CHARTER PROHIBIT?

If decades of radical transformation in the political system have left the law of the Charter standing, they have not been without impact on its scope and meaning.

Article 2(4) clearly intended to outlaw resort to traditional war,*

---

* Arab claims from 1947 of right to wage war against Israel were difficult to justify in international law and found no support outside the Arab world; when Israel

but the framers obviously excluded also other uses of forces, whether or not in declared war, whether or not in all-out hostilities. Force is outlawed, however, against "the territorial integrity or political independence of any state, or in any other manner inconsistent with the purposes of the United Nations." Does the prohibition of force against "the territorial integrity" of another state forbid only force designed to deprive it of territory, or also force which merely violates territorial borders however temporarily and for whatever purpose? Does the prohibition of force against "the political independence" of another state outlaw force only if its aim is to end another state's political independence, or also force to coerce another government to take a particular decision? In what other circumstances would a use of force be "against the purposes of the United Nations?" There has also been debate as to whether economic pressure—the oil embargo, economic boycott or other sanctions—is a prohibited use of force.*

A different and wider set of debates has involved the scope of the exception in Article 51. On the face of it, that article provides that despite the prohibition on the unilateral use of force in Article 2(4),

---

resorted to force, it claimed to be acting in self-defense under Article 51. There has been wide support of Arab claims that Israel should return territories conquered in the 1967 war, and Israel has asserted its readiness to do that in a peace settlement.

* Article 2(4) may have had the effect of superseding the "laws of war"—especially notions of neutrality between belligerents to be treated alike. The Charter may be seen as declaring that the aggressive war is "unjust" while the victim is justified in fighting in self-defense. Other members of the United Nations may not remain neutral: at least if the United Nations takes action against the aggressor, they are obliged to assist the United Nations and refrain from assisting the aggressor. Article 2(5). See L. Henkin, "Force, Intervention and Neutrality in Contemporary International Law," cited in n. 5, this chapter, at 159–61. Compare the address by Attorney General Robert Jackson, 35 *Am. J. Int'l L.* 348 (1941). Compare also the resolution of the Council of the League of Nations, concerning a dispute between Poland and Lithuania, that "a state of war between two members of the League is incompatible with the spirit and the letter of the Covenant." 9 LNOJ, no. 1, Jan. 1928, at 177; see *id.*, at 148–53. A state of belligerency, like that asserted by the Arab states in relation to Israel, would seem to be incompatible with the normative conceptions of the U.N. Charter.

a victim of an armed attack may use force to defend itself, and others may join in force to defend the victim, pending action by the Security Council. No one has doubted that the right of individual or collective self-defense against armed attack continues to apply if the Security Council does not act at all. It has also been generally accepted that self-defense against armed attack includes the right to take the war to the aggressor in order effectively to terminate the attack or even to prevent or deter its recurrence. It is generally accepted, too, that states are permitted to organize themselves in advance, *e.g.*, NATO, in bona fide collective self-defense arrangements for possible action if an armed attack occurs.[10]

Especially in the wake of Suez-Sinai (Chapter 13), however, some publicists began to argue that the "inherent right of self-defense" incorporates the traditional pre-Charter right of self-defense which was not limited to and did not have to await "armed attack"; that the right of self-defense "if an armed attack occurs" does not mean "only if an armed attack occurs."[11] The only limitation on self-defense, they have argued, was that implied in the famous *Caroline* dictum, that self-defense was limited to cases in which "the necessity of self-defense is instant, overwhelming, and leaving no choice of means, and no moment of deliberation";[12] and the use of force had to be "reasonable" and "proportional."

To me, the argument is unfounded, its reasoning is fallacious, its doctrine pernicious. The fair reading of Article 51 permits unilateral use of force only in a very narrow and clear circumstance, in self-defense if an armed attack occurs. Nothing in the history of its drafting (the *travaux préparatoires*) suggests that the framers of the Charter intended something broader than the language implied. Since the Charter was drafted, the world for which it was written has changed; the United Nations has changed; the quality of force has changed. But neither the failure of the Security Council, nor the Cold War, nor the birth of many new nations, nor the development of terrible weapons, suggests that the Charter should now be read to authorize unilateral force even if an armed attack has not occurred.

The argument most frequently given in support of "anticipatory self-defense" is based on the new military technology. Of this I have written:

> They misconceive both the significance of the United Nations and the character of new war who suggest that the basic concept of the Charter—outlawing unilateral use of force—cannot apply in the day of modern weapons. It was that mild, old-fashioned Second World War which persuaded all nations that for the future national interests will have to be vindicated, or necessary change achieved, as well as can be by political means, but not by war and military self-help. They recognized the exception of self-defense in emergency, but limited to actual armed attack, which is clear, unambiguous, subject to proof, and not easily open to misinterpretation or fabrication. Surely today's weapons render it even more important that nations should not be allowed to cry "vital interests" or "anticipatory self-defense" and unleash the fury. It is precisely in the age of the major deterrent that nations should not be encouraged to strike first under pretext of prevention or pre-emption.
>
> The argument that "anticipatory self-defense" is essential to United States defense is fallacious. The United States relies for its security on its retaliatory power, and primarily on its second strike capability. It does not expect that it would be able to anticipate an attack and it could not afford to be mistaken, to bring about total war by a "pre-emptive strike," if the Soviet Union were not in fact striking or preparing to strike. In all probability, then, only an actual take-off by Soviet planes or missiles would cause the United States to strike, and in that case the United States is not "anticipating" an armed attack, for the attack would have begun.
>
> In fact, of course, for determining what the Charter means or should mean, the nuclear attack and the pre-emptive strike are not the relevant concerns. A nation planning all-out attack will not be deterred by the Charter, though it may well talk "anticipatory self-defense" to any left to listen. Nor does one prescribe rules for the nation threatened with such an attack. If a nation is satisfied that another is about to obliterate it, it will not wait. But it has to make that decision on its own

awesome responsibility. Anticipation in that case may have to be practiced; it need not be preached. The Charter need not make a principle of it; the law need not authorize or encourage it. But surely that extreme hypothetical case beyond the realm of law should not be used to justify new rules for situations that do not involve the impending mortal thrust. Anticipatory self-defense as a rule of law has meaning only in less extreme cases. There, anticipatory self-defense, it should be clear, is a euphemism for "preventive war." The U.N. Charter does not authorize it. Nothing in international relations, including the new weapons, suggests that international society would be better if the Charter were changed—or read—to authorize it.[13]

I would add the following. If the reason for a new reading of the Charter permitting anticipatory self-defense is the hypothetical case of a country which learns certainly and unimpeachably that another is about to destroy it, responsible readings of the Charter and responsible concern for international order would limit the new reading to that extreme case. One might perhaps argue that the scheme of the Charter did not contemplate the extreme case. Article 51 recognized that a nation cannot and should not be expected to refrain from defending itself and rely wholly on the protection of the United Nations. A nation might suffer great losses or be overwhelmed before the forces of the United Nations could come to its aid. Collective action may be effective only if the victim can do something in its own defense pending collective mobilization. For that reason, self-defense against armed attack was provided for, until the United Nations acts. Surely, with the Security Council neutralized and no United Nations forces in being, Article 51 has proved its foresight and practical wisdom: nations will defend themselves against armed attack, and some will defend each other collectively, say, through NATO or the OAS. That will give time to the United Nations to mobilize forces—military, political, moral—against the aggressor. None of this, clearly, is relevant to a sudden all-out nuclear attack. If deterrence fails there is no defense, individual or collective, or possibility of protection by the United Nations. If there were clear evidence of an attack so imminent that there was no time for political action to prevent it, the only meaningful defense for the potential victim might indeed be the preemptive attack and—it may be argued—the scheme of Article 2(4) together with Article 51 was not intended to bar such attack. But this argument would claim a small and special exception for the special case of the surprise nuclear attack; today, and one hopes for a time longer, it is meaningful and relevant principally only as between the Soviet Union and the United States and, fortunately, only for a most unlikely eventuality. But such a reading of the Charter, it should be clear, would not permit (and encourage) anticipatory self-defense in other, more likely situations between nations generally.

There has been no authoritative resolution of these questions and no concentrated discussion of them since Suez (1956) and the Cuban missile crisis (1963). Since then, too, frustration and impatience with perceived injustice have released pressures favoring the use of force—to end colonialism (in Namibia and Rhodesia, as in Goa a generation earlier) or racism (South Africa). India's incursion into East Pakistan during the creation of Bangladesh, too, was justified as support for "self-determination" or as "humanitarian intervention." [14]

To me, these pressures eroding the prohibition on the use of force are deplorable, and the arguments to legitimize the use of force in those circumstances are unpersuasive and dangerous. Neither the U.N. Charter or any other international law forbids rebellion, whether against local or colonial authority. But to suggest that because colonialism is wrong, and now perhaps even illegal, the continuing presence of colonial authority constitutes "armed attack" and brings into play Article 51, is surely a distortion. Similar arguments might be made, with as little warrant, whenever one state claims sovereignty to territory held by another in any of the numerous disputed areas, say British Honduras (Belize), or the Western Sahara, or on the Somalia-Ethiopia border. If any presence or exercise of authority perceived to be illegal or unjust is an "armed attack" against the "proper sovereign" of the territory, any use of force against it becomes plausible as "self-defense," and Article 51 will have destroyed the prohibition of Article 2(4). Even "humanitarian intervention" can too readily be used as the occasion or pretext for aggression. Violations of human rights are indeed all too common, and if it were permissible to remedy them by external use of force, there would be no law to forbid the use of force by almost any state against almost any other. Human rights, I believe, will have to be vindicated, and other injustices remedied, by other, peaceful means, not by opening the door to aggression and destroying the principal advance in international law, the outlawing of war and the prohibition of force.

Surely, any extension of Article 51 is especially to be resisted, for whatever is allowed to come within its "armed attack" exception to Article 2(4) might permit full-scale war against the "attacker" and bring in allies on both sides. If there are hard cases where it is commonly accepted that temporary use of small force is justified, its legality might better be sought in the limitations on the prohibition perhaps implied in Article 2(4). The hijacking of a French plane to Uganda and the retention of its passengers as hostages there, apparently with the connivance or consent of the government of Uganda, was not an armed attack by Uganda against France or against the countries whose nationals were being held, and did not permit these governments to wage war against Uganda "in self-defense." But Israel could plausibly argue that in the circumstances its raid at Entebbe was not a use of force against the political independence or territorial integrity of Uganda, or in any other way contrary to any purpose of the United Nations.*

If "humanitarian intervention" is to be permissible it should be sharply limited to actions the purpose of which is unambiguous and limited, for example, to release hostages or execute other emergency evacuations. Even those might better be left to collective (not unilateral) action, for example by special U.N. "humanitarian evacuation forces" (akin to the various U.N. peace-keeping forces), created in advance for that purpose and immunized so far as possible from larger international political tensions.

* Compare the argument in the Cuban missile crisis, Chapter 15.

HAS THE LAW AGAINST FORCE
BEEN OBSERVED?

Observers have expressed doubt that one could "suppress the chaotic and dangerous aspirations of governments" by "legal rules and restraints," that one could "subordinate states to an international juridical regime, limiting their possibilities for aggression and injury."[15] Sovereign nations cannot be expected to give up the power to vindicate ultimate interests as they see them, by force if necessary. Some who originally thought the law would work because it would be enforced by the dominant powers through the Security Council of the United Nations changed their views when the Cold War destroyed illusions of great power cooperation to maintain peace and even involved them in actual hostilities, as in Korea. Divergent interests of major powers also prevented agreement on peaceful change, and on meeting the demands of other nations for justice and welfare so as to reduce their frustrations and their temptations to resort to force.

And yet, the norm against the unilateral national use of force has survived. Indeed, despite common misimpressions to the contrary, the norm has been largely observed, and the kinds of international wars which it sought to prevent and deter have been infrequent, although threatening to become less so, alas, in the late 1970s. (I am referring, I emphasize, to wars between states, to the use of force by one nation against the political independence or territorial integrity of another; I will speak separately of subversion, intervention, internal wars, and the difficult-to-characterize Vietnam war.) I repeat: the norm against unilateral force has been largely observed. With the exception of Korea (in some respects an "internal war"), the brief, recurrent Arab-Israel hostilities in 1956, 1967, and 1973, the flurry between India and Pakistan over Kashmir in September 1965, the invasion of Czechoslovakia by Soviet troops in 1968,* nations have not engaged in "war," in full and sustained hostilities or state-to-state aggression even in circumstances in

---

*One might add, unhappily, Ethiopia-Somalia and Vietnam-Cambodia-China in 1978–79.

which in the past the use of force might have been expected. In the period since the Second World War there have not been analogues to the conquests and wars that followed the First World War—the Japanese conquest of Manchuria, Italy's aggression in Ethiopia, Hitler's invasion of Poland, Japan's attack at Pearl Harbor, the long Gran Chaco war.[16] Most important, despite acute hostility, the law against unilateral force has been observed among the big powers; the most significant fact about the Cold War is that it remained cold. It is commonly suggested that the war of our times is the internal war and that waging war between nations is no longer "done." If it were so, the society of nations would have achieved a new level of evolution, and one might conclude that the foundations of international order were finally established. Even a decade ago that conclusion would have been premature: within a brief period in 1963–65 the world saw increased Arab threats against Israel, Greece and Turkey close to war over Cyprus, Indonesia asserting a right to attack "colonialism" in Malaysia, India and China in dispute over borders, India and Pakistan actually if briefly at war, the beginning of United States involvement in Vietnam. Again, perhaps the significant fact is not that these threats occurred but that they did not result in war, and that even actual war between India and Pakistan over the long-festering problem of Kashmir was probably not wholly intended, did not become "all-out" war, and was soon terminated. Since then, there have been two wars in the Middle East, and no one can say there will not be another. But recurrent Middle East hostilities also were quickly ended, the world acting on the view that states no longer have the right to fight wars when and for how long they will. Cyprus erupted again, but did not become extended war. And there were war-like maneuverings in the Western Sahara and about the Horn of Africa, even an eruption between Lybia and Egypt in 1977. Cambodia and Thailand have fought frequently but briefly. Confidently one may now assert that although the possibility of international war or violence cannot be discounted, the expectation of violence no longer underlies every political calculation of every nation. Most nations, surely the bigger powers, know that, even as to issues in which the stakes are very high, they are limited to peaceful settlement—or, often, peaceful "nonsettlement"—of their disputes or occasional forcible flurries (*e.g.*, Kashmir, Cyprus).*

To speak of war and peace in terms of observance or violation of law may appear naïve. Those who do not accept such law as "realistic" will not agree that it has any relevance to decisions of this import. Nuclear war is deterred by consequences so unthinkable that to speak of the influence of law in deterring it is supererogatory. Lesser powers have also hesitated before the terrible consequences of modern war even if no nuclear weapons come into play; they have also feared possible involvement of the big powers and consequent escalation to nuclear war. Some nations have no doubt been saved from the sin of aggression by the inadequacy of their arms and the fear of failure. But there has been no war initiated by the strong against the weak,† by nuclear powers against others whom they could annihilate without fear of significant retaliation. In any event, whatever the reasons, the fact is that the law against the unilateral use of force is commonly observed.‡ The sense that war is not acceptable conduct has taken some hold; nations more readily find that their security and other national interests do not require the use of force after all; even where force is used, the fact

---

* There are exceptions, notably in Arab-Israel relations. Whether the possibility of war will continue to be an ever-present calculation may depend on what comes out of a mood for settlement that appeared to emerge in the mid-1970s. Even in Arab-Israel relations, the law of the Charter and the United Nations organization have been the bases and means for limiting or terminating the use of force. See Chapter 8, pp. 172–73, and Chapter 13.

† Except in the view of those who consider that the United States committed aggression against North Vietnam. See Chapter 16.

‡ Perhaps the law against war could not really work until war became prohibitive, and until most differences between the strong and weak became immaterial. The cause of peace is no doubt also helped by increased territorial stability. Previous efforts to invoke law against war were attempted in a world society that was territorially unstable and changeable. While there remain numerous border and territorial disputes creating tensions between states, today's instabilities are largely internal and political, not due to hopes of territorial realignment that were often in the past a substantial inducement to external war.

that it is now illegal must be taken into account and limits the scope, the weapons, the duration, the purposes, the justifications.*

Again the reasons must be sought in an accounting of cost and advantage to the national interest and in internal forces and pressures. But in regard to the law against force these considerations and pressures weigh quite differently. In regard to some violations, at least, we approach the limits at which terms like cost and advantage cease to be meaningful. All-out war today would not be a deliberate policy or Clausewitz's continuation of political intercourse by other means; it would signify instead a tragic failure of foreign policy and of diplomacy. A major violation that brought world war with nuclear weapons would be suicidal, rending the fabric of international society and possibly destroying human society as well. Nations that even risk approaching the "brink" of nuclear war would do so only for global political stakes. As between smaller, non-nuclear powers, too, all-out war today seems incredible as a rational policy, especially as there is the ever-present danger of great power involvement and escalation. More likely, nations might stumble into war, rather than plan it.† Since the issues that lead to war often engage the deepest passions, hardly conducive to careful assessment of cost and advantage, a nation may be swept to action regardless of law or consequences. Perhaps one can speak meaningfully of cost-and-advantage accounting only in regard to non-nuclear, planned wars (like Hitler's) or to isolated, discrete, limited uses of force.

Even where it is plausible to imagine careful weighing of very different kinds of consequences, the accounting of the pros and cons of law observance is very different for this particular law. It is

*Compare, for example, the limitations on United States involvement at the Bay of Pigs, the Greek and Turkish roles in Cyprus; at Suez the actions of France and Great Britain were circumscribed; even the Arab-Israel wars were pressed to "premature" ends.

† Only the 1973 attack by the Arab states against Israel was planned and calculated, although it appears unlikely that the Arab states expected victory and counted it worth the cost; more likely they were pressed by political forces and hoped to gain some political advantage from having fought and "bloodied Israel's nose."

ludicrous to say that nations observe the prohibition against war because violation would jeopardize friendly relations with the victim, or because war would damage international order or stability. Specific advantages to be gained and the costs to be incurred also have a special look. The advantages will generally be contingent on success and on degree of success, but no nation deliberately goes to war unless it expects victory (or at least non-defeat). The costs will be the costs of war and will depend on its course and outcome; they will include domestic losses and suffering and possibly political losses in the event of failure and defeat. Domestic restraints on going to war also have special relevance: war distorts the life of a people; sometimes there are also constitutional and institutional obstacles.

Where violations of the norm have occurred, the threats or uses of force have been limited, indirect, and conditional, so that the risks and uncertainties made possible some rational balancing of cost and advantage (although it is far from clear that such careful consideration took place). Against Israel in 1948, one may guess, the Arab states acted in passion, without balanced consideration of costs, but they might have acted the same way in expectation of a quick, easy victory at low military or political cost. When the Arabs failed, the end came quickly, in response to the authority of the big powers and the United Nations. In June 1967, the Arab states did not believe that their provocations would really lead to war. For its part, Israel found the sudden removal of U.N. forces and the blockade of Aqaba intolerable; it considered war inevitable and preferred to choose the time, and it was confident that it could win. In 1973 the Arab states sought to establish their military respectability and to destroy the myth of Israeli invincibility, counting on surprise and Israel's overconfidence and the expectation that, if necessary, big-power intervention would save them from defeat.

Korea was probably the result of a miscalculation: the Communists assumed that the deed could be quickly done and there would be no adequate and timely response. In the event, too, it was a violation, and a war, the cost of which was limited. The Soviet

Union succeeded in staying out of it; the United States and Communist China tacitly agreed to limit hostilities to Korean territory; the United States refrained from using nuclear weapons. Hungary was not properly a war between states, and Russia was able to becloud the legal issue by invoking an "invitation" by the "Government" of Hungary.[17] In any event, Hungary reflected Soviet assumptions—and perhaps neutralist and even Western reluctant acceptance—of a Communist sphere of influence within which, somewhat as in a civil war, the law against force does not apply. There, and in Czechoslovakia in 1968, the Soviet Union could assume—correctly as it proved—that there would be no military response and that adverse political consequences would not outweigh the political cost to Russia of Hungary's escape from the Soviet sphere. India took Goa in part in response to domestic pressures, and in expectation that there would be no response and little political cost.

The Hungarian revolution may teach, too, that even where big powers are involved, a single, quick and forceful *fait accompli* is less likely to be deterred than an extended, continuing violation. Such isolated attacks, made possible by the bomber and the missile, have also been infrequent, but they are encouraged by the temptation to achieve a single purpose which cannot be undone, and the expectation that any likely response would not be too costly. The United States, we shall see, considered bombing to eliminate Soviet missile bases in Cuba; in 1964, Turkey dropped "warning" bombs on Cyprus.[18] At Suez, the governments of France and Great Britain probably expected that their mission would be quickly accomplished. In the very different Belgian–United States airdrop to save hostages in the Congo in 1965, the governments thought that there would be a single action quickly done.[19] Sporadic, limited actions (for example, recurrent incidents over the years between Israel and its neighbors, Indonesia's sending of guerrillas to Malaysia in the 1960s[20]) are similarly not subject to the same restraints as would be an all-out war expected to continue for some time. (I do not consider here whether any of the actions cited violated international law.)

Continued observance of the prohibition on the use of force will also depend on the changing political forces of the postwar world. Technology has produced nuclear stalemate. It has substituted deterrence for defense, has made war unthinkable and therefore, one hopes, unlikely. It has also produced the supersonic airplane, the missile, and the bomb which make easier and encourage the sporadic attack and the *fait accompli*. Ideological conflict underlay the tension that led to war or limited action in Korea, Hungary, and at the Bay of Pigs. The new nations have been eager to avoid war between the big powers and to prevent the use of force by Western powers in Asia or Africa, as at Suez in 1956 or in Angola in 1975–76. The new nations have not been as concerned to prevent force against a colonial power, as at Goa, and some have asserted— and may yet exercise—a right to use force against colonialism in Rhodesia, and South West Africa. Big-power conflict has precluded a common interest in international peace and stability and has frustrated cooperation and weakened their influence, sometimes their desire, to maintain peace.

Other forces restraining small powers also seem to have loosened. The market in ever-more-sophisticated non-nuclear weapons is flourishing, with buyers able and eager, sellers at best insufficiently reluctant; and with weapons available there is some disposition to use them. States which did not exist or did not suffer much during the Second World War have no memories to deter them and are perhaps not as dedicated as are the European powers to the U.N. Charter's commitment to save future generations from the scourge of war. With big powers not likely to become involved, smaller powers may feel freer to consider war;* and the continuing competition by big powers for their alignment or realignment may

---

*This, and the emergence of China as a dominant force in Asia, helps to explain why, in 1965, after eighteen years, India and Pakistan should resort to fighting over Kashmir, and later India could help Bangladesh achieve independence.

Or, a nation may feel confident of the protection of one side. Egypt was probably encouraged to restore the blockade at Aqaba (which led to the Arab-Israel war of June 1967), and the Arabs generally to resort to war in 1973, by the expectation of Soviet support.

bring them big-power support in weaponry that can be used against neighbors, *e.g.*, in the Middle East, between Ethiopia and Somalia, Sudan and Egypt, Uganda and its neighbors, Iraq and Iran, Algeria and Morocco, Vietnam and Cambodia.

Both big-power competition and Third World solidarity tend to exclude big-power cooperation or unilateral big-power "interference" even to restrain hostilities, while the Third World has not replaced them as an effective monitor of peace. It has been insufficiently united, determined or effective to deter, prevent or terminate unlawful uses of force by Third World powers, even against other Third World states: Indonesia grabbed Timor; Morocco and Mauritania took the Spanish Sahara and skirmished with Algeria over it, contrary to cherished principles of self-determination; Somalia fought for old territorial claims against Ethiopia, which invited help from Cuba and the U.S.S.R.; Vietnam invaded Cambodia and China responded, but the Third World stood helplessly by.

INTERNAL WARS AND INTERVENTION

We turn now to a different matter: the state and influence of the law in regard to the use of military force within one's own territory, and to military intervention by other nations in such internal struggles.* Since World War II, there has hardly been a time without at least one such struggle in progress, and there have been numerous interventions and counter-interventions. These, it has been commonly assumed, have replaced international war as the wars of the nuclear age.

Intervention by foreign powers in domestic or civil wars has been regarded as a special form of foreign intervention generally. (Intervention, strictly, means dictatorial interference by force or threat of force; lesser forms of interference are also resisted and sometimes considered as "intervention.") Every nation resists inter-

---

*One must add instances when internal struggles were stirred up by outside powers, which then intervened.

ference in its affairs, and no nation admits that it has in fact interfered in another's affairs. Indeed, many of the acts specifically prohibited by international law are forms of foreign intervention or other improper interference, *e.g.*, aggression, lesser territorial intrusions, forms of espionage;[21] in addition, customary international law prohibits "intervention" generally.[22] By treaty and in various declarations and resolutions of international bodies, nations have unanimously and repeatedly accepted absolute prohibitions on "intervention" in the affairs of other states.[23]

Prohibitions of intervention and interference, it should be clear, are part of the quest for an ideal of equally sovereign and independent nations. Complete independence is, of course, an illusory goal; if, indeed, it was ever otherwise, today the interdependence of all nations is a commonplace. Some act of any nation may reverberate everywhere. Big powers, in particular, affect domestic affairs in other nations by their mere existence. American political and economic policies, whether of action or inaction, may "intervene" in the national life of other states as effectively as would sending the Marines. In a sense, to "intervene" to influence the policy of another government is the very purpose of all diplomacy and of all international agreements. International society could not deal with all these interventions by general "rule" even if it wished to. The broadest of the prohibitions on intervention has never been held to reach every action that clearly affected the interests or "independence" of other nations. There has been little success, however, in defining or enumerating the forms of intervention that are forbidden;[24] many nations have been particularly reluctant to agree to any suggestion or implication that intervention—by any means, for any purpose—was permissible.*

Our concern here is with intervention in internal wars, especially with military intervention. There are additional reasons why international society has dealt with such interventions in our time. Resistance to it has evoked particularly the principle of "self-deter-

---

* On the relation of "intervention" to concern for human rights in other countries, see Chapter 12.

mination"; also, such intervention, has often threatened international peace. But here international law has been subject to particular uncertainties and strains. Revolution and internal wars have been a common phenomenon. Not surprisingly, revolutionary movements sought external assistance for themselves, but condemned as intervention any assistance to the governments against which they were rebelling. Not surprisingly, governments (including those which themselves came to power by revolution) saw objectionable "intervention" when other nations supported rebellion, whether by financial, political, or military means. Not surprisingly, governments saw no objectionable "intervention" in financial, military, or political support for themselves, even to shore them up against possible rebellion.

The result was that international society struggled to achieve consensus and law on such questions as: What kinds of assistance may be given to legitimate governments? At what point does such assistance cease to be permissible because the government's right and power to rule are being challenged? At what stage may nations begin to accord rebels limited rights as "insurgents"? When may they decide to accord them belligerent rights equal to those of the government previously in power? When may they recognize them as the legitimate government? What are the rights and duties of states in regard to one side or the other in full-blown civil war? The absence of international standards or procedures for recognition has left nations with wide discretion as to when and whom to recognize, which they are able to exploit for their own "interventionist" political interests. Some of these issues became acute during the Civil War in Spain, when the actions of several countries battered whatever norms there might have been about intervention or neutrality or about that assertion of neutrality which becomes a kind of intervention because it accords belligerent status to rebel forces.[25]

When, in the U.N. Charter, the nations decided to outlaw wars and the use of force, they said nothing explicit about internal wars; clearly, they did not intend to prohibit revolution or civil war. The Charter, too, though it enshrines principles of "independence," "sovereign equality," and "self-determination," says nothing explicit about outside intervention in internal struggles. It is not commonly insisted that the Charter itself forbids intervention in internal wars by political and economic means.* The question that has divided lawyers is whether the Charter provision that members shall not use or threaten force against the political independence or territorial integrity of another member forbids also intervention by force in a civil war.

For this purpose one might perhaps distinguish different kinds of intervention. One can readily argue the unlawfulness of "subversive" intervention: it is just as much a violation for an outside power to use force subtly or covertly to subvert an existing government and impose a puppet government as it is to send its armies to conquer the victim and impose a puppet government. On this view, the Charter bars external participation in internal struggle by force, at least if this intervention threatens the political independence or territorial integrity of the victim. The United Nations has in effect taken this position when its resolutions condemned "indirect aggression"; the definition of aggression which it adopted, the Declaration of Principles on Friendly Relations, the Code on the Rights and Duties of States, all condemn "indirect aggression."[26]

Some lawyers have argued that, when nations come to the support of one side or the other in cases of independent insurrection or *bona fide* civil war, it is not a violation of the norms of the U.N. Charter† but only of some customary rule against such intervention which, if it was ever sound, may not have recovered from the wounds it suffered in the Spanish Civil War. Many believe that there is no agreed norm forbidding active military support for the

---

*It is only the United Nations itself which is expressly prohibited by the Charter to intervene in the domestic affairs of nations. Article 2(7).

†It is argued that even if intervention is not considered a use of force against the territorial integrity or political independence of the victim state [Article 2(4)], it may . yet constitute a threat to international peace, especially when nations intervene on both sides. No doubt, in a given case, U.N. organs may conclude that such competing interventions threaten the peace, and may invoke their authority accordingly. It has been suggested that even civil war itself (without intervention) may constitute a threat to the peace which the United Nations is authorized to suppress.

recognized government of a country, at least before rebellion has made great headway. The United States has invoked the right to give such aid to Greece, Lebanon, Nationalist China, and South Vietnam.[27] The Soviet Union claimed a similar justification in Hungary. Some may even assert the right to recognize and support rebel causes, as in Angola (against Portugal), and even in the Congo in 1964–65. International law was not much invoked when different powers supported different factions competing for authority, as in Angola in 1975–76, or even when India recognized Bangladesh, or Tanzania recognized Biafra while civil war was still in progress.

In our time, some forces for intervention have been particularly strong and unlikely to heed an uncertain law. The difficulties of defining and preventing "unlawful intervention" have been multiplied where domestic and international interests are entangled and internal conflicts have special international significance. There were interventions to help end colonialism, as when Tunisia actively supported the Algerian rebels, and when other nations supported rebels against Portuguese rule in Angola. The major interventions involved, of course, Communist expansionism and Western efforts to contain it. Even interventions not unlike those of past days, and not obviously related to colonialism or communism, have looked different in our times—for example, Egyptian troops in Yemen in the 1960s, and open, full-blown and continuing intervention in Lebanon in 1976–77.*

It is the ideological conflict which has given the problem of intervention new significance, and made new difficulties for law. Intervention, as much as external aggression, has been the focus of the "containment policy" and the Cold War. The competition between

* Our times also raised special problems of intervention where there is no internal war. We were not too far from traditional accusations of foreign intervention when West Germany protested recognition of East Germany as a separate state, but this division—and those in Vietnam, Korea, China—was hardly a traditional instance of rebellion or secession. The People's Republic of China continued to protest recognition of the Nationalist regime in Taiwan, whether as the Government of China or even as having authority over Taiwan.

East and West in economic assistance and in other forms of wooing (including the supply of arms) is at bottom a competition in interventions. What becomes of the rules against intervention when promoting "people's revolutions" and "wars of liberation" is official Communist policy, Soviet and Chinese, and the prevention of Communist "take-over" is a pillar of American foreign policy? The dynamic of communism backed by tremendous military power, the control exercised by the Soviet Union (or China) over Communist parties elsewhere, and the avowed policy of exporting and promoting revolution have transformed earlier notions of intervention. As early as 1948 with the Communist coup in Czechoslovakia, the international community faced a political change accomplished ostensibly through domestic forces but largely engineered by an external power and backed by the threat of its military force. In Greece, rebel forces attempting to seize power were supported and supplied by neighboring Communist countries. In other parts of the world, particularly Indochina, local groups were supported from without, first against the French, then in civil war.* In Hungary, Soviet military force intervened to prevent revolution which might have taken Hungary from the Soviet orbit, and in Czechoslovakia in 1968 to prevent liberalization.

The powers determined to contain Communist expansion have resorted to "counter-intervention" by aiding non-Communist governments to suppress rebellion (Greece), and anti-Communist forces to rebel against pro-Communist regimes (Cuba, Guatemala), or to attempt to win full-blown civil war (Vietnam). Political and economic assistance and providing arms to help a government maintain stability are forms of "preventive intervention." Fear of Communist take-over led to alleged "preemptive intervention," although there was no government asking for support, when United States Marines landed in the Dominican Republic in April 1965—in the face of express treaty undertakings against intervention and a foreign policy in the area carefully built and nurtured on

---

*Korea appeared different because there was a clear division of the country before the Communist government in North Korea launched its attack.

a principle of nonintervention.[28] The Soviet Union encouraged Cuban support for a sympathetic faction in Angola, and the United States was discouraged from active military support to another faction by memories of Vietnam and domestic political opposition. Even where the United States and the U.S.S.R. are not involved, or are only in the wings, regional ideological competition may provoke interventions—say, by "radical" or "conservative" Arab states, or African states.

In the exploitation of internal forces, the stirring of internal struggle, and military support and intervention, which have become weapons in the political-ideological struggle of our times, the law against intervention has inevitably suffered.[29] Laws against intervention are acceptable and viable only if both sides in a worldwide ideological struggle agree to abstain. As soon as one side intervenes or threatens to intervene, the other side may feel that it cannot afford to abstain. Surely, many would deplore it if "forces of evil" felt free to intervene while "forces of good" insisted on abstaining. Other political influences also have not supported the rule of law in this regard. Even the new technology, by rendering international war prohibitive, has only reinforced the tendency of Communist forces to promote and exploit internal wars; in these wars new technology has not proved decisive, and nuclear weapons may not even be wholly relevant. In Vietnam, new technology was effectively frustrated.

The multiplication of new nations and emergence of the Third World have not helped the law against intervention. New "artificial" states in territory reflecting the accidents of colonial history tend to be unstable states, riven by tribal and religious antagonisms, vulnerable to the world's ideological conflicts, breeding civil war and inviting intervention by states in the area or by ideological leaders outside. The new nations themselves have not all been able to resist intervening in each other's affairs (Nkrumah's Ghana intervened in Togo, and more recently there have been repeated charges of intervention in Zaire, or between Uganda and its neighbors). Some themselves stirred or supported internal wars against colonialism (Angola, Rhodesia) and even against an African government

considered Western-oriented or controlled (the Congo in
1964–65).[30] More recently, too, they have not taken an active role
or a strong position against ideological interventions generally, even
by distant governments, e.g., Cuba's support for one faction in
Angola in 1976.

The obstacles to a rule of law in regard to military intervention
in internal wars were epitomized by the war in Vietnam that finally ended in 1973. (See Chapter 16.) Since internal factions often
feel impelled to invite aid from one major power or another, and
these feel impelled to provide it, many an internal struggle is potentially a Vietnam, and promotes resistance to law against intervention. In particular, Vietnam showed the political difficulties of
bringing law to bear on intervention that finds the superpowers on
opposite sides and reflects their major ideological political struggle.

Vietnam also served to confuse legitimate distinctions between
subversive intervention against the political integrity of a country
and military support for either side in internal wars. Thus it continues to be politically difficult to obtain wise consideration of the
relevance of Article 2(4) of the U.N. Charter to any kind of intervention by force in internal struggles and other internal affairs. For
the present, then, it may be better to leave the authority of Article
2(4) clear and undisputed to cover at least cases of direct, overt
aggression that are generally capable of objective and persuasive
proof. The battle of interventions, for the present, will have to be
fought with little help from law. Perhaps stronger regional coher-
ence and determination will lead the governments of particular
areas themselves to isolate internal struggles from outside intervention, to influence their own members as well as the big powers to
leave competing internal forces alone to work out—or fight for—
their own solutions.

The laws against intervention in internal struggle have been uncertain; the facts of internal struggle and intervention are also often
uncertain or, at least, easy to confuse; contemporary politics has
enhanced the interests at stake in internal wars, tempting external
intervention. Together they have combined to weaken the influence of laws and obligations prohibiting forcible intervention. This

is not to say that the law has been without influence to deter intervention. Deterrence is always difficult to prove, but one may assert confidently that there have been numerous instances in which nations had the interest and ability to intervene but refrained from doing so because of law and obligation barring intervention and the fear of the consequences of violation, as when a regime distasteful to the United States came to power, *e.g.*, Allende's government in Chile.* Even some of the cases where intervention took place prove the influence of law. United States intervention at the Bay of Pigs had to be covert, limited, and less than halfhearted; further forcible interventions within Cuba have not taken place. United States experience with intervention in the Dominican Republic and Vietnam makes it less likely that such episodes will readily happen again. Compare the Nixon Doctrine; U.S. abstention in Angola (1976), and Zaire (1977). On the Communist side, the Soviet Union intervened in Hungary (1956) and again in Czechoslovakia (1968), but both proved highly expensive politically; it has not been prepared to pay the price of intervening to suppress centrifugal forces within other Eastern European countries—in Yugoslavia or in Albania on the one hand or Rumania on the other.

In sum, whereas the law against international war has fared well, the law against intervention in internal wars has fared less well; and it has fared rather badly where internal wars reflected the major ideological struggle of our day. This may still represent an important advance in international order: it is not always possible to promote or maintain internal wars; intervention in internal war is not so great an aggression against sovereignty and independence; internal wars are generally limited in area and in scope of military operation and therefore less terrible in their destructiveness. One may hope that with increasing interest in stability, especially in the new nations, changing political forces may make internal wars, too, more amenable to the influence of law. Immediately, alas—witness Vietnam—the danger is that the reverse might happen, that inter-

---

*If the United States contributed to the fall of Allende, it did not do so by military intervention.

nal wars may spread and ignite international wars. Militarily and politically as well as legally, it may not be possible to maintain the distinction between internal and international wars. The use of force is contagious and can easily spill over a country's borders and cause major conflagration. Force applied by big powers in internal wars may suggest to others that use of force is not indeed intolerable, weakens the influence of the powers over others, sets examples that ignore nice legal distinctions: if force is used in Vietnam and in the Dominican Republic, why not between the Arabs and Israel? The emergence of the Third World tends to insulate its members from influence by big powers, even if these were united in desiring peace. Black Africa is determined to end white rule in Southern Africa, by force if necessary, and the Third World (and the Communist powers) will condone or support it. Third World condonation or support might extend to other uses of force to which important elements in the Third World might resort, *e.g.*, another Arab attack against Israel. The prevalence of force, moreover, even if only in internal wars, creates an atmosphere of instability which weakens the observance of all norms, not least the rule against international war.

THE RULE AGAINST FORCE AND GENERAL LAW OBSERVANCE

If the norm against the use of force between nations has been largely observed, some think the norm may have discouraged observance of other norms of international law. For the result is, they say, that unilateral use of force has not been available as a response by the victim of injustice or of a violation of international law. Even weaker nations, then, may feel more free to violate international law or to challenge its norms or to insist on their modification. For this reason, it has been suggested, the Charter should not be interpreted as outlawing force to rectify violations of international law or other injustice.[31]

The resort to war to "enforce" international law, I agree, is today politically unacceptable, and the threat of such force by the "victim" would be generally incredible.* It does not commonly figure in the calculus of cost of a violation and is not usually available as a deterrent to violation. That the unavailability of force encourages violation of law, however, is difficult to accept in principle and is not supported by evidence. The suggestion assumes, apparently, that wars have been fought to right wrongs, whether of law or of justice, and that threat of war has deterred such wrongs. History will not support that conclusion.† Unilateral force was not commonly used to enforce international obligations, nor did the fear of such force commonly deter violations. Weaker nations did not have a patently better record of compliance with law than did stronger states. Nations which initiated hostilities may have invoked the rhetoric of international law and of justice, accusing the victim of violation, but it is far from clear that in most cases, in the eyes of an impartial judge, there had in fact been violation. In principle, the suggestion that the elimination of the use of force leads to increased violations is wrongly focused. It concentrates on physical force as the principal method of law enforcement; in fact, other "horizontal" responses are effective. It focuses on enforcement and sanctions as the principal inducements to compliance; in fact, other forces, internal and external, may be more significant. In most contexts, there is little reason to expect that the elimination of force would reduce common compliance with international law; nations did not stop paying their debts when forcible collection of debts was outlawed at The Hague in 1907.[32] Indeed, one might more plausibly urge that the prevalence of force—even the threat that it might be used, for whatever reason—makes for international instability, which generally discourages the observance of international

---

*I do not refer to the possible invocation of force by the Security Council under Article 94 of the United Nations Charter to enforce judgments of the International Court of Justice, although even that has never yet occurred.

†I refer to violations of international law generally. Force will be used, of course, to reply to armed attack or other illegal uses of force. The Arab states have claimed that they attacked Israel in 1973 because Israel improperly refused to give up the occupied territories. Israel denied any legal obligation to do so, insisting that it would return territory only as part of a peace settlement, which the Arab states refused.

law. On the other hand, if force is unavailable, there may be greater disposition to pursue consensus, to develop and maintain law.

But if, in fact, the risk that the victim would use force were a deterrent to some violations of law, it is better, I believe, that this deterrent be sacrificed. I am one of those who have urged that order is essential for international society, and self-help is fundamentally disorderly; justice and vindication of law will have to be worked out separately and by other means.[33] It may be that in a more developed international society there would be organized force to enforce law. Even without international force, one might then seek to accommodate peace to justice, to permit self-help in some cases, not in others, to draw lines and to measure degrees. But in the primitive state of international society today—primitive in all but the weapons of war—peace is fundamental; there must be no occasion or pretext for nations to decide that their rights have been violated and they may resort to force. And, in the long run, as Judge de Visscher put it, "peace will serve justice better than justice will serve peace."[34] (But justice, perhaps, must come not too long after, if peace is to endure.)

THE
eight
UNITED NATIONS

Although students of international relations would probably agree that technology, cold war, and the proliferation of nations shaped international politics in the decades following the Second World War, few would argue that the United Nations ranks with these in significance. For the influence of law on foreign affairs, however, the relevance of the United Nations cannot be denied. The major development in contemporary international law is contained in the United Nations Charter. The organization is charged with enforcing this law and has involved itself in the creation and enforcement of other international law. The effect on law of modern technology, of cold war, and especially of the proliferation of new nations is enhanced and modified through the United Nations.

The United Nations is a political body, but its principal *raison d'être* was to have been the enforcement of law, the law of the Charter against war and the use of force between nations.[1] Its other purposes—political, social, and economic—have also engaged various U.N. organs in the development and enforcement of international law, usually of international agreements. In some areas, the principal organs have exercised legislative influence, the General Assembly promoting law in many fields—outer space, disarmament, defining aggression, the sea-bed, human rights. Sometimes it has purported even to declare law by "parliamentary" majority.*

THE UNITED NATIONS AND
THE LAW AGAINST FORCE

The extent to which the existence of the United Nations and its processes have influenced nations to observe the norm against unilateral force need not be exaggerated; neither should it be discounted, although that influence was far greater in earlier years. Because the United Nations has existed, issues of war and peace have become the active business of all its members, and they have not been able to avoid taking a stand and doing so in support of peace. All of the nations there assembled are eager to avoid a nuclear holocaust. All have had some sense that the norm against force is important and that the organization, which they value, is diminished when it fails in its principal purpose of maintaining international peace. All have had some recognition that any war concerns them, that peace is indivisible, that war anywhere might

---

*The United Nations is not the only international body with influence on the development of law or on its observance. Regional organizations like the OAS play a similar, if smaller, role. One should not overlook also the impact of "functional" international organizations, notably the specialized agencies of the United Nations. All have, of course, contributed their own charters and other constitutional documents to the body of international law. The contribution of some is far greater. For half a century the ILO has been midwife to international agreements promoting minimum standards on conditions of labor and other social welfare. The IBRD and the IMF have had a profound influence on international financial order, on the domestic economic policies of nations, and on their external economic relations. These and arrangements like GATT have also influenced the observance of trade agreements, which constitute a substantial portion of international legal obligations. See also Conclusion.

spread and escalate. All have had some desire to assert authority and influence events in world affairs. In the absence of special factors, principally colonialism or racial oppression, only private quarrels have threatened war (Arab-Israel hostility, Sudan-Ethiopia, Somalia-Ethiopia, Cyprus, Indonesia-Malaysia, India-Pakistan, Latin American quarrels), while almost all the other nations pressed for peace. Where international fighting broke out, U.N. organs have generally called for an end to hostilities, and the call was generally heeded, although sometimes only after some delay to achieve some political end.

At the center of efforts to maintain international peace, the United Nations was for many years the focus not only of world opinion but of the many diplomacies concentrated there.[2] We sensed its influence, even if we are unable to weigh it, in the early confrontation between the Soviet Union and Iran in 1946; in the Indonesian case, when the forces for peace may have been more significant in resolving the controversy than the new forces for ending colonialism; in continuing tension and occasional fighting between the Arab states and Israel, in Korea, where virtually all the nations outside the Communist bloc followed the lead of the United States and placed the resistance to aggression under the aegis of the United Nations; in the Congo and in Cyprus, where internal hostilities threatened to ignite external wars; in ending actual fighting over Kashmir. In different cases, in different ways, the United Nations intervened to discourage, prevent, or terminate hostilities, and provide "peace-keeping."

Perhaps the United Nations' greatest influence for peace can neither be measured nor proven. But it is not wholly an assertion of faith to insist that the existence of the organization reaffirmed the norm of the Charter and enhanced its deterrent influence. (Corridor diplomacy in the United Nations also serves to discourage threatened violations and helps terminate any that materialize.) A nation could initiate the use of force only with full awareness that it would have to answer in this world forum, a prospect which few nations faced with equanimity. Even if a proceeding produced nothing more than condemnatory addresses and resolutions and hostile headlines in the world press, the prospect of being accused was a significant cost of violation that all governments take into account. (The universal and intense concern of members with the outcome of votes on U.N. resolutions is evidence that resolutions matter.) The effect of a violation on the aggressor's relations with the victim was also magnified by public accusation; because others had to take sides, its relations with other nations would also be affected. Though rare, there was also the threat of sanctions—as against North Korea and Communist China.[3] Even the response of an individual nation to a use of force by another had increased justification and effectiveness because the United Nations and the Charter exist: in 1956, the Russian threat to intervene if invading forces were not withdrawn from Suez-Sinai was more credible and effective because the United Nations was seized of the issue and was prepared to find that there had been a violation of the Charter.

Even in earlier years the deterrent influence of the United Nations, however, was not simple and certain. For the United Nations is legislator as well as judge and executive, and its judgments are political, not juridical. Its members have adverse national interests as well as the common ones reflected in their U.N. membership. No matter what a court might do, the members of the U.N. political organs will reach political judgments. They may condemn where a court would not; they will not condemn if they do not wish to. And the response of the United Nations will continue to reflect both ideological conflict and the emergence of the Third World which effectively dominates the organization.

In regard to the law against force in particular, I have written:

> The law of the Charter forbidding unilateral force is, of course, intertwined with the institutional pattern created by the Charter. One may say, indeed, that the primary purpose of the institution was to implement and enforce the law of the Charter against war. . . . The relation of the law to the institution, however, is more complicated than merely that of law to law enforcement. Authority to enforce includes the power not to enforce. . . . In order to decide whether and how to

enforce, moreover, the Security Council and the General Assembly must first sit in judgment on the action of member nations. And in the process of judgment and enforcement, inevitably the Council, and particularly the Assembly, exercise also legislative influence modifying the law of the Charter. In the first instance, of course, the actions of members, and the reactions of other members, have the effect of interpreting what the Charter obligations mean. Then, deliberations, recommendations, resolutions, and actions in the Council or Assembly inevitably determine what the law of the Charter means or may be held to mean in the future.[4]

Policy-makers considering whether to use force had to take into account what might or might not happen in the United Nations. The expectation that members would condemn and the organization would take a strong stand was likely to serve as substantial deterrent. On the other hand, would-be violators might expect—and find—protection against effective U.N. judgment. In 1964, Indonesia was saved by Soviet veto from condemnation by the Security Council for its attacks on Malaysia.[5] The veto did not of course save Indonesia from criticism by a majority of the Council. Surely, the promise or hope of U.N. blessing, acquiescence, or even inaction or mild reaction would not discourage violation. India, for example, may well have been encouraged in its action in Goa by an estimate—proven correct—that the United Nations would do nothing,* that some members in the Communist bloc and among the new nations would condone or approve, some even condemning the "victim" in the case.[6] In such a case the organization not only fails to deter, or prevent, or restore, or punish; it may also prove a haven for the violator, serving as a lightning rod to help protect him even against sanctions outside the United Nations. In fact, when the U.N. majorities fail to condemn, its failure tends to

* Its actions, as India might have guessed, would present a *fait accompli:* it was inconceivable that the United Nations would insist on measures which would restore Goa to the colonial rule of Portugal.

remove the stigma of a violation by suggesting that the Charter provision, properly interpreted, was not violated.*

Goa might have proved to have been a "sport" or a case of the special "law" of anticolonialism, but it reflected, quite early in the U.N.'s history, the temptation of political bodies to judge by a double or multiple standard, or by no standard at all but only on the basis of political sympathies in the particular case. It showed that this might become a common occurrence, and war and peace might revert from the domain of law to that of politics and power. Concerned observers began to warn that the influence of the U.N. organization too might not survive, for even small nations will not respect unprincipled votes of powerless majorities.[7]

Different weaknesses in the United Nations were revealed in the Kashmir war of 1965. As a matter of international law for our hypothetical court, the hostilities that erupted in September 1965 did not perhaps represent a clear violation by one party or the other. Politically, too, Kashmir was a unique situation: a territory long in dispute and in joint occupation without political solution in sight; military forces in close confrontation; political maneuvers that became a military skirmish and, both sides probably unwitting, exploded into war. Still, the fact that war happened seemed to bode badly for the United Nations. In South Asia, in particular, political forces conspired to weaken the forces for peace. The United States and the Soviet Union were effectively neutralized, politically and militarily, leaving nearby China dominant, and emboldening China's friend (Pakistan) which had a grievance against China's enemy (India). The influence of the United Nations was at its weakest: Chinese exclusion from the organization and Indonesian

---

* It is commonly assumed that a court, deciding the question immediately, would have found India guilty of a violation of the Charter. But while not every "violation" which remains uncondemned necessarily effects a change in the law, the result of the proceedings in the United Nations might be to modify, *pro tanto*, the meaning of the Charter. It might prove only a small and special exception, based on Goa's position as a colonial enclave surrounded by Indian territory. Some nations may claim it as authority that the Charter permits unilateral force against "colonialism"; others may seek to stretch it to justify force against racism, and even beyond.

withdrawal[8] had created a focus independent of, even hostile to, the United Nations, and attracted countries, like Pakistan, which might see their future in China's friendship. The United Nations' authority was further weakened by its long failure to achieve a political solution in Kashmir. For its part, India had lost its position of political and moral leadership in the United Nations and was less concerned with the institution; on Kashmir, it had long been in embarrassed opposition, refusing the plebiscite that had been U.N. policy for many years.[9]

But whatever the particular explanation of Kashmir, it represented the first war between established nations since the Charter had been signed,* the kind of war that the organization was designed to prevent. It led to wonder and to worry whether there was worse to be expected, especially in Asia; whether the weakening influence of the institution might impair the authority of the Charter and its law against force; whether assumptions of the Charter that nations will forgo the use of force to change the existing order were in fact accepted in Asia; whether nations elsewhere might also begin to think of force to effect political change; whether the big powers and the U.N. members were prepared to enforce the status quo against threats of forcible change; whether, in short, the skeptics were right who had insisted that the law of the Charter was an idle hope, that war cannot be governed by law. But the war was quickly terminated, under pressure of a strong and unanimous stand in the Security Council; the influence of China did not prevail, but rather impelled the United States and the Soviet Union to assume a common position for peace; in the end, perhaps, the law of the Charter and the influence of the United Nations were enhanced rather than weakened. (Subsequently, agreement at Tashkent bolstered the peace in Kashmir, the disruptive influence of China was further weakened, and Indonesia changed direction and returned to the United Nations.)

---

* The Arabs attacked Israel as it came into existence, and never recognized it as an established state; the U.K.-France-Israel seizure of the Suez Canal was a special, limited action, not seen as a war even by the parties.

The United Nations was tested again by the Arab-Israel wars of June 1967, and October 1973, chapters in a long unhappy story that began soon after the United Nations approved the creation of a Jewish state in Palestine. In 1948, claiming that the establishment of Israel in Palestine was a continuing "aggression" against the former inhabitants of that territory, the Arab states went to war against Israel. Despite the armistice agreement that followed Israel's victory, the Arab nations later insisted that a state of war continued, denied to Israel's shipping passage through the Suez Canal and blockaded its port on the Gulf of Aqaba, launched or encouraged border raids, and threatened eventual revenge. From time to time, Israel retaliated by single military actions. On two occasions there were major hostilities. In 1956, Israel (in "collusion" with France and Great Britain) launched a major attack at Suez and Sinai; the invading forces were withdrawn at the request of the United Nations, but a U.N. peacekeeping force was stationed on Egypt's side of the border, and the blockade of Aqaba was lifted. The fighting in June 1967 began after Egypt requested the withdrawal of U.N. forces and reimposed the blockade of Aqaba; Israel, claiming self-defense against armed attack, again fought and defeated the Arab states. In 1973, the Arab states launched a surprise attack on Israel; again, under pressure from the United States and the U.S.S.R., there was a cease-fire pursuant to a U.N. resolution.

During the first two decades of Arab-Israeli hostilities the law of the Charter and the U.N. organization made important contributions to peace in the area. After their defeat in 1948, the Arab states continued to threaten revenge but refrained from resuming major hostilities. While no doubt they were deterred by their military weakness in comparison with Israel, they also knew that nations outside their own bloc would consider any attack on Israel a violation of the Charter. Israel, too, was deterred by law and U.N. authority. Despite its confidence in its military superiority, despite substantial provocation and the temptation to take the old city of Jerusalem and other border territories which would strongly improve its defensive position, Israel refrained from major action from 1948 to 1956 and again from 1956 to 1967. Israel knew that, although there was considerable sympathy for its position, even its friends in the United Nations would not tolerate offensive action in violation of the Charter. Major actions—in 1956 and 1967—came in response to intensified Arab threats and pressures, in circumstances which gave Israel a respectable claim that it was acting in self-defense consistent with the law of the Charter. In 1956 the United Nations was the stage for great drama: it compelled the United Kingdom, France, and Israel to justify their action, helped concentrate the other pressures that brought about the withdrawal of their forces from Egypt, established a U.N. force to prevent and deter further hostilities. For eleven years U.N. forces helped maintain the peace in the area; fighting erupted only after these were withdrawn. In 1967, too, the United Nations helped limit the war and terminate it in a few days. The resolution which was adopted, acceptable to both sides and to the powers, served as a kind of armistice agreement and offered the outline of a peace settlement.

Alas, the peace settlement did not come, and has not come yet, though another war and another cease-fire, an Egypt-Israel interim disengagement agreement and dramatic meetings and negotiations have intervened. The law of the Charter was hardly mentioned when the Arabs attacked Israel in 1973; perhaps the Arab-Israel hostility has been accepted as one continuing violation or deviation. The cease-fire was adopted after extended U.N. debate and pursuant to U.N. resolutions, but, skeptics might say, the United Nations added nothing to the influence of the United States and the U.S.S.R., both of which desired the cease-fire. Since then, surely, the United Nations' influence in the Middle East has sharply declined as substantial Third World solidarity and the particular influence within the Third World of the Arab states—"its own rich," on whom others depend for oil and aid—impelled majorities to support pro-Arab, anti-Israel resolutions in various contexts, including the infamous resolution identifying Zionism with racism. For Israel the United Nations—for the present, at least—became the enemy. For the United States and some others, U.N. majorities have, especially where Israel is concerned, abused their voting power, and violated constitutional limitations, fair process, and equal treatment.

The dominance of the Third World has politicized U.N. implementation of the law of the Charter in other ways. Although the five permanent members retain their veto, Third World members have important weight even in the Security Council. Peace-keeping, however, is not as high on the Third World agenda for the United Nations as other purposes—ending white rule in southern Africa and a new economic order. Big-power wars would indeed concern them but these are highly unlikely, and the Third World has little disposition to invoke and assert U.N. machinery in hostilities between Third World countries (where hostilities are increasingly likely to occur, as they have, *e.g.*, between Somalia and Ethiopia). It remains to be seen, of course, whether Third World solidarity will continue to politicize also issues of war and peace. Some hope that increased responsibility, increased recognition of the crucial importance of international peace and stability, and concern for the organization which they value might yet restore both the law and the institutions of the United Nations to their intended major significance in international relations. A settlement in the Middle East would make a major contribution to that end.

THE UNITED NATIONS AND
INTERNAL WARS

International law, including the Charter, we know, has not been notably successful in controlling internal wars and external intervention in such wars; the influence of the organization has also been less than decisive. In the absence of external intervention or the clear danger that an internal war will otherwise threaten international peace, the jurisdiction of the United Nations is open to question: it, too, is not supposed to intervene in strictly "domestic affairs,"* and presumably the strictly civil war, contained within

---

* U.N. Charter, Article 2(7). There has not been agreement as to what matters are "essentially within the domestic jurisdiction" of a state, and some may question whether the United Nations would ever in fact deny itself jurisdiction on this ground.

national boundaries, would be deemed "domestic." Nor would the United Nations wish to become involved in every struggle of power between factions in unstable countries. Even when there is a basis for its jurisdiction and concern, its opportunities are circumscribed. It is hampered by lack of a clear Charter mandate and other uncertainties of law, and by uncertainties and disputes as to fact. And where there is war between two *bona fida* internal forces, even where there are no cold war overtones or subversion from outside, the sympathies of the U.N. membership may well be divided. In any event, the United Nations cannot prevent revolution; it cannot readily provide peaceful solutions to prevent or end civil war. It may attempt to mediate or conciliate, but there are often issues not susceptible to accommodation or third-party settlement. In regard to external intervention, especially in the absence of an agreed Charter norm forbidding assistance to either side, the United Nations cannot easily obtain agreement that there shall be none. Where big powers become involved, moreover, there is even less likelihood that the United Nations can act in a way that will defeat the interests of one of them (*e.g.*, Vietnam). In internal wars, then, often it can only hope to help contain the war in the territory of the country in question, to keep the internal war from becoming international.*

The United Nations could do nothing in Vietnam, or in Angola. In general, the "candidates" for intervention are Third World countries, and while the Third World might exert some influence to exclude big-power intervention, it is not likely to unite against intervention by Third World states. (In Angola, even the African states supported different factions and accepted the victor, who had important help from Communist Cuba.)

Still there are internal wars and internal wars, and in some the United Nations acted effectively in the cause of peace. It superseded "preventive intervention" by the United States in Lebanon in

---

* It is the fact that the United States "spread" the war in South Vietnam into North Vietnam, with the risks of further involvement of other nations, that gained for the United States particular reproach among U.N. members.

1958.[10] It has tried to continue its pacifying activities in Cyprus.[11] It attempted to end intervention and civil war in Yemen in 1963.[12] It was a major participant in the dramatic events of 1960 in the Congo to prevent a race of military interventions between the Soviet Union and the United States.[13] Indeed, since existing law is uncertain and new law at present unlikely, it is the political face of the organization, not the law of the Charter, that offers hope for the increased independence and self-determination that are the aim of any law against foreign intervention. Of course, the United Nations might contribute most if it promotes the welfare and stability that render internal wars less likely.

THE UNITED NATIONS AND OTHER INTERNATIONAL LAW

The Charter's rule against force, though most important, hardly exhausts the influence of the United Nations on the normative content of international law or on its observance.[14] The other face of the United Nations, the organization and the organs established by the Charter, has exerted a legislative influence, developing language in the Charter, in some cases beyond the hopes of the most hopeful, in ways "which could not have been foreseen completely by the most gifted of its begetters."[15]

Whether in regard to the use of force or other issues, the deliberations, resolutions, and judgments of U.N. organs inevitably have had a legislative effect. Political organs have had to determine the scope of their own authority under the Charter; they have applied general language to specific situations, including many not envisioned by those who wrote the Charter. The General Assembly, in particular, which cannot be prevented from acting by any veto, can interpret and apply the Charter when and how its majorities wish, subject only to their own self-restraint. (That the Assembly usually only "recommends" measures does not involve it any the less in interpretation and application of legal provisions.)

Interpretation by the United Nations of the Charter and of other law inevitably reflects views of the majority in that political body.

For some years, the United States and its allies dominated the General Assembly, and the Assembly adopted resolutions reflecting their attitudes and preoccupations, including, for example, resolutions directed against Communist subversion and "indirect aggression." [16] Later, the dominant influence shifted to the newer and poorer nations, in regard to issues on which they were agreed.

It is in the Assembly, in particular, that the new nations, in their numbers and influence, have made an impress on law. It is they, principally, who have taken the Assembly into other areas of legislation. While the United Nations Charter reflects Western democratic values, aspirations, and hopes, the generality of its phrasing, inevitable in a constitutive document, lends itself to new interpretations and new emphases. I have mentioned the greatest triumph, begun by the new nations of the immediate postwar years, with each subsequent new nation joining the battle, in which the United Nations raised to pre-eminence the almost incidental phrase in the Charter, "self-determination." [17] That principle, originally more a political ideal and program than a legal norm, [18] has had important effect on law. It has washed away treaties of political hegemony and compelled their renegotiation or abandonment. It has given some support for a new legal principle that "unequal treaties," at least as to political treaties, are not enforceable.* In support of self-

---

*Such a concept might inject into the law of treaties the defense of national "duress," which puts into question peace treaties following a surrender by one party. To extend it to other treaties reflecting unequal bargaining power, whether military, political, or economic, would cast doubt on many extant treaties. It may be too radical a doctrine for the law to swallow whole, but already we have seen its political force extending even beyond strict self-determination to impel renegotiation of treaties like the Panama Canal Treaty.

For the future at least, the Vienna Law of Treaties, adopted in 1969, provides: "A treaty is void if its conclusion has been procured by the threat or use of force in violation of the principles of international law embodied in the Charter of the United Nations." The Vienna Conference also adopted a Declaration that "solemnly condemns the threat or use of pressure in any form, whether military, political, or economic, by any state in order to coerce another state to perform any act relating to the conclusion of a treaty . . ." but it did not declare that such pressure vitiates consent and nullifies the treaty.

determination, as earlier in Angola, and still in Rhodesia and Namibia, some nations have already claimed a right to use force, collectively through the United Nations if possible, unilaterally if necessary. Self-determination has been asserted as a human right, although it is far from clear which humans have this right [19] and what it entails. Some new nations have attempted also to invoke "economic self-determination" to nullify agreements, particularly those made by their colonial masters, which conferred on foreigners economic rights or concessions to exploit natural resources.[20]

Self-determination may cease to be an active concern of the United Nations as Western colonialism in Asia and Africa comes to an end. Other Charter interpretations may have a greater future. Already the Assembly has helped give some uncertain normative content to the human rights provisions of the Charter, at least as applied to discrimination against non-whites, as in South Africa.[21] (See Chapter 12.) The Assembly has promoted new cooperative law designed primarily to benefit the many poor and underdeveloped nations, to the extent that the few nations that bear the largest financial burden have been persuaded to go along.[22] It has sponsored and promoted international conferences for developing multilateral conventions and has urged the ratification of such conventions.[23] In some cases it considered actual texts of conventions and contributed to their final form.[24] On selected questions the Assembly has also undertaken more direct action in legislating international law. It has "recommended" new international norms.[25] It has adopted resolutions declaring what the law is on a particular question, or recommending policy based on particular interpretations of law.[26] It has adopted a Charter of Economic Rights and Duties of States that includes provisions of normative purport. (See Chapter 10.)

The legal significance of various actions and resolutions of U.N. organs is hardly agreed.[27] Scholars continue to debate, in particular, whether a resolution of the General Assembly which purports to "recommend" or declare a norm of international law, or which recommends an action reflecting a particular position on such a norm, is binding on everyone, or no one, or on those who voted for it. There have been suggestions that such resolutions constitute a contemporary manifestation of the process of making customary international law. A more traditional view, on the other hand, insists that it takes "practice," not speeches or votes, to make customary law, and that customary law is universal and cannot be made over dissenting views. Some have suggested that these Assembly resolutions be treated as informal agreements binding, at least, on those who do not dissent from them, or on those who affirmatively vote for them. Others ask whether such a view accurately reflects the significance of the votes: a state voting for a resolution may be expressing an opinion on the present state of the law; it may even be asserting an opinion as to what the law ought to be; is it also asserting an intention to bind itself to that view, a willingness to enter into an agreement to that effect with others of like mind? Yet another view has it that nations which publicly declare something to be the law are later "estopped" from denying it. Again, some ask whether this is consistent with the assumptions of international society and whether this would be a desirable principle.

Time will probably show that different kinds of General Assembly resolutions have different significance for law. An occasional resolution may fairly be seen as tantamount to a multilateral treaty. This might perhaps have been said of the resolution approving a law for outer space.[28] The principal space powers proposed the resolution; the other members supported it with virtual unanimity. There was no reason to expect that future space powers would not be content with the approved regime. Everyone also seemed satisfied with the provisions that affected them immediately—*e.g.*, rights and obligations in regard to terrestrial consequences of space mishaps. (Still, the principal powers involved saw fit not to rely on the legislative character of this resolution and followed it with a formal treaty.[29])

Such "legislative resolutions" have been few. For the rest, the legislative character of General Assembly resolutions is inevitably more limited. To begin with, there are the resolutions that do not purport to make or declare law. Originally, surely, the Universal

Declaration of Human Rights, for example, was approved as an aspiration and an ideal; not as a statement of present law.[30] If the Declaration, or any of its provisions, has since acquired some of the character of law, it is not the resolution itself that achieved that result but subsequent resolutions and events and the actions and reactions of nations that combined to make law.

In a number of instances the General Assembly has purported to declare what international law is on a particular subject. A resolution purporting to state existing law does not claim to legislate. If the asserted proposition is indeed law, one would have to show how it became law—in treaty, or custom, or other accepted "source" of international law. The General Assembly resolution in such circumstances is, of course, an expression of opinion on the state of the law by the governments which support it; that this opinion is expressed in a formal resolution may give it even more significance and may sometimes authoritatively prove that such is the law. The weight to be accorded to such declarations of law may depend upon other factors. One might distinguish, for example, the case where majorities are asserting law which meaningfully applies to all, from resolutions in which they purport to declare law which in fact would apply primarily to others. Inevitably, one must give less weight to a majority vote declaring that the use of nuclear weapons is unlawful (even in self-defense),[31] when one of the two principal nuclear powers (the United States) stoutly denies that this is the law;* when the affirmative vote of the other principal nuclear power is commonly interpreted as an attempt to curry favor with the majority rather than as an accurate reflection of its views on what the law is or even what it ought to be;[32] when other members of the majority, one may suspect, might themselves look at the law differently if they saw a reasonable prospect that they too might become nuclear powers. On the other hand, an overwhelming resolution declaring *apartheid* to be contrary to international law, against the strong views of South Africa, the one nation which admittedly practices it, is entitled to greater weight.[33] Here,

---

*The United States insists that such weapons may be used when force may lawfully be used, *i.e.*, in self-defense under Article 51 of the U.N. Charter.

at least, the resolution reflects a virtually universal ethical standard. The asserted norm condemns that which other nations have also practiced and may wish to practice again. It is a declaration of law that might apply to other countries today, and might be relevant to potential forms of segregation or discrimination in virtually every country in the future. Again, even such a resolution purports only to declare existing law, and our hypothetical impartial tribunal would have to find that such law had largely come into existence apart from the confirming resolution, although the resolution itself may be seen as contributing to the law-making process.

What seems clear is that no single statement can describe the juridical significance of all these General Assembly resolutions, or even their political import. At least, the resolutions contribute something to the subtle, uncertain process by which law grows. At least, they may predict what the law will become someday, in some cases even what the law would be held to be tomorrow, or today, whether by governments or by international tribunals, real or hypothetical. But whatever a court might say about the binding effect of these resolutions, inevitably they have some effect on national policy and national behavior. Nations that vote for a particular statement of law cannot act quite as though they had not done so. Those who do not agree with a resolution cannot wholly disregard the views of a majority.

LIMITATIONS ON
PARLIAMENTARY DIPLOMACY

Whatever the effect, in law or in politics, of its resolutions, the General Assembly has continued to adopt them, including declarations of law, on an increasing number of subjects. Its "jurisdiction" under the Charter is very broad, there being little in an interdependent world that is not related more or less intimately to international peace and security. Other purposes of the United Nations, as set forth in Article 55 of the Charter, would support Assembly deliberation on anything that relates to justice and the well-being of nations and peoples.

If the effect of the Assembly on the law has not been greater, it is not principally because of doubts as to the legislative authority of the Assembly or the legislative quality of its resolutions. Nor has it necessarily been due to doubt as to the qualifications of the Assembly to deal with legal questions, or its suitability as a forum for making or revising law. Rather, I believe, there has been little interest in involving the Assembly in international law at large. On law generally there is no cohesive majority with a common attitude. Perhaps no nation is confident that it will always be in the General Assembly's majority, and every nation is reluctant to build up a power in the Assembly to "legislate" against its interests. Those who constitute majorities may prefer to deal with issues *ad hoc* as political decisions rather than to promote law which would bind them as well some future day.

In practice, then, the Assembly's law-making ventures have been limited to selected areas. There has been no difficulty in adopting resolutions of legislative import which appear idealistic and which no nation sees as directed at its own behavior: the Assembly, for example, early approved the Nürnberg principles.[34] All, of course, were happy to affirm as law the regime for outer space which the two principal space powers promoted. The members were always prepared to ask for law on disarmament, even general and complete disarmament, which had no immediate relevance to any but the big powers.[35] Only one member (the Soviet Union) of the majority that declared unlawful the use of nuclear weapons had such weapons, and few had good prospects of having them soon. Other "law," too, they do not usually see as relevant to them—*e.g.*, law against genocide or racial discrimination. Even favored principles have not been applied to areas that might affect members generally or that would involve taking sides in the ideological conflict. There was no apparent disposition to apply "self-determination" to establish a right to secede (whether of the Katangese in the Congo or the Kurds in Iraq), to be free of foreign domination (as with Soviet satellites under Stalin), or for the individual to vote for a representative government. Human rights provisions have been invoked to condemn mistreatment of political opposition or denials of freedoms or inadequate systems of criminal justice or even torture only in selected cases of unpopular governments.

But the area in which majorities can "legislate for others" is broad, and the pressures will be great to increase the Assembly's jurisdiction and competence and to obtain maximum observance of its "legislation." For many nations the temptations to confuse votes in the Assembly with power will not be easy to resist. The majority of U.N. members, poor and without major military significance in the nuclear age, would probably prefer a society in which it would not be possible for a few nations ultimately and autonomously to dispose of their wealth and power. Reluctant to remain dependent on the generosity of the wealthy or even their enlightened self-interest, impatient with extended and unequal negotiations, the majority may be tempted to "legislate" huge development programs and new trade patterns in their favor. Unfortunately for them, such legislation cannot succeed, and efforts to achieve it by votes will only dilute the significance of the votes and of the Assembly.[36] The wealthy few will obey the "law" of modest resolutions for practical programs. Even the United States—the largest contributor to all programs and the one that long insisted that General Assembly assessments are obligatory[37]—would not honor assessments for grossly unrealistic, improvident, or irresponsible programs. Surely, as regards economic policy, the wealthy nations will not agree to sacrifice their control over their wealth. It remains to be seen to what extent such "legislation" might become a basis for negotiation, accommodation and compromise, as in the Law of the Sea or the New Economic Order (Chapters 10 and 11).

The Assembly might have somewhat greater say in regard to controlling military power. Here it would not be the have-nots boldly exploiting their majority to take from those who have.[38] The majority has a real and valid interest in common with the big powers in reducing the likelihood of war, and it is at least plausible for all nations to claim a voice in controlling armaments, as they have in controlling the use of force. Here, too, revolutionary law is not in prospect, and whatever new law may come will not be imposed by majorities. The realistic promises of disarmament are modest:[39] in particular, unless shaken by some terrible event, governmental leaders of the big powers will not give up their superweapons or put out of their own control these "basics" of national security. Moreover, no inspection system to give adequate assurance of compliance with such disarmament is technically feasible today; if one could be achieved, it is not likely to be accepted by the Soviet Union, perhaps not by the United States either. Inspection apart, national power might be given up only if a secure international force were available to protect against major violations and to assure peace; in today's world it is difficult to see how an international force could be strong enough to afford defense against major violation without creating the danger that it might be subject to abuse or usurpation. I do not think the major powers will agree; all the votes of all the nations will not get them to agree. In fact, majorities have stopped asking it, reasonably content with continuing Strategic Arms Limitations Talks (SALT) which, no matter how they may succeed, will not produce a world without nuclear arms.

The modest promises of disarmament also reflect the crucial limitation on the influence of majorities. Surely the many nations cannot hope to make disarmament law for the big powers alone. All their efforts to date seem to be devoted to getting agreement between the United States and the Soviet Union to eliminate or control their superweapons; there is little indication of any interest in disarmament for themselves by nations which have pursued their own armaments races for their own purposes—Indonesia, India and Pakistan, the Arab states and Israel, Greece and Turkey, and many others. Clearly, not all nations are prepared to forswear future entry to the "atomic club," and with India proliferation may already have begun.* Surely, from this posture, they cannot hope to persuade the big powers to give up the weapons which assure their commanding position and are also instrumental in maintaining peace.

---

* The efforts to achieve a nonproliferation agreement have evoked the counterclaim that the big powers are seeking to impose limitations only on others and are not prepared to control their own armaments. This is doubtless intended to spur strategic arms limitations agreements; it may also be a pretext for some who do not wish to give up the "nuclear option."

Continued efforts to control and reduce armaments and to contain the arms race and limit the number of nations participating in it are, I believe, of the highest importance to the prospects of peace. But the plausible agreements are limited, and major changes cannot be imposed by majorities, especially those not ready to control themselves. In the control of arms, as in the better distribution of wealth, progress will not be in legislation by majorities, but in slow, patient negotiation and compromise by all, including the majorities.

There is little to prevent majorities from further sitting in judgment and asserting authority. But whether the actions of such majorities achieve legislative influence and obtain obedience will depend on whether they will act modestly, providently, reasonably. New submissions to majority rule will not appeal to the rich and powerful, or to many others. The Soviet Union and France have resisted even when all that the majorities demanded were moderate financial contributions to peace-keeping efforts that were already in fact implemented.[40] They, or the United States, or China, or others, will not soon accept majority law regulating their important interests.

THE UNITED NATIONS AND GENERAL LAW OBSERVANCE

The existence of the United Nations, I have suggested, creates a threat that certain violations of law will be aired there. As in regard to the use of force, the United Nations has had influence to undo and to deter other violations that might come into its ken. While a member can bring virtually any dispute to the organization, if only because it spoils friendly relations and may threaten the peace, to do so would generally further aggravate the dispute and impair relations; the membership at large may also resent being drawn into the controversy. The political fare of the United Nations, therefore, still consists almost entirely of the especially "political" issues that were expressly made its business. The questions of law they involve are those relating to use of force, threats to the peace, colonialism and race, and kindred subjects. (U.N. bodies have assumed some small responsibility for monitoring gross violations of human rights.) As to these political issues, the influence of the United Nations—like that of law—is complex and not readily demonstrable. Although there is no way of proving it, one may assert confidently that the existence of the United Nations tends to discourage some of the grosser and more devastating programs of racial discrimination.* In regard to colonialism, too, the United Nations has largely achieved its goals; in Rhodesia and in Namibia, the United Nations is, again, the "legislator" of sanctions imposed against states that are charged with "violations."[41]

Whether the political influence of the United Nations will be extended to seek observance of other law or agreement is uncertain. There have been isolated cases where the United Nations was invoked to vindicate other law. The future may bring additional cases, but until they begin to multiply, the fear of accusation in the United Nations will not be sufficient to figure in a violator's accounting.

THE INTERNATIONAL COURT OF JUSTICE

One organ of the United Nations deserves special mention in any discussion of contemporary influences on compliance with law. The likelihood of being brought before the International Court of Justice would be a deterrent to a violation,[42] even if a nation did not fear enforcement of its judgments by the Security Council (Article 94). The judgments of the Court are complied with,[43] the onus of noncompliance with a judicial judgment weighing substantially in world opinion.

Still, the existence of the Court has not proved a major deterrent, because nations have not been prepared to submit to its jurisdiction or even to invoke it when the other side had accepted jurisdiction. The reasons for this negative attitude of nations—old and

---

*Even the progress of the United States on civil rights may owe something to the subtle influences of the United Nations' concern to end racial discrimination.

new, capitalist and socialist—have been much discussed.[44] Briefly, it is based on a reluctance by political officials to let their interests in a dispute get out of the control of their own diplomacy for final determination by others; a sense of ignorance and unfamiliarity about the world of law and adjudication; a preference for flexibility and possible compromise rather than the all-or-nothing of a law suit; the law's delay and uncertainty; the weakness—in many cultures or countries—of the habit of adjudication; a lack of confidence in "foreign judges" and fear that a court might extend its authority and the scope of law to "strictly internal" matters; the feeling that a law suit is an unfriendly act that might exacerbate relations, and that loss of a case would be a blow to national prestige.* Resentment over a particular action of the Court—as in the South West Africa case in 1966—may also enhance mistrust of the institution or of the process. The issues of particular cases, moreover, will often discourage its adjudication. A nation will not normally come to court where its case is weak and its chance of winning slim. Political law or agreement, where the stakes are high, are especially unlikely candidates for adjudication: nations will not adjudicate matters which, they feel, they could not afford to lose or where, if they lost, they could not afford to obey the judgment. Those confident of political support for their cause, as in the General Assembly, will not risk a loss in court. That the Court is an organ of the United Nations and is invoked by majorities for advisory opinions to support political actions has "politicized" the Court to some extent and made it less acceptable to all as an impartial supreme court on international law.

Many of these reasons are "irrational." None of them explains reluctance to turn to the Court in some cases, say, for interpreta-

---

* As a result of having lost a case to Cambodia in the International Court of Justice, Thailand, to show its displeasure, refused to attend SEATO meetings and the Geneva Conference on Laos. *N.Y. Times*, June 20, 1962, pp. 1, 6. Thailand also recalled its ambassador to France, presumably because two French lawyers represented Cambodia in the case, and cut off trade with Poland, apparently because the President of the Court at the time was a Polish national. *N.Y. Times*, June 23, 1962, p. 2.

tion of multilateral treaties, or for advisory opinions.[45] The Western observer is committed to hopes that adjudication may yet play a greater role. At present, few would claim that it figures significantly as an inducement to law observance. It is relevant to add that reluctance to submit to adjudication is not necessarily evidence of an intention to violate international law. Even the nations with the best records of compliance and with every intention to comply in the future, have not been willing to submit to the Court.[46] Nations seem eager to maintain that extra measure of "freedom" to decide whether they will observe the law, even when they know that they will probably do so.

THE QUEST FOR

PART THREE

NEW LAW

International society is disorderly and poor. It could be destroyed in minutes. Masses of sophisticated weapons are everywhere, and nuclear weapons are ever on the verge of further proliferation. Relations between some nations or groups of nations are tense or troubled, and terrorism is common within and across national boundaries. Some colonialism and some racism still persists, and much blood may be shed in the attempt to end them. There are gross inequalities in the power and influence of nations in the system. Powerful transnational companies bestride the world with insufficient responsibility and inadequate external control. There are a few rich and many poor, and some starving. The population of the world continues to grow and threatens to outstrip its living resources. The world is hungry for fuel, but it is scarce, expensive and effectively monopolized by an international cartel of states; monopoly gives these few states both the ability to exploit the rest and a powerful political weapon. Pollution of air and sea worsens. In all societies, individual human rights are vulnerable and largely immune to international improvement; in some countries their condition is unspeakable. There is still slavery and child labor; the status of women is deplorable in many places. There is still massive illiteracy.

Much of this disorder and dis-ease could be alleviated by international cooperation, most of which might take the form of law. But international law remains primitive and develops slowly. The contemporary forces that have transformed the political system—new technology and weaponry, ideological conflict, the proliferation of states and its effect on the political complexion of the system—have indeed underscored needs and generated pressures for new or different law, but they have also complicated the effort and the process of achieving it. Conflicting or divergent interests cannot frequently be bridged or compromised, universal law is difficult to achieve, and less-than-universal law is often less than effective (for example, to establish a working monetary system, or to suppress hijacking).

The agendas of various states for new or changed law are different, often conflicting. The Western world remains essentially content but seeks new law to shore up stability and order: for example, strategic arms limitation, cooperation to prevent nuclear proliferation and to resist or suppress international terrorism; an economically "sound" trade and monetary system on tried models, requiring cooperation but based essentially on laissez-faire free market forces, respect for property and investment; protection against the oil cartel and the oil weapon; control of population and protection of the environment. The Third World wants law that will establish a new economic order, even more, perhaps, a new political order. It united behind Black African demands for law that will outlaw and help eliminate white colonialism and racism in Southern Africa. The Third World suspects terrorism but supports it for some purposes, and many states will not cooperate to suppress it. It resists being told what to do about population or pollution. The Communist world shares Western concerns about nuclear proliferation and reluctance to put its wealth at the disposition of other states, or to submit to strong international institutions run by majority. But it tries to conceal or mute its resistance to Third World demands and supports those that are at the expense of the West or that can be deflected from itself and directed at the West, as it has largely succeeded in doing, for example, as regards bearing the costs of development.

In 1967 the world began a most extended and most complicated legislative process to revise the law of the sea. Division between developed and developing states, ideological-political differences as well as competing economic interests and aspirations, both reflected and were related to comparable divisions on land, but these were complicated by differences between geographically fortunate and geographically disadvantaged states. Coastal states "grabbed" for themselves much that might have been the heritage of mankind (the seabed "beyond national jurisdiction"), and the various vectors of political influence pulled in different ideological, political, economic directions. If the process succeeds, it will produce a complex legal and institutional regime that seems destined for difficulty and dispute.

Politics had similar yet different impact on the international law of human rights that had been growing quietly since the Second World War, receiving little attention even from governments. But that law has deep ideological roots and potentially powerful political importance. It exploded into prominence in the middle 1970s when the United States Congress made respect for human rights a condition for its aid and trade, President Carter wove it into U.S. foreign policy, and the West wrote it into détente at Helsinki in 1975. The dramatic escalation of the place of human rights in international relations dramatized the unique problems of regulating national behavior in respect of this law.

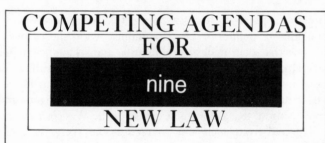

COMPETING AGENDAS FOR

nine

NEW LAW

Some of the manifestations and causes of disorder and injustice in the contemporary world are universally condemned. The need to control armaments, for example, is on every state's agenda, but it stands higher with some than with others; and there are differences as to which arms of which states should be regulated, by what means, on what terms. The superpowers continue to negotiate on strategic arms limitations and have made some small agreements.[1] Neither of them is prepared to sacrifice much or risk anything, and surely they have not ventured as far as they might to foreclose evermore radical weapons in the future, as many of their people and many other nations would like to see them do. The superpowers are united in their desire to prevent nuclear proliferation;[2] but their different predilections, their mutual rivalries, and the general context of their relations with other countries have prevented them from determined cooperation by effective means and mechanisms to prevent new members from joining the club.

Other, lesser powers which have nuclear technology to export—
France? West Germany?—also doubtless would not wish to see it
put to military uses; but they seem to be more sanguine about the
risk of such diversion, or perhaps hopeless that it can be prevented,
and do not wish to sacrifice a highly lucrative export market and a
continuing participation in a major technological development.

In sum, one may conclude that armaments have not been effectively controlled because governments—however blindly or fool-
ishly and extravagantly—seem generally to prefer the security and
confidence they get from their own arms to that which they might
gain from controlling the armaments of others in exchange for
limiting their own.[3] That the world has lived with ever-deadlier
nuclear weapons for more than thirty years, without nuclear war
and indeed with incredible insouciance, has relaxed early drives for
controlling even such weapons; limiting conventional arms is not
even on any meaningful agenda. Armaments, both nuclear and
conventional, have become a hallmark of prestige and influence, a
key investment for buyers, a major industry for sellers. For too
many countries armaments are a political lever in the region and a
bulwark against domestic change.

All have participated in reworking the Law of the Sea. (Chapter
11.) All states have participated also in the development of a law of
human rights, and few would confess to opposing further development both in adding some new norms (though there may not be
agreement on which to add) and even some new machinery for
their implementation (though, again, there is no agreement as to
which). (Chapter 12.)

For the rest, however, matters that cry for remedy remain
unregulated, or inadequately regulated, because, in a system that
essentially can legislate only unanimously and with the consent of
the regulated, there are conflicts in values, in judgment, or in perceived national interests. Some seem so hopeless that even those
most vulnerable to present disorder do not dare to suggest regulation. Surely, say, those states which have a large monopoly in oil
resources, have exploited it for great gain, and have used the monopoly successfully as a political weapon will not agree to control

such economic arms by law forbidding cartels or concerted economic boycott. Other states which dream of emulating them as
regards other scarce resources will also resist such law, at least until
they came to see acute danger to themselves from the availability of
such economic weapons.* Some items, however, are on the agenda
of one or another group of states, and not surprisingly, the agenda
of the developed states differs widely from that of the Third
World. The Communist powers are generally less interested in
new universal law, but tend to support or to appear to support the
Third World to the extent that it costs them little.

THE LAW AGENDA
OF THE DEVELOPED STATES

The developed Western states remain reasonably content with
the present system and its law. Especially in a system in which
they are an ever smaller minority, they insist on their essential autonomy and resistance to majority pressure whether in the United
Nations or elsewhere, while keeping the advantages they have enjoyed, *e.g.*, the veto in the U.N. Security Council for the permanent members. They will join in some sanctions against Rhodesia
or against South Africa (over Namibia or even *apartheid*) but will
not end all trade with the latter or embargo all arms to it.[4]

The new law which the developed states have sought is law that
would reinforce the system as they have known it and its values of
stability and order. They have sought to maintain, extend, and
strengthen the ban on nuclear proliferation. They have sought to
reinforce traditional law holding states responsible for acts of terrorism against others originating in their territory; they have
sought new universal agreements of cooperation against aerial hijacking and related forms of terrorism.[5] But while all governments
recognize their own vulnerability to terrorism, and almost all will
join in decrying it, international law to deal with it effectively is

* Western developed states have also used economic weapons, especially during
the Cold War.

slow in coming, for every cause which different terrorists claim to represent evokes some governmental support or condonation; and many governments resist outlawing those who terrorize under the banner of "self-determination," "people's liberation," "people's socialism," or other slogans of new order. An effective international law against hijacking would require agreement by virtually all states to prevent potential hijackers from preparing and arming for their venture, to deny them haven, to punish them severely or extradite them to a country that will. But no Arab state, for example, has been prepared to adhere to an agreement that would require it to extradite or punish a Palestinian hijacker, and these and other terrorists have in fact been justified in their confidence that they would find some country to harbor them.[6] Some libertarian countries, too, are reluctant to agree to law that would require them to deny asylum to a refugee who hijacks a plane to escape tyranny. They may be willing to agree to punish them, but not to extradite them, and other states may find, or purport to find, that to be unacceptable and a barrier to agreement.[7]

It may be possible to develop narrower agreements limited to terrorist actions that are commonly decried, agreements which states can feel politically free to support without incurring the onus of opposing causes to which they are sympathetic. Thus states have been especially concerned to protect diplomats and have felt free to develop an international agreement to that end, regardless of whatever causes might choose to indulge in such acts.[8] It is not yet true but it is hoped that the taking of hostages has acquired sufficiently general opprobrium in world opinion that states may feel free to adhere to agreements outlawing it, giving all states jurisdiction to try violators, and requiring states to cooperate in preventing or suppressing such crime and to punish or extradite those who commit it.[9]

In economic matters, too, the developed states wish to maintain and improve the system they have had. They wish to maintain substantial autonomy and laissez-faire in trade and finance, in a substantially free market, calibrated by cooperative mechanisms like the International Monetary Fund, GATT and similar institutions in which the developed states have a dominant say or at least maintain their essential autonomy. The developed states have continued to insist on the integrity of the properties and investments of their nationals in other countries. They are prepared to consider increasing their aid to poorer countries if others—the Communist powers and the "Third World rich"—will also do their share; but they resist any attempt to impose a legal obligation upon them to extend such aid.

The Western world has also attempted to reverse the tides of pollution and restore or maintain the world ecology and environment. It has been far from united in this effort, for its own commitments are uneven and its interests divided: maritime states, for example, have resisted and reduced measures which coastal states have sought; no one has emerged to champion the general interest against pollution of the high seas.[10] But the Western developed states have sought some universal standards. Underdeveloped states have been required to include environmental protection measures in projects for which they sought financing, *e.g.*, from the World Bank. But developing states resisted stringent environmental controls as an obstacle to rapid, less-expensive development and as a luxury which developed states can now afford only after centuries of environmental degradation.

The Western world has sought universal cooperation in population control; the Third World resisted coercive conditions or assistance and other external participation as improper interference in their internal affairs; some also had religious and other cultural objections; some purported to see in such programs racism and even genocide, and an effort to deny the Third World the population countries needed for development and security.

The Western world has sought other universal attacks on social problems: the remnants of slavery, slave trade and forced labor, the oppression of women and children, other violations of human rights, and illiteracy. The Third World has closed its eyes to some of these (slavery); it has been prepared to receive aid for other of these ends but without strings or strict scrutiny, even by international bodies (ILO, UNESCO), and with a minimum of Western world participation.

The Western world has also sought law to assure freedom of international communication, whether audio-visual or print, and cultural exchange. But the Third World has seen this as cultural imperialism, and some states have asserted the need to protect their cultural heritage from foreign corruption.[11]

THE THIRD WORLD AGENDA
FOR LAW REVISION

The new states and their allies in the Third World have asserted a right to re-examine and to question the international legal system and to take full part in its codification, development or modification. Although many of them have but few lawyers, they have insisted on "geographic distribution" and their share in bodies contributing to law-making, *e.g.*, the International Law Commission; they have participated fully in other bodies that contribute to law, *e.g.*, the U.N. General Assembly including its Sixth (legal) Committee; they have participated in major international lawmaking conferences, *e.g.*, the Vienna Conference on the Law of Treaties and the Third U.N. Conference on the Law of the Sea. They have participated in other international conferences which considered the possibilities of law-making: conferences on the environment, population, food, and numerous others under the auspices of the United Nations or one of its specialized agencies. They have promoted special organizations in which they might exert influence leading to new law, for example, the U.N. Conference on Trade and Development (UNCTAD).

The Third World has sought maximum freedom from those norms of traditional law which they found objectionable. They resisted a fixed rule tying states to agreements made by the colonial governments they succeeded, as well as the opposite rule that held they were not automatically party to such agreements (and could not automatically claim the advantages). Perhaps from sympathy or embarrassment of the developed states or because no vital interests were involved, the new states largely succeeded in having an option as to whether to succeed or not to succeed to these agreements, and even to take some time to decide.[12]

The Third World has also left its mark on new law. The new states put political self-determination as well as the principle of sovereignty over natural resources ("economic self-determination") at the head of both the International Covenant on Civil and Political Rights and the International Covenant on Economic, Social and Cultural Rights, over objections that these were not rights of individuals at all and did not belong in either covenant. They made the Convention on the Elimination of All Forms of Racial Discrimination the strongest convention with the clearest and most effective enforcement machinery and influenced many states to adhere to it. In the Security Council they obtained normative sanctions against Rhodesia and against South Africa to compel it to give up Namibia; they obtained also an advisory opinion of the International Court of Justice on the legal status of Namibia and the obligation of states in regard to it. They reasserted the favorite norm of small powers—nonintervention in internal affairs—and had it enshrined in new declarations and treaties.[13] They challenged the traditional rules protecting foreign investment, in particular the obligation to give effective compensation for nationalized foreign properties.[14] They have searched for international law that might give them protection from the power of transnational companies, but have not yet developed any that would add much to what can be done by national laws and informal cooperation with other particular states.

Some of these changes in the law are aspects of the principal item on the Third World agenda—development, primarily economic development. To that end also the Third World is seeking new trade and aid patterns; high prices for their raw materials and low prices for fuel, and for the industrial products they must buy; access to sophisticated technology on favorable terms. It seeks these by law, as of right and without strings, not by grace or charity of Western powers, not under Western tutelage and scrutiny. This is the significance of the New Economic Order.

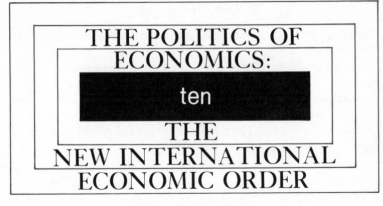

THE POLITICS OF ECONOMICS:

ten

THE NEW INTERNATIONAL ECONOMIC ORDER

The last quarter of the twentieth century is witnessing a concerted drive by the majority of the nations of the world to establish a "new international economic order." By new international arrangements and agreements based on "welfare principles" rather than on free-market forces, the majority hopes to satisfy basic human needs for their people, narrow the gulf between rich and poor states, accelerate economic development for all, bring the fruits of science and technology everywhere. The developing states hope to persuade the developed countries to provide them with capital, manufactured goods, technology and know-how, at low cost on liberal terms, and to import their raw materials at high prices and on terms favorable to exporting states. In a separate but not unrelated effort, the Third World seeks economic control and opportunity in the exploitation of the resources of the deep seabed. Some see the drive for a new economic order as a major step to a new political order in which the nations of the Third World can shape if not determine the future.

The particular economic issues are beyond the purview of this book (and beyond my competence). But the drive for a new economic order is a major political campaign to remake international economic law and the fundamental principles that have animated it for hundreds of years. The politics of economics provide a different perspective on the politics of law-making.

TRADITIONAL INTERNATIONAL ECONOMIC LAW

International relations in time of peace have been primarily economic relations since nations began, and the seed for modern international law can be found in primitive, rudimentary economic "law" between peoples. Ancient and medieval times already knew complex commercial systems, explicit trade and monetary agreements (and privileges on condition of reciprocity, as in Magna Carta), unified standards of coinage, protections for aliens and their property, the predecessors of modern consuls protecting commercial interests in foreign countries. Modern times brought more sophisticated bilateral agreements and networks of agreements and multilateral cooperation and organization.

The foundations of international economic law have been, and remain, pre-historic notions of property and its protection in tort principles and of contract common to virtually all domestic societies. As regards the property of individual aliens (as distinguished from governmental property), international law developed protections subsumed in a notion of "justice" for foreign nationals, though exactly what protection the law has given to alien property in time of peace has been hotly disputed. (See Chapter 6.) The most important principle of international economic law, as of all international law, is *"pacta sunt servanda"*—agreements are to be kept—and the sanctity of undertakings, whether in treaties and other international agreements, or in commercial contracts between governments or between governments and foreign nationals, has been the foundation of international trade and finance.

In principle, international economic law has assumed freedom of contract: governments are free to enter or not to enter contracts, and the terms of such agreements would reflect free bargaining and the interplay of market forces. Of course, as all recognized, nations were not in fact equal in bargaining power, and powerful states could extract terms favorable to them. That duress, fraud, or unconscionability might vitiate an arrangement was a notion slow to enter even into enlightened domestic law, and it has only recently penetrated the international legal system.[1] Even in domestic societies, moreover, unfair contracts are common, and could be voided, if at all, if the victim complained and resisted and if courts vindicated his objection. In international trade, resistance came harder and less frequently and there have been no institutions to resolve disputes or give judgment or relief.*

Despite inequalities among states, the international system developed patterns of commerce and intercourse of wide applicability. Except for war, with its special regimes of belligerency and neutrality, international relations in peace generally assumed and implied "friendly relations" and commercial as well as diplomatic intercourse between states. The common charter of bilateral relations was a treaty of friendship, commerce and navigation, and although there were differences among such treaties, the network of these treaties effectively established a regime of common principles, standards and practices. A treaty might define the right of one party's ships, goods, and nationals to enter the territory of another, regulate tariffs and other trade limitations, establish terms of payment for goods, prescribe means for resolving disputes. It might spell out the protections for the foreign national or his property, in accordance with or differing from the asserted customary law. Or each state might accord the other "most favored nation" treatment, terms as regards tariffs or other matters as favorable as it accords to the most-favored of other governments. Or, a state might accord to

* International economic law based on freedom of contract assumed bargaining between independent states. The age of colonialism removed many areas from international law because arrangements between dominant and dependent powers were seen as of domestic not international concern, not subject to international regulation and law.

nationals of another "national treatment"—the same rights enjoyed by its own citizens as regards, say, the right to own property, invest capital, engage in trade, seek employment, or practice a profession.[2]

There have also been bilateral or multilateral agreements on specific subjects relating to trade and commerce: monetary agreements; agreements governing the importation of labor; agreements for networks of transportation and communication; patent, copyright and trademark agreements; commodity price agreements; agreements to provide goods—arms, machinery, food and other raw materials, nuclear reactors. There have been agreements to share and divide markets, or sources of supply, or the resources of areas of the seas; or to boycott particular states for some political end, *e.g.*, Rhodesia, Mussolini's Italy. There have been agreements on the settlement of disputes, on choice of law in cases of conflict, on reciprocal judicial assistance.

In the absence of any governing agreement, international economic relations were *ad hoc*, and policies of different states and of the same state at different times or about different products or toward different trading partners have fluctuated between unilateralism and cooperation, between special bilateral arrangements and common international standards (as reflected in the principle of the "most favored nation" clause), between free trade and "protectionism." Regional free trade zones (and customs unions) have existed in different parts of the world at various times, and in Europe, since World War II, there have been both a free trade area and a "common market." After the Second World War the General Agreement on Tariffs and Trade (GATT) sought to establish a trade regime of general applicability. Also since World War II there have been monetary arrangements, generally under the umbrella of the International Monetary Fund. Both GATT and the monetary system responded primarily to the needs and interests of developed states; both were essentially under their control.

"ECONOMIC SELF-DETERMINATION"

The contemporary attack on the traditional economic regime began, of course, with the attack on colonialism and other dependent arrangements. Political self-determination created new independent economic actors, and political realignments following the end of the age of colonialism transformed economic relations and trading patterns. Economic relations between "metropole" and "dependency" themselves, of course, became relations between independent states, but pre-existing arrangements could not be abruptly terminated or radically changed. Independence often entailed an agreement continuing or modifying economic relations between erstwhile "parent" and erstwhile dependency, and though such agreements were often abandoned or modified in the following years, economic relations between them usually retained some special character.

Political self-determination early began to suggest also "economic self-determination," the right of new, weak states to control their own economic resources and to shape their economic destiny.[3] Asserting freedom from traditional principles about succession to the obligations assumed by their colonial governments, new governments were allowed to free themselves from international agreements they found intolerable, often being allowed to pick and choose, keeping those arrangements they found to be in their interest. But it was less easy for them to liberate themselves from the "burdens" of foreign holdings, concessions to foreign companies, or other commitments to private foreign individuals or companies. Western governments which might be prepared to waive their own rights or accommodate new governments in regard to inherited intergovernmental obligations, could not as readily sacrifice the holdings and claims of their citizens and of big companies that bore their nationality. These claimed, in particular, the protection of customary international law requiring "justice" to alien property—specifically, no expropriation without just compensation.[4]

Third World states have been increasingly troubled by political and social as well as economic consequences of their over-dependence on one or more multinational companies.[5] The size and economic power of some companies dwarf that of many governments with which they deal, distorting their bargaining relationship, breeding corruption, with unhappy consequences for their societies. The company may effectively determine the shape and content of the local economy, the use of local resources, the allocation of available capital and distribution of the labor force, the interests of consumers; it directs and limits the development of technology. The domestic society remains dependent on the needs and wishes of the company and bears its imprint.

Every host state can, in principle, regulate the activities of multinational companies operating in its territory. States have denied or conditioned entry, cancelled or rewritten concession agreements, terminated investments, replaced foreign concessions with joint-ventures, limited company earnings, regulated the repatriation of their capital, imposed strict labor laws. But the local government is often unequal to the task of taxing and regulating its giant guest and often cannot prevent the unhappy consequences of its unequal relations with such companies, for many of them are inherent and inevitable. Much of the distorting power of a large company comes from activities outside a particular country and therefore is not subject to its control. A state cannot regulate unduly lest the company take its investment and activity elsewhere. If regulations become confiscatory or discriminatory, the host state jeopardizes its relations with the state whose nationality the company bears.

There have been many calls, especially by new states, for international protection against multinational companies. Some seek bilateral and group agreements that would prevent companies from playing one country off against another. Proposals include the adoption of an international anti-trust law, the establishment of an international regulatory agency, the chartering of companies by an international body, international protection against pressures by the home state of the company. But many of the unhappinesses of developing states with multinational corporations seem to have no easy solution.

The controversy over expropriation was a principal issue of the first decades after the Second World War, and is still with us. I have told the story of the effort to change this law, of Western resistance, of the skirmishings and compromises, of growing Third World aggressiveness on the issue with their growing solidarity and confidence. (See Chapter 6.) Although the issue is less frequently the subject of controversy, in fact it remains important because the capital-importing countries are determined not to lose their "economic sovereignty" and to retain the power and right to assert it. But economic self-determination served only to rid new nations of the shackles of the past so they might start afresh on their own terms; it only "cleared the decks" but did not move them far toward their economic goals and aspirations. To meet their societal goals, to achieve their development, to bridge the chasm between them and the affluent, needed much more. It needed capital and other financial aid, higher prices for their goods, lower prices for what they needed to buy, support for their currency, access to technology, and much more.

The developed world recognized the needs of poor countries and there was some willingness to help. Recognition early took the form of new institutions like the U.N. Economic and Social Council, the U.N. Specialized Agencies, and regional economic commissions and other such bodies. It took the form of technical assistance and other aid programs. Traditional international law being a law of laissez-faire and freedom of contract, it could hardly have addressed itself to assistance by state to state, even by rich state to poor state, in the absence of special agreements freely undertaken. Since the Second World War, foreign assistance has become a common ingredient of foreign policy, whether from humanitarian, economic or political motivation, or some of each, with the political significance of aid increasing as the international system divided along varying political alignments; but as it has been seen as voluntary, at least by the donors, recipients were not happy to be dependent on the grace of the rich and the powerful. Slowly they turned to multilateral intergovernmental organizations where the aid, though contributed largely by a few rich states, is in principle given by all, is "laundered" through the international organization, and the terms of the aid could be shaped by the receiving majority and their sympathizers. The majority also developed the "welfare" rhetoric: assistance by rich to poor is not a matter of grace but of justice, even of obligation, in part for past exploitations, unjust enrichment, and other injustices, in part because present inequalities required something akin to "from each according to his ability to each according to his need."

Even multilateral aid could not begin to give the Third World what they aspired to. Despite resolutions calling on developed states to give more, few met the "quotas" established for them, and the level of assistance remained low; donors, moreover, sought to control how their "donations" were spent. Industrial development, gross national product increased manifold, but bridging the economic gap would depend largely on trade, and the international rules of trade and finance were "stacked" against the developing countries. Law based on freedom of contract and free trade served countries in a strong bargaining position, the developed states and those few developing states with a near-monopoly of an essential commodity such as oil; with the wealth from oil revenues, and their bargaining power, the latter could move as far and as fast toward development as money can buy. But freedom of contract and free trade with occasional protection does not help other developing states that cannot get high prices for their raw materials, whose manufactured goods get low prices and are sometimes wholly excluded by import restrictions or high tariffs, and furthermore must pay high prices in expensive currency for manufactured goods they import and for oil and other sources of energy. The result is not only that they cannot make major steps in development but are heavily in debt, and the cost of carrying that debt sets them further back and makes their progress painfully slow if not hopeless. The Third World soon began to recognize also that for the longer run it needed continuing access to technology and education, training and participation in its use. But while some of it was for sale to them, the market price was high and much could be had only under controls and strings held by developed states or their companies.

THE NEW INTERNATIONAL
ECONOMIC ORDER

Slowly the outlines of the new economic order desired by the
Third World unfolded, full-blown finally in a "declaration," a
"programme" and a "charter" adopted in 1974.[6] Its rhetoric and
justification were "justice" and equality. It began with "economic
sovereignty," "economic self-determination," and "economic non-
intervention," including the right to nationalize alien like citizen
property, with compensation only as seemed appropriate; it included also the right to regulate and supervise foreign companies,
not least the so-called "multinational companies." The developing
states sought protection for their exports by preventing fluctuations
in the market and the market price. They sought new institutions
that would stockpile commodities and use them to help maintain
prices, establish special contracts, and arrange for special financing.
On the other hand they sought special rights of access to the industrial world markets without tariffs or other restrictions. And they
wanted their debts "rescheduled," and some of them perhaps for-
given. Finally they wanted quick and ready access to Western technology, whether publicly or privately held. In all respects they
wished full and equal participation in running the new economic
order, including institutions like the International Monetary Fund,
the World Bank, and GATT. Trade on these terms would not, of
course, reflect the ordinary market forces but would require the developed states to pay more and accept less than they have to,
whether as an act of generosity, of prudent politics, or from some
new developing principle modifying freedom of contract as necessary to achieve a measure of economic redistribution.

THE POLITICS OF ECONOMICS

The stress on the quest for new economic law should not suggest
that economics are separable from politics. All law is political, and
economic law is integral to that which governs other relations in
the system. Even in narrow senses in which economics can be distinguished from politics, economic law spills over. It is not easy to

separate the economic concerns of new states for developing nuclear power as an answer to their needs for sources of energy from their attitudes toward the proliferation of nuclear weapons. In other respects, too, their economic needs are confounded by their security needs as they see them. The international regime which new states desire for the deep sea-bed responds in part to desires for political authority that will enable them both to meet their economic needs as well as to further their larger political purposes. The desire of developing states to narrow the economic gap and to obtain access to developed technology have deep political as well as economic implications.

The politics of the New International Economic Order began when the Third World emerged, when new states and older undeveloped states began to sense a common history, a common condition, common interests. Beginning as a caucus in the United Nations, they established the U.N. Conference on Trade and Development (UNCTAD), which became the focus of their economic demands on the developed states and the expression of their solidarity.[7] Ever increasing numbers enhanced their "clout" and their confidence. That some developing states—the oil cartel—could impose their will on the developed states somehow increased the confidence of the whole group (although it also greatly increased their "fuel" debts as well); perhaps some Third World states think that the "oil weapon" will be available to the Third World as a whole to compel the developed states to accept the New International Economic Order. In any event they have learned that the developed world, at least the Western world, wants and depends on stability and order, and have dared make the implied threat that "development is a new name for peace." The Communist states, notably the U.S.S.R. and China, compete in enthusiasm to support the rhetoric and even the specific demands of the Third World, doubtless hoping that the Third World will continue to overlook that the Communist powers too are developed states, and that they will continue to avoid having these demands directed to them as well.

It goes without saying, perhaps, that the developed states have not rushed to accede to Third World demands. They strongly resist the "welfare system" rhetoric and insist on their sovereignty, their freedom of contract, their right to continue to run an economic system on traditional principles and terms. They resist international institutions based on "one-state, one-vote" and run by the resulting majority. They fear institutions that will organize the Third World and give them power in relation to other commodities akin to that enjoyed by the oil cartel. They do not wish their investments and those of their companies to be at the unlimited mercy of developing host states, although they might agree to an even-handed international code of behavior for and toward multinational corporations. They insist on the sanctity of international agreements. They think trade is a two-way street based on reciprocal agreements and arrangements, not on preference for the Third World. They want debts paid. They will give some assistance, but in amounts and on conditions acceptable to them. They will sell their technology, but only with due regard to their national security interests and the patent and other rights of their nationals (which they will not and perhaps cannot sacrifice).

And yet, after stunned and frosty beginnings, they have not broken off discussions with the Third World, and the blueprint for a New International Economic Order has in fact become an agenda for an extended and continuing dialogue. For the fact is that the rhetoric of equality and justice, if not quite accepted by the developed states, is not rejected either. Guilt over past exploitations, and some guilt over present affluence in a world of many hungry millions, mutes or discourages the counter-rhetoric of laisser-faire and freedom of enterprise. And Western citizens, if not their governments, have a deep sympathy for at least some Third World aspirations. Perhaps their vulnerability to the oil cartel and the oil weapon has added sincerity to their protestations of "interdependence" between developed and developing states. They recognize the weaknesses of the old international economic order* and in cor-

---

* The United States deemed it in its interest to violate its International Monetary Fund obligations in 1971 by terminating the convertibility of its currency.

recting them are willing to give some concessions to some of the poorer states in some respects, but on an ad hoc, not on an organized, Third World, all-countries, all-subjects bases.

Those who believe in *Realpolitik* and "business is business" may be particularly skeptical of the influence of "morality" in this dialogue. Yet, while rhetoric is easy and the strident militancy of some Third World pronouncements is irritating and evokes resistance, there is a Third World weapon that is in fact difficult to deny. If "development" is only a word, and "gross national product" only a number, the Third World has the undeniable truth of poverty. When they stress that for more than a billion people in the poorest states the per capita income is $150 a year, that more than 600 million people do not have enough food, that life expectancy is very low, infant mortality very high, illiteracy still rampant, the developed world is disarmed. As Third World countries begin to talk less of economics, of prestige products (like national airlines or useless steel mills), are concerned to show that development more than merely trickles down and as they begin to reform internally, and to talk of programs to satisfy basic human needs, the likelihood of at least some success brightens markedly. It is not irrelevant, I think, that even while the economic dialogue simmers, developed and developing states are meeting about population, food, the environment, human settlement, women, water, deserts, science and technology, the seas, suggesting a new kind of agenda in international relations and international law-making, alongside the political-security and old-order economic agendas we have known. And those who represent nations at these conferences on "soft" subjects are now getting the eye and the ear of national policymakers, and sometimes have been the foreign ministers and secretaries-of-state themselves.

I cannot foresee the outcome of dialogue and eventual negotiation, and, in fact, there is not likely to be an "outcome," only a series of continuing developments and changes over years and decades. One can say with some confidence, however, that although the developed world holds most of the cards today, the influence of numbers, of rhetoric, of ideas whose time have come—if slowly—will be strongly felt in the politics of economics; and the international economic order at the end of the century, if not new, will be substantially different from what we know today.

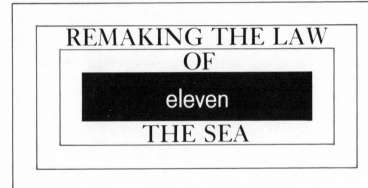

REMAKING THE LAW OF
eleven
THE SEA

A law of the sea is as old as nations, and the modern law of the sea is virtually as old as modern international law. For three hundred years it was probably the most stable and least-controversial branch of international law. It was essentially reaffirmed and codified as recently as the First U.N. Conference of the Sea in 1958. By 1970 it was in disarray. After years of studies, negotiations, declarations and resolutions in the United Nations, the Third Law of the Sea Conference began to remake the law of the sea. It began in 1973; it had not finished its work by 1979.

The process and politics of law-making in our time can be studied (and nearly understood) in this most ambitious, most populous, most extended, most complex law-making effort in international history. To understand better, one should begin at the beginning.

Virtually from the birth of modern international law, the international law of the sea was subsumed generally in the principle of freedom: except in a narrow band of water adjacent to coasts, which came to be called the territorial sea, there was freedom for all to navigate, and freedom for any one to fish or to appropriate other resources. (Even in the territorial sea there was a right of "innocent passage" for all.) The powerful, influential maritime states favored that freedom and, with a few minor exceptions, resisted occasional claims by a coastal state to reach farther into the sea.[1]

After World War II, the United States, aware of the wealth of petroleum in the subsoil of the seabed off its shores, and determined to reduce its dependence on foreign sources (starkly demonstrated during the war), proclaimed exclusive rights as a coastal state to the mineral resources of the seabed of its continental shelf.[2] Other states acquiesced. Some coastal states saw opportunity for themselves to do likewise; others saw a precedent for breaking out beyond a narrow territorial sea in other ways, including extended exclusive fishing zones. No developed maritime state saw fit to oppose the extension, although it implied sacrificing a right they might have had to mine the continental shelves of other states, and might encourage coastal states to claim other exclusive rights. A customary law of the continental shelf,* therefore, grew quickly by general acquiescence, even before it was codified by Convention at the First U.N. Law of the Sea Conference in 1958.[3]

At the same time, the United States insisted that the waters above the continental shelf remained high seas as before, and that the regime of the high seas included the freedom for all to fish outside the narrow territorial sea of coastal states. Other coastal states, however, saw it differently. Some depended heavily on fishing and could not compete with the technologically advanced "fishing factories" of developed "distant-fishing states" in waters not far from their coasts (though outside their traditional territorial sea). Some suggested that a state can unilaterally assert a wider territorial sea

---

*The continental shelf is a geological notion and, where it is regular, generally goes out to where the water is 200 meters deep: the "200 meter isobath." The 1958 Convention defined the shelf as going out to the 200 meter isobath, or beyond it "to where the waters permit of exploitation." It was not anticipated that exploitation would soon be possible (technically if not economically) anywhere, regardless of depth of water.

(in which they would have complete sovereignty, subject only to "innocent passage"). At least, some argued, since coastal states had successfully claimed exclusive rights in the resources of the seabed beyond their territorial sea, why could they not claim also exclusive rights to fish in the waters above?

Soon claims to wide fishing zones burgeoned and proliferated. For years, powerful distant-fishing states fought these extended claims,* but their weapons were limited. The day of "gun-boat diplomacy" was past. The use of force was outlawed by the Charter; the emerging Third World would strongly condemn the use of force by a developed against an underdeveloped state (and the Communists would join in the condemnation). And so, Peru could arrest "invading" American tuna boats, and Iceland could shoot at the codfishers of its NATO ally Great Britain, but neither the United States nor Britain could afford the political onus of using force to protect the right to fish which they believed they had under international law.

REMAKING THE LAW, 1967–

In 1967 the representative of a small country (Malta) placed for consideration on the agenda of the U.N. General Assembly the future of the resources of the deep seabed. The subject seemed "futuristic" and hardly relevant to the world of affairs, but the Maltese initiative catalyzed a variety of national interests and international political forces and brought about a new, if yet undetermined, law of the sea.

The launching of this agenda item found governments wholly unprepared, ignorant of geology and geography, of technological development and prospects, of economic opportunities, even of

---

*At the First U.N. Law of the Sea Conference in 1958, and at the Second Conference in 1960, the issue for most of the participants was still whether coastal states had exclusive rights to fish only in a zone of three miles (the traditional, narrow view of the width of the territorial sea), or beyond that to 6 miles, or 12 miles from shore. But those conferences failed to reach agreement on the issue.

their own particular interests. But while developed states were skeptical, cautious and reluctant, Third World states embraced the subject and fired it with rhetoric, some apparently dreaming dreams of great wealth that would transform the world economic system and eliminate the chasm between rich and poor. Early the General Assembly unanimously declared the seabed beyond national jurisdiction to be "the common heritage of mankind."[4] The seabed became a continuing preoccupation of the United Nations for more than ten years: committees were established, studies commissioned, declarations and resolutions were adopted, blocs formed and re-formed, and negotiations were continuous until the Third Law of the Sea Conference convened and continued during its long life.

The documents emerging from the conference contain the new law of the sea. They were shaped by a complex process, novel procedures and imaginative adaptations of old ones, intricate negotiations within and between blocs and sub-blocs, the interplay of personalities. But at bottom, the law that emerged was the result of "political vectors," the interplay of political forces reflecting the influence of governments (and of domestic influences on government) trying to realize national interests as they saw them. These included sometimes competing interests in and about the sea; they included also the relevance of sea issues to other economic-political issues, and their place in the totality of national interests in an interdependent, highly complex international system. The forces were modified by the process, by the greater need that some had to obtain agreement, and by different advantage or disadvantage if the conference failed. The vectors were drawn at the conference tables in Caracas, Geneva, New York, but the forces and their true negotiation and interplay took place elsewhere, everywhere, before as well as during the actual conference proceedings. Some of the resulting law was effectively realized even before the conference formally began; most of it, surely, before the conference ended.

THE EXPANSION OF
COASTAL-STATE JURISDICTION

The Maltese initiative was directed to the resources of the seabed "beyond national jurisdiction" but, ironically perhaps, its principal impact, rather, was on the extent and character of national jurisdiction of coastal states in the seas. While attention and discussion focused on the future and on mining the deep seabed, developing coastal states concentrated on modifying the reach of national jurisdiction. Repeated declarations by Latin American coastal states, soon supported by similar expressions from African states, asserted the right of coastal states to determine how far out they needed to extend their jurisdiction. Specifically, without rejecting individual claims to wide, even extravagant territorial seas, they developed the notion of a "patrimonial sea" 200 miles wide (or wider) in which the coastal state had exclusive rights to all economic resources.[5] They sought to persuade their fellow members of the Third World, grown in numbers and influence, that their coastal claims were an aspect of "economic self-determination" and that fishing and mining by distant states was "economic imperialism." And they sought to assure that the proposed U.N. Conference would not be limited to the deep seabed but would be a full-fledged conference to revise the law of the sea, including, in particular, accepting enlarged jurisdiction by coastal states.*

The geographically disadvantaged states[6]—those that were landlocked, had short coast lines or narrow submerged land masses, or whose coastal areas were not rich in minerals or fish—stood to gain nothing from coastal-state expansion. Indeed, they might have benefited, rather, from leaving more of the seas as "the common heritage of mankind" in which they might claim a share. But apparently they deemed the demands of Third World solidarity more

*The big powers succeeded in keeping control of armaments in the sea out of the Law of the Sea Conference and within the context of arms control negotiations. See, for example, the Treaty on the Prohibition of the Emplacement of Nuclear Weapons and Other Weapons of Mass Destruction on the Seabed and Ocean Floor and the Subsoil Thereof, 10 *Int'l Leg. Materials* 146 (1971). Issues of navigation and the environment were also left largely to other forums.

compelling, perhaps seeing all Third World interests in the seas as an aspect of a drive for a new economic order. Perhaps they did not perceive their particular interests clearly, or organize themselves effectively and in time. Perhaps they expected some compensation from their coastal-state neighbors who would gain from this expansion.

Developed maritime states early resisted coastal-state expansion. As distant fishing states, they rejected the notion that a coastal state might exclude them from wide coastal zones in which they had long fished. They feared, too, "creeping jurisdiction." Already they had seen how exclusive mining rights for coastal states on the continental shelf (beyond their territorial sea) had created pressures for exclusive fishing rights for coastal states in wide zones beyond the territorial sea. Developed maritime states feared that if the coastal state acquired exclusive fishing rights, its jurisdiction would continue to expand to other uses and would interfere also with navigation, scientific research, and military uses in wide coastal zones.

But developed maritime states are also coastal states and have important national interests that stood to gain from coastal-state expansion. They had some sympathy with the economic needs of poor coastal states. They were reluctant to confront developing coastal states (supported by the rest of the Third World), especially since the latter had effective "possession" of the coastal areas and could seize them (or threaten to seize them) unilaterally. Pressed from without and by national interests from within, they acquiesced in the concept of an exclusive economic zone. (This, in fact, unleashed domestic forces that pressed unilateral expansion. While the conference was in process, the United States Congress declared a 200-mile fishing zone for the United States.[7]) Developed states, however, hoped to assure that the coastal states' jurisdiction in the zone should apply only to the exploitation of economic resources, and that the zone should remain "high seas" for navigation, military and other uses.

On this as on other sea issues, the U.S.S.R. did not differ markedly from the United States and other maritime states. It had perhaps an even stronger interest to preserve distant fishing, and was equally concerned for retaining freedom of navigation and military maneuver. But the Soviet Union was perhaps even more eager than was the United States not to appear in opposition to Third World interests, and eventually also supported the expansion of coastal-state jurisdiction.

It was a foregone conclusion that an exclusive economic zone would be written into law if the Conference succeeded; it would emerge as the law in fact, even if the Conference failed. That doubtless strengthened the hand of developing coastal states to resist limitations. The geographically disadvantaged states sought to deny the coastal states rights (under the 1958 Convention) in the submerged land mass where it extended beyond 200 miles; at least, they insisted, the coastal state should share revenues there with the rest of mankind. They sought special rights for disadvantaged states in the 200-mile economic zones of their coastal-state neighbors. But although the geographically disadvantaged were sufficiently numerous, if united, to prevent a two-thirds majority for any Conference decision, they had made their commitment to Third World solidarity and had few "bargaining chips" left.

The hopes of the developed states to impose limitations on the jurisdiction of the coastal state were also substantially disappointed. There being large agreement on the zone in principle, there was no *quid pro quo* or other inducement for the developing coastal states to accept limitations. The developed states did not succeed in having the zone explicitly identified as high seas, or in explicitly preserving the freedom of scientific research there without coastal-state veto. They did succeed in getting agreement on complex, limited machinery for compulsory settlement of disputes arising in the zone, perhaps because refusal to agree to a settlement of disputes is not an appealing position for any state to insist on.[8]

OTHER COASTAL ISSUES

There were other coastal issues and interests at stake in the redevelopment of the law of the sea, and they too were resolved by the interplay of national forces and influence in the context of the system and of geography. None was apparently important enough in itself to engage major national interests and efforts, or to affect significantly the outcome of other issues or of the Conference as a whole.

With the growth of the idea of an exclusive economic zone, the pressure for expanding the territorial sea relaxed. But earlier pressures had already shaken the narrow three-mile zone, and had moved states toward a 12-mile sea when that would have provided them twelve miles of exclusive fishing. Perhaps, too, some developed states considered that a modest widening of the territorial sea in which the coastal states would have full sovereignty (subject only to the right of "innocent passage") might reduce tendencies for a coastal state to move its economic zone toward becoming a 200-mile territorial sea. Soon, then, developed states were prepared to move to a 12-mile territorial sea. That expansion, however, would be particularly troublesome to far-roaming fleets and navies, for it would convert important international waterways—those which somewhere were less than 24 miles wide—into territorial sea where passage might be hindered by riparian states if deemed not to be innocent. The developed states therefore insisted that the price of their acceptance of a 12-mile territorial sea was a regime for international straits and waterways that provided for "free transit," regardless of the kind of vessel or of any "innocence" or "non-innocence" of its passage. Riparian states did not see fit to resist strongly. The special claims of archipelagic states to treat waters "connecting" their islands as internal found sympathy among other Third World states and resistance from maritime and naval states, and were also compromised.

The issues of regulating pollution were resolved differently. Coastal states sought maximum protection against pollution of coastal seas and beaches, urging their right to set standards and assert other police authority over vessels that might approach their shores, navigate their territorial seas or even their economic zones. Maritime states resisted, claiming that this would give the state with the most stringent standards the power to determine vessel construction for the whole world. They sought instead internationally agreed standards. Again a compromise, reflecting the different influences that could be brought to bear. Protection of the marine environment from land-based pollution or activities in the economic zone is left to national laws, although states are required to enact and coordinate such protective legislation and to seek agreement on global or regional standards. But vessel-source pollution is to be governed generally by international standards (like those in conventions promoted by the Intergovernmental Maritime Consultative Organization (IMCO),[9] with the international standards to be enforced by the flag state generally, and by coastal states as regards vessels that come within their jurisdiction.

"BEYOND NATIONAL JURISDICTION"

The direction and magnitude of the forces brought to bear on mining the deep sea were different and produced a different result. While no government cared to dissent when the U.N. General Assembly declared that the seabed beyond national jurisdiction was "the common heritage of mankind," governments disagreed widely as to what that implied and differed as to what they hoped to make of it.

Originally, perhaps, the many poor states hoped that the wealth of the seas might somehow all go to them and bridge the economic chasm between them and the rich. The developed states were more sanguine about the early economic prospects of deep-sea mining, and in any event were not prepared to give the wealth of the seas to the poor; they accepted only that some revenue from deep-sea minerals might go to aid less-developed countries. As that and other differences simmered, the Third World majority sought to improve its bargaining position by adopting a General Assembly resolution declaring a moratorium forbidding mining (by the developed states) until an agreement was reached and a new regime was established; developed states, of course, challenged its authority and legal effect, insisting that under existing international law any state was free to mine in the deep seabed just as it could fish freely on the high seas.[10]

Perhaps because it soon appeared that the wealth of the deep seabed would not in fact produce tremendous wealth right away, the general agreement that there should be some revenue-sharing was soon submerged beneath other, largely ideological differences. "Radical" Third World states sought arrangements that would not only give the Third World virtually all the economic benefits, but would also give the exclusive right to mine to institutions which the Third World would control, which would enable Third World governments and citizens to have access to and be educated in the technology and to manage as well as operate the enterprise.* The United States and other developed states, on the other hand, insisted on a regime that would permit free enterprise and profit for states or their national companies. The Communist states, although generally fearful of multilateral institutions and wishing to retain a role for their state enterprises, did not favor a large role for Western companies and banks.

Here, the pressures of majority votes and rhetoric were not enough, since the developed states had "possession"—the technology and the capital—and could "go it alone," as domestic forces were pressing the United States to do. Efforts were made to compromise the issues. The right to exploit was divided between national enterprise and a new international enterprise run essentially by the developing states, with the developed states giving the international enterprise the capital and technology it would need in order to get started on one set of mining operations. The Seabed Authority would combine equal voting on some matters with weighted voting on others. The interests of consumers in access to resources were set against some concern for land-producers of minerals whose markets would be affected.

In 1978 the issue was not yet resolved. But whether the result is

*Some developing states wanted such control in order to prevent exploitation of minerals that would compete with their land-based minerals in world markets. Some observers think that effective control of mining may have been seen by some as a step toward Third World control of other uses of the oceans, in turn a step towards other powerful institutions with authority in other aspects of international life.

agreement or deadlock (and breakdown of the negotiations), the result will reflect, among other forces, the "power" of large numbers of states voting together (even in the context of the principle of unanimity); of the Third World, especially when it can maneuver big powers to compete for its support; of ideas, that the political system is a "welfare society" and must move toward a new economic order with less inequality—ideas that found some support in Western guilt over past imperialism and present wealth and in some sympathy for Third World aspirations. But the result will be shaped also by the forces of inertia, the resistance to change of established principles and ways and of the rights they vest and the expectations they build; and by the bargaining power which the developed states enjoy by virtue of their ability to proceed to take the resources of the seabed if agreement failed.

DOMESTIC FORCES AND
NATIONAL SEA POLICY

The remaking of the law of the sea provides an opportunity for studying also the interplay of domestic interests and of agencies, and the vector of forces that determine national policy as to how important law might be modified or updated in the complex society of the United States.

As a highly developed country and a major maritime and naval power, the United States wished to maintain maximum freedom for navigation, military maneuver, exploitation of resources, scientific research, waste disposal, and other uses, in as much as of the sea as possible, including areas close to foreign coasts. On the other hand, the United States also has long coasts and as a coastal state would prefer exclusive rights in its coastal waters as far, and for as many purposes, as possible. In the seas as elsewhere, the United States was prepared to promote international cooperation, develop international institutions, and generate revenue for less-advantaged countries; but as it also wished to maintain maximum economic opportunity for itself and for American companies, free of restrictive international regulation, it resisted international institutions which might be controlled by unfriendly majorities. The United States also had to see a new law of the sea, and the process of achieving it, as part of an integral national policy, with implications for American security, economic interests, prestige and influence, for its friendships and enmities, for world peace, order, and general welfare, and for the needs and aspirations of other states.

The various interests of the United States had different constituencies and spokesmen in the policy-making process. In the executive branch, political and diplomatic considerations were espoused by the Department of State, and security and military interests by the Department of Defense. The Department of the Interior, charged with responsibility for mineral resources in the coastal seabed, aspired also to represent United States interests as regards the resources of the deep seabed. The Department of Commerce was in charge of sea-fishing. The Treasury Department was concerned for the financial implications of any policy adopted. These, and other executive departments and agencies with relevant responsibilities, had more-or-less intimate links with private interests and their pressure groups, and the public at large had the ear of all of them. In turn, the executive branch had to maintain continued liaison with Congress, with the Senate whose consent would be necessary for any new Law of the Sea treaty, and with both houses for they could destroy anything the executive branch built, *e.g.*, by enacting unilateral extensions of U.S. jurisdiction at sea or by authorizing American companies to mine in the deep seabed and protecting their investments, without regard to any international agreement. The various national interests were also reflected in the different jurisdictions of a variety of Congressional committees and subcommittees and in the different views of individual members of Congress responsive to diverse constituencies. Both within the executive branch and in Congress, each national interest weighed differently, and the various interests were not equally, or equally-well, represented. Personalities, and personal and bureaucratic interests, further complicated this process and shaped the outcome.

The process could be observed most clearly, perhaps, in the development of United States policy as regards one set of issues, the

scope of coastal-state jurisdiction over the sea's resources. Along
many of the coasts of the United States, the seabed was large and
rich in minerals, especially oil and gas; from the beginning, therefore, the National Petroleum Council (an advisory body) and
the Department of the Interior exerted influence in support of international law that would establish wide coastal-state jurisdiction.
But as a naval and maritime power, the United States wished maximum freedom to navigate or maneuver in a maximum of sea, and
the Department of Defense feared that exclusive coastal-state jurisdiction over resources in a wide area might "creep" to other uses
and become coastal-state jurisdiction there for all purposes. Fishing
interests, not yet fully mobilized, were divided, the distant-fishing
industry favoring a narrow coastal-state jurisdiction so that it might
fish in foreign coastal areas, while domestic-fishing interests wished
a wide zone to keep foreign fisherman far from our shores. In the
public at large more "enlightened" interests favored, while more
"egoistic" interests opposed, leaving more of the sea to "the common heritage of mankind," with generous revenues for the less-
developed countries.

The result originally was a United States position favoring essentially a narrow coastal-state jurisdiction, with an intermediate zone
in which the coastal state had control but subject to international
regulation, and sharing the revenues with the international community.[11] On fishing, it took a mixed, compromise position, giving
the coastal state greater rights as to some species but subject to
some recognition of historic claims of distant-fishing states, while
denying the coastal state any special rights over migratory species
beyond the territorial sea. But the Department of the Interior and
oil interests persuaded the Defense Department to withdraw or
mute its opposition to a wide coastal-state jurisdiction; and encouraged by the example of other nations, domestic fishing interests organized and gained a dominant voice in Congress, eventually
leading to a unilateral assertion of a 200-mile fishing zone. United
States policy responded also to foreign needs and pressures, and
some domestic voices, it is said, inspired other coastal nations to
maintain an uncompromising stand for a wide economic zone. Be-

fore long, the United States had effectively joined the supporters of a wide coastal-state jurisdiction, while trying to deny coastal states any authority that might interfere with freedom of military maneuver outside the 12-mile territorial sea.

The U.S.S.R. provides another illustration. Its economy has no private sector, and its government is less diffuse and more centralized, but it, too, has to respond to different constituencies within the bureaucracy representing competing national (and perhaps bureaucratic and personal) interests. The Soviet Union cared about the security of its coasts but had less to gain from coastal-state expansion, and more to lose from interference by other coastal states with its freedom of navigation, military maneuver, oceanological activity, and distant fishing. But the Soviet Union was also sensitive to Third World interests, and was not eager to stand in strong and open opposition to coastal states asserting resistance to "economic imperialism" by distant-fishing states or developing mining states. In the result, the U.S.S.R. moved from early resistance to substantial acquiescence in coastal-state expansion.

As regards the seabed beyond national jurisdiction, different domestic interests dominated and were variously arrayed. Here, too, the Department of State espoused international political considerations, pressing for accommodation with the more moderate segments of the Third World. The Defense Department did not see its concern as seriously engaged (except insofar as positions on deep-sea issues might affect coastal-state attitudes on other issues, *e.g.*, navigation in the economic zone or in international straits); but it considered carefully the implications for U.S. military interests of establishing powerful international institutions, not under U.S. control, which had authority that might extend to, or impinge on, freedom of military maneuver. The principal private interests at stake were represented by the "hard mineral" companies, desiring to exploit the manganese nodules that richly populated the seabed. They were supported by other companies with an interest in the oceanological technology, by banks interested in investment, and by the "private sector" generally concerned for freedom of enterprise and opportunity and fearful of institutions and precedents that might limit opportunities for American companies. Representing interests not as critical to the national interest as petroleum, nor as extensive, well-organized and influential, they nevertheless had the support of the Departments of the Interior and of Commerce and of important Congressional bodies. Repeatedly Congressional committees threatened to press legislation that would "unleash" American companies to start mining; repeatedly the Department of State begged for more time to allow international negotiation to run its course, warning of dire consequences to American interests if the Conference on the Law of the Sea failed: coastal states would be encouraged to assert wider and fuller jurisdiction unilaterally; the Third World would unite in condemning the United States, threatening to disrupt "illegal" U.S. mining in the deep seas and to challenge its title to any minerals extracted, and spilling over to other subjects on which the Third World could injure U.S. interests. For several years the executive branch prevailed on Congress to delay; in 1977 it could resist no longer and sought instead to insure that proposed legislation would be as "internationalist" as possible, temporary in character, and not too difficult to replace by international agreement if any were achieved.[12]

Whether by agreement at a successfully concluded Third Law of the Sea Conference, or as a result of customary law deriving from unilateral acts, reciprocal legislation or smaller local agreements, the law of the sea will not be the same in 1990 as it was in 1960. The new law will reflect less the narrow wishes of superpowers than the growing influence and solidarity of the Third World.

The principal outcome will be something which Ambassador Pardo of Malta surely did not intend or anticipate, but probably helped to achieve. By throwing open the law of the sea to change at a time of political militancy and daring by small nations, he unleashed, in particular, egoistic nationalist forces of coastal states blessed by geography which, by expanding their coastal jurisdiction, were reaching for immediate gains at the expense both of traditional freedom (*i.e.*, laissez-faire) and the common heritage. Beyond national jurisdiction the Third World saw an opportunity to develop new institutions which they might control and thereby extend their authority and preclude that of developed states in the large oceans, and to add a dimension to their drive for a New International Economic Order. There, however, they met strong opposition from established law and expectations, and the powerful, wealthy and technologically developed states which these favored. From the ever-changing law of the sea the student of politics will learn much about the politics of law-making in the international political system of the last quarter of the century.

IDEALISM AND IDEOLOGY:
twelve
THE LAW OF HUMAN RIGHTS

Process and politics have a different place and dimension in the new kind of international law, the law of human rights.[1]

Law to control how states behave toward their own inhabitants, developed during the decades since the end of the Second World War, has faced extraordinary obstacles. Unlike other international law, the law of human rights serves idealistic ends, not particular national interests, although it becomes entangled in international politics especially when they are heavily ideological. The law of human rights contradicts the once deep-and-dear premises of the international system that how a state behaved toward its own citizens in its own territory was a matter of "domestic jurisdiction," *i.e.*, not any one else's business and therefore not any business for international law. Governments have not been eager to submit the manner in which they govern at home—the core of their "sovereignty"—to external standards and scrutiny. Officials of national governments who make and negotiate foreign policy have not been eager to scrutinize what goes on in other countries; by tradition, experience, and inclination they are concerned with furthering national political and economic interests, and tend to look at efforts to make international human rights law as officious, unsophisticated, unrealistic, diversionary if not disruptive of real international politics, and detrimental to friendly relations between nations. In the face of these important obstacles, the impressive growth of an international human rights law tells of the influence of ideas and rhetoric, the sensitivity of modern governments to "public opinion," and the effectiveness of international organizations for exploiting that sensitivity to transform ideas and rhetoric into law and national policy and behavior.

ANTECEDENTS

International law was not absolutely indifferent to the fate of individuals—some individuals—before our time. Diplomats have enjoyed extraordinary protection, and the law requires states to provide all aliens a minimum standard of "justice." By treaties, some going back to the early days of the modern international system, governments promised other governments to accord religious toleration, basic rights of equality, or other protections to their own citizens or inhabitants with whom the other government had religious, ethnic or other identity. In the nineteenth century and again after World War I the big powers imposed on lesser ones treaties guaranteeing basic rights to specified ethnic or religious minorities. Early treaties outlawing slavery and the slave trade in effect gave all persons in many states freedom from slavery. In the aftermath of World War I, the International Labor Office (later the International Labor Organization) began its long and successful history of promoting international conventions setting minimum labor and social standards for all inhabitants of all parties.[2] The treaties that concluded peace with Italy and with several central European countries following the Second World War imposed obligations to respect human rights. Without claiming that violations of law had been committed, powerful states sometimes interceded privately, or condemned publicly, egregious infringements of human rights, whether czarist pogroms or other massacres.

This earlier international law afforded important protections to many people, but most protections did not apply to all the inhabitants of a state and all were rooted in political (rather than strictly humanitarian) considerations. Mutual religious toleration and respect for ethnic minorities identified with other governments reduced international tensions and helped keep the peace. The World War II peace treaties were law imposed by the victors upon the vanquished only. The ILO conventions were capitalism's response to the blandishments of socialism; nations, moreover, had a national interest in shaping the labor conditions in countries that competed with them in world markets.

The war against Hitler identified violations of human rights as a major threat to international peace, and they were linked in the rhetoric of the war and in plans for the peace. Human rights were prominent in the constitutions of the new nations that began to emerge in the postwar years, *e.g.*, India, and of almost every new nation that came thereafter.[3] But the coalition of *Realpolitik* and idealism did not long survive the victory. In the aftermath of victory, there was some pressure on all governments to give meaning to the humanitarian rhetoric that had been invoked to articulate the aims of the war. Heads of state and foreign ministers, however, might have been content to satisfy their wartime commitment by imposing respect for human rights on the defeated countries and paying homage to human rights in ringing declarations and in generalities and exhortations like those in the United Nations Charter. But the existence of the United Nations (and other intergovernmental organizations), the opportunities which their procedures provided and the momentum they generated, the influence of national and transnational nongovernmental organizations on governmental policy in international organizations, the influence of personalities of international stature (*e.g.*, Eleanor Roosevelt) who came to represent their governments and worked together toward a common aim, the support given their work by intellectuals and media of information, all combined to launch an international human rights movement, with law-making one of its principal elements.

Because, in general, the condition of human rights seemed to have little relation to the foreign policy interests of states, traditional policy-makers and diplomats tended to have little concern for the human rights movement, but neither did they see any need to court the public embarrassment of opposing it. In the United Nations General Assembly and the Economic and Social Council and their sub-organs, governments were impelled to participation and surely could not lightly resist it. Protected by the principle of unanimity,[4] governments could take part in the law-making process without any commitment to adhere to the final product, trying nevertheless to shape emerging international norms so that their country's behavior would not be found wanting in their light; and it might even be possible to adhere to them without undue burden if that later appeared desirable.

THE NEW INTERNATIONAL LAW OF HUMAN RIGHTS

The law took root and spread. When a dedicated individual created the term "genocide" and developed a convention to outlaw it,[5] governments readily adhered, wishing to avoid the slightest suspicion that they condoned Hitler's monstrosities, or that they wished to remain free to emulate him; in fact, too, governments did not consider that eschewing genocide would limit their freedom to govern in any way. The Charter's general exhortations, which few originally saw as having any normative significance, were converted into a Universal Declaration, a masterly blend of Western libertarianism and "welfare state" principles adopted almost unanimously by the nations of the time.* Nations felt free to do so since it was generally considered as having no binding legal character. Although some governments articulated misgivings (and others doubtless had, but suppressed, them) a long slow process began to convert the Declaration into binding international law.[6]

It took eighteen years to complete the process. Every new nation that emerged increased the number of law-makers and helped

---

*The Communist bloc, Saudi Arabia, and South Africa abstained.

change the political complexion of the system, complicating and slowing the process. Differences emerged early between those committed to Western libertarianism and limited government, and the growing appeal of the socialist commitment to activist-interventionist government and economic and social development. The West insisted that the latter could not imply individual rights with concomitant state obligations, but only societal aspirations, and surely could not be enforced as international law. The result was a bifurcation into two covenants, one on civil and political rights in the Western tradition, one on economic and social rights as in the welfare state or socialism. States that had been prepared to support articulation of general principles in a universal declaration, wished legal obligations to be more precise and more limited. Some rights articulated in the Universal Declaration did not survive the lawmaking process completed years later in a transformed political system, notably the right to property.* Some rights were added or expanded. Despite objection by Western states that self-determination was at most a right of "peoples" not of individual human beings, it was placed at the head of both emerging covenants. Over similar objections the covenants included national sovereignty over resources and other "economic self-determination."[7]

The human rights norms set forth in the international covenants, particularly that on civil and political rights, compare with those in enlightened libertarian national constitutions. Even the derogations and exceptions, *e.g.*, for national security or public order, are not on their face extravagant or unduly permissive. The weakness in the law is in its enforcement, a weakness far greater here than in other international law. Since a violation by a state of the rights of its own inhabitants does not ordinarily infringe the national interests of other parties to the agreement, they have no compelling interest to scrutinize the violating behavior and call it to account.[8]

The international law of human rights, then, cries for special

---

*The omission of the right to property reflected largely the disagreement over compensation for expropriation of alien properties (see Chapter 6), not any denial of a human right to property in other contexts. See Universal Declaration, Article 17.

machinery to enforce it, but governments have generally not been eager to create such machinery. Divisions emerged, requiring complex compromises when the law-makers struggled with methods of implementing and enforcing the Covenant on Civil and Political Rights. Most governments resisted "activist" international bodies that could scrutinize, investigate, call violators to account. It was provided that parties would report voluntarily on their compliance to a Human Rights Committee created by the Covenant, but it was not clearly provided even that this Committee should scrutinize these reports and interrogate governments about them. The Committee can hear complaints by one party that another has committed a violation only if the parties have agreed in advance to that effect.[9] That the Committee might hear complaints from private individuals or organizations was relegated to a separate optional protocol to the Covenant.[10] Even when the Committee was accorded this jurisdiction, it could only act upon complaints discreetly, with public criticism possible only after extended private efforts failed to obtain rectification. Perhaps because enforcement was weak and not threatening, states adhered to these covenants, including some—like the U.S.S.R.—whose human rights performance was found by outside observers to be less than satisfactory. But few accepted the optional provisions for either state-to-state or private complaint.[11]

The International Covenants did not exhaust the efforts to make human rights law. Particular human rights were the subject of special agreements, as earlier in the Genocide Convention. The Convention on the Elimination of All Forms of Racial Discrimination was quickly drafted; few states saw any need to resist it; many wished the political kudos, and the approval of the Black African states, that came with adhering to it.[12] Even the enforcement provisions were somewhat stronger than those in the Covenant on Civil and Political Rights, the Committee created having authority to receive "state-to-state" complaints, although it had authority to receive private complaints only if states expressly declared their submission to that procedure.[13]

Other human rights law was made regionally, in Europe and in

Latin America. The countries of Western Europe saw in human rights another acceptable cooperative integrating effort. Their institutions and values favored human rights; their relations were strong enough so that they could withstand even the strains of reciprocal scrutiny. Beginning with "core" libertarian rights and adding others by successive protocols, they created also an elaborate blend of administrative, political and judicial machinery to implement and enforce their Convention.[14] The Latin American nations, also building on common Western traditions and confident in their hemispheric relations, adopted a strong convention and some promising enforcement machinery.[15] That human rights law is difficult to enforce makes it easier to accept, since one can get the political benefits of adhering to the law without the onus of having to comply with it. While more and more states slowly adhere to the International Covenant on Civil and Political Rights, say, there is little evidence that all of them do so intending to take the obligations they assume seriously. Some states, however, will be more reluctant than others to adhere on that basis. The United States, it can fairly be said, does not enter international agreements lightly, in substantial measure because it takes commitments seriously. Its failure to adhere to human rights agreements to date is doubtless due not to any desire to remain free to act without regard to international norms, but to a reluctance to submit its behavior to scrutiny and to an insufficient interest in creating a legal basis for concerning itself with how other nations behave. It remains to be seen whether developments in the late 1970s will bring the changes they promise.[16]

The amorphous international legislative process sometimes offered possibilities for other law-making in human rights, even in the face of the principle of unanimity. The temptation and the opportunity came when states sought a legal basis for condemning, say, apartheid. Some began to argue that the U.N. Charter itself outlawed at least some egregious, universally condemned violations of human rights, like racism. Or, that the Universal Declaration, though itself not binding, served to realize and particularize the general, inchoate obligations assumed by all in the Charter. Or that the Charter, the Declaration, repeated resolutions of international bodies, and the nearly unanimous opinion and practice of states together had combined to make customary law prohibiting egregious violations, like apartheid.[17] Even nations fearful of law-making by uncertain procedures undercutting the requirement of unanimity were hard-pressed to resist such arguments when applied to racism. And African states eager to make such law against racism were impelled to consider that it might apply also to other egregious violations which no one dared justify—slavery, genocide, even torture, perhaps other forms of repression.[18]

COMPLIANCE WITH
HUMAN RIGHTS OBLIGATIONS

The forces that induce compliance with other law (Chapter 3) do not pertain equally to the law of human rights. That law is not reciprocal between states; there is no other state that is the victim or is otherwise offended when a state violates its human rights undertakings. Violations do not ordinarily affect friendly relations with other states or international credit or prestige.

Human rights law also has its own reasons for violation. Some violations, *e.g.*, apartheid, reflect important national policy; others, *e.g.*, political repressions, are indispensable to particular regimes. National police forces have their own mores and methods and are often effectively immune to control even by governments desiring that rights be respected. Governments still have not shed the attitudes that, even when they have promised to do better, how they treat their own habitants is their own business. The international covenants permit derogations from rights when necessary for an important public interest, and governments are tempted to interpret and apply those permissible derogations and exceptions as they deem appropriate. There is no meaningful scrutiny by international bodies; complaints which might be brought to U.N. bodies can be effectively smothered by the solidarity of the Third World, or by a Communist-Arab bloc that has cooperated against effective international action. Violations generally will not bring a response from other governments; and "world opinion," even if it becomes aware and condemns, can often be shrugged off. In many countries domestic institutions and other forces to support human rights are lacking or deficient.

There are also, however, forces that influence governments toward compliance with the law of human rights. Human rights have assumed a high place in the rhetoric of international relations and most governments, moved to adhere to international covenants, cannot lightly disregard them. While there is no other state that is directly "offended" by mistreatment of local inhabitants elsewhere, there are external knowledge and reaction to many human rights violations, and offending governments are sensitive to them. Some human rights, *e.g.*, freedom from racial discrimination, have become major international political issues, and many governments will be quick to react to and to seek international sanctions against violations. Other human rights, too, become major political issues and subject to sharp scrutiny and reaction. (Apartheid has even led to formal sanctions. [19]) Gross violations affect relations with some countries, and are the subject of attack in the press and by nongovernmental organizations. The obligation to report on compliance generates some inducement to comply, and international committees receive the reports and might be moved to scrutinize and act upon them. Even in the face of strong resistance, for example by the Communist-Arab bloc, there have also developed special official international mechanisms for "enforcement" "against a consistent pattern of gross violations of human rights" that help deter or persuade offending governments to discontinue them. In the European and Latin systems sophisticated institutions might bring embarrassing condemnation, and gross violations might affect relations with fellow members (*e.g.*, for the Greek Colonels in 1967–69). In many countries domestic forces with a personal or ideological interest in individual rights serve to encourage compliance even by repressive regimes, *e.g.*, vis-à-vis Jews desiring to emigrate or dissidents in the Soviet Union.

In the 1970s, forces in the United States and Western Europe began to exert influence in support of human rights in other countries. The American Congress enacted laws that made trade concessions to the U.S.S.R. depend on increased respect for human rights. Other legislation would deny or reduce military assistance and economic aid to governments that engage in "a consistent pattern of gross violations of internationally recognized human rights."[20] When the Soviet Union sought a Conference on Security and Cooperation in Europe (Helsinki, 1975) to achieve political acceptance of the status quo in Eastern Europe, Western States exacted in exchange political (if not legal) human rights commitments. The United States, at least, has seemed determined to try to hold the U.S.S.R. to that "deal."[21] Emboldened dissidents, particularly in Communist countries, invited and received support from Western governments. Communists in Western Europe spoke out for greater individual freedom. Torture and repression by some regimes that were otherwise "unpopular" (*e.g.*, in Chile) aroused reaction in the United Nations and the Organization of American States. Beginning in 1977, a new Administration in Washington spoke out vigorously against human rights violations in various countries; it seemed prepared to considered concern over such violations as a national interest to be weighed with other national interests in making foreign policy generally or toward particular countries; it promised to be least generous and less friendly to gross violators.[22] While U.S. pressures on other countries were not linked to international legal commitments (which the United States itself had not assumed), its influence supplemented other forces in the international system to promote adherence to and compliance with the norms which international law had developed. New attitudes promised that the United States itself might consider adhering to conventions and move into the main stream of the international human rights movement.[23]

INTERNATIONAL HUMAN RIGHTS IN NATIONAL POLITICS

The impetus within nations to promote or participate in international human rights depends on a nation's own ideological traditions and commitments. It comes from idealistic, libertarian, or religious constituencies, especially those with links to counterparts in other countries. It is supported by domestic constituencies eager to improve the condition of human rights in particular foreign countries, say, to help end white racism in Southern Africa or the denial of freedom of expression and movement to dissidents or Jews in the Soviet Union. Middle-level officers in foreign offices assigned responsibility for activities of international organizations, and often particularly dedicated to their ideals, recommend support for human rights measures. Secretaries of State and traditional diplomats often find it expedient to go along, so long as it is not too "expensive" and does not entail too strong a commitment to intervene against violations elsewhere.

Resistance comes not from any particular domestic constituencies threatened by such law, but from ideological-political forces that do not wish domestic matters to be subject to international law and scrutiny, and their concern is aroused only late in the process, to prevent national adherence to the law. For example, in the 1950s when the prospect that the United States might adhere to human rights covenants seemed real, members of the U.S. Senate and "activists" in the American Bar Association rose to prevent it, but they did not curtail American participation in the extensive process of developing the law. Even the Genocide Convention lay on the shelf of the Senate for some thirty years, and promises by President Carter to press for its ratification and that of other principal covenants may not succeed. In the Soviet Union, by contrast, a more centralized law-making process could decide for a long time to abstain or even resist the movement; then to participate grudgingly; later to reverse direction so as to gain political advantage abroad (and some at home) by adhering to the covenants while resisting external scrutiny and machinery to implement it and to challenge restrictive interpretations and applications.

Domestic influences on observance of human law are essentially different than for other law. In libertarian countries the forces for respect for human rights tend to invoke constitutional or other national laws and institutions; it is infrequent that international human rights add appreciably to such constitutional rights; though where there is a conflict between national and international standards, there will be a constituency to press for respecting the international standards.* Where, however, domestic laws fall appreciably short of international standards, the international standard may become a rallying point for change, and domestic forces will strive to achieve compliance with the international norms, sometimes at great risk to themselves, as in the case of Soviet dissidents.

* But there may be constitutional obstacles to doing so, as in the United States. The International Covenant on Civil and Political Rights, for example, requires every state to forbid propaganda for war of racial hatred. But unless such propaganda constitutes "incitement," laws forbidding it would probably violate the First Amendment to the U.S. Constitution.

If the character of the law's influence is as I have described it, it should be reflected in the behavior of all nations, everywhere, all the time. Given all the facts and all the other forces at play, whether rational or irrational, one should be able to understand why nations make law and why particular law does or does not emerge; further, why nations generally observe the law (even when the temptation to violate it exists), as well as the occasional violation when it occurs, the decision to postpone violation while lawful alternatives are explored, or the choice of alternative policies that are lesser violations. One should be able to see the different effects of different norms and agreements, the special character of the law of the U.N. Charter prohibiting the use of force, of political agreements, the influence on national behavior of ideological differences and competition, of Third World aspirations and solidarity, of the United Nations organization.

In this part, I attempt to look at the law's influence in operation—in the formulation of national policy in actual instances from contemporary international life. Unfortunately, as I have noted, this exploration cannot be made with full confidence and precision: policy is often not planned or deliberate; records of the process of reaching decisions are not available; the elements of decision are often confused and cannot be identified, analyzed, weighed, even by the decision-makers themselves. In substantial measure, then, the "case studies" must be speculative. One may have to rely on insufficient glimpses and debatable insights, guess why nations acted or refrained from acting (knowing only that they did so), assume their motivation principally on the basis of probabilities of international behavior, of what appears "reasonable" in the circumstances (if they acted "rationally").

The cases I have selected are not typical or random. They are, I believe, politically interesting, but principally they are the cases about which enough has been said in the public print to make speculation about them somewhat less speculative. This requirement suggests cases involving the United States or other "open societies" or cases that have received major public attention.* It has also seemed instructive to look

* One could study cases other than those I have chosen, such as U.S. intervention in the Dominican Republic (1965), or non-intervention in Angola (1976), or Soviet intervention in Hungary (1956) or Czechoslovakia (1968), though as to most of these and other less dramatic events and non-events, the study might have to be even more speculative. Communist aggression against the Republic of Korea in 1950 might be studied to determine why the Communists decided to violate law, and why the overwhelming majority of the United Nations, under United States leadership, acted to vindicate the law. But the Korean War was, in some respects, a civil war with its special law; the motivation of the many members of the United Nations, or even of some of them, would probably be difficult to disentangle. The strange failure of law in the Middle East over 20 years might well repay study if one had access to regional sources. It would be interesting to have evidence on the extent to which law was considered and the influence it had in the U.S. liberation of the *Mayaguez* or Israel's raid on Entebbe.

at the law's different influences and to see—and explain—its failures as well as it successes. But the result is inevitable distortion and misimpression: the law's essential success—the daily observance of law and obligation—does not lend itself to "case study." And to give equal, or more, attention to the law's failures may obscure the fact that the law succeeds almost all the time.

The principal effect of law—how it shapes policy in the daily operations of governments—can be best illustrated by reference to the process of making decisions. In addition, occasionally one is informed or one can see what a government might like to do but refrains from doing because of its legal obligations. Or one can compare different actions of a government to show how they reflect different obligations applicable in each case. Infrequently, the deterrent influence of law in a particular case is admitted by principal decision-makers, as in Great Britain's reaction to Nasser's nationalization of the Suez Canal, discussed in Chapter 13.

I begin the "case studies" with two international incidents where, most would agree, law failed to deter violation: the Suez-Sinai crisis of November 1956, and the abduction and trial of Adolf Eichmann. These two events or series of events are hardly representative of international behavior. That they involved violations of law, or serious allegations of violation, *ipso facto* gives them special character. Nor are they, even, representative of the small category of actions contrary to international law. Suez involved that unique and most political of norms, the rule against unilateral force. In background and context, the events resounded with undertones and overtones of colonialism. The stakes, political and economic, made for high drama and deep passion. To understand Suez, moreover, one must recapture a sense of the forces in international relations as thy were before the radical transformations of the last two decades: important changes in governments and personalities; Sputnik, and the recognition of Soviet military and technological prowess; the Sino-Soviet schism and lesser fissures in the Western bloc; the many new nations making for major changes in the political complexion of international society (reflected particularly in the United Nations); the rise (and sometimes the fall) of confident aggressive leaders in Africa and Asia.

At Suez, the law was vindicated. Two of the violators at least retained no advantage from violation and suffered unhappy consequences. The Eichmann affair teaches no such lesson. There was, in a sense, judgment on the violator, but Israel "got off" with an apology, retaining the fruits of its violation. Eichmann, too, was a very special case. The crimes for which he was tried were without precedent in history. As part of the Hitler machinery and a relic of a defeated Nazi Germany, his fate was almost totally isolated from contemporary political forces. Israel felt deeply. No other nation cared about Eichmann or dared to admit that it did. The events long antedated Arab success in exploiting the United Nations for its cause and achieving "automatic majorities" against Israel.

Still, though unique, the cases are worth stuying. The special factors I have stressed may indeed suggest that almost all violations are special, the important ones reflecting particularly the realities of international life at the time. If no two times and no two cases are alike, every case may offer insights that are applicable elsewhere.

To illustrate how law may help determine choice between alternative policies, I deal with the missile crisis in Cuba in 1962. This, too, was hardly typical of international actions. The crisis involved the global interests of the superpowers and the peace and survival of international society. But the missile incident may well illustrate what role law might play even where the stakes are the highest, when the temptation is great to see law as immaterial if not irrelevant ("*inter arma silent leges*"), when the difference between law and "policy" seems unbridgeable, when diplomats are impatient and lawyers are pressed to see the law as supporting what political officers deem to be in the national interest. Cuba may also afford a footnote to the dictum that hard cases make bad law. The Cuban quarantine has lessons, too, on the importance for law and for its influence of what nations say about what they do.[1] And it can suggest how future law may deal with past events, the uses of precedents, the responsibilities of nations and of lawyers in handling these dangerous legal weapons.

Finally, Vietnam is a more recent case, continuing while the Third World was emerging and the system changing, yet largely impervious to those changes. No volume on international law and politics in the second half of the twentieth century can neglect that major event in the international political system; no American book can be silent on that national tragedy. Even years later it is not easy to trace how the United States found itself involved in a major ground-war in Asia, contrary to all the conventional military wisdom and the lessons of Korea. It is not clear whether there was ever a single, major decision to become so involved, or a clear realization that it was likely to result if other lesser decisions were taken. But there is a common impression that in this important segment of its postwar history the United States acted in violation of international law. It seems important to understand whether this was so; if so, what forces induced the violation; if not, why the impression. Vietnam shows the consequences of confused fact and uncertain law, weighing less in the balance against major interests of major powers.

THE LAW WORKS DAILY

Most difficult to study in operation is the influence of law when law "works"—in regard to the mass of governmental actions that are consistent with international law and national undertakings. There is first the uncertainty as to whether law was at all in issue. When a government's action violates law or agreement, one may assume that the policy-makers were aware of it but decided that the action had some preponderant advantage. When conduct is consistent with law or obligation, on the other hand, one cannot even be sure that the law was considered, or relevant. There may have been no temptation, no interest in violating law. Even when the interest existed and gave way to law, the ways of the law do not lend themselves to neat demonstration. One can only assert, not prove, that the Egyptian Desk Officer in the State Department has probably not even considered proposing U-2 flights over Egyptian territory to monitor military activities. One does not know when, or whether, an Assistant Legal Adviser redrafted an instruction to the embassy in Paris because the action it proposed might violate the NATO Status-of-Forces Agreement, or objected to proposed visa regulations because they were inconsistent with United States obligations under the Headquarters Agreement with the United Nations. One cannot even guess intelligently whether voices in the government have suggested stretching the area of permissible action—say, under the Nuclear Test-Ban Treaty—and been rebuffed. The clear case—a foreign minister ruling against policy brought up to him for final decision, in substantial part because of legal considerations and the undesirable consequences of violation—is uncommon and would rarely be public knowledge. Governments do not announce that they seriously considered violating the law, or even that they might have liked to do so but were deterred.

And yet the law works all the time. With few, isolated, sporadic exceptions, nations daily live up to the obligations of thousands of treaties, to the responsibilities and duties of states under customary law, even when there might be substantial interest and substantial temptation to violate law or when, if there were no law, nations would freely act otherwise. Even when the Cold War was most bitter, the United States and the U.S.S.R. left each other alone, respecting each other's territory, property, diplomats, nationals; they carried out numerous treaties, bilateral and multilateral; they lawfully pursued trade and other forms of intercourse.

Law observance is the daily habit of government officials. They live by the law even—or especially—without the intervention of lawyers: generally, the government official does not need the lawyer to tell him what he may and may not do; it is when the non-lawyer "administers" and applies the law, when arrangements work as contemplated and there is no issue about compliance, that the law is working at its best. In less usual cases, if officials, wittingly or unwittingly, suggest what may conceivably be a violation of law or obligation, the lawyers in the foreign ministry are available to alert the political officers to possible unlawfulness. A day in the office of the Legal Adviser of the State Department finds some seventy lawyers monitoring, advising, amending, resisting, to help assure that the law is being carried out.

We may see the observance of law from another perspective. Take the Nuclear Test-Ban Treaty of 1963. When that treaty was before the United States Senate for its consent to ratification, opponents of the treaty stressed the limitations which it would impose upon the United States.[2] Among other things, they urged that the treaty will prohibit the use of nuclear weapons in self-defense, or in defense of invaded allies; it will retard development of antiballistic missile systems; it will prevent the United States from overtaking the Soviet Union in "high-yield" weapons; it will limit knowledge of the effects of nuclear explosions upon missile sites; it will prevent testing whether a nuclear weapon and its carrier will function together as a dependable system; it will prevent "prooftests" of the readiness of our nuclear stockpile; it will prohibit or restrict nuclear explosions for peaceful uses, like blasting a new interoceanic canal. Some of these arguments were denied by proponents who claimed that the treaty, properly interpreted, did not prohibit the actions in question, or that other ways consistent with the treaty could be found to achieve the same results.[3] In some of their arguments, no doubt, the critics were right: the test ban did prohibit some activities and prevent some achievements. These, then, are precise assertions of what the United States might have liked to do, and presumably would still like to do, but refrains from doing—because it has undertaken not to do them. Other activities not yet even thought of when the treaty was approved are also deterred by its terms. The unquestioned assumption of both critics and proponents was that the United States would abide by its undertakings. And, no doubt, in these respects and in others, the United States has honored the limitations, forgoing the advantages of violation in favor of the advantages of observance.

Another treaty affords another perspective. When the Department of State was urging the United States Senate to consent to the Southeast Asia Treaty, the Department was careful to underscore the differences in obligation between that treaty and the North Atlantic Treaty.[4] The latter provided that an attack on one member shall be treated as an attack on all; the Southeast Asia Treaty provided that an attack on one member shall be deemed to endanger the peace and safety of the others. This difference in language reflected, presumably, a judgment as to the different degree of American interests in the two areas. The difference of interest led to a different degree of undertaking, avoiding in SEATO an obligation of virtually automatic response. The different language was deliberate, indicating that the United States was prepared to promise more to its European allies and to carry out a greater obligation. Unlike NATO, the Senate was also told, SEATO did not imply any undertakings by the United States to join in establishing an elaborate organization or to station American forces in the area.

In both these respects the Senate was told that in SEATO the United States was promising less and would be carrying out less. The administration, the Senate, the public, and America's allies accepted that difference; they understood that it made a difference that the United States promised more in one case than in the other; they accepted, too, that what the United States promised, it was obliged to carry out, was expecting to carry out, and will be carrying out. And, in fact, the United States did carry out different obligations in regard to the two treaties. In neither case was the United States called upon to meet the basic undertaking to fight in defense of an ally.* In both "organizations" the United States carried out its "preparatory" undertakings. But in NATO, though not in SEATO, the United States joined in establishing an elaborate organization and military structure, established bases and stationed troops, made itself ready and able to carry out the ultimate obligation to defend its allies, created the credible impression on friends and others that it would do so "automatically" if the occasion arises.†

Occasionally, the influence of law is focused, and one sees law at work to deter (or impel) particular action. Great Britain, it was reported, had decided to break its agreement with France to develop the Concorde airplane; it changed its mind and carried out its agreement when France threatened suit before the International Court of Justice.[5] From time to time the American Congress, in considering legislation, bows to objections that the provision would violate some treaty provision. Occasionally the memoirs of a former policy-maker tell how law led to a particular decision. One such instance was the aftermath of the nationalization of the Suez Canal in 1956.

* Except, perhaps, in Vietnam, where the United States claimed that it was acting pursuant to its SEATO commitments.

† The difference in the national interests of the United States and of other countries involved, reflected in the difference in commitments, also helps explain why NATO has survived and SEATO has lapsed.

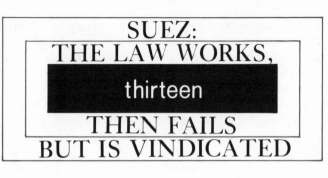

SUEZ:
THE LAW WORKS,
thirteen
THEN FAILS
BUT IS VINDICATED

In contemporary international relations "Suez" has come to suggest a military action, probably in violation of international law, a turning point in the use of force between nations and in the history of the influence of major European powers in the Middle East and beyond. Those climactic events in the fall of 1956 have swallowed up the early acts in the drama, events in which international law fared far better.

THE LAW WORKS:
NATIONALIZATION OF THE SUEZ CANAL
AND INTERNATIONAL RELATIONS

The nationalization of the Suez Canal is an instance where law helped deter, at least delay, important measures in the face of powerful pressures and with major interests at stake.[1]

On July 26, 1956, Egypt's President Nasser announced the na-

tionalization of the Universal Company of the Suez Maritime
Canal, seized its property, and expelled its officials.* The decree of
nationalization provided that compensation would be paid to the
Company's shareholders. The governments of France, the United
Kingdom, and the United States—representing shareholders in the
Company, users of the Canal, parties to the treaty governing its
status—protested this "arbitrary and unilateral seizure."[2] During
the next months there were proposals, conferences, negotiations,
but none produced any agreement between the erstwhile owners
and users of the Canal and the government of Egypt. A resolution
of the United Nations Security Council setting forth six principles
was adopted with Egyptian acquiescence, although Egypt's formal
acceptance of them was later withdrawn.[3]

Nationalization of the Canal under International Law

Although my principal concern here is with the influence of law
in determining the reactions to the nationalization of the Canal, it is
interesting to examine, too, how law influenced President Nasser's
action itself. For that purpose one must consider the legal issues
which that action involved, and they can perhaps best be deduced
from the objections to the nationalization which were raised
later by those whose interests were deeply affected.

The issues here were not the issues common to controversies
over nationalization. Ordinarily, governments do not question the
right of any government to expropriate alien properties in its territory; the controversy has been (see Chapter 6) whether international law requires compensation and, if so, whether the compensation for the taking satisfies the requirement. At Suez, the
governments owning the shares in the Suez Canal Company did
not object to the compensation as inadequate, although they did

---

* It is generally accepted that Nasser acted in angry response to a decision by the
United States not to help finance the construction of the Aswan Dam. There are
reasons to believe, however, that the idea of nationalizing the Canal did not come to
him suddenly at that time, and that anger at Western powers merely precipitated
what was already in contemplation for some later time.

have doubts as to Nasser's ability to pay.* Rather, they objected to the nationalization, as a whole, as a violation of international law and treaty.

The argument against the lawfulness of the nationalization was made by the three Western powers in a joint memorandum:

> But the present action involves far more than a simple act of nationalisation. It involves the arbitrary and unilateral seizure by one nation of an international agency which has the responsibility to maintain and to operate the Suez Canal so that all the signatories to, and beneficiaries of, the Treaty of 1888 can effectively enjoy the use of an international waterway upon which the economy, commerce, and security of much of the world depends.[4]

The argument, then, was that Egypt could not undertake nationalization because the Canal was an international waterway and the Company had "international character," as Egypt had repeatedly recognized in the various agreements it had negotiated with the Company. The government of Egypt purported to nationalize the ownership of the Canal, but ownership in this unique body of international character cannot be dissociated from the question of control of the Canal and its operation as an international waterway.[5] It was also argued that in the package of arrangements, including the Treaty of 1888 and the concessions to the Company, Egypt had expressly or by implication agreed not to terminate the concession (and therefore not to nationalize the Company) before 1968.[6]

The objections made later (and those not made) show clearly that President Nasser had legal advice and tailored his actions, his statements, and his later arguments in its light. He was careful to strengthen his legal position by not challenging the Western view that international law required just compensation for nationalized alien properties and by providing for compensation for the stock of

---

* To have argued the adequacy of compensation might have implied acceptance of Egypt's right to nationalize upon acceptable compensation.

the Company at its full value on the Paris Bourse. He was careful to separate the question of ownership of shares in the Company from the question of control and use of the Canal: he nationalized ownership of an Egyptian company organized under Egyptian law and enjoying a concession under Egyptian law; he reaffirmed Egypt's treaty obligations to permit free use of the Canal.[7] To nationalize an Egyptian company raised no problem under international law; to nationalize its ownership in no way implied interference with the freedom of use protected by treaty. That Egypt had given a concession until 1968 would not prevent the nationalization, although it may be a factor in determining compensation.

The skeptic may suggest that law did not influence Nasser in any fundamental way: it did not deter him from seizing the Canal; at most, he attended to the law only as to the way in which he acted and in what he said. Of course, if nationalizing the Canal was in fact lawful, there is no reason in law why he should be deterred. In fact, however, the law molded his action in important ways. For Nasser to undertake adequate compensation was neither easy nor inevitable; there have been numerous nationalizations before and since that did not offer adequate compensation.* For Nasser to guarantee continued freedom of passage was also not inevitable; the temptation to assert "My canal is my own"[8] might also have been great. Of course, Nasser was making a bold move and failure to compensate or to assure freedom of movement would have made strong reaction even more likely—but fear of such reactions, we know, is often why governments observe law.

Lawyers have disagreed as to whether the nationalization violated any norm or agreement and, if so, how serious the violation was.[9] President Nasser might have been told by his lawyers that

*E.g., the Cuban nationalization of properties owned by United States nationals. Compare *Banco Nacional de Cuba* v. *Sabbatino*, 376 U.S. 398, 401–403, nn. 3, 4 (1964).

That Nasser was careful to provide effective compensation would support the argument of the capital-exporting nations that international law requires it; and, since he had to pay, Nasser himself might to that extent be less eager to support those who had already begun to claim that they can nationalize without paying.

his action would pass legal muster. Even if he had some doubts about his case, he clearly sought to reduce any illegalities there might have been; obviously, he was not prepared to give up the whole idea.*

The Response of the "Victims"

International law had different relevance to the decisions of the principal victims of Nasser's action. The Suez Canal was vital for European powers dependent on the oil of the Middle East.† In 1955 almost 15,000 vessels had gone through the Canal, three-quarters of them belonging to NATO countries, one-third of them British. [10] From the viewpoint of Great Britain, in particular, Presi-

---

*If Nasser's lawyers told him that his action could be deemed a violation of law, he might still have decided to do it. A later report by a reputed confidant of President Nasser tells that he had two policy papers prepared, one setting forth the reasons in support of nationalization, the other anticipating the probable reactions of the Western powers. (See N.Y. Times, Oct. 9, 1966 § 1, p. 21.) The advantages must have loomed large: he could slap at the Western powers, and enhance his prestige at home and abroad. The Canal would be an important weapon in his hands and a source of income he sorely needed for major domestic development programs and ambitious international designs. The probable costs of his action, on the other hand, did not seem high. The legal case against him was not clear and nationalization of a company redolent of colonialism would be widely accepted if not applauded. Nor did he need to fear judgment, judicial or political. (He made it clear that while he was prepared to submit some questions for adjudication his authority to nationalize was not one of them.) In the U.N. Security Council, he could count on the Soviet veto; in the General Assembly, he had at least enough support to prevent a two-thirds vote necessary for action against him. The only danger he ran was that some powers might attempt to seize the Canal. But the use of force was illegal and was no longer "done." The Soviet Union would afford some protection, and even the United States would not wish to risk action which might throw the Arab states wholly into the Soviet camp. (The report cited above alleges that Nasser's intelligence estimates indicated Great Britain was militarily unprepared, and he expected that if Great Britain could not act promptly, it was increasingly less likely to act later.)

† Later, the closing of the Canal caused diversion to other routes and means of transport; when it finally reopened in 1976, much of the oil traffic through the Canal was not restored.

dent Nasser's action called for prompt and effective response.*
Habits of empire, indeed, called for force, and a generation earlier
it would have been invoked promptly and without hesitation.
There were voices in the British government urging force now.

Their arguments might have seemed overwhelming. Great Britain had "protected" Egypt for decades. Only recently (1954) it had
generously given up its remaining authority and perquisites.[11] Nasser's move was an intolerable affront. It was a violation, at least in
spirit, of important international agreements. Most important it
was essential that the Canal run, and Nasser could not run it. In
any event it was unthinkable that this "lifeline of empire" should be
in the control of another government, and one less than wholly
friendly and responsible. Efforts to restore international control by
negotiation were futile, for Nasser was a difficult man and he held
all the cards. It was important, moreover, to deal firmly with him,
for he was an upstart and a troublemaker and, unless put in his
place promptly, he would continue to trouble British interests in
the Middle East, French interests in Algeria, and the Western position in Asia and Africa generally. A quick and limited military action would restore the Canal and assure its future operations. President Nasser would be humbled and might have to go. Stability
would be restored.

The advantages of action were clear. The cost would not be
high.† There need be few casualties and little damage to property.
The act would be quickly done, and the *fait accompli* could not easily be undone. British relations with Nasser and with the Arab
countries that supported him were not very good and could not
seriously worsen; some of Nasser's neighbors, moreover, might be

* Although there is even less evidence as to the motivations of French policy, one
may guess that the attitudes of France were not too different from those of Great
Britain except that its interests in the Canal were not as great. France, no doubt,
deeply resented Nasser's support of "rebellion" in Algeria.

† The other "costs," *e.g.*, "world opinion," the effect on order and stability and
on the influence of law, if considered, were probably too intangible and too indeter-
minate to be given much weight.

pleased to see him humbled. The matter would probably be brought to the United Nations, but Great Britain could survive that readily. The Soviet Union might attack the action in the Security Council, but there would be no adverse action in the face of unanimous Western opposition (even apart from any veto). Legal justification for the action could be found in the fact that it was strictly limited to achieve the obviously necessary purpose of protecting an international waterway against unlawful seizure and the interruption of its operations. Politically—even in the General Assembly—the action would command substantial sympathy and some support, since many nations were shocked by Nasser's high-handed action and most believed that he could not keep the Canal operating. And Great Britain could be very conciliatory, disclaim any selfish interests, indicate willingness to negotiate with any Egyptian government, promise to withdraw promptly upon the assurance of international control, offer something to Egypt, give the United Nations some new authority in the operation and protection of the Canal. In the end, the United Nations would do nothing or very little and might even help assure an international status for the Canal (which even the Soviet Union basically favored).

I do not know whether any policy paper along these lines was ever written or how the counsels of government divided. We do know that Great Britain (and the other governments) did not at the time respond with force and for several months engaged in various diplomatic efforts to achieve an acceptable status for the Canal. Later, Prime Minister Eden wrote that from the beginning the British government had determined that

> our essential interests in this area must be safeguarded, if necessary by military action, and that the needful preparations must be made. Failure to keep the Canal international would inevitably lead to the loss one by one of all our interests and assets in the Middle East, and even if Her Majesty's Government had to act alone they could not stop short of using force to protect their position.[12]

Eden then tells us that the British did not act for two reasons:

The first answer is political. As signatories of the Charter of
the United Nations, we were bound first to seek redress by
peaceful means. Though we were conscious of the Soviet veto
and of the weakness of the United Nations as an executive
body, we knew that we must at some time take the issue to the
Security Council. We might even be able to prod them into
action. To accept this did not mean abandoning the use of
force as a last resort.[13]

The second reason given by Eden for British failure to react with
force was that Great Britain was militarily unprepared to take effective action.

One cannot, of course, weigh the two reasons given to determine
how much each contributed to the decision. The skeptic about law
may suggest that the military reason was wholly sufficient to explain what happened. (There is evidence that Great Britain began
immediately to improve its military posture in the area.) But military preparedness is often a matter of degree, and Britain obviously
had some military forces in the area.* One cannot disentangle, either, the "political" reason given by Eden into its legal component
and others. Important, no doubt, was opposition by the United
States to any military action; but that too reflected, in part, the influence of the U.N. Charter. Eden did expressly assert that Great
Britain (and France presumably) were deterred in some measure by
Charter obligations and were motivated, at least, to postpone action
which might be deemed unlawful until lawful efforts proved inadequate to safeguard their interests.

The importance of the law's achievement should not be underestimated. Violations that are not committed immediately often do
not occur at all. Lawful alternatives can develop. (In the present
case, some progress was being made at the end of October, when
the situation exploded.[14] Inertia and other forces set in. Even the
sad aftermath at Suez does not wholly contradict this. Great Britain, France and Israel, we later learned, acted in concert. But one

* That Britain was militarily unprepared may itself be some indication that the use
of force had become less acceptable and a less usable option for governments.

can only speculate whether if other developments had not pressed
Israel to action and given Britain and France an ally, and another
reason (or pretext), the British and French would have attempted to
seize the Canal (even if negotiations had not produced a satisfactory
solution). Perhaps, despite Eden's later statement that Britain
"could not stop short of using force," having failed to act promptly
and decisively, the political factors which earlier deterred military
action—including the influence of law—might have become even
stronger and prevailed. Indeed it is difficult to imagine that having
failed to react immediately, the British and French could have
taken military action later, when the shock and the tension had
ebbed, the Canal was running, and some kind of compromise had
been offered by Nasser and approved in the United Nations.[15]
Perhaps they later recognized that nationalization of the Canal gave
no plausible legal justification for the use of force, whereas acting
in Israel's wake afforded at least some colorable justification. If so,
one might say, the use of force occurred later only because, for
reasons mostly independent of the nationalization of the Canal,
Israel was prepared to attack Egypt.

One cannot deal confidently with the might-have-beens of history. One need not claim more than the evidence supports. One
can say with some confidence that in regard to the nationalization
of the Suez Canal, law helped at least to postpone the use of force
and give diplomacy an opportunity.

SUEZ-SINAI:
THE LAW FAILS BUT IS VINDICATED

At Suez and at Sinai, in the autumn of 1956, international law
failed in its primary purpose: to maintain order by deterring violations of agreed norms. But law was later vindicated, its authority
reaffirmed, and the violations largely undone.

Major hostilities in the area began on October 29, when Israeli
forces moved into the Sinai Peninsula. These hostilities had a background and context—in Arab opposition to the creation of the state
of Israel, the war of 1948, the armistice agreements of 1949, con-

tinued Arab hostility (including periodic border incidents thereafter), the closing to Israeli shipping of the Suez Canal and the Gulf of Aqaba.

The outbreak of hostilities had their immediate cause. Since 1955, Israel had been subjected to hit-and-run guerrilla raids by armed "Fedayeen" operating from Egypt and other Arab countries with the knowledge and support of the Arab governments.[16] Such raids took place again on October 20 and 24, 1956, and several Israelis were killed. On October 23, Egypt, Jordan, and Syria announced a unified command of their military forces. On October 27 Israel began mobilizing. On October 29 its forces crossed the armistice lines into the Sinai Peninsula and routed the Egyptian forces.

In consequence of the Israeli attack (and its success), the governments of France and the United Kingdom, on October 29, issued an ultimatum calling on both sides, within twelve hours, to cease hostilities and to withdraw their forces to a distance ten miles from the Suez Canal. They asked the Egyptian government to agree that Anglo-French forces should move temporarily into the area to protect the Canal. Israel accepted the ultimatum, but Egypt did not.[17] British and French airborne forces landed at key points around the Canal.[18]

The United States and the Soviet Union both condemned the resort to force, the latter even threatening military intervention. After efforts to deal with the situation in the Security Council were frustrated by veto, the General Assembly adopted resolutions calling for cease-fire and withdrawal of forces, and establishing a United Nations Emergency Force to supervise and secure the cessation of hostilities.[19] Eventually all British, French, and Israeli forces were withdrawn from Egyptian soil.

The Attack at Sinai under International Law

It was Israel that initiated major military action in the area, on October 29. Was this in violation of international law? If so, why did international law fail to inhibit Israel?

The members of the United Nations at the time, and most

writers, have taken the view that the action of Israel was a violation of Article 2(4) of the U.N. Charter.[20] There was clearly a use of force against the territorial integrity and political independence of Egypt.* The only question is whether Israel's action was within the exception permitted by Article 51 for self-defense against armed attack. The argument for Israel would recite that Egypt had insisted that there was still a state of war with Israel (which the Arab states had created in violation of the Charter, and which Egypt continued to invoke to justify its denial of the Suez Canal to Israeli vessels); that this state of war, plus repeated Arab threats to destroy Israel, the recent announcement of a joint Egyptian-Jordanian-Syrian High Command, and the recurrent "Fedayeen" raids were part of a single, recurring armed attack that began in and had continued since 1948. The denial of the Suez Canal to Israel in violation of the Treaty of 1888, of the armistice agreements, and of an express resolution of the Security Council would be cited as additional evidence of the continued aggression.[21] And Israel's action was not a disproportionate response since only destruction of the "Fedayeen" bases and their equipment could assure its security.[22] There also are those who might justify Israel with the argument that the Charter did not outlaw the use of force in "anticipatory self-defense" or to protect vital interests,[23] but the government of Israel eschewed such broad readings of the Charter.

Israel's situation was unique and its arguments were not implausible. Still, Israel's lawyers, one may guess, recognized that the contemplated action might be viewed as a violation of the Charter. And there are many reasons why one might have expected Israel to obey this international law. Although Israel was a new nation, it drew on long roots of law and law observance. It had well-developed legal institutions and many lawyers trained in Western legal traditions. As a small country surrounded by enemies, Israel also needed the protection of international law, particularly of the United Nations Charter. It owed its existence, in substantial measure, to the United Nations organization and it was concerned for

* As commonly interpreted. See Chapter 7.

the support of the majority of its members.* It had a strong legal and political case against renewed Arab attacks (which it continued to expect) and did not wish to jeopardize its case by unlawful and unwise action.

If nevertheless Israel disregarded the probable law, there must have been much on the other balance. There was domestic pressure on the government to "do something" about the "Fedayeen" raids. There were, principally, Israel's security needs as it saw them. The cost of inaction loomed high, with increasing Arab armament and aggressiveness and harassing border attacks that took lives and interrupted the life of a struggling country; unless something was done, the Arabs might be emboldened to strike harder, or to goad Israel into striking, at a time of *their* choosing. The Sinai action, then, would, at the very least, dramatize the situation as intolerable. If successful, it would put an end to border attacks and the danger of all-out attack for some time thereafter. It might permit capture of important equipment. It could provide a buffer on Egyptian territory against further Egyptian attacks. It could open the Gulf of Aqaba to Israel. If it truly succeeded—and if Anglo-French cooperation helped seize control of the Canal—it might finally open the Suez Canal to Israeli shipping. And it might even topple Nasser, cause instability and disarray in Egypt and additional humiliation to all the Arabs, thus further reducing the threat of Arab attacks for a long time and perhaps even leading to a true peace in the area.

The gains to be anticipated were substantial. On the other hand, the cost of the action and of the possible violation of international law did not seem very high. Israel had confidence in its military prowess and disdain for Egypt's army and the other Arab military forces; Anglo-French military support was promised.[24] Off the battlefield, Israel had little to suffer in response from the Arabs; there were no relations with them and their hostility was already acute.

* That concern largely evaporated much later, when the Arabs began to muster Third World majorities against Israel on various issues (in Israel's view without justification) and by distorting and abusing the Charter, the organization, and its processes.

In the United Nations, there might be some criticism, but Israel had a politically sympathetic position even if not an undeniable legal case. Israel had been making friends in Africa and Asia and had some sympathy in Latin America; Nasser had lost friends and sympathy by the seizure of the Canal (even if he also had gained prestige in some quarters).[25] Israel could, of course, count on British-French political support. Soviet hostility could be expected but it would not matter; the United States, in the face of British and French support and just before a national election in which a large "Jewish vote" was at stake, might chastise mildly but would not urge or permit strong action.

The Anglo-French Action under International Law

On October 30, British and French forces landed around the Canal. If the decision was carefully considered, the governments must have been aware that most lawyers would consider the action a violation of Article 2(4) of the United Nations Charter.[26] The action at Suez was clearly a use of force against the territorial integrity and political independence of Egypt. Nor could that use of force be justified within the exception of Article 51. On its face, at least, that provision permits unilateral force only to defend oneself or another member if an armed attack occurs; the British-French attack could hardly fall within that exception.[27]

Whatever the lawyers said, the governments did not claim that the use of force was justified because Nasser's nationalization of the Canal had violated international law or had jeopardized their vital interests. After the passage of months and intervening negotiations with some prospect of success, that justification would have appeared ludicrous. Their ultimatum, and the arguments later made in support of it, principally asserted a right to act as "volunteer policeman," to use force to separate Israel and Egypt in order to protect the Canal—akin to the right, in some municipal systems, for a private citizen to intervene to put down a breach of the peace if the police failed to do so.[28] Accepting the *bona fides* of the justification, the ultimatum offered a novel interpretation of the Charter. Note that it was a narrow exception to Article 2, tailored to the circumstances, not likely to recur often, and not subject to the dangers of some broader theory which would have permitted force at any time in support of vital interests as each nation saw them. Still, the United Kingdom and France might have expected that it was not a theory that would be acceptable to most nations. One may even wonder whether these countries would be prepared to promote this proposition as a general principle of law.

Why did the law fail to deter them? Again, one can only speculate. France and the United Kingdom played important roles in the creation of the United Nations and the drafting of its Charter. They had no doubt taken seriously their undertaking to eschew unilateral force. Both were generally law-abiding countries with an interest in law observance and developed institutions to take account of law. In both countries there were domestic forces, including powerful opposition parties, that might condemn such violations of the Charter.[29] On the other hand, perhaps, although the Charter had been influential in the decision not to respond to the nationalization by immediate use of force, its influence was not yet strong enough to rule out force altogether. There were long traditions, old habits, established institutions involving reliance on military power, in particular to support interests of empire and trade in Asia and Africa. Perhaps neither France nor Great Britain had yet fully recognizecd that the day of white force against independent nations on the non-white continents was over.

There was, of course, the calculation of cost and advantage. No doubt the principal motivation of the Anglo-French action was to take the Canal from Egypt. If their action on the heels of Israel's victories also toppled President Nasser, so much the better. As regards the Canal, they had refrained from prompt military action because of American insistence and to see what political pressure could achieve. But President Nasser had not given way, and indeed his action had brought him new prestige and new confidence. Diplomatic efforts, including those in the United Nations, had produced some concessions to the international character of the Canal but would still leave Egypt with more control than was desirable or safe. Most of the reasons for moving against the Canal—the great advantages and the low cost—remained persuasive. Perhaps it would be difficult, expecially after the intervening delay and the diplomatic efforts, to act in admitted response to the nationalization, but Israel's problems, interests, and plans gave a new and better opportunity. Now force could be used not in response to Nasser's nationalization but for the purpose of protecting the Canal against destruction due to Israeli-Egyptian hostilities. In this context the costs of the action might be even lower. Militarily, Egypt, defeated by Israel, could do little to frustrate the operation. Politically, the United Kingdom and France could "ride out" whatever the defeated President Nasser and his friends, even the Soviet Union, could attempt. In the Security Council, the Soviet Union could muster few votes against the united opposition of all the Western powers and their friends; in any event they could veto action in the Security Council, as indeed they did after Israel marched.[30] In the Assembly, there might be criticism, particularly from the Asian-African bloc, but especially if Nasser was humbled or even replaced, the United Kingdom and France could be very conciliatory. They could stress the limited and temporary nature of their action, their concern for the international waterway so essential to world trade, their readiness to withdraw after settling the Canal question with a new Egyptian government, and perhaps even their contribution to relieving another world sore spot by bringing a measure of peace also between the Arabs and Israel. In such circumstances even those most concerned for the Charter and for international law might accept the justification claimed for the action or treat it as a small violation—in any event, one best quickly forgotten after the situation was restored.

Such might have been the position paper written in the Foreign Office or the Quai d'Orsay, taking into account the views of the lawyers. And the policy might have succeeded in some measure if the military operation had been more successful. In the end, these calculations, even more than those of Israel, went awry, partly because they did not anticipate the strong threat of intervention by the Soviet Union, largely because of erroneous assumptions as to what the United States would say and do. Israel, in fact, despite all that happened later in the United Nations and the eventual withdrawal of its forces, did not miscalculate badly. If it did not succeed in getting passage through the Canal or toppling Nasser, it dealt a severe blow to his prestige and that of the Egyptian army, dramatized an intolerable situation, halted the "Fedayeen" raids, obtained access to the Gulf of Aqaba, and succeeded in bringing into the area a United Nations force as a buffer against attack and further raids. The British and French, on the other hand, suffered deep humiliation and mortal injury to their aspirations to maintain big-power status, important damage to their relations with the Arabs, and the end of any hope of restoring some international control over the Suez Canal.

The Law Vindicated

If the law worked during the early months of Nasser's nationalization of the Canal, the second part of the Suez story is an instance of the law's failure: it did not deter violations. It is also an instance of the law's vindication: the violations were judged and condemned, the unlawful acts largely undone, the law of the Charter reaffirmed and established. The law was applied by the General Assembly, a highly political body. The members were no doubt moved by a variety of motives, among which the authority of the Charter and of the United Nations itself were not insignificant.

It is pertinent to ask, in particular, whether international law played any role in the major determinants in the drama, in the attitudes of Russia and the United States. In political terms one can explain their attitudes without mention of international law. The Soviet Union was delighted with events that diverted attention and political pressure from its military action against the rebellion in Hungary. The Soviet Union also seized an opportunity to pursue the policy it had already initiated of wooing the Arabs and trying to replace Western influence with their own. Condemnation of Israel, even more of Britain and France, suited that policy. Russia could gain great kudos with the Arabs even if French and British forces were not in fact withdrawn. That in part under threat of Soviet military intervention the Western powers had to withdraw gave the Soviet Union a new standing as friend of the Arabs.

It was exactly this political gain for the Soviet Union which Secretary of State Dulles sought to avoid or minimize, and which largely determined the policy of the United States.[31] Dulles strove to maintain Arab friendship and to prevent an Arab-Soviet alignment. Perhaps Dulles also feared that the Soviet Union might indeed send troops to aid Egypt and obtain a military toehold in the Middle East.* The position of the United States, on the side of Soviet Union and against its principal allies, can be explained, then, as an effort to keep Russia out of the Middle East and to keep the Arabs from aligning themselves firmly on Russia's side. But many are persuaded that the United States, at least, was substantially influenced by its view of the law. It saw the attacks on Egypt as violations of the Charter, which, if tolerated, would damage the principles against the use of force and the future of the United Nations as an influence for peace and security. American spokesmen, including Secretary Dulles and President Eisenhower, repeatedly invoked the Charter and expressed sorrow that they felt obliged to vindicate the law even against their country's best friends.[32] Others in the United States, including lawyers sympathetic to Israel, felt that it would be a serious blow to the United Nations and the law against force if the attacks were not disowned and condemned. (It is another question whether, even as a matter of good law, the United States should not have pressed for United Nations action, which, while requiring the withdrawal of the attacking forces, would have achieved some settlement between Israel and Egypt and perhaps imposed some international control over the Canal.[33])

That Russia, too, cared about the law of the Charter is a possibility that few in the West would even consider. Still, it may well be that the law against external force is in the Soviet interest to maintain. The Soviet Union may have begun to recognize by 1956

---

*Domestic opposition to this policy in the United States was not effective against President Eisenhower's tremendous popularity; perhaps it was decided that the Republican party could not command "the Jewish vote" in any event.

that war is too dangerous, that external aggression could not succeed, that the world community will no longer tolerate it, that Soviet interests do not require it, indeed that dynamic communism must use indirect, more subtle methods, and that outlawing war would improve the climate for internal "wars of liberation." [34] The Soviet Union, then, it is plausible to suggest, also was partly concerned to vindicate the law against unilateral, external force.

I conclude that, at Suez, after helping to induce Great Britain and France not to react immediately with force to Nasser's nationalization of the Canal, the law failed to deter them from collusion with Israel in important violations of the Charter of the United Nations. But the transgressors were called to order, and members of the United Nations, including at least the United States, were motivated, in some measure, by concern to uphold the principles of the Charter and the effective authority of the United Nations organization for maintaining peace and security.

In turn, the actions in the Suez-Sinai drama had their effect on international law.* The position of the United States and the Soviet Union, supported by the overwhelming majority of members in the United Nations, reaffirmed the norm of Article 2(4), and did so against major powers. Rejected too, in effect, were arguments that the Charter took a broad view of "armed attack" which justified self-defense, that it permitted anticipatory self-defense, national "police action," or the use of force to protect vital interests against injustice. The facts of the case indeed demonstrated that what each nation believes is necessary (or important, or conducive) to its survival (or security, or national interest) is a very uncertain affair. What may at one moment seem essential may prove hardly so at the next; within the same government there will be many views as to whether a particular action is essential to survival, or only possibly convenient to some immediate interest; those outside

---

* By nullifying all efforts to establish some permanent international control for the Canal, the Suez-Sinai affair helped confirm the right of a nation to exercise eminent domain within its territory, even as to property which had some international character, and even in the face of undertakings not to do so.

will often see the situation quite differently. Suez enhanced the authority of the United Nations, showing its particular effectiveness when the United States and the Soviet Union joined to lead it; and it is credible, as claimed, that the United States, perhaps others, felt compelled to act as it did because of the existence of the United Nations and the influence of its members. Suez helped confirm that, despite provocation, external unilateral force against another nation was not acceptable international behavior, at least by big powers against small, at least by Western nations against Asian or African states.* It remained to be seen whether the principle could also withstand other forces—opposition to colonialism or racial oppression, the rising influence of Communist China, the declining influence of India, new instabilities, new configurations of power and influence in and out of the United Nations, the sad example of the Kashmir war of 1965, and, most seriously, the spreading hostilities in Vietnam.

*Later Israel-Arab hostilities, in June 1967, and October 1973, do not vitiate these conclusions. See pp. 172–73, above.

THE LAW FAILS:

fourteen

THE CASE OF ADOLF EICHMANN

The abduction and trial of Adolf Eichmann in 1960 involved violations of international law. The law in issue was not some new, controversial political norm or agreement but an old, traditional norm, dear to all nations—the exclusive sovereignty of a state in its own territory. The case did not involve major political interests but only the fate of one man who was accused of heinous crime. Charged with violation, and virtually pleading guilty, was Israel, a state which, at the time surely, had unusual interest in and concern for international law. Why did the law fail to deter Israel? Exceptionally, the case was brought to the United Nations, but Israel "got off" with an apology instead of the reparation usual in such cases, and it kept the fruits of its violation. Why was the law not vindicated by an adequate response?

In May 1960 Adolf Eichmann was seized in Argentina by Israeli citizens, abducted, and brought to Israel.[1] Argentina protested and brought a complaint against Israel in the Security Council for viola-

tion of international law.[2] The Security Council reaffirmed the
principle of territorial integrity and called upon Israel to "make appropriate reparation in accordance with the Charter of the United
Nations and the rules of international law."[3] Argentina accepted
Israel's public apology as full reparation for the offense.[4]

The government of Israel brought Eichmann to trial under an
Israeli statute enacted in 1950 to punish "crimes against the Jewish
people" and "crimes against humanity" committed in various European countries before and during the Second World War.[5] The
prosecution presented evidence that Eichmann was a principal ar-
chitect and the principal executor of the Nazi policy to bring a
"final solution" of the "Jewish problem" by extermination of all
Jews wherever Nazi power reached. He was convicted, the conviction was affirmed on appeal, and Eichmann was executed.

ISSUES OF INTERNATIONAL LAW

The details of Eichmann's identification, seizure, abduction, and
transportation out of Argentina have not yet been wholly revealed.
When Argentina later brought the issue to the United Nations Security Council, the debates revealed an issue of fact: were the persons who abducted Eichmann in Argentina agents of the government of Israel or—as the Israeli spokesman insisted—private
persons who, though citizens of Israel, in no way represented the
government? If Eichmann was abducted and spirited from Argentina by private persons, brought to Israel and handed to the authorities "on a silver platter," there was presumably a private violation of Argentine law but probably no violation of international law
by Israel, even when it decided not to return him to Argentina.*
There is evidence, however, that the Israeli government was involved, that the persons who abducted Eichmann acted with the
blessing if not under direct orders of the government.[6] There is evidence, too, that he was brought from Argentina on an airplane of

* Israel's public approval of what these abductors had done might, however, have
been considered an unfriendly act toward Argentina.

Israel's government-owned airlines; indeed, that the plane had come on an official mission, to bring Israel's Minister of Security to Argentina to represent Israel at Argentina's Independence Day celebrations, and returned to Israel without the Minister but with Eichmann.[7] Also, Israel's later public apology to Argentina may be viewed as an admission of its involvement.

Assuming that the Israeli government initiated, or joined, or ratified the abduction, it committed an international tort. The international norm in this case is clear beyond dispute; all nations would resent and insist on rectifying its violation. Israel violated the territorial integrity of Argentina by purporting to exercise powers there without the consent of the Argentine government, indeed in gross violation of its laws against kidnaping.

Different issues of international law were raised when Israel proceeded to bring Eichmann to trial. Israel probably did not view seriously the legal objections to trying Eichmann under a 1950 Israeli statute for crimes committed earlier than that date. Although the Universal Declaration on Human Rights had declared against *ex post facto* laws, international law as yet knew no such principle. As applied, in particular, to the crimes of the Nazis, other states (including the Federal Republic of Germany) had adopted statutes to enable them to punish earlier Nazi atrocities.[8] The Nürnberg Trials—on which the Israeli law was based—were not inhibited by the *ex post facto* argument.[9] Also, while Israel's statute authorizing trial and punishment was enacted after the fact, Eichmann's acts—participation in murders—were probably violations of the laws of all nations, and were presumably criminal in the countries in which they were committed at the time they were committed.*

The issues of international law raised by the trial involved questions of "prescriptive jurisdiction"—the right of a state to prescribe and apply its laws to persons and actions like those in this case.[10] Traditional international law clearly permits the application of a

---

*Even if committed during military occupation. The occupied countries later commonly "restored" their laws and applied them to occupation actions.

nation's laws to acts committed on its national territory by anyone, or to acts committed by a state's own national even in a foreign country.[11] Eichmann did not fall into either of these categories: he was not a citizen of Israel; he did not commit his crimes in Israel. Beyond these cases, as to whether and when a nation may punish an alien for an act committed abroad, there was confusion and disagreement (and there still is). It is generally accepted that a nation may punish a few limited acts against its security or national integrity: for example, if it can catch them, a nation may bring to trial and punish foreign nationals who counterfeit its currency abroad.[12] This principle could not avail Israel. Some nations have claimed a right to punish crime committed abroad where the victim of the crime is one of their nationals. But that principle—the right to vindicate the "passive personality" of a state in the person of its nationals—was (and is) widely rejected.[13] In Eichmann's case its invocation would be particularly questionable since the victims were not citizens of Israel. Israel's occasional claim to represent the Jewish victims of Hitler may be a political and sentimental claim for a political or sentimental representation: such representation has not been commonly accepted as legally equivalent to the relation of a state to its nationals under international law. Israel's claim to jurisdiction, then, would probably have to depend on some basis of "universality"—that international law directs or permits all nations to exercise jurisdiction over crimes like Eichmann's, which have been denominated "international crime," as they do for piracy or (by treaty) for counterfeiting or traffic in slaves or narcotics.[14] It has also been argued that in many circumstances public international law permits the enforcement of criminal law "by proxy": any nation may punish an offense which it deems criminal if it was a crime where the act was committed.[15] How an international court would have decided this issue of Israel's right to try Eichmann cannot be asserted with confidence.

For Israel, then, the Eichmann affair involved one clear violation of international law—the abduction from Argentina—and one questionable action—the application of its laws to Eichmann for the acts in question. To explore the influence of law in Israel's decisions, or the reasons why Israel decided to act regardless of law, one can dispose first of the question of jurisdiction. Leaving aside how Israel expected to obtain the criminals, it had apparently decided the legal questions as to its jurisdiction to its own satisfaction in 1950, when it adopted the law providing for these trials, and later when it proceeded to hunt for Eichmann and others in the hope of bringing them to trial. In that decision Israel apparently thought it had at least a colorable claim that its action was permissible under international law. Perhaps it thought it could create new law establishing universal jurisdiction of Nazi crimes; perhaps it thought it could establish a right in the state of Israel to try Nazis charged with crimes against the Jews. The law of prescriptive jurisdiction was sufficiently fluid, and the case of the Nazis and the position of the state of Israel sufficiently exceptional, that holding these trials might prove not to be a violation after all.

In regard to Eichmann in particular there were other reasons why traditional limitations about prescriptive jurisdiction might prove immaterial, if not irrelevant. In traditional theory, international law governs the actions of states against other states, and it is not clear what other state would be "offended" by the exercise of jurisdiction over Eichmann. The abduction was an offense against Argentina since its territorial sovereignty was violated; but Eichmann was not a national of Argentina and his trial, if improper, was not a wrong to Argentina. He had been a national of Germany but may have forfeited that nationality, at least the right of its protection, by passing himself as a stateless refugee;[16] Germany, too, then may have had no basis for objecting to Israel's exercise of jurisdiction. This conceptual difficulty apart, Israel might well have considered that any violation of the law involved would bring no undesirable consequences because no other nation would object. In fact, the Federal Republic of Germany announced that it would not object to the trial;[17] and Poland and Soviet Russia, in whose territory some of the crimes had been committed, officially approved Israel's trial of Eichmann.[18]

In the case of Eichmann himself, of course, Israel no doubt viewed the abduction and trial as a single policy. Any possible

violations involved in the trial were submerged in the original violation by the abduction. If Israel was prepared to commit that violation, it would not be deterred by debatable additional illegality in
holding the trial. The question remains: why did the forces which
motivate nations to observe law fail in this instance? It may well be
that the decision to seize Eichmann was taken quickly and without
thorough consideration of law or of political consequences. It may
be that domestic pressures were so strong as to render international
costs of violation immaterial. (A regime which had found Eichmann and allowed him to escape would face serious difficulties
even within the governing party.) For our purposes, I assume careful consideration of all the factors and alternatives.

As a democratic country with a developed respect for law, Israel
had special need for the protections of international law, for
friendly world opinion, and for friends among governments. The
good will of Argentina had a particular importance in view of the
large Jewish population in that country. Unlike Suez, the Eichmann case did not involve Israel's security or other "vital interests."

But for Israel there were the advantages of violation and the costs
of nonviolation. Chiefly, there was the fear that if Eichmann were
not seized, he might escape judgment completely, or that, in any
event, Israel would not be the one to bring him to trial. Neither of
these possibilities seemed tolerable. Israel has claimed a special
relationship to the Jewish victims of Hitler. Many of its citizens
were themselves survivors of Hitler's efforts and blood relatives of
the victims. There were tremendous domestic pressures in Israel
for the capture and punishment of remaining Nazi criminals, and
Eichmann was a "big fish" believed to be particularly responsible
for the murder of six million Jews. And Israel's leaders saw the
right of Israel to try Eichmann as a "historical imperative."[19] Israel
may have wished also, by the trial, to establish the principle of its
"succession" to the rights and status of the Jews killed by Hitler, as
well, perhaps, as some basis for representing all Jews today. Israel
also wished to hold the trial to publicize the Nazi crimes
against the Jews for the education of the world, the new generation of Germans, perhaps even the new generation of Israelis.[20]

If Eichmann were not seized but his extradition from Argentina requested, Eichmann would be warned and might again disappear. And although Argentina had once promised to surrender any war criminals,[21] it might claim that its promise only contemplated delivery of war criminals for trial before international, Nürnberg-type tribunals. Or, it might say, Eichmann should be tried by other countries—Germany, or the countries in which Eichmann had operated, or the countries of nationality of the Jews killed. Argentina might be unwilling or unable to extradite him to Israel, particularly since there was no extradition treaty between the two countries, since the crimes charged were committed before the state of Israel existed, and since they might even smack of "political crimes" that are not usually extraditable.[22]

Israel guessed—correctly, as it proved—that the costs of violation would not be high and would be forgotten in the drama of the trial. First, it was hoped, perhaps naïvely, that where Eichmann was found and how he got to Israel might remain a secret, that Argentina might never know that its territory had been violated. Perhaps, too, there was some small hope that Argentina would accept the story that the abduction was the work of private Israeli "volunteers," hence not a violation of international law. In any event, it was probably expected that Argentina would not wish, or dare, to make too much of an issue on behalf of Eichmann (especially as he had, apparently, come to Argentina on false papers and under false pretenses). At least, Israel was confident, it could keep the fruits of the action (i.e., bring Eichmann to trial). Argentina would not insist on Eichmann's return; general relations with Argentina would not be jeopardized since the extraordinary passions of the case would render the offense pardonable.

In fact, Israel did not guess far wrong. Its authorities may not have expected Argentina to bring the case to the Security Council, but even that did not prove too costly. Argentina and other nations were, as anticipated, reluctant to appear to champion Eichmann or to interfere with his trial, even in order to vindicate the universally accepted principle of territorial integrity. The Council required Israel to make "appropriate reparation," but the debates revealed some understanding, if not sympathy, for Israel's position.[23] Argentina accepted a public apology and did not insist on Eichmann's return, the usual remedy in such cases.[24] Argentina may even have been relieved to be quit of the Eichmann problem cleanly. And some countries—West Germany?—may have been relieved that they did not have to hold the trial themselves.

The Eichmann case may be so unique as to afford no precedent for anything—not for development in law, not for national or international reactions to violation. But it will inevitably be necessary in the future to consider the case and its effect on international law. Argentina's protest, the Security Council's resolution, and Israel's apology reaffirmed the principle of territorial integrity. It is unlikely that nations will be more tolerant of such violations, although ideological conflict, guerrilla operations, and more efficient means of concealment may increase kidnapings and make it more difficult to prevent, detect, or prove them.[25] Kidnaping will surely remain an unmitigated violation; there is no evidence that Argentina's failure to insist on Eichmann's return had set a precedent for milder responses in the future and weakened the deterrent effect of the law. There may be a different kind of precedent in that Argentina brought the case to the Security Council and the Council acted upon a basically bilateral dispute that did not involve peace and security. In the Eichmann case, then, international law may have taken another small step in moving from tort to crime, from a system in which there is response by the victims alone to one of communal responsibility.*

For the law of jurisdiction, again, the Eichmann case may be too extraordinary to serve as precedent. Unpunished Nazi criminals will not long be with us. The possibility of new genocides cannot, alas, be totally discounted; but it is far from clear that their perpetrators will be brought to judicial trial, and the coincidence of factors impelling exercise of jurisdiction solely on the "universal" principle would in any event be rare. Still, one may expect that the

---

*Compare the Report of the International Law Commission, p. 90 n.

Eichmann case will be cited as some authority for "universality" for the crime of genocide, and for "proxy" as a basis of jurisdiction, perhaps even for "passive personality" generally. The case may also contribute to a re-examination of the law of prescriptive jurisdiction—to what actions, by whom, a state may apply its law. We can begin to ask anew why there should be any limitations on jurisdiction, what they should be, who should be able to vindicate them and in what ways? Conceptual limitations that assume territorial sovereignty but some "inherent limitations" on the authority of states to act outside their borders are losing persuasiveness. Conceptual arguments which see issues of jurisdiction exclusively in terms of the rights of states, rather than of individuals involved, are also becoming outdated.* Surely, the bases for jurisdiction must be redefined to reflect fairness to the individual, the competing or conflicting interests of states, the needs of a growing world community. The Eichmann case reminds us of an area of the law that has not yet been shaken by the new winds.

The Eichmann case, surely, does not suggest that law is without effect on the conduct of nations. Rather, it suggests the hard case, the exception that tests the rule. Despite clear violation, one may say that the particular norm was violated but emerged unscathed. That Argentina insisted on its rights but reacted moderately and soberly, that the case gained the attention of the world, and that the Security Council acted to reaffirm the law may make further

---

* If the rights of another state only, and not of individuals, are violated by an improper exercise of jurisdiction, some "violations" might not, in fact, be subject to law. Ordinarily the state affronted is the state of nationality of the person to whom law is "improperly" applied, but what state is affronted when law is applied improperly to a stateless person? Some argument might be made that there is an affront to the state in whose territory an act is committed when another state seeks to apply its laws to that act, but that suggestion is still questionable.

Growing concern for the rights of individuals suggests that international law might impose some limitations on the exercise of jurisdiction by a state as a matter of fairness to the accused, whether or not any state is affronted thereby. It has not yet entered into the human rights conventions, *e.g.*, the Covenant on Civil and Political Rights.

violations of this character less likely and enhance the influence of the United Nations in support of law generally. Whether the case would have had the same progress and outcome in the international system and the United Nations of more recent days is an interesting but hypothetical speculation.

THE LAW'S OTHER INFLUENCES:

fifteen

THE CUBAN QUARANTINE

The Cuban missile crisis of 1962 saw the world's superpowers in deadly confrontation in circumstances involving their security, their global interests, and the peace and survival of international society. Since it ended successfully for the United States, it has become a highlight of American foreign policy after the Second World War. Friend and enemy have expressed deepest respect for President Kennedy's policy and diplomacy during those fateful days; it has become a standard by which American actions since then have been measured (and sometimes found inadequate).

To explore the influence of law on the political actions that comprised the "missile crisis," we should look for law in the decisions of many governments: what was said about law in the Kremlin, in Havana, in the foreign offices of naval powers whose vessels were interdicted by the blockade, in the councils of governments instructing their delegates to the United Nations or the Organization of American States, in the meetings—and in the corridors—of those organizations, in the office of U.N. Secretary General U Thant. Hopefully, scholars may someday shed light on the different influences of law in different places. I, of necessity, limit myself to the decisions and deliberations of the government of the United States.

International law, I believe, influenced the policies of the United States, the decision to do what was done and to say what was said. The processes of decision are not yet available for public scrutiny, but fortunately our speculations need be less than wholly speculative: American society is open, and adroit journalists have again succeeded in pulling apart the curtains of policy-making.[1] In the decision taken, we know, lawyers were present at virtually all the deliberations. The Attorney General of the United States was the President's brother and enjoyed a special working relation with him. George Ball, a lawyer, was Under Secretary of State. The legal advisers of the State Department took part at all stages. Adlai Stevenson, the United States representative to the United Nations, also a lawyer, was consulted.[2]

On October 22, 1962, President Kennedy addressed the people of the United States by television in an atmosphere of crisis. He announced that the United States had clear evidence that the Soviet Union was in the process of installing in Cuba "large, long-range, and clearly offensive weapons of sudden mass destruction." These weapons constituted "an explicit threat to the peace and security of all the Americas," and their introduction was "a deliberately provocative and unjustified change in the *status quo* which cannot be accepted by this country." The President announced that the United States would impose a defensive maritime quarantine to prevent the further introduction into Cuba of offensive missiles, and to induce the Soviet Union to withdraw the missiles already there.[3]

On the same day, the United States placed the Cuban situation before the United Nations Security Council and asked for an urgent meeting of the Council.[4] The Council met on the following day, October 23, and discussed the crisis and the proposed quarantine but took no action.[5] On that day, the Organization of American States, acting under the Rio Treaty of 1947, adopted a resolution recommending that the members

> take all measures, individually and collectively, including the use of armed force, which they may deem necessary to ensure that the Government of Cuba cannot continue to receive from the Sino-Soviet powers military material and related supplies which may threaten the peace and security of the Continent and to prevent the missiles in Cuba with offensive capability from ever becoming an active threat to the peace and security of the Continent.[6]

In the evening of October 23, after the action of the OAS, President Kennedy proclaimed the quarantine to take effect on the following day.[7] Under the quarantine all vessels, of whatever nationality, in defined zones would be intercepted but would be allowed to continue to Cuba if they were not carrying prohibited materials.[8]

Pursuant to the quarantine, vessels of the Soviet Union and of other nations were trailed, boarded, inspected. Soviet submarines were located, tracked, surfaced, and photographed. Other vessels apparently destined for Cuba changed course and proceeded elsewhere. No vessels were forcefully seized or diverted, and military force was not actually used.

The outcome is well known. The Soviet Union agreed to discontinue bringing missiles into Cuba; it agreed to discontinue building its missile bases in Cuba and to dismantle and remove missiles that had already been installed. The United States agreed to end the quarantine and gave assurances against an invasion of Cuba.[9] When Premier Castro refused to agree to United Nations inspection in Cuba to monitor Soviet compliance with its undertakings, the Soviet Union permitted its vessels going to and from Cuba to be inspected (from alongside) by American officials.[10] The United States also maintained surveillance of Cuba from the .air.[11]

CONTEXT FOR POLICY

What happened in and about Cuba in October–November 1962 can be understood only in a complex context that included the basic confrontation between East and West, the strategic import of the new military technology, the significance for both the Soviet Union and the United States of Castro's alignment with the Communist powers, the history and politics of the Western Hemisphere, domestic politics in the United States, and much more. None of these can be ignored in any examination of the effect of law on American decisions, particularly in an attempt to assess cost and advantage of compliance with or violation of international law as seen by American policy-makers at the time.

Let me assert some over-simple propositions. The United States had been deeply disturbed by Castro's Cuba as a foothold for Soviet communism in the Western Hemisphere. A Soviet satellite in Cuba is inconsistent with the policy of the United States, dating from the Monroe Doctrine of 1823, to exclude new European penetrations of the Western Hemisphere. An aggressive Soviet satellite in Cuba not only set a bad example, but also was dangerous as a base for propaganda and subversion in Latin America. The people of the United States and congressional leaders were also disturbed by the presence of a Soviet military base in the Caribbean, so close to the shores of the United States.

In an earlier day the United States might have dealt with this disturbing occurrence by using military means to replace Premier Castro by Cuban leadership with a friendly orientation. But by 1962, in Latin America surely, the day of overt unilateral intervention by the United States seemed over, replaced by collective judgment if not by truly collective action. Military and geographic realities had compelled the governments of the area to accept United States protection for the Western Hemisphere against external attack, as well as its power and influence to maintain peace within the hemisphere, but they have insisted that action must be based on collective judgment and have been vehement against unilateral intervention in the affairs of any state in the region. The Cuban revolution, moreover, had stirred sympathetic echoes in various Latin American countries; it was only Castro's alignment with the Soviet Union that led to collective adverse judgments and actions, but even that alignment would not bring support or tolerance for unilateral use of force by the United States against Cuba.

The United States, then, aware of its obligations under the United Nations Charter and the Charter of the OAS and of the new postwar attitudes against force, and concerned both to avoid antagonizing the nations of Latin America and to obtain their support for anti-Castro measures, had been deterred from overt military action against Cuba. Involvement in the Bay of Pigs incident in 1961 only underscored the limitations on action by the United States; it had promoted and supported action by Cubans in rebellion, but its support was ambivalent and on a small scale. Even that action had admittedly been a mistake, and apparently no other military action against Castro was contemplated.

October 1962 was different. Observers have not been agreed as to the motives and significance of the Soviet attempt to emplace missiles in Cuba, but in retrospect, at least, most of them see it as a challenge and a threat which the United States could not tolerate.[12] Many have seen the Soviet action as primarily of psychological-political significance: particularly since the United States had just proclaimed that the "missile gap" was in its favor, the Soviet Union sought to dramatize and flaunt its strategic "parity" with the United States for the sake of its prestige at home and influence abroad. It would permit Khrushchev to reopen the Berlin issue from a new strategic posture.[13] From the point of view of the United States, Soviet intrusion into its "sphere" and unilateral disturbance in the array of strategic forces were a gauntlet that had to be taken up.[14] The United States also feared the political and psychological impact of this sudden, dramatic move on Latin America. Other observers saw the Soviet action as having important implications for hemispheric security and U.S. strategic policy.[15] The security of the Western world and its global political alignments depended on deterrence—a state of mind reflecting a perception of the balance of nuclear power. The new Soviet program in Cuba might disturb the balance of forces, or at least the perception of those forces on which the policies of nations were built. A missile base in Cuba, even if control of the missiles remained firmly in Soviet hands, threatened to disturb the delicate strategic balance between East and West. Soviet missiles could reach anywhere in the hemisphere and could circumvent the defense-warning system of the United States, depriving it of most of the critical minutes of notice that an attack was on the way.[16] Within the hemisphere, Cuban missiles could be used for political blackmail and in support of subversion. They might sufficiently offset American military power so as to create questions as to whether the United States would act in defense of the hemisphere. With no danger to itself, the Soviet Union could hide behind Cuba, letting Cuba be the counterpoise to United States power.

On the global scene, too, Cuban bases would have had immeasurable effect on the delicate balance of power and terror. Until the Cuban crisis, it was believed that Soviet missiles could not reach the United States in sufficient numbers to destroy it, while the United States, with more, longer-range missiles, could largely destroy the Soviet Union. On the other hand, the Soviet Union had plenty of medium-range delivery vehicles and could destroy Western Europe. As hostage for the West, Western Europe found its security in the promise that if it was subjected to a Soviet attack, the United States would retaliate against the U.S.S.R., risking whatever further "strike" the Soviet Union might still be able to launch. This had been, and promised to be for some time, the basis for security and peace between the East and West. Cuban missile bases threatened this balance, by putting the United States itself within reach of Soviet medium-range weapons. In sufficient numbers, some argued, they would have neutralized United States weapons enough to distract or deter them from coming to the aid of Western Europe.

Such appeared to be the significance of Cuban missile bases in the logic of the deterrent and its political role in international relations. Within the United States, moreover, it would be difficult to exaggerate how deeply troubling was the new presence, at its doorstep, of Soviet missile bases with the capacity of destroying the

United States.* Were they to remain there, the shock would severely shake the country, with far-reaching consequences for the administration and for political parties and institutions. Determined to eliminate this threat, President Kennedy and other American policy-makers prepared to face a major political and military confrontation that carried the risk of total war. In the calculus of cost and advantage the United States found the price of inaction very high, and may well have been prepared to violate international law and face the substantial costs of violation.

CHOICE AMONG ALTERNATIVES

What were the possible courses of action open to the United States? † First, the evidence could be presented to the Soviet Union with a demand that the missiles be removed. Instead, or in addition, the matter might be brought to the United Nations as a threat to the peace, and the world organization asked to take measures to have the missiles removed and to see that no new ones were introduced. Either of these moves, without more, would have raised no questions under international law. But, it is clear, American policy-makers had little faith that these steps would succeed, and their failure might make other measures more difficult. Bilateral talks might have led only to Soviet denials. The U.N. Security Council would have been frustrated by veto. The General Assembly would have debated at length, and it was not sure that a majority would have been prepared to act in a global confrontation between the two giants. There would have been delay, confusion, and obfuscation rather than the firm action needed to impress the Soviet Union—during which time the Soviet Union would have been warned, might have expedited construction of the bases to

* In fact, the assumption that the Soviet Union would anticipate and be deterred by the strong reaction led to initial disbelief of the reports that Soviet missiles were indeed being installed in Cuba. Travis, cited on p. 380 n. 9 below, at 164–65. See also Schlesinger, pp. 798–811, 831–32.

† The situation being "intolerable," I exclude the possibility that the United States might say and do nothing. Compare Sorensen, pp. 682–83.

achieve a *fait accompli*, or taken other measures to frustrate further reactions by the United States.

It was early decided that the United States would act directly to meet the Soviet threat. Three main lines of action seemed open. The most serious would be an invasion of Cuba, which would not only dispose of the missile problem but would also topple the Castro regime. Short of invasion, the United States could move in one of two ways: either destroy existing bases by bombing, and deter future installations by threat of further bombing or prevent them by blockade; or, begin by blockade to prevent completion of the installations; then, with that show of strength, demand the removal of existing missiles; held in reserve would be the threat and possibility of bombing.

No one can say exactly what factors, in what degree, weighed in the decision among these alternatives. Even the versions of the deliberations which have been published to date do not tell exactly the same story, and much remains untold. From available sources I conclude that legal considerations were not insignificant. While law was not expressly stressed, it lay, I am satisfied, behind much of what was said. Arguments in terms of "morality," "moderateness," "responsibility," "low-key response" in effect subsumed legal considerations.* Discussion of the possible costs of the various alternatives included those reactions and consequences reflecting, among other things, views as to the lawfulness or unlawfulness of proposed U.S. action.†

---

*Attorney General Robert F. Kennedy, for example, argued that a bombing attack, especially without warning, would be another "Pearl Harbor" and would blacken the name of the United States. Hilsman, pp. 203–6, 288; see also Abel, pp. 64, 88; Schlesinger, pp. 803, 806–7. "In retrospect most participants regarded Robert Kennedy's speech as the turning point." Schlesinger, p. 807. The arguments for and against the various alternatives may be found in Sorensen, pp. 678–705; Abel, pp. 50–110; Hilsman, pp. 202–9; Schlesinger, pp. 801–8.

† In an address on December 9, 1964, Dean Acheson said: "Those involved in the Cuban crisis of October 1962 will remember the irrelevance of the supposed moral considerations brought out in the discussions." *N.Y. Times*, Dec. 10, 1964, p. 16. On the basis of other sources, I do not share his conclusion that these considerations were irrelevant. In fact, Mr. Acheson admitted that there were in the balance of decision considerations of "prudence," and the consequences of "doing too much."

An immediate invasion of Cuba, it appears, was an alternative soon discarded.* Unlike the earlier Bay of Pigs mishap, this would presumably have meant not support of Cuban rebels but a direct attack with American forces. Although the purpose of the attack would not have been conquest, it would clearly be a violation of the most important norm of international law—Article 2(4) of the United Nations Charter.† Of course, one might guess, it was not only the wish to obey the law that deterred the United States. Such an attack could not afford to fail, and adequate preparation might have taken some time. The ever-present possibility of a Soviet military response could not be totally discounted: Soviet weapons would be destroyed and Soviet personnel probably killed; and the loss of Cuba might have seemed to the Russians a serious blow which they would seek to prevent, as in Hungary in 1956. The United States would have faced a storm of adverse world opinion from allies and others both within and without the United Nations. Its influence for order and against force, nurtured in Korea and at Suez, would have been gravely damaged. Latin American approval for this action would have been difficult to obtain and would have jeopardized the essential surprise; if done without such approval, it would have revived the specter of "Yankee intervention" and destroyed the delicate balance of trust and mistrust which supports United States relations with Latin America. But these political reasons merely vindicate the international norm and reflect the interests that lead nations to accept it. In our world, international law is observed because of political reasons—the fear of political sanctions, of responses and consequences.

The remaining two alternatives differed in the likelihood of their effectiveness as well as in their legal and political import. Bombing

* Sorensen, p. 683. Of course, invasion remained available as an ultimate possibility. And there was a view that bombing would in fact have to lead to invasion. *Id.* at 684.

† The United States would have been compelled to argue "anticipatory self-defense," an argument hardly likely to have been accepted. See pp. 295–96, below. Even those sympathetic to such argument might have agreed that the United States response was out of all proportion to the threat.

would more likely achieve the military objective even if at some cost in casualties. The deed would be done quickly and irrevocably. It would not depend for its success on Soviet compliance and the acquiescence of other nations. But bombing the missile sites would probably have killed Soviet personnel in charge of the missiles, increasing the likelihood of a Soviet military reaction.[17] Despite the photographic evidence which the United States was able to spread before the world, it might have been easier, after the sites were destroyed, for the Soviet Union to deny the evidence as fabricated. Even if the evidence were believed, a bombing attack by the United States in violation of Cuban territory, causing loss of lives and the danger of world conflagration, would have been deplored if not condemned. Again, legal justifications for such bombing would be questionable and would have received little hearing. The desire for surprise would have made it difficult to seek the authorization of the OAS; if sought, it is not clear that it would have been obtained.

The quarantine, on the other hand, might be less effective. Even if successful, it was inherently only a partial measure. It might prevent the introduction of additional equipment; it would not by itself eliminate from Cuba what was already there. The quarantine, moreover, depended for its success on Soviet acquiescence if not submission. It would affect the shipping of third nations.[18] Being an action which might continue for some time (unlike the *fait accompli* of a bombing), it might cause festering disputes both with the Soviet Union and with others. But the quarantine also had important political advantage. The United States would show itself determined, but moderate and responsible, aware of the stakes for the whole world. There would be no invasion of Cuban territory, no loss of lives, no irreversible course of action. Arguments for its legality might be heard with some sympathy. Being a continuing action involving no irrevocable consequences, it could be taken to the United Nations in accordance with the Charter; hopefully, it might lead the Soviet Union to negotiate instead of reacting by force; it would also permit time for mediation after the flow of missiles halted. The same factors would make it easier for Latin

America to support, and even for the Soviet Union to swallow the quarantine.

On balance, the immediate military objective could better be assured by bombing; the political factors seemed to weigh on the side of the quarantine. There are reports that lawyers helped carry the day for the quarantine.[19] In that decision, clearly, legal and political considerations were deeply entangled; but for some of the lawyers, at least, it mattered that bombing would be a serious breach in the fabric of law, a damaging blow to the efforts of the Charter to establish order by outlawing the unilateral use of force.[20] A bombing attack, even one strictly limited in purpose and effect, would probably be deemed a use of force against the territorial integrity (and perhaps the political independence) of Cuba. The quarantine would be less difficult to defend as a modest extension of law to a new situation. The quarantine could also be more readily combined with initiatives in the Organization of American States and in the United Nations—measures which would strengthen the legal foundations for the proposed action and thereby also political support or acceptance of it. Of course, it should be clear, there were risks in these steps too: if the OAS refused to act, the major legal foundation on which the United States wished to base its action would vanish, and it would be even more difficult for the United States to act than if it had not sought OAS authorization.* But law and politics impelled that the risk be taken. Building the best legal case, making the action of the United States as legal and reasonable as possible, would help persuade other nations to cooperate or comply, perhaps also help persuade the Soviet Union to a moderate reaction, even to acquiescence.†

If this informed speculation is correct, concern for maximum legality and maximum appearance of legality, and fear of the political reactions to violation of the most political norm of international

---

* It would also be easier for other nations to defy the blockade.

† Abel, pp. 87, 131. The use of the word "quarantine," a legally neutral term, also suggests the lawyer's influence; it recalled President Roosevelt's Chicago speech of 1937 and emphasized that the action was limited and "pacific," while "blockade" might have suggested war and belligerency. See Abel, p. 115.

law, helped persuade the United States government to adopt the more moderate quarantine.*

THE LEGAL JUSTIFICATIONS

When the decision was made, the lawyers of the United States government assumed their second task—presenting the case for the United States to justify the action under law.† Some of the case for the United States appears in the President's proclamations and in the statements by its spokesmen in the United Nations and in the Organization of American States. The Legal Adviser and the Deputy Legal Adviser of the Department of State have also set forth the basis in international law on which the United States felt justified in doing what it did.[21] They admitted that the action of the United States implied new interpretations of old law and perhaps, too, some new law; they denied that it involved any violation of established norms.

Principally, United States lawyers based their case on the authorization from the Organization of American States. The OAS is a regional organization contemplated by Chapter VIII of the United Nations Charter; indeed, it was the inter-American system which the framers of the Charter had principally in mind.[22] As the later embodiment of the inter-American system, the OAS can take collective action, or can authorize action by its members, in defense of the hemisphere.[23] Just as the United Nations Charter was interpreted as permitting the General Assembly to act in support of

---

*At least in the first instance. No doubt, some who concurred in this decision did so on the understanding that if the quarantine failed, bombing would be available as a later resort. Compare Sorensen, p. 694. We cannot know, of course, whether, had the quarantine failed, the United States would have proceeded, after all, to commit serious violations of law and to court their cost and consequences.

†Officially, the United States would not say, as some critics said later, that the action may have violated international law but was necessary for the security of the United States and world peace. See p. 333 below. Compare also D. Acheson, "Remarks," *Proceedings of the American Society of International Law, 57th Annual Meeting* 13 (1963), quoted below, Conclusion, p. 333–34 n.

international peace and security when the Security Council proved
ineffective, so, argued the lawyers for the United States, the
Charter should be interpreted to allow a similar role to such
regional organizations when the organs of the United Nations cannot be effective.[24]

It is true that Article 53 of the Charter provides that "no enforcement action shall be taken under regional arrangements or by
regional agencies without the authorization of the Security Council." But the resolution of October 23, it was argued, was not "enforcement action"; it was only a recommendation. Also, the authorization required from the Security Council need not be prior
authorization nor need it be expressed. The Security Council was
informed of the OAS resolution and of the proposed action of the
United States thereunder, and, in the words of the Deputy Legal
Adviser of the State Department, "did not see fit to take action in
derogation of the quarantine. Although a resolution condemning
the quarantine was laid before the Council by the Soviet Union,
the Council subsequently, by general consent, refrained from acting upon it."[25] Finally, it was argued, Article 2(4) forbids only
force or the threat of force which is "inconsistent with the purposes
of the United Nations." It does not outlaw a use of force, like the
defensive quarantine, that supports the aim of the United Nations
of maintaining international peace and is in accordance with the
role contemplated by Chapter VIII of the Charter for regional organizations.[26]

I do not wholly support all of the arguments just outlined. The
Cuban case apart, I could not accept an interpretation of Article
2(4) as outlawing force against the territorial integrity and political
independence of other states only when that use of force is also inconsistent with the purposes of the United Nations. The argument
suggests that war and conquest may be permissible to vindicate
human rights or self-determination or even "justice"—all "purposes" of the United Nations—though I do not think the spokesmen for the United States contemplated such a reading. To me,
the Charter, in both language and intent, outlaws any use of force
against the territorial integrity or political independence of other

states for *any* purpose, such use being *ipso facto* contrary to the purposes of the United Nations.[27] Other force—not against the political independence or territorial integrity of nations—is also outlawed if it is inconsistent with U.N. purposes. Some may question
the State Department's reading, too, because it would seem to give
to the OAS—and to less responsible groupings claiming the title of
regional organizations—authority to give its blessing to full-scale
attack on some state in support of some proper purpose, say, to
promote self-determination or to rectify inhumanity or injustice.
Without disagreeing, I would also express caution about Security
Council authorization which is subsequent or implied. Perhaps it is
permissible under Article 53 to act in advance of Security Council
authorization when there is warranted expectation of getting it; the
danger is that a regional organization having little reason to expect
authorization from the Council might act and present a *fait accompli*. Also, while authorization by the Security Council under
Article 53 need not perhaps be expressed, implications of authorization are more ambiguous and to be found with caution.

It is not my purpose here to judge the action of the United States
under international law, or to debate the justifications given by
government lawyers. I cite the justifications because they reflect
how international law helped shape the action of the United States
and helped determine the steps and procedures followed. The
United States may have gone to the OAS and the Security Council, as it did, because its political interests suggested those steps,
but among those interests was the desire to comply with legal commitments to those institutions and their members. The United
States wished also to strengthen the legal foundations for its quarantine by invoking the authority of the OAS and some acquiescence from the Security Council.

It is interesting to note, too, how international law and an appreciation of its role in world affairs determined what the President of
the United States said in justification of the action and what lawyers for the United States argued in its support.

[O]fficials of the Government were well aware of the novelty
and difficulty of the question presented. They were concerned

that any actions to be taken by the United States should rest on the soundest foundation in law and should appear in that light to all the world, including the Government of the Soviet Union. . . .

No new doctrines of wide application were enunciated. One single situation was considered on its individual facts, and the limited action decided upon rested on the narrowest and clearest grounds.[28]

The justification claimed by the United States was virtually limited to action pursuant to recommendations by the OAS, the only regional organization clearly contemplated by the framers of the Charter, the only pure regional organization in existence dedicated to peace-keeping. While some of the arguments might also justify bombing, or even invasion, if authorized by the OAS, that is less clear; and, in any event, such authorization is less likely to be forthcoming.* The United States and its lawyers recognized, of course, that a narrower extension of law is more likely to be acceptable than some broad new doctrine.† American leaders also recognized that the action of the United States and what was said in its justification had important consequences for international law and therefore for the behavior of nations: the justifications invoked would reflect what the United States thought the law should be, what law it was prepared to live by, what it wished that it (and others) should be free to do another time. Responsible spokesmen were concerned to keep to a minimum any extensions of existing law. In particular, they were concerned not to assert or act on a view of international law that would substantially enlarge the area of permissible use of force by nations acting on their own authority.

---

* While the resolution of the OAS, p. 281, above, on its face, would justify such extreme uses of force, one may assume that the resolution was adopted with only the quarantine in mind. If invasion or bombing were perhaps also contemplated as a later resort, these would have been "recommended" only in order to eliminate the missile threat, not for other purposes or in other contexts.

† Recall that at Suez-Sinai the governments also invoked narrow and special justification.

THE JUSTIFICATIONS WHICH
THE UNITED STATES AVOIDED

What the United States did not say about Cuba—just as what it did not do—may have been more significant than what the United States did and said. This is brought home by what others have suggested in justification of the quarantine. A favorite argument found support for the United States action in Article 51 of the Charter: "Nothing in the present Charter shall impair the inherent right of individual or collective self-defense if an armed attack occurs against a Member of the United Nations." In brief, the argument is that the "inherent right of self-defense" is not conferred by the Charter but is preserved by it and is as broad as it was before the Charter. The right of self-defense "if an armed attack occurs" does not mean "*only* if an armed attack occurs"; as before the Charter, nations continue to have the right of self-defense if an armed attack is imminent, and in the age of nuclear weapons, surely, no nation can be denied this right of "anticipatory self-defense."[29] (See Chapter 7.) The United States therefore had the right, in anticipatory self-defense, to use force against Cuban soil, surely against the missiles. Of course, there was the traditional requirement that force in self-defense be "proportionate,"[30] but clearly the use of force involved in the quarantine was not excessive.

This argument echoes others made earlier, particularly after Suez-Sinai, but American writers largely rejected it;[31] the Cuban events apparently changed the views of some of them. It is interesting that the United States government scrupulously avoided this argument. Although the President and others invoked the needs of American defense and security in political justifications, no responsible spokesman mentioned Article 51, even as possible alternative legal support for the quarantine. Repeatedly, the Legal Adviser and the Deputy Legal Adviser stressed that the United States "did not rest its case" on that ground.[32] Report has it that reference to Article 51 was several times proposed for insertion in statements by the President and others, and every time alert and insistent lawyers succeeded in eliminating it.[33]

The temptation must have been great. Pressed to justify the action of the United States, the lawyers relied on the authorization of the OAS, although some may have found that authorization flimsy and the argument under it strained. They eschewed Article 51, although, as some would interpret it, that article would have handsomely justified the quarantine, as well as bombing and perhaps even invasion of Cuba, without need of OAS authorization. But spokesmen for the United States apparently recognized the dangers which the argument entailed.

We are not told why the United States avoided that justification. I have suggested why, in my view, the United States government rightly avoided it. As I have said, to me the argument is unfounded, its reasoning is fallacious, its doctrine pernicious.[34] The fair reading of Article 51 is persuasive that the Charter intended to permit unilateral use of force only in a very narrow and clear circumstance, in self-defense if an armed attack occurs.[35]

As a general extension of Article 51, anticipatory self-defense would replace the requirement of armed attack—"clear, unambiguous, subject to proof, and not easily open to misinterpretation or fabrication"—with a standard which is ambiguous, deceptive, and dangerously flexible.[36] To have invoked it in Cuba would have extended it to meaninglessness. Traditional self-defense, as reaffirmed at Nürnberg, was at least limited to cases in which the "necessity of that self-defence is instant, overwhelming, and leaving no choice of means, and no moment for deliberation."[37] Cuba was not such a case. No attack was imminent; there was no evidence that an early attack was planned or contemplated. To say that whoever sets up "offensive weapons" justifies pre-emptive use of force would justify unilateral force by everyone everywhere. All nations are now faced by someone with power to strike them. Most weapons are "offensive" or could be used offensively. Nations that would attack could always claim the threat of "offensive weapons," and, after a *fait accompli*, let the victims try to challenge the claim or let the United Nations attempt to judge whether the actor's security had been truly at stake and whether his response was "proportional." To have argued "anticipatory self-defense" on the facts of the Cuban case is to distend the self-defense exception of Article 51 until it swallows up the rule of Article 2(4) against the use of force. It would have dealt a severe blow to the principal contemporary development of international law and destroyed its influence as a deterrent to national violation.

The lawyers for the United States who resisted the argument dealt responsibly with international order and international law. Of course, they did not, and had no occasion to, explicitly reject the argument. The Deputy Legal Adviser stressed that "reliance was not placed" on Article 51 but added that the "United States took no position" on the scope of that article and its relevance to Cuba.[38] The legal adviser does not needlessly foreclose arguments which his government may have to consider another day. He does, and did in this case, recognize the consequences of his government's actions and justifications as a precedent and encouragement to other nations, and the responsibility of his government for the future of international order and law.

THE QUARANTINE AS PRECEDENT

International law influenced what the United States did in Cuba as well as what it said in justification. In turn, as an important action by an important nation, acquiesced in by all other nations (including the Soviet Union, the principal "victim"), what the United States did in the Cuban quarantine became part of the corpus of international law and practice. The statements, justifications, and legal interpretations announced by the United States (and others) at the time of the action have influenced and will continue to influence the legal significance of the Cuban case. Unlike the actions at Suez-Sinai, condemned by the United Nations and largely undone, the Cuban quarantine has not been seen and will probably not be seen as a violation leaving the law as it was; probably it made new law, but what that law is cannot yet be told. Much will depend on how the United States itself later interprets what it did and why it was justified, and what other nations seek to make and succeed in making of the incident. Happily, the Cuban missile case has not been invoked by any other state in the intervening years as precedent permitting other uses of force or near-force; one may hope that none or few will in the future. If occasions arise, nations will, of course, consider this precedent in the light of their national interest;* responsible nations will include in such consideration their interest in an international society from which unilateral force is largely eliminated.

Some of the possible legal "uses" of the Cuban affair have been suggested. The United States has expressly made it a precedent for action—any action?—pursuant to authorization by regional organizations, like the OAS. Others may seek to seize on that justification as authority for other organizations—say, the Organization of African Unity—to authorize force in support of United Nations purposes like self-determination in Rhodesia and Namibia or human rights in South Africa. There are those who will invoke it to support any use of force in "anticipatory self-defense," broadly conceived. I suggest that governments and judges and writers have responsibility to use the precedent with due concern for future law, and that the quarantine lends itself to very cautious "use" indeed.

In longer retrospect, the Cuban quarantine will doubtless look different from the way it appeared to government officials defending it then, even to scholars debating it in the afterglow. Their readings were inevitably colored by the sense of crisis and the possibility that further action beyond the quarantine might yet be taken. Later, perhaps, when the quarantine is recollected in tranquility, discussion of it as an exercise in the use of force might seem a distortion of emphasis. Future lawyers might see the action of the United States principally in terms of its purpose, secondarily in terms of the limited means used.

The United States was asserting a right not to permit the introduction of Soviet missiles into Cuba. At its narrowest, it is an assertion that when world peace hangs on a delicate balance of terror, measures that threaten substantial destabilization are intolerable. Even if the assertion is to be generalized, it may mean only

---

*Maritime nations may be particularly careful to limit the "precedent" of the blockade.

that particular deployments of weapons outside a nation's territory may create a threat to the security of another nation to which the latter is entitled to object. The United States also asserted a right to take measures to prevent the new deployment. It did not assert the right to do so by all means: it did not claim the right to wage war against the Soviet Union, which was deploying the weapons, or against Cuba, on whose territory the missiles were being placed. It did not, in the event, invoke any right to attack Cuban territory to destroy the weapons.

Carefully analyzed, the United States was asserting different rights in regard to missiles already in Cuba and to those which might be heading there. It asserted the right to accost vessels to assure that they were not transporting offending weapons—a limited type of blockade for this limited purpose, a special Cold War analogue to traditional wartime blockade. As to missiles already there, on the other hand, the United States only called upon the Soviet Union to remove them, and the Soviet Union agreed. A threat that the United States would destroy them if not removed never came to the test; in any event, nations may threaten more force than they intend to use.[39] One need not assume that if the Soviet Union had refused to withdraw the missiles, the United States would in fact have bombed them. If the United States were assured that the further importation of missiles had been halted, it might not have felt compelled to destroy those already emplaced. If future lawyers see the Cuban affair as establishing the legality of the United States action, it may be said that it was the objection to the missiles and the blockade to "enforce" the objection that were accepted as legal, not the implied threat, if any, to bomb Cuba if the missiles were not removed.

To accept the legality of the blockade also entails some interpretation of the Charter's prohibitions on unilateral force.[40] One would argue that Article 2(4) was not really involved. That article intended to outlaw war, and the major uses of force not formally designated as war. Article 2(4) does not deal with such use or threat of force as is incidental to the enforcement of accepted rights—say, to enforce prohibitions on intrusion in territorial sea or air, or to capture pirates or slave traders. The quarantine may be seen as falling in this category. The quarantine did not involve the actual use of force, and the threat of force in the background (naval and air power if the quarantine were violated or resisted) was minimal and conditioned on legitimate demands. It could be argued that the force threatened was not against the political independence or territorial integrity of Cuba, or of Russia, or of other nations whose vessels were affected. Nor was such threatened force inconsistent with the purposes of the United Nations; its purpose was not aggressive but rather defensive, to eliminate a potential threat to peace. Moreover, such force was not threatened unilaterally but only pursuant to the authorization and recommendation of the OAS, a regional organization contemplated by the Charter and furthering its purposes.

The future, I am suggesting, might well see Cuba not as an extension of the area of permissible use of force, but rather as recognition of a new small limitation, in special circumstances, on the right of transfer or deployment of weapons between nations.[41] Whether or not such transfer or deployment is itself illegal, where the aggrieved nation has a right to object it may also enforce this objection by limited means, including a modicum of force if necessary. In regard to transportation of such weapons by sea, this right to object and to enforce the objection (*e.g.*, by interdicting vessels, inspecting them, preventing them from proceeding) is an additional limitation on the "freedom of the seas," that political slogan which subsumes legal norms. (The law has long recognized other limitations on freedom of the seas—including those inherent in prohibitions of piracy, slave running, arms running.) International law and agreements generally apply at sea as well as on land and constitute, *pro tanto*, limitations on the "freedom of the seas." Although we do not know whether some traditional limitations on freedom of the seas—principally the wartime blockade and the limited "pacific blockade"—have at all survived the end of lawful war and the prohibitions on unilateral force, the days of the Charter have seen new forms of limitation on the freedom of the seas. Big powers have temporarily blocked off substantial segments of the sea while they conducted nuclear tests; [42] the contemporary regimes for the continental shelf and the exclusive economic zone are also limitations on the erstwhile freedom of others. [43] (See Chapter 11.) Nations have also imposed and accepted limitations on the free use of the air, as in requirements of identification upon entering Air Defense Zones far beyond the territorial airspace. [44]

Events in international relations, like cases in law, have a life of their own. They are available as possible precedent beyond their original facts, context, or justification in doctrine. Responsible nations, in their own behavior or in reacting to the behavior of others, avoid hardened categories and deal imaginatively with precedents with due concern for their impact on international law. Cuba, I am suggesting, might well be limited to its facts. It might be seen as applicable only between the superpowers in regard to the nuclear balance. At least, nations might be concerned to treat it not as a basis for extending the permissible use of force, but as a right to interfere with the deployment of weapons outside a nation's territory in special circumstances by limited means pursuant to collective decision.

AERIAL INSPECTION

A different precedent was established in Cuba by American aerial reconnaisance. The United States freely admitted that its planes had photographed Cuban territory; the evidence thus obtained was invaluable to the United States in proving its case before the world and in pressing Russia to concede. There have been claims that United States airplanes took photographs by methods of peripheral photography, without violating Cuban airspace; but early in the episode it was reported that an American pilot had been shot down over Cuba. [45] Since the end of the quarantine, it appears undisputed that United States planes have flown over Cuban territory to continue surveillance against the possibility of the reintroduction of missiles. [46]

Overflight of the territory of another nation without its consent has been universally considered a violation of a fundamental norm, and has been universally resisted. The U-2 incident of 1960 over the U.S.S.R. found the United States, in effect, confessing violation. Small nations have shot down planes of larger powers over their territory in full confidence of their right to do so and the victims have never challenged the right (though they may have denied being over the territory, or claimed that it was an unintentional violation). Cuba surely does not imply any early and wide breach in this rule. Neither the United States nor any other nation has since claimed the right to fly over other countries; they have continued to assert their right to exclude foreign planes from their territorial airspace.[47] In Cuba the United States apparently claimed special justification for the aerial reconnaissance, as for the quarantine, in resolutions of the OAS.[48] The United States might perhaps also claim justification in its agreement with the Soviet Union leading to the withdrawal of the missiles and the end of the quarantine, which provided also for inspection. Although Cuba was not a party to the agreement, it can be argued that it conferred on the Soviet Union authority to bind it, if only by implication, as a result of the original arrangement permitting the installation of the missiles.

Still, while the law against overflight remains "good law," United States persistence and Cuban acquiescence (even if only under protest) may suggest that the significance of this law is changing. The objection to overflight has been couched in conceptualistic terms: the territorial sovereign owns the space above its territory "up to the sky."[49] But we now know that there is no sky. The practical reasons supporting the conceptual objection are also changing in impact. Overflight was feared as a threat of attack and a source of "espionage." But today the missile is replacing the airplane, and attacks even by airplanes have to be met long before planes enter the territorial airspace; in any event there is now law against attack whether from within or without the territorial air. The plane may still be feared as a source of intelligence, but planes can now perform surveillance from altitudes at which few nations have the military means to prevent them. Technical advances, moreover, have made it possible to carry out photographic reconnaissance from the air outside the territory, from ships at sea, from installations in other lands, from satellites. Such surveillance from outside the territory cannot easily be known or prevented; it is probably not a violation of any law that is, or any that is likely to be agreed. Every society has to this extent become an open society.

No doubt overflight will continue to be a national concern if only for aviation control. Obtrusive flights without consent will be resisted "on principle"—although these will usually be unintentional violations. But the unobtrusive and virtually unnoticed flight—as by U-2 planes over Cuba—may come to be accepted and may cease to be a problem for international law. If so, that and other technical advances which modify the import of the law of territorial airspace can lead to new law to control armaments. The hope for substantial agreements on the control of armaments rests in part on the ability of nations to verify whether others are complying with agreed limitations. Agreement apart, moderation in the arms race depends on satisfactory information that other nations are also exercising moderation and are not engaged in developing, manufacturing, acquiring, deploying new weapons. Unobtrusive, unilateral "inspection," whether by expressed or tacit agreement, can supply knowledge about what others are doing and encourage nations to seek security in mutual limitation of armaments rather than in arms races. That is what has made Strategic Arms Limitation Talks (SALT) possible and hopeful.

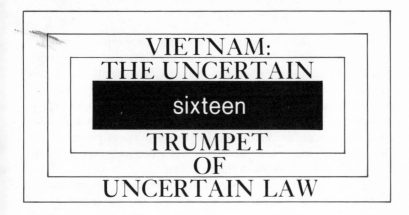

VIETNAM:
THE UNCERTAIN
sixteen
TRUMPET
OF
UNCERTAIN LAW

"Vietnam" appears deeply etched in American history as one of the few great national tragedies. At home, it was a cause of unprecedented malaise and dissension; internationally, it meant near-defeat in war, loss of prestige and credibility, damage to "image" and leadership, friction even with allies. Both in the United States and abroad there was common agreement that the United States had made a big mistake. Both in the United States and abroad there was a disposition to assume that what was deemed stupid or immoral must also be illegal, and there was a common impression that American Presidents had committed gross constitutional transgressions as well as serious violations of international law. The executive branch, however, denied constitutional improprieties, and official American spokesmen rejected charges that the United States committed any violation of international law, insisting, rather, that U.S. involvement was dictated by international undertakings in the spirit of the U.N. Charter to assist victims of aggression.

Accusations of violations of law are common weapons in political controversy, often with little warrant. For their part, on the other hand, those who in fact violate the law, commonly plead "not guilty." As regards Vietnam, however, even supporters of the U.S. position recognized that various of the tortuous developments in Indochina between 1954 and 1973 required justification and raised legal issues wanting resolution. Even the judiciously-minded and the impartial were hard put to reach a clear judgment as to the merits of the legal claims of the two sides.

The legal uncertainties about Vietnam revealed uncertainties in the law of the U.N. Charter; they revealed, too, the importance of facts and their characterizations in legal determinations. The legality of the actions of the United States (and those of other parties to the war) turned on difficult issues as to the status and character of the territory and the government of South Vietnam, and their relation to the Vietcong, to North Vietnam, and to the North Vietnamese government. Was the war in Vietnam civil war or international war, and what was the status of the United States in that war? Of course, if the facts were confused, if what they amounted to was disputable, and the governing legal principles uncertain, they were less likely to exercise restraining influence on the policies of governments.

Even the barest, briefest narrative of American involvement in Indochina must go back at least to 1954.[1] At a political conference in Geneva following years of fighting, France signed a cease-fire and agreed to transfer sovereignty to a "State of Vietnam." The Final Declaration of the Conference affirmed the unity of Vietnam and envisioned holding elections in July 1956. But while the rival governments in North and South Vietnam committed themselves to unifying the country, the South Vietnamese government did not accept the Geneva Conference and the United States did not sign the Final Declaration, although it announced that it would abide by the Declaration's terms.

It soon appeared that the South Vietnam government would not agree to general elections, claiming that the elections could not be free in the Communist-controlled North. The United States supported that view. Instead, it led in the establishment of the South-East Asia Collective Defense Treaty (SEATO), and a protocol to that treaty made its provisions applicable to Cambodia, Laos, and "the free territory under the jurisdiction of the state of Vietnam."[2]

General elections were not held in 1956, and in the years that followed Communist-led dissident groups (known as the Vietcong, or later, the National Liberation Front) in terroristic activities, rebellion and war against the South Vietnamese government. Supported by Southern Communists trained in North Vietnam, the Vietcong made important headway and by the end of 1960 controlled substantial areas of South Vietnam.

United States support for the South began early and increased slowly. In the early years it helped build up the South Vietnamese army; in 1961 it began to send combat advisers to accompany combat-support units, and by 1963 there were some 16,000 U.S. military personnel in South Vietnam. Following a coup d'état, apparently with U.S. knowledge if not support, President Johnson concluded that stronger U.S. support was necessary. In August 1964 a North Vietnamese attack on two U.S. destroyers in the Gulf of Tonkin led to a resolution by Congress authorizing the President to "to take all necessary measures to repel any armed attack against the forces of the United States and to prevent further aggression," and to assist any member or protocol State of SEATO "requesting assistance in defense of its freedom."[3] In October 1964 American aircraft began to attack supply trails in Laos; in March 1965 they began to bomb in North Vietnam; in April 1965 President Johnson sent combat troops. Beginning in the latter months of 1965, North Vietnamese troops entered the South to support the Vietcong. In 1967 the United States began to bomb in Laos, and in 1970 in Cambodia, claiming that the Communists were using those territories to support their aggression, and the local governments were unwilling or unable to prevent them. Despite intermittent efforts by both sides and by third parties to end the war, it continued for years more, terminating finally with the Paris agreements of 1973.[4]

THE LAW AND THE FACTS

What international law would say about U.S. involvement in Vietnam depends on disputed questions of fact, even more on debatable characterizations of those facts. The lawyer seeking to apply norms needs first to decide what was going on. He might begin by asking which side was responsible for the failure of a political solution and the resort to arms. It seems agreed that the South refused to go along with elections; was it legally obligated to do so? If so, was it excused by the fact that elections would probably not be "free" in the North? Assuming the South was responsible for the failure of general elections, was the North justified in responding by supporting the Vietcong in the South and helping it achieve control by force?

It is difficult to conclude that the United States breached international obligations by supporting the South in its refusal to proceed with elections, since the United States was not party to the 1954 Declaration. But was it permitted by law to support the South Vietnam regime, build its army, advise its troops in combat? Political and auxiliary military support to the South Vietnam government was probably seen by the North as intervention in the internal affairs of Vietnam, but the United States was free to treat the government of South Vietnam as a legitimate government and to support it accordingly. More serious allegations against the United States came after the Tonkin Gulf incident with direct U.S. participation in hostilities, particularly by bombing in North Vietnam and by committing ground troops to combat.

There are at least three possible models to characterize the Vietnam War and the U.S. role in it, and the judgment of international law will largely depend on which characterization it accepts.[5]

Model A saw the war as civil war within an independent South Vietnam, with North Vietnam an outside state helping one side, the United States another outside state helping the other. Military intervention in civil war was not acceptable under traditional international law, but that law may never have recovered from the wounds it suffered at many hands during the Spanish Civil War.[6] On its face at least, such external intervention is not obviously a

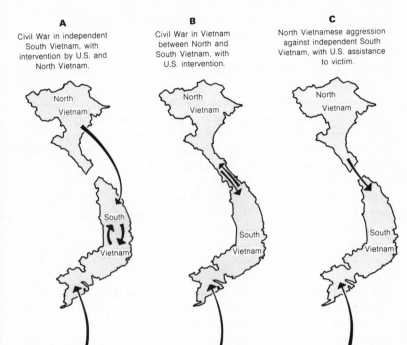

A

Civil War in independent
South Vietnam, with
intervention by U.S. and
North Vietnam.

B

Civil War in Vietnam
between North and
South Vietnam, with
U.S. intervention.

C

North Vietnamese aggression
against independent South
Vietnam, with U.S. assistance
to victim.

violation of Article 2(4) of the U.N. Charter as a use of force against the political independence or territorial integrity of another state, if the support was bona fide and the intervenor was not seeking to dominate the side it supported and establish a puppet regime.

On this view of the Vietnam War, neither the United States nor North Vietnam violated a vital contemporary norm of international law, as long as both confined themselves to supporting activity. But U.S. bombing of North Vietnam added an unacceptable dimension, converting an essentially civil war into an international war. (In the Spanish Civil War, intervenors did not, nor claimed the right to, attack each other's territory.) Indeed, world reaction to U.S. participation appeared to harden appreciably after the United States began to bomb in the North, in part perhaps because the world saw the war as an internal affair in South Vietnam and held the United States responsible for expanding it.

A second view (Model B) also saw the war as civil war, not between the Vietcong and the Saigon government in a separate independent South Vietnam, but within the single state of Vietnam, between North Vietnam and the Vietcong on one the hand and Saigon forces on the other. In such a war, U.S. intervention, even bombing North Vietnam, was—again—perhaps a violation of traditional international norms against intervention in civil war, but not clearly of the U.N. Charter. Bombing Laos or Cambodia would be more difficult to justify, even if they were viewed as tacit supporters of North Vietnam; toleration of mutual interventions in civil war does not contemplate attacks by one intervenor against another.

Officially, the United States saw the war in Vietnam in yet a third perspective (Model C).[7] North Vietnam launched an armed attack against the territorial integrity and political independence of an independent country, the Republic of South Vietnam, using the Vietcong as its agent. This was a use of force in clear violation of Article 2(4) of the Charter. In the face of this armed attack, the Republic of South Vietnam had its inherent right of self-defense under Article 51 of the Charter, and the United States could come to its aid in collective self-defense—as indeed, it had obligated itself to do in the South East Asian Collective Defense Treaty. The United States and the Republic of South Vietnam had every right to carry the war to the territory of the aggressor in order to defeat the aggression;* they could carry the war to the territory of any other countries that involved themselves in the aggression, or permitted the aggressor to use their territory for its aggressive purposes, i.e., Laos and Cambodia.[8]

---

* Ironically, a similar argument was made in 1979 to justify China's invasion of Vietnam after the latter had overrun Cambodia.

THE LAW AND ITS INFLUENCE

No international or other disinterested tribunal was ever seized of these issues, and political and moral passion clouded findings of fact, characterizations, and legal determinations. Subsequent attempts to recollect and reflect on those issues in tranquility are still troubled by abiding passion and hampered by unavailable or confused data and by inherent ambiguities of fact and uncertainties of law.

If a judgment on the United States were at issue, one might venture a highly tentative guess that an impartial body might find that United States officials believed in their characterization of the status of South Vietnam as a separate entity, and the war as an external attack rather than authentic civil war; that, as in Korea, the governing groups in South Vietnam and perhaps the aware and the concerned among the "masses" wished to be left alone rather than be swallowed by a Communist North, thus reflecting an authentic "self-determination" that others should honor and international law should protect, as was being recognized in other once-unified countries: in Korea, in Germany, even to date in China. A tribunal might nonetheless have concluded that the separate character of South Vietnam had not sufficiently congealed, either within Vietnam itself or in the international system at large, and that North Vietnam did not violate international law by trying to unify all of Vietnam under its own rule. The war, then, was civil for international purposes, and if one had to choose among the models suggested above, the war was most closely characterized as Model B, civil war between North and South Vietnam, or perhaps as both Models A and B, a civil war between North and South superimposed upon another within South Vietnam. Since the United States had no designs on Vietnam's independence or any of its territory, the Charter was not violated by U.S. intervention in those civil wars; but, despite the Spanish War, traditional international law still forbids intervention in civil wars. The use of territory of adjacent states by one side in a civil war did not necessarily permit the other party (surely not an intervenor) to attack that adjacent territory.

Whether that would in fact be the judgment of a hypothetical court is not the issue here. We are concerned with the influence of law in the decisions of U.S. officials. If they asked the question, perhaps their conclusion as to what the hypothetical court would decide was different from the one suggested; or, even if they accepted my guess, perhaps that conclusion did not appear to them so clearly the common view of other national governments in the political system so as to discourage the action.

More important, the Vietnam experience reveals the unstructured, unplanned, not wholly deliberate quality of many political events or series of events in international life. It may be that, although a long war eventuated, there was never in fact any single, discrete, clear decision by American foreign policy-makers to engage in war in Vietnam. Policy was not made, but happened, the accumulation of small steps each of which seemed not too significant. There was then no advance evaluation of benefits and costs of a total policy that included all foreseeable cases and consequences; at later stages, failure to take the next step—even one legally questionable—may have appeared too costly in considerations of foreign policy or in domestic consequences. Early involvements were small and promised to be sufficient and readily terminable, not requiring any further commitments nor pulling the United States down a "slippery slope" to war; surely, they seemed to raise no serious issues under international law. If there was any particular decision on a new and major involvement, notably after the Tonkin Gulf incident, that seemed a "natural," necessary and proper consequence of what had already been invested and of what had flowed therefrom. It had, moreover, plausible provocation, and therefore plausible justification under international law; it promised, and kept promising, to be brief and decisive. International law seemed at worst ambiguous, and the cost of any violation that might be claimed seemed comparatively low while the advantages expected from possible violations were prompt and great.

Whether international law figured in official American deliberations in the way and to the degree I suggest cannot be determined from available data. It is, I think, a plausible guess as to probable conscious considerations, and a fair perspective on the attitudes implicit in what was said and done, if one may assume rational policy-making and planning.

Vietnam epitomizes the obstacles to a rule of law in regard to military interventions in internal wars in an age of ideological conflict. The traditional law is extant but too often disregarded, and there is no consensus between East and West or even between North and South that would support new law against such intervention. Invitations to intervene are common and tempting. The facts of internal struggle and intervention and their significance are often difficult to disentangle and easy to confuse. Vietnam did not help the development of a meaningful distinction between subversive intervention against the political integrity of a country and military support for either side in internal wars. The legitimate hope that Article 2(4) of the U.N. Charter may yet become a rule against disguised force threatening the independence of a nation was not in fact encouraged when the United States was seen as invoking it in a situation where, as many nations believed, independence was the inevitable victim between competing imperialisms, or worse where the West appeared to be defending the interests which stand in the way of self-determination and independence.

Vietnam also represented the political difficulties of bringing law to bear on intervention that found the superpowers on opposite sides, and reflected their major ideological-political struggle. The United States was deeply involved in what its government believed to be defense of a small ally against Communist aggression. In that view and that policy it was not without support. But many of the governments of the world, including some of the allies of the United States, were unhappy with its intervention; some sharply condemned it. Some governments may themselves have been uncertain of the facts, but were not willing to accept the United States version. They were not eager to find that such "subversion" violated the Charter. Some may not have been wholly persuaded that so-called subversion was not support for legitimate aspirations to independence and that, by contrast, the "legitimate" government in Saigon was not a vehicle of "neo-imperialism." At best, to some nations the conflict over subversion was just another aspect of the ideological war, in which they did not wish to take sides. They chose not to side with the United States (considered "soft" on colonialism) against the Soviet Union and China (seen as strongly anticolonialist), in support of intervention by a big white power in a small country of non-whites. Many governments may have resented and feared the escalation of local conflict into a big war which threatened to involve them all.

A nuclear world, a world divided between East and West and North and South, a world in which the "order" of colonialism suddenly exploded, shooting forth new unstable nations, a dynamic, developing world identified by common attitudes and aspirations—in short, the world since World War II—has not abandoned traditional international law or radically departed from its principal tenets. The old infrastructure of principles, assumptions, and institutions has survived. New law for cooperation in the common welfare has taken root. The new foundation for international order—the law of the U.N. Charter outlawing war—is occasionally shaken, but stands.

The world tomorrow might be wholly different, but, almost by hypothesis, radical transformations cannot be foreseen or planned for. Assuming essential continuity though with continuing change in the foreseeable future, and despite pervasive explosive disorder in southern Africa and periodic eruptions elsewhere (as around the

Horn of Africa and in the Middle East), the importance of law will be no less. If society survives, law is indispensable and inevitable, and new law to meet new needs will come, if slowly. The health of the law, however, will depend largely on the health of the society, on its ability to contain explosive forces and mobilize creative ones for general welfare.

Powerful political forces and recurrent political drama conceal the efficacy of law and feed skepticism about its importance. In a kind of self-fulfilling prophecy, this skepticism can lead to laxity in observing law and reluctance to accept new law—short-sighted attitudes that are damaging to international order and to the national interest.

THE OUTLOOK FOR LAW
AND LAW OBSERVANCE

The unexpected, cannot, of course, be anticipated, but neither the international political system nor its law promises radical transformation in the decades ahead. There will be many nation-states enjoying large domestic autonomy even in an interdependent world; international political institutions will not be substantially stronger (or weaker); the reach and influence of international law on the behavior of governments and other transnational actors will be familiar if not essentially the same. There will be the same need to understand the role of law and its limitations, the politics of lawmaking and law-observance, the influence of contemporary political forces on the legal system.

The international legal system remains primitive and its radical development is not in sight. The principle of unanimity and other weaknesses in the legislative process will continue, and diverse interests of many states will not easily be accommodated and resolved. But necessity will produce some virtue. The law will be further codified, clarified, developed. Some further agreements to limit strategic weapons and nuclear proliferation will be reached. A new law of the sea is inevitable, even if takes some time to stabilize. Efforts to rationalize the world's economic and monetary system will continue, and if the economic order does not become quite the new one which the Third World asks, it will take some steps in that direction. Modest cooperation will continue and some will take legal forms—on safeguarding the environment, controlling the world's population, and feeding it. Even the market in fuels and other resources may acquire some stability. With some political improvements, *e.g.*, some settlement in the Middle East, new or widened agreements may even help bring international terrorism under legal controls. There will be other new law to meet needs not yet perceived or acute enough to bestir the international legislative processes.

Internal impulsions and international inducements, I believe, will continue to promote the observance of law and obligation. The prospects are good that nations will observe the body of law and the mass of treaty undertakings governing their multivaried daily relations. The fate of the more political norms and agreements will be shaped, if not determined, by the extent to which the principal political forces of our time emphasize the advantages of law observance, by the general state of international order and the climate of interstate relations, by the example of influential nations, and by their stand toward the violations of others.

The major forces in international relations are ever changing but will continue to affect law and law observance, modifying the content of the law, rendering some norms obsolete and giving others new importance, affecting national attitudes toward law. Technology will continue to govern the observance of the law forbidding war. There is basis for hope that, for "technical" reasons, major war will remain unthinkable. Improvements in communication, in methods of detection, in safety devices may further reduce the danger of war by accident, mistake, or miscalculation. The big dangers are in expansion and escalation of local or regional conflicts, as in the Middle East. There is danger too that additional nations may acquire nuclear weapons without a concomitant sense of responsibility.

The ideological conflict has changed; but whether there is cold war, "coexistence," détente, or some new phase, we shall see the effects on the law of continuing competition, of the forces which have created the irregular triangle of China, the Soviet Union, and the United States. If among the three giants we anticipate a balance conducive to good behavior, other nations might conclude that the ideological confrontation no longer dominates the stage and that they can escape its influence; some may even see in it, or in one side or another, protection against their lawlessness, as in the Arab attacks on Israel. The emergence of the Third World that has helped immunize its members from big-power influence does not promise to substitute its own influence for peace. There is no certain resolution of all the explosive tensions in southern Africa, or warrant to hope for an end to competing interventions, no new agreement to achieve the stability and order indispensable to a *bona fide* rule of law. There is no bright hope either for an early end to national attitudes which see the adverse interests of nations more readily than the common, which focus on armaments and on some diplomacy for immediate goals but distrust the promises of law.

In our times, improved law observance may depend particularly on increasing the interest of the many new nations in international order and in "friendly relations" generally. That will require a willingness by older and wealthier nations to give serious consideration to the aspirations of the "New Economic Order," to help satisfy the legitimate aspirations of newer and poorer countries for quicker development and favorable trade, and the special concern to find a way to eliminate white colonialism and white racism from black Africa. If the new nations acquire a greater stake in order, they will re-dedicate themselves to the law of the Charter in regard to their own disputes; they will be better able to resist interventions and counterinterventions, even by the big powers or their surrogates. Then, too, the United Nations will more probably see its majorities mobilized in support of order and its machinery used to police law observance. A peace in the Middle East not only might eliminate a tinder box for world conflagration but also might end Arab-Communist and the Arab-Third World alliances that have disrupted and abused the processes of the United Nations and politicized it to create "double standards" and otherwise frustrate effective action, *e.g.*, to promote human rights.

If the major powers come to see a common interest in order (as they have in the avoidance of nuclear war) they can do much to make law observance decisively more advantageous than violation. If diplomacy can maintain a climate of order and provide lawful means for achieving change, these will induce the acceptance of law and the development of institutions for its observance. Habits of accepting and observing law will, in turn, contribute to international order and stability. On the other hand, if international order and stability are weakened—universally, regionally, or locally— laws of more political character will not fare well, and the observance of even the basic, "routine" laws and agreements may be weakened. Regardless of law and in spite of the terrible consequences, there may even be international war if the big powers see their interest in disorder and promise to support or protect those who breach the peace.

The law's prospects, then, will prosper or falter with the forces making for healthy international society. No doubt, these prospects might also be substantially brightened by deliberate effort to improve law and law observance. The influence of law will grow as it continues to rid itself of abiding conceptualism and outdated concepts, to eliminate elements which feed a sense of injustice, and bases itself firmly on contemporary ideas of equity and on mutual interest. Law will fare better as the processes of law-making are re-examined and new nations participate fully in its codification, adaptation, and development. It is increasingly important to make a virtue of less-than-universal law, to concentrate on the needs of regions and other interest-groupings, and to foster in them effective law and legal institutions.[1] Observance will also be enhanced if law is better known and more certain and if events that might involve violations are open to verification; and regional efforts to these ends are more likely to be effective.

Internal forces in support of law observance also depend on more healthy, open, stable domestic societies with freer institutions. These are still rare and slow to develop. There will be need, in addition, for deliberate effort to raise the status of international law in individual countries, widen the education of lawyers, enhance their role in the process of making foreign policy, and improve public administration to take account of law and obligations.

Important consequences for law observance will flow, of course, from the examples of important nations. Whatever the comparative interests and legalities, when the United States bombed North Vietnam or sent Marines to the Dominican Republic, it could not hope to be persuasive in urging President Nasser to withdraw his forces from Yemen or to lift a blockade at Aqaba, or in urging Israel not to use force in response to border raids or other Arab acts of belligerency. Nations with special interest in and avowed dedication to order have special responsibility: it is time that such nations take an affirmative lead in demonstrating the importance of law to international stability. They need to be scrupulous about their own behavior, shed their own suspicions and hesitations about international law, reverse the trend to erode law and reduce once-legal questions to issues for diplomacy or unilateral decision, and affirmatively seek extension of the law's domain. Nations dedicated to human rights can form a "human rights bloc" to promote observance and try to reduce violations wherever they may occur. If universal law cannot be easily achieved or maintained, law between particular nations and groups of nations is nevertheless an important beginning. A willingness by more nations to resort to third-party determination in the light of law—whether by the International Court or otherwise—would enhance the likelihood that others will do likewise and would develop adjudication as an additional deterrent to violation of law.

In short, law observance can be enhanced by an improved climate of international order, by better law, by stronger domestic institutions, by the special efforts of influential nations. Law observance can be enhanced, too, by increasing the disadvantages of violation—by more open societies where violations will be more readily detected; by more effective verification, including international observation, to deter violation; by threat of adverse judgment, judicial or political, in support of law and international obligations; and by credible, commensurate, and effective responses.

Most important, I am convinced, is the need for a firm, clear, and credible stand by international society against unilateral use of national force; in particular, a firm, clear, and credible policy of self-restraint by the powerful and a firm, clear, and credible promise of effective response by them and by the community, notably by the Third World or regional bodies within it, to any such use of force by any nation. I have characterized the prohibition on unilateral force as a political norm. But this is not to say that it is only a political expedient; it is law, with the force of law, designed to control the behavior of nations. After hundreds of years, nations finally agreed to add the influence of law as a further deterrent to war. It would be tragic if nations allowed force to descend again to the level of national political interest as each nation saw that interest. It would be tragic if the observance and enforcement of this norm became a political football, encouraging violation by any nation which was secure in its military or political power, or which felt confident that it would be protected or its conduct condoned by political forces in or out of the United Nations. If this norm fails, we may not even be able to revert readily to the days when law applied in peace although it did not forbid war. Failure of the principal norm of contemporary international law can only cast doubt on the efficacy and legitimacy of all international law. All will be to do again, if there are any left to do it.

THE LAW'S SUPPORTERS
AND ITS CRITICS

International law is an assumption, a foundation, a framework of all relations between nations. Concepts of statehood, national territory, nationality of individuals and associations, ownership of property, rights and duties between nations, responsibility for wrong done and damage inflicted, the fact and the terms of international transactions—all reflect legal principles generally accepted and generally observed. The law provides institutions, machinery, and procedures for maintaining relations, for carrying on trade and other intercourse, for resolving disputes, and for promoting common enterprise. All international relations and all foreign policies depend in particular on a legal instrument—the international agreement—and on a legal principle—that agreements must be carried out. Through peace treaties and other political settlements, that principle has also helped to establish and legitimize existing political order as well as its modifications—the identity, territory, security, and independence of states, the creation or termination of dependent relationships. Military alliances and organizations for collective defense also owe their efficacy to the expectation that the undertakings will be carried out. International law supports the numerous contemporary arrangements for cooperation in the promotion of welfare, their institutions and constitutions. Finally, there is the crux of international order in law prohibiting war and other uses of force between nations.

The law works. Although there is no one to determine and adjudge the law with authoritative infallibility, there is wide agreement on the content and meaning of law and agreements, even in a world variously divided. Although there is little that is comparable to executive law enforcement in a domestic society, there are effective forces, internal and external, to induce general compliance. Nations recognize that the observance of law is in their interest and that every violation may also bring particular undesirable consequences. It is the unusual case in which policy-makers believe that the advantages of violation outweigh those of law observance, or where domestic pressures compel a government to violation even against the perceived national interest. The important violations are of political law and agreements, where basic interests of national security or independence are involved, engaging passions, prides, and prejudices, and where rational calculation of cost and advantage is less likely to occur and difficult to make. Yet, as we have seen, the most important principle of law today is commonly observed: nations have not been going to war, unilateral uses of force have been only occasional, brief, limited. Even the uncertain law against intervention, seriously breached in several instances, has undoubtedly deterred intervention in many other instances. Where political law has not deterred action it has often postponed or limited action or determined a choice among alternative actions.

None of this argument is intended to suggest that attention to law is the paramount or determinant motivation in national behavior, or even that it is always a dominant factor. A norm or obligation brings no guarantee of performance; it does add an important increment of interest in performing the obligation. Because of the requirements of law or of some prior agreement, nations modify their conduct in significant respects and in substantial degrees. It takes an extraordinary and substantially more important interest to persuade a nation to violate its obligations. Foreign policy, we know, is far from free; even the most powerful nations have learned that there are forces within their society and, even more, in the society of nations that limit their freedom of choice.[2] When a contemplated action would violate international law or a treaty, there is additional, substantial limitation on the freedom to act.

The varieties of law that permeate international relations maintain international society. They shape the behavior of nations. They achieve substantial order, and even welfare and justice, in significant measure. One may protest, then, that international law is misunderstood and grossly underestimated, that it is a vital force in international affairs and a dominant influence in national policy. But one must not protest too much. The fact is that international law and international society are still "underdeveloped." Some of its deficiencies the society shares with many domestic societies. It remains tense with political-ideological conflict and awesome arms races, destabilized by increasing numbers of unstable nations, disturbed by the impatient striving of the unfortunate many for more goods, power, influence. International society is still far from dedicated to the general welfare, to elevation of the living standards of all, to reduction of the disparities in well-being among nations. International law, in some respects, fares less well than does the law in developed domestic societies. Large areas of international life remain effectively unregulated. Governments do not yet find violation of law unthinkable, nor are they yet deeply persuaded that law and law observance are in their ultimate interest; there is yet no confident reliance by others that a nation will observe important law. If there have been few traditional wars, there are increasing rumblings of them, *e.g.*, between neighbors in Africa; surely, there is as yet no confidence in peace, no assurance that war will not come, no security against the threat implied in the proliferation of terrible weapons. Law has not effectively deterred several indirect aggressions and other gross interventions, including military interventions that, as in Vietnam, have assumed the outlines and proportions of international war.

A lawyer might answer that for inadequacies in justice and welfare, in stability and order, the fault is not in the law but in society. Law does not achieve these goals in the best of societies unless its members desire them and are prepared to pay their cost. But if international law can blame its inadequacies on the society, still it cannot deny them.

If the thesis of this book is correct, those who fail to recognize the law's limitations are wrong; they too are wrong who fail to see the law's uses and its strengths. Those who exaggerate the law's significance need no depreciation, since they are commonly disregarded; I would say something more to particular critics and other deprecators of law who have been explicit, authoritative, and persuasive. In the world since midcentury the American voices commonly associated with depreciation of the role of law in international affairs are those of a distinguished and thoughtful diplomat, George Kennan, and a distinguished and thoughtful political scientist (trained in law), Professor Hans Morgenthau.*

Outside the professional universe of political scientists, I believe, the best-known contemporary criticism of law in foreign policy may be Kennan's in his *American Diplomacy, 1900–1950:*

> . . . I see the most serious fault of our past policy formulation to lie in something that I might call the legalistic-moralistic approach to international problems. . . .
> It is the belief that it should be possible to suppress the chaotic and dangerous aspirations of governments in the international field by the acceptance of some system of legal rules

---

*Some might add a distinguished and thoughtful Secretary of State, statesman, and lawyer, Dean Acheson. See pp. 325 n. and 333–34 n., below.

and restraints. This belief undoubtedly represents in part an attempt to transpose the Anglo-Saxon concept of individual law into the international field and to make it applicable to governments as it is applicable here at home to individuals. . . .

In the first place, the idea of the subordination of a large number of states to an international juridical regime, limiting their possibilities for aggression and injury to other states, implies that these are all states like our own, reasonably content with their international borders and status, at least to the extent that they would be willing to refrain from pressing for change without international agreement. . . .

. . . History has shown that the will and the capacity of individual peoples to contribute to their world environment is constantly changing. It is only logical that the organizational forms (and what else are such things as borders and governments?) should change with them. The function of a system of international relationships is not to inhibit this process of change by imposing a legal strait jacket upon it but rather to facilitate it: to ease its transitions, to temper the asperities to which it often leads, to isolate and moderate the conflicts to which it gives rise, and to see that these conflicts do not assume forms too unsettling for international life in general. But this is a task for diplomacy, in the most old-fashioned sense of the term. For this, law is too abstract, too inflexible, too hard to adjust to the demands of the unpredictable and the unexpected. . . .

Finally, this legalistic approach to international relations is faulty in its assumptions concerning the possibility of sanctions against offenses and violations. . . .[3]*

It is not wholly clear what Kennan included in the "legalistic-moralistic" approach that bothered him. He has been interpreted as

*Published in 1951, that criticism may no longer exactly represent Kennan's views. Later restatement gives them a different emphasis with the same positive focus on political "realism" but a less negative accent on "moralism" or "legalism." I discuss here the original statement, in view of its common citation and the widespread audience it has received.

opposing or deprecating international law. But, in the same lectures, Mr. Kennan insisted that getting away from the legalistic approach "will not mean that we shall have to abandon our respect for international law, or our hopes for its future usefulness as the gentle civilizer of events."[4] Surely, he was not objecting to traditional international law (say, on territorial integrity or diplomatic immunity), to treaties on traditional subjects (say, extradition) or even the contemporary agreements for international cooperation. Nor could he have been criticizing reliance upon legal instrumentalities and forms for resolving disputes: a settlement must have some kind of agreement, and agreement means a legal agreement. He did cite arbitration treaties and the Hague Conferences, but these, as such, do not appear to have been the focus of his concern.[5] Today, surely, no nation—certainly not the United States—places third-party determination high in its foreign policy. Third-party decision, moreover, is not a substitute for diplomacy, but an alternative for which diplomats are often grateful when the parties cannot reach agreement. Even advance undertakings to arbitrate disputes or to go to court do not hinder diplomacy; such adjudication occurs, if at all, only as a last resort after diplomacy has failed. I can think of no instance where the availability of arbitration or adjudication hindered the diplomatic process or proved undesirable.

If the approach to which Mr. Kennan was objecting was reflected in any particular law, it is the law against war.[6] Among the purposes of the legalistic approach he notes the desire "to suppress [by law] the chaotic and dangerous aspirations of governments," to limit "their possibilities for aggression and injury to other states." His arguments against this "legalism" may be grouped. Some are that such law is unrealistic: many nations are not content with their status and their boundaries and will press for change, by force if necessary. The law, moreover, is inadequate because it has no effective sanction against violation; and it attempts to control only external aggression, ignoring "ideological attack, intimidation, penetration, and disguised seizure of the institutional paraphernalia of national sovereignty." Such law is also undesirable: it imposes a strait jacket where what is needed is the flexibility of diplomacy; it drags along "moralism" with undesirable consequences.[7]

Thirty years of experience with the law of the Charter do not support the assertion that nations will not accept this law or the conclusion that it cannot work.* All nations have appeared willing, even eager, to adhere to the United Nations Charter: they have found it at least desirable, perhaps necessary, to outlaw force as an instrument of change; and they have largely abided by this law. If there was reason to be skeptical about this law a generation ago, the new weapons have rendered this idealistic law realistic and viable. If nations have not all accepted "at heart" what they formally agreed to, nuclear weapons have, to date, persuaded them of the wisdom of the law which they adopted. The fact is that in the nuclear age nations generally do not have the option to achieve ex-

* But compare the statements of former Secretary of State Dean Acheson in an address delivered on December 9, 1966: "But, you will say to me, at least one moral standard of right and wrong has been pretty well agreed to be applicable to foreign policy. Surely, the opinion of the world has condemned the use and threat of force by one state against another, as the United Nations Charter bears witness. Does this not give us a firm ground on which to stand?

"Well, does it? Ever since the Charter was signed, those whose interests are opposed to ours have used force, or the threat of it, whenever it seemed to them advisable and safe—in Greece, Czechoslovakia, Palestine, Berlin, Korea, Indochina, and Hungary. Each side used it in regard to Suez.

"Is it moral to deny ourselves the use of force in all circumstances, when our adversaries employ it, under handy excuses, whenever it seems useful to tip the scales of power against every value we think of as moral and as making life worth living?

"It seems to me not only a bad bargain, but a stupid one. I would almost say an immoral one. For the very conception of morality seems to me to involve a duty to preserve values outside the contour of our own skins, and at the expense of foregoing much that is desired and pleasant, including—it may be—our own fortunes and lives.

"But, however that may be, those involved in the Cuban crisis of October 1962 will remember the irrelevance of the supposed moral considerations brought out in the discussions. Judgment centered about the appraisal of dangers and risks, the weighing of the need for decisive and effective action against considerations of prudence; the need to do enough, against the consequences of doing too much." *N.Y. Times*, Dec. 10, 1964, p. 16. Compare R. Aron, *Peace and War* 608–10 (1966).

ternal change by conquest—as was learned in Korea and at Suez.*
Smaller nations—*e.g.*, Somalia—have found little success and little
sympathy when they tried to achieve international change by force.
If the result has been to channel some international conflict into
"internal" wars, the latter, in any event, are less dangerous; despite
disappointments to date one may hope that the tendencies supporting the rule against international war will help confine and limit internal wars, too. Of course, this law is subject to constant pressures, and one cannot be certain that it will survive. Many may still
believe that its failure is inevitable;[8] that tragic failure, I believe,
must and can be avoided.

Mr. Kennan suggests that the law is a "strait jacket" to be eschewed in favor of the flexibility of diplomacy. In context, this dichotomy between law and diplomacy is difficult to grasp. I have
called diplomacy a stage on the way from force to law in the progress of civilization. But in the conduct of foreign policy, law and
diplomacy are not alternatives, either in purpose or in means. Diplomacy is "flexible," but its purpose is often to achieve "inflexibility," *i.e.*, stability, credibility, confidence. And the law (*e.g.*, international agreement) is one of diplomacy's most important
instruments. Is it diplomacy as distinguished from law that produced the bases-for-destroyers deal of 1941, Lend-Lease, the Marshall Plan, NATO, the Common Market? In regard to the use of
force, in particular, if a major aim of American foreign policy is to
achieve a maximum of peace and stability, the law is a major instrument for diplomacy to use to that end. In any event, here the
choice is not between law and diplomacy; it is between law and
force. The law against force does not bar diplomacy; on the con-

* Even "realists" tend still to agree that if the superpowers wished, they could
maintain the peace. In fact, at least the United States and the Soviet Union recognize that war is undesirable. They have not only avoided war themselves but, even
when political obstacles prevented their overt cooperation to that end, they have
helped prevent or terminate war by others (*e.g.*, at Kashmir in 1965, in the Middle
East in 1967 and 1973). However, their influence against war depends substantially
on the fact that it is invoked in support of law, that war is illegal for everyone,
including themselves.

trary, it insists on it. By outlawing force it makes diplomacy possible, indeed inevitable. It is not diplomacy that prevails when force is paramount, whether at the Congress of Vienna or at Munich, or in Paris in 1973.

Beneath the dichotomy between law and diplomacy may lie a misunderstanding about law, and a confusion between what the law prescribes and how it responds to violations of the prescription. Like enlightened domestic law,[9] international law is replete with standards of substantial flexibility, as when it prescribes "reasonable" or "just" behavior, or permits a nation only "proportional" response to a violation. "Rigid" requirements are usually procedural; for example, an undertaking to submit to arbitration or adjudication. Occasionally, a substantive prohibition will be universal and near-absolute; because they deemed it essential to eliminate war, the nations decided that the prohibitions on the use of force should be clear and firm, the permitted exceptions small and defined. Even so, the Cuban missile crisis surely does not suggest that in regard to important interests the United States found itself bound in a strait jacket of inflexible law. As regards responses to violation, moreover, nothing in international law directs how a victim or its allies or the United Nations must respond to a particular violation.[10] Surely, United Nations reactions in the Middle East and elsewhere do not suggest rigid application of rigid rules. Even at Suez, if there was any inflexibility in the reaction at the United Nations, it was not in the law but in the parliamentary diplomacy played there. (Indeed, the danger is rather that pressure for greater flexibility, in the norms of the Charter and in the judgments of the United Nations, may threaten the deterrent influence of law.)

This confusion between occasional firmness in the law's prescription and flexibility in the law's response may also underlie Mr. Kennan's objections to "the inevitable association of legalistic ideas with moralistic ones." This "inevitable association," he believes, carries over into the affairs of states the concepts of right and wrong, and leads to self-righteousness, a desire to punish "lawbreakers," a refusal to compromise with evil, an insistence on "unconditional surrender" by the violators, which among nations means all-out war.[11] "Moralism" apart, there seems little basis for blaming these excesses on the law. Those who sincerely strive to build the kingdom of international law do so with beams taken from their own eye, not with motes taken from others. To those who wish to be moralistic, the violation of law is only a convenient pretext. In international society, it is not the violations of law that have provoked the violent reactions and the cries for retribution or all-out victory. The hatred felt for Hitler or for the Japanese during the war had little to do with the fact that they had committed violations of law. Surely, it was not those who were concerned that there had been a violation of the U.N. Charter who pressed for "all-out victory" in Korea, or those who cared most about law who were "hawks" in Vietnam.

Perhaps it is not to any particular law that Mr. Kennan objects, but to the attitude which seeks in law "easy" answers to difficult political problems. Although his principal example, the law against force, may have been overtaken by revolutionary events, I agree with what may be his principal thesis—that one does not resolve political problems by "machinery," especially not by paper laws and paper institutions.[12] In a world that is unwilling to disarm, general and complete disarmament cannot be achieved by drafting agreements which nations will not adhere to or observe. Disputes are not settled or peaceful relations promoted by fabricating "gimmicks" that will not be adopted, or by piling up agreements which nations will not invoke, or by setting up tribunals they will not use. Basic conflict is not eliminated or bridged by creating a United Nations;* nor is a strong and effective world institution built merely by drafting new Charter provisions, so long as international society is not strong enough to support them and the nations that compose it are not prepared to accept them.† As Mr. Kennan has

* Nor does one solve problems that powerful nations are not prepared to solve (e.g., Berlin, Vietnam) merely by taking them to the United Nations. Compare L. Henkin, *The Berlin Crisis and the United Nations* 9–10 (1959); "The United Nations and Its Supporters: A Self-Examination," 78 *Pol. Sci. Q.* 504, 513–16 (1963).

† There is nothing basically inadequate in the present Charter for creating an institution to enforce and maintain peace in contemporary society, but it will work

pointed out, many laws have not prevented subversion and intervention.

But to say that law cannot achieve what nations do not wish is
not to say that it is undesirable to maintain and extend the domain
of law, to persuade nations that it is in their interest to agree and to
abide by their agreement. The fact is that nations do generally observe law, and, pursuant to law, they do what they would not have
done were there no law. It is of little use to attempt to make law
where nations clearly have no interest in being bound, clearly will
not be bound, regardless of what they sign or profess. But in large
"gray areas," nations can be persuaded to agree, if only hesitantly:
they may insist on the right to denounce the agreement or on other
escape clauses—themselves indication that they intend to observe
as much as they agree to. And if they agree, the forces for law observance will generally prevail. There will be law, giving confidence to international relations and adding to order and stability.

Mr. Kennan's strictures were directed principally against law as
an instrument of American foreign policy. Similar views, generalized as principles of political science, appear widely in Professor
Morgenthau's writings.*

. . . the legalistic approach to essentially political problems is
but an aberration from the true laws of politics. . . .[13]

On the international scene . . . the legal decision of isolated
cases is particularly inadequate. A political situation presenting itself for a decision according to international law is always
one particular phase of a much larger situation, rooted in the
historic past and extending far beyond the issue under legal
consideration.[14]

Law and political wisdom may or may not be on the same
side. If they are not, the insistence upon the letter of the law
will be inexpedient and may be immoral. . . .

. . . the questions which the law and the lawyer can answer

only to the extent that it reflects political forces in society and so long as these forces
combine to seek peace.

*He, too, has written in other veins (see p. 330 n.), but the materials I cite are
still staples of study and discussion.

are largely irrelevant to the fundamental issues upon which the peace and welfare of nations depend. . . .[15]

The common denominator of all these tendencies in modern political thought is the substitution for the national interest of an assumed supranational standard of action. . . .[16]

Again, the full import of these and other passages is not clear. Obviously, no one would espouse the "legalistic approach" if that is to be distinguished from appreciation of the uses of law. No one would insist on the "letter of the law" if that is to be distinguished from its spirit. For the rest, these views were perhaps intended to be limited by the time and contexts in which they were expressed. But if they are intended as generalizations suggesting the irrelevance of law,* they reflect a narrow—and unreal—view of the law, as well as a narrow—and inadequate—view of "national interest."

Professor Morgenthau seems to think of the law exclusively in terms of judicial decisions on particular questions, rather than as a pervasive system supporting the society and influencing national behavior within it. And he aims his blows at straw men of legal unsophistication.[17] Even judgment as to the lawfulness of a nation's conduct, which cannot be avoided by those who would act or those who would judge the actions of others, does not apply merely "the letter of the law"; nor does it look at either norms or actions without regard to "the much larger situation," "the historic past," and the implications of the decision "far beyond the issue under consideration." That narrow view of the law was familiar enough in days gone by, but it has never been the perspective that sophisticated American lawyers have taken, whether in interpreting a constitution or a doctrine of private law; one need not take a narrower approach to law in international affairs.

---

* Elsewhere Professor Morgenthau stresses that international law has been scrupulously observed, and concludes that "to deny that international law exists at all as a system of binding legal rules flies in the face of all the evidence." But, Professor Morgenthau says, the "spectacular" rules—like the Kellogg-Briand Pact or the Covenant of the League of Nations—have not been observed. And violations of international law have not been effectively punished, because international law is "decentralized." Morgenthau, *Politics Among Nations* 265 (4th ed., 1967).

It is perhaps this circumscribed view of the law which has caused Professor Morgenthau to take also a narrow view of "national interest." There follows "that iron law of international politics, that legal obligations must yield to the national interest." [18] Of course, that statement may suggest merely the truism that nations, like individuals, balance the advantages and disadvantages of law observance and may decide to violate the law and accept the consequences. But the implications of Mr. Morgenthau's "iron law" are broader. It seems to set up a dichotomy between law observance and national interest, to treat their concurrence as coincidental and their opposition as common. If so, it seems to see immediate tangible advantage—the gain from a violation—as the only national interest. It does not seem to consider that the law of nations may be in the interest of all nations, as the law of an enlightened society is in the interest of all its citizens. It does not see national interest in law observance—in order and stability, in reliable expectations, in confidence and credit, in the support of other nations and peoples, in friendly relations, in living up to a nation's aspirations and self image, in satisfying the "morality" of its own officials and of its own citizens. It tends to discount the national interest in avoiding other, immediate, "concrete" responses to violation. The issue of law observance, I would suggest, is never a clear choice between legal obligation and national interest; a nation that observes law, even when it "hurts," is not sacrificing national interest to law; it is choosing between competing national interests; when it commits a violation it is also sacrificing one national interest to another. At the Bay of Pigs, for example, was the issue whether the interest of the United States (eliminating Castro) should yield to its obligations under the U.N. Charter and the Rio Treaty? Surely, the statesmen who made the decision to limit U.S. participation in that enterprise, and refrain from attempting it again, decided that the national interest in maintaining legal obligations and avoiding the consequences of violation outweighed the interest in displacing Castro.

Governmental decisions to disregard law, I have argued, reflect a conclusion—or at least an impression—that violation would bring a preponderant advantage to the national interest. Obviously, reasonable men may differ about the weight to be accorded to various costs and advantages, as well as on the probability that a particular cost or advantage will accrue. Tendencies to "realism" or "idealism," to skepticism or confidence about international law and international order, will inevitably color the computation. The effects of violation on order, on national credit and credibility, on prestige and influence, on friendly relations are imponderable and incalculable and particularly open to argument. There is easy temptation to think that one can violate without tempting others to violate, that one can commit "just a small violation," that one can violate "just this once" and then atone and recoup any damage incurred.[19] Even the most skeptical see some national interest in avoiding the consequences of violation. It involves some faith to insist that every violation damages the total structure to the detriment of all, or that in a particular case the specific advantages of violation are less weighty than incalculable costs, the immediate benefits less important than eventual loss. Attitudes which see law observance as being in opposition to national interest inevitably discourage policy-makers from including in the balance any but patent and immediate interests. The policy-maker is even reluctant to consider law observance at some immediate cost if he sees himself as "sacrificing national interest" to some legal obligation. In deciding whether or not to send Marines into the Dominican Republic in 1965, for instance, it might have made all the difference in the world whether the policy-maker saw the issue as national interest versus legal obligation or as a choice between competing natonal interests. Professor Morgenthau's "iron law" then becomes an inducement to favor the immediate tangible interest as the dominant national interest and to depreciate the national interest in observing legal obligations. I am convinced that this attitude—deeply ingrained—is harmful to enlightened national interest, as well as to international order. One may hope that increasing awareness will expose the basic fallacy of this "iron law of politics" and, by exposing, destroy it.

A narrow view of law and of national interest also underlies the attitude commonly expressed by other critics—as in regard to the intervention in the Dominican Republic in 1965 or Israel's raid at Entebbe—that what the United States (or Israel) did may have been illegal but it clearly had to be done, and the United States (or Israel) was right in doing it. Similar expressions come even from those who in national life are deeply law-abiding and see clearly the basic interest in law observance, who might not tolerate even the special case of civil disobedience, who surely would not agree that there may be common instances in which one "has" to violate the law and one has the "right" to do so.

For my part, I cannot agree that there can be behavior that "has to be done" but which violates the law. No legal system accepts as law that which "has to be" violated. No view of international law, no interpretation of any norm or agreement, could concede that a nation may be legally required to do that which would lead to its destruction, or jeopardize its independence or security. Nations, surely, would not accept such law for themselves or impose it on others. If this issue has any reality, it may perhaps arise in a novel situation in which an act not contemplated when a norm was established appears to fall within its prohibition. In such circumstances, if there is a prevailing view in international society that the act in question should not be deemed a violation, governments, scholars, and courts would seize on any ambiguity in the law to conclude that it was in fact lawful. Even if there is no obvious ambiguity, exceptions might yet be carved out in order to avoid an absurd result.[20] (This, I believe, can be said, for example, of the law as applied to Israel's raid at Entebbe.).

What should be clear is that we are talking about change in what was or had been thought to be the law when there is common agreement that the law should be different. This is not to suggest that any nation can itself violate or reject law because it deems that existing law jeopardizes its security or other interests.* That would destroy the very concept of law. No society could tolerate such

* Dean Acheson's views are different. In a comment on the Cuban quarantine, he said, *inter alia:*

"In my estimation, however, the quarantine is not a legal issue or an issue of international law as these terms should be understood. Much of what is called international law is a body of ethical distillation, and one must take care not to confuse this self-judging exemptions from important principles. Of course, a nation may assert that the law is or should be different, but it takes the risk that, unless its assertion is accepted, it will face the consequences of violation.

Differences of opinion as to the place of law in international af-

---

distillation with law. We should not rationalize general legal policy restricting sovereignty from international documents composed for specific purposes.

* * *

"I must conclude that the propriety of the Cuban quarantine is not a legal issue. The power, position and prestige of the United States had been challenged by another state; and law simply does not deal with such questions of ultimate power—power that comes close to the sources of sovereignty. I cannot believe that there are principles of law that say we must accept destruction of our way of life. One would be surprised if practical men, trained in legal history and thought, had devised and brought to a state of general acceptance a principle condemnatory of an action so essential to the continuation of pre-eminent power as that taken by the United States last October. Such a principle would be as harmful to the development of restraining procedures as it would be futile. No law can destroy the state creating the law. The survival of states is not a matter of law." *Proceedings of the American Society of International Law* 13, 14 (1963).

Mr. Acheson's remarks were brief, and I am not confident that I wholly understand his position. His comments about international law generally are especially succinct; he may be denying that much or any of international law is "law," but he does not tell us why. I also have great difficulty with his more concrete propositions. Clearly, the nations sought to deal "with questions of ultimate power" when they adopted the United Nations Charter to outlaw war. If he means that such law is undesirable or futile, I have indicated my disagreement at length, here and in Chapter 7. Perhaps Mr. Acheson means only that no law can, or does, or should, bar a state from taking measures necessary for its survival. The United Nations Charter recognized some such principle when it made an exception permitting force in self-defense against armed attack. But, in context, Mr. Acheson's statement seems to equate challenge to "power, position and prestige" with challenge to survival. His remarks, further, might be interpreted to imply that law cannot, and does not, deny to any state the right to decide for itself when its survival is threatened, or what measures are necessary to assure it. Such a view would, indeed, be a negation of law that no legal system could tolerate. In the Cuban situation, surely, international society could not accept the view that the *ipse dixit* of the United States that its action was necessary to its survival (if indeed the United States ever claimed that) *ipso facto* made the action lawful. It is a very different argument, on the other hand, to suggest that if a society agrees that the action was necessary for the survival of the United States, it would be absurd to interpret the law as forbidding it. See p. 143, above.

fairs have often been confused by differences as to whether morality has any place in relations between nations. Critics of reliance on
law have often joined in condemning the "legalistic-moralistic" approach (hyphenated by both Mr. Kennan and Professor
Morgenthau), and criticized it for injecting notions of morality borrowed from relations between individuals.[21] Frequently cited is
Alexander Hamilton's famous essay opposing American support
for France in its war against England:

> It may be affirmed as a general principle, that the predominant
> motive of good offices from one nation to another, is the inter-
> est or advantage of the nation which performs them.
>   Indeed, the rule of morality in this respect is not precisely
> the same between nations as between individuals. The duty of
> making its own welfare the guide of its actions, is much
> stronger upon the former than upon the latter; in proportion to
> the greater magnitude and importance of national compared
> with individual happiness, and to the greater permanency of
> the effects of national than of individual conduct. Existing
> millions, and for the most part future generations, are con-
> cerned in the present measures of a government; while the
> consequences of the private actions of an individual ordinarily
> terminate with himself, or are circumscribed within a narrow
> compass.[22]

Hamilton was arguing that the sentiment of gratitude was less
appropriate to national policy than to individual behavior; the rule
of morality "in this respect" is "different" for nations. He did not
say that notions of morality do not apply to national behavior.
Clearly, he was not suggesting that, in the name of national interest, governments may freely violate law or obligation. Indeed, earlier in the essay he wrote:

> Faith and justice between nations are virtues of a nature the
> most necessary and sacred. They cannot be too strongly incul-
> cated, nor too highly respected. Their obligations are absolute,
> their utility unquestionable; they relate to objects which, with
> probity and sincerity, generally admit of being brought within
> clear and intelligible rules.
>   But the same cannot be said of gratitude.[23]

If one accepts "morality" at all, if one agrees on the general contours and content of a particular moral code, it is difficult to avoid the conclusion that nations, too, may act morally or immorally. Certainly, men judge the actions of governments by moral standards. People react in moral terms to the behavior of other governments; many impose moral standards on their own governments. The behavior of Hitler's Germany has surely been adjudged immoral by standards common to many contemporary societies. Others have judged as immoral the dropping of atomic bombs on Hiroshima and Nagasaki, or the use of napalm in Vietnam.

If governments are judged by moral standards, it would be strange if there were no overlap between international law and international morality; it does not follow, of course, that violation of law is itself immoral, or that all violations should be adjudged immoral. Even in developed national societies there are violations of law that are punished but are not generally condemned as immoral—*e.g.*, traffic violations, perhaps drunkenness or even tax evasion in some countries. In international society, while nations may not treat breaches of international agreements as lightly as some individuals treat breach of contract, few would insist that it is immoral to break any treaty. Other activities which may involve violations of international law have also gained the respectability of old, universal practice—*e.g.*, various forms of espionage. But some violations of law, at least, would surely be deemed immoral by common contemporary standards—say, the systematic killing of prisoners of war or the crime of genocide. Many would today condemn naked aggression by the strong against the weak as immoral.*

If there is no agreed international moral standard, many will judge governments by their own standards. Officials of governments cannot shed their own moral codes. Representative govern-

---

* In the 1970s some attacked as "moralism" some inclination by the United States to shape its national policies in response to the condition of human rights in various countries. The United States, itself not a party to principal international human rights law, was not invoking international law, but its own ideology.

ments, at least, cannot be indifferent to the morality of their own people, and some violations of law clearly offend that morality. It may also be offended by violation generally, as when people think that their government violates its undertakings, that it "breaks its word."

Law, I sum up, is a major force in international relations and a major determinant in national policy. Its influence is diluted, however, and sometimes outweighed, by other forces in a "developing" international society. Failure to appreciate the strengths and weaknesses of the law underlies much misunderstanding about it and many of the controversies about its significance. "Realists" who do not recognize the uses and the force of law are not realistic. "Idealists" who do not recognize the law's limitations are largely irrelevant to the world that is. Those who resist new law because of general skepticism about international law or the expectation that others will not abide by it, or from a reluctance to see their own government limited by it, may frustrate their own nation's interest, including its interest in general welfare and greater order in international relations. Those who press for optimum laws or agreements which would not be accepted, or which if accepted would not be observed, indulge in futility that may damage the cause of law generally and frustrate more modest, realizable progress.[24]

Today, extremes of "realism" or "idealism" about law are rare. The lawyer may sometimes place too much faith in law. The diplomat or policy-maker too often errs on the side of skepticism. He resists persuasion as to the desirability of some new undertaking—from inertia, from undue confidence in his diplomacy, from a desire for "flexibility" and the avoidance of commitment. He sees in *laissez faire* the benefits of freedom for his country; he tends not to see the disadvantages to his country in the unbridled freedom of others. (He sees, for example, security in his country's weapons, not the security that might come from controlling the armaments of others.) Skepticism may also affect governmental attitudes toward existing law, exaggerate the need or benefit of violation, and underrate the advantage to the national interest of law observance in general and of keeping a particular norm or obligation.

The important questions that divide the lawyer and the diplomat today are not whether and why law is insufficiently effective, or whether in a very different world—the distant hope of some for more-or-less world government—law would be more effective. In its extreme form, the question is whether, admitting the inadequacies of international society, law really matters—whether it makes sense for nations to bother with law, to depend on it, to uphold it, to seek its extension.

To me, the answer is clear. In the society we have, international law sustains what order we have and promises better. There is bound to be controversy about its application and interpretation, but that does not vitiate its significance or effectiveness. Nor is law destroyed by the fact that it is sometimes violated, even by the fact that it is sometimes hypocritically invoked by the violators. (We do not reject scripture merely because the devil may cite it.) In regard to the law against force, there is no longer any doubt about its validity, its desirability, its necessity. The question is whether men and nations will live by it or will violate it and be destroyed. Despite Vietnam and the Dominican Republic, Yemen and Cyprus, Biafra and Angola, and the ever-present threat of new civil wars and new interventions, I do not believe that the failure of the law against intervention vitiates the law against war, the total impact of international law, the general record of law observance, or the substantial measure of order that it affords.

International society "works"; at least it "muddles through." There has been no big war and there are cogent reasons to hope that there will be none. There has been progress beyond wildest hopes in giving peoples independence—the national analogue to individual liberty. There is a spreading law of human rights. There has been some recognition of responsibility for general welfare. If the present levels of law can be maintained, they will be surpassed. Risking analogies, one may suggest that international society is not yet secure in a *laissez faire* stage, where institutions can barely hope to assure individual nations their "security," the right to be let alone. From there to a welfare society is a long road, as it has been in national societies; but if wars can be avoided, progress toward a more just welfare society is a reasonable expectation. The need is clear, the ideas are launched, institutional framework exists. Slowly, slowly, technology will begin to meet its promise; poor nations will be less poor; new nations will be less new and have more of a stake in stability, order, and law; increasing welfare will begin to supply basic human needs for all; a growing consensus on at least a core of political-civil as well as economic-social human rights will attenuate even ideological conflicts and translate them into acceptable channels and forms. The process is under way, however gradually or imperceptibly. Its progress depends on maintaining the order we have, through the law there is. It depends on nations paying more, not less, attention to law, extending its domain, and sacrificing some often superficial, immediate interest for law's longer, deeper promises.

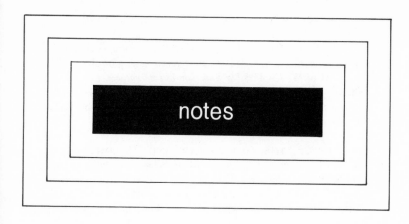

notes

INTRODUCTION

1. But *cf.* G. Kennan, Conclusion, n. 4, below.
2. G. Kennan, *American Diplomacy, 1900–1950*, 95 (1952); see text, Conclusion, pp. 322–23.
3. *Southern Pacific R.R. Co.* v. *Jensen*, 244 U.S. 205, 222 (1917).
4. Some relevant writings include: P. Corbett, *Law in Diplomacy* (1959); E. Hoyt, "The United States Reaction to the Korean Attack: A Study of the Principles of the United Nations Charter as a Factor in American Policy-Making," 55 *Am. J. Int'l L.* 45 (1961); E. Hoyt, "National Policy and International Law: Case Studies from American Canal Policy," *The Social Science Foundation and Graduate School of International Affairs, University of Denver, Monograph Series in World Affairs*, vol. 4 (1966–67); see also C. Ronning, *Law and Politics in Inter-American Diplomacy* (1963); also R. Fisher, "Internal Enforcement of International Rules," in *Disarmament: Its Politics and Economics* 99 (S. Melman ed., 1962). Compare C. de Visscher, *Théories et Réalités en Droit International Public* (4th ed., 1970; Corbett tr., rev. ed., 1968); M. Kaplan and N.

Katzenbach, *The Political Foundations of International Law* (1961); *Proceedings of the American Society of International Law, 58th Annual Meeting* (1964). Also, W. Coplin, *The Functions of International Law* (1966); H. Dillard, "Some Aspects of Law and Diplomacy," 91 *Recueil des Cours* 449 (1957). See also the materials cited in the notes to the Preface to this edition.

CHAPTER 1.   THE ROLE OF LAW AND ITS LIMITATIONS

1. The word was coined by Judge (then Professor) Philip Jessup, "to include all law which regulates actions or events that transcend national frontiers. Both public and private international law are included, as are other rules which do not wholly fit into such standard categories." P. Jessup, *Transnational Law* 2 (1956).

2. See, *e.g.*, the Security Council debates arising from the U-2 incident, 14 U.N. SCOR, 857th–860th meetings (1960), and those dealing with the shooting down of a United States RB-47 by the Soviet Union in the same year, 14 U.N. SCOR, 880th–883rd meetings (1960). See also, the debates in the General Assembly on the same subject, 15 U.N. GAOR 696–700, 701–9 (1960).

   In 1955, Bulgaria shot down an Israeli passenger plane that had entered Bulgarian airspace, and Israel instituted suit in the International Court of Justice. The decision of the Court, disposing of the case on preliminary motions, is at [1959] I.C.J. 127.

3. See W. Friedmann, *The Changing Structure of International Law* (1964).

4. The United States belongs to some eighty international organizations and arrangements.

5. O. Holmes, *Speeches* 68 (1934), speaking of "historic continuity with the past."

6. L. Henkin, "Disarmament—The Lawyer's Interests," in Association of the Bar of the City of New York, *Background Papers and Proceedings of the Fourth Hammarskjold Forum* 1, 28 (1964). On the legality of the oil embargo and other forms of economic coercion, see the various articles in *Economic Coercion and the New International Economic Order* (R. Lillich ed., 1976); also the Symposium in 12 *Tex. Int'l L.J.* 1–60 (1977). Propaganda "warfare" is also inadequately regulated. See A. V. W. and A. J. Thomas, *Non-Intervention, The Law and Its Import in the Americas* 273–81 (1956), and the symposium, "International Control of Propaganda," 31 *Law & Contemp. Prob.* 437–634 (1964), especially A. Larson, "The Present Status of Propaganda in International Law," *id.* at 439. On the regulation of international terrorism, see Chapter 9.

7. The "Connally Amendment" to the United States declaration recognizing the Court's compulsory jurisdiction, 61 Stat. 1218, T.I.A.S. No. 1598 (1946), [1946–47] I.C.J.Y.B. 217–18, 228, which reserved to the United States the right to determine whether a suit against the United States involved a matter that was "essentially within the domestic jurisdiction of the United States," and was therefore not subject to the jurisdiction of the Court. This has been interpreted as reserving to the United States the power to reject any suit against it; as a consequence, under the Statute of the Court, in any suit brought by the United States, the defendant can similarly refuse the suit. See the disposition by the Court in the case of Certain Norwegian Loans, [1957] I.C.J. 9; see also the case concerning the Aerial Incident of 27 July 1955 (*United States of America* v. *Bulgaria*), [1960] I.C.J. 146. Compare the concurring opinion of Judge Lauterpacht in the Norwegian Loans Case at pp. 34, 43 *et seq.* and his dissenting opinion in the Interhandel Case, [1959] I.C.J. 6, 103–4. Compare Henkin, "The Connally Amendment Revisited and, Hopefully, Contained," 65 *Am. J. Int'l L.* 374 (1971); also "Pending Repeal of the Connally Amendment," 19 *Record of N.Y.C.B.A.* 162, 163 (1964). See Wilcox, "The United States Accepts Compulsory Jurisdiction," 40 *Am. J. Int'l L.* 699, 710–14 (1946).
8. See J. Austin, *The Province of Jurisprudence Determined* 1–31, 138–39 (1832). But compare *id.* at 140–45.
9. Exceptions are few: Albania in the Corfu Channel case is the outstanding example. Iran in 1951 and France and Iceland in 1973 ignored orders for interim measures; [1951] I.C.J. 89; [1973] I.C.J. 99, 135. See Kearney, "Amid the Encircling Doom," in *The Future of the International Court of Justice* 105, 112–13 (L. Gross ed., 1976).
10. See R. Falk, *The Role of Domestic Courts in the International Order* 93, 170–77 (1963); compare Mr. Justice White dissenting in *Banco Nacional de Cuba* v. *Sabbatino*, 376 U.S. 398, 439 (1964).

CHAPTER 2.   THE POLITICS OF LAW-MAKING

1. See, generally, A. Nussbaum, *A Concise History of the Law of Nations* (2d ed. 1954).
2. On the principle of unanimity, see, for example, Waldock, "General Course on Public International Law," *Recueil des cours* 1962 (II) 1, 50. Compare the development of procedure for seeking "consensus" (instead of putting matters to majority vote), as in the Third U.N. Law of the Sea Conference, p. 215, above.

3. Compare the development in the United States of the "restrictive theory" of sovereign immunity, culminating in the "Tate Letter," 26 *Dep't State Bull.* 984 (1952), and finally in the Foreign Sovereign Immunities Act of 1976, P. L. 94-583, Oct. 21, 1976, 28 U.S.C. § 1330, 1602 *et seq.* (1976).

4. Compare G. I. Tunkin, *Theory of International Law* 133 (Butler tr. 1974) with C. de Visscher, *Theory and Realty in Public International Law* 161–62 (rev. ed. Corbett tr., 1968).

5. For a discussion of the issue in American Constitutional jurisprudence see Henkin, "Privacy and Autonomy," 74 *Colum. L. Rev.* 1410 (1974).

CHAPTER 3.   THE POLITICS OF LAW OBSERVANCE

1. M. McDougal, "A Footnote," 57 *Am. J. Int'l L.* 383 (1963). For a full exposition, see McDougal, "International Law, Power and Policy: A Contemporary Conception," 82 *Recueil des Cours* 137 (1953). Compare, generally, M. McDougal and F. Feliciano, *Law and Minimum World Public Order* (1961).

2. See my statement in *Proceedings of the American Society of International Law* 147, 165, especially at 168 (1963).

3. Professor McDougal has also been interpreted as suggesting that nations do, and properly, determine law and obligation for themselves in the light of fundamental values. See, *e.g.*, W. Friedmann, Book Review, 64 *Colum. L. Rev.* 606, 612–13 (1964). Of course, in the first instance, every nation determines for itself the lawfulness of any action it contemplates. Inevitably, it also determines, in the first instance, the standards and considerations that determine lawfulness. But if, as has been suggested, Professor McDougal believes that the determination of some nations, in the light of values they deem fundamental, is *ipso facto* proper and their actions are *ipso facto* lawful, such a view would seem mistaken as well as pernicious. The emphasis on fundamental values to guide a determination of a particular law might be appropriate, again, to judgment from on high, where there is some body with competence and authority to determine such values and apply and impose them as law. It is not appropriate where law is not imposed from above but depends ultimately on consensus and common interest, where there is no arbiter of values, where there is no agreement on basic values and on what laws these require. Nations do, often enough, confuse their own immediate interests, as they see them, with absolute principle, and they may invoke these values to bolster their

legal position or to justify a violation. Some of them may even insist that their values determine the law. But international society has usually not accepted such actions or assertions as law, and the actors themselves probably do not consider them valid as law.

4. But see H. Morgenthau, *Politics Among Nations* 270 (4th ed., 1967).
5. See *Whitney* v. *Robertson*, 124 U.S. 190, 193–95 (1888); *Chinese Exclusion Cases*, 130 U.S. 581 (1889); also, *United States* v. *Gredzens*, 125 F. Supp. 867 (D. Minn. 1954); *United States* v. *Rumsa*, 212 F. 2d 927 (7th Cir. 1954); *cf. Moser* v. *United States*, 341 U.S. 41 (1951). See Henkin, *Foreign Affairs and the Constitution* 163–64 (1972).
6. In the "Byrd Amendment," Congress legislated to prevent U.S. compliance with a U.N. Security Council decision that all members shall prevent importation of Rhodesian products. The Byrd Amendment was repealed in 1977. See S.C. Res. 253, U.N. Doc. 5/INF/23 (1968); Section 503 of the Military Procurement Act of 1971, 50 U.S.C. 98(h) (1970), effectively repealed in P.L. 95-12, 95th Cong., March 10, 1977, amending 22 U.S.C. 287c.
7. 42 *Dep't State Bull.* 818–19 (1960).
8. See P. Corbett, *Law in Diplomacy* 274–75 (1959); compare L. Henkin, Book Review, 9 *J. Pub. L.* 229, 232–33 (1960).
9. In 1914 Germany paid dearly in "credit" and in public opinion for spurning rhetoric when its Chancellor, in a conversation with the British Ambassador, referred to Germany's agreement to observe Belgian neutrality as a "scrap of paper." See the dispatch of Ambassador Goschen to Lord Grey in 108 *British and Foreign State Papers*, Part 2, 785 (1914). But see the German explanation in *N.Y. Times*, Jan. 25, 1915, pp. 1, 2.
10. Or, some think, the oil embargo. Compare Chapter 1, n. 6, above.
11. Perodic efforts to improve law observance often concentrate on seeking new sanctions against violators. One might do well to consider strengthening other inducements to compliance. See R. Fisher, "Internal Enforcement of International Rules," in *Disarmament: Its Politics and Economics* 99, 106–20 (S. Melman ed., 1962). Compare L. Henkin, "Enforcement of Arms Control: Some Basic Considerations," 1 *J. Arms Control* 184, 185 (1963).
12. The bilateral treaty represents ordinarily an undertaking by the nation itself engaging its "honor." The multilateral treaty, in addition, represents wide acceptance in the community and its violation will not "sit well." These advantages are among the reasons for conventions codify-

ing customary law—despite the danger that some nations will take the occasion to deny the customary law, and refuse to accept the convention. That may be one lesson of attempts in 1958 and 1960 to codify the width of the territorial sea, although, it seems clear, the norm was uncertain and challengeable. See Chapter 11.

13. The United States insisted that it must live up to its commitments to protect South Vietnam, in part so as not to jeopardize the credibility of its commitments to other allies. See, *e.g.*, D. MacArthur, "The Free World's Stake in Viet-Nam," 55 *Dep't State Bull.* 745, 748–50 (1966).

14. In 1966, the Chinese Communists detained the Dutch Ambassador to Peking after Dutch authorities sought to interrogate several Chinese officials who took refuge in the embassy at The Hague. See *N.Y. Times*, July 19, 1966, p. 6; July 23, 1966, p. 2; Aug. 20, 1966, p. 4. Another unusual instance occurred in October 1966, when Guinea placed the United States Ambassador under house arrest in retaliation for supposed American involvement in the detention by Ghana of the Guinean Foreign Minister while in transit to a diplomatic conference. 55 *Dep't State Bull.* 789–91 (1966).

15. In 1963, the United States blocked all Cuban assets in the United States. 28 Fed. Reg. 6974–85 (1963). In 1964, Congress authorized the President to vest the blocked Cuban assets and to sell them to pay the expenses of a Foreign Claims Settlement Administration set up to determine the losses suffered by American nationals from Cuban nationalization decrees. 78 Stat. 1110, 22 U.S.C. § 1643 (j) (1964), modified, 79 Stat. 988, 22 U.S.C. § 1643 (j) (1976). See S. Rep. No. 701, 89th Cong., 1st sess. (1965).

16. See 26 *Dep't State Bull.* 7 (1952).

17. See the "Hickenlooper Amendment," 76 Stat. 260–61 (1962), 22 U.S.C. § 2370 (e) (1976). Aid to Ceylon was canceled under this legislation. It was resumed after the Government of Ceylon agreed to an acceptable measure of compensation for the nationalized property. See Chapter 6, p. 132.

18. For example, on April 19, 1965, Turkey announced that Greek nationals resident in Turkey would be expelled and the Ecumenical Patriarchate "controlled." *N.Y. Times*, Apr. 20, 1965, p. 1. The Turkish announcement was generally regarded as an effort to overcome Greek resistance to high-level negotiatons on the problem of Cyprus. *N.Y. Times*, Apr. 25, 1965, p. 13. Greek officials replied by pointing out

that the provisions of the Treaty of Lausanne, which governed the rights of the Greek minority in Turkey, were also the source of guarantees for the Turkish minority in Greece. *N.Y. Times*, Apr. 23, 1965, p. 5.

19. Political scientists have written of tacit agreements particularly in regard to international competiton in armaments; *e.g.*, T. Schelling, "Reciprocal Measures for Arms Stabilization," in *Arms Control, Disarmament, and National Security* 174–77 (D. Brennan ed., 1961).

20. *N.Y. Times*, Nov. 27, 1961, p. 8; Nov. 28, 1961, p. 4; Nov. 29, 1961, p. 3. See n. 7, above.

21. There is, of course, the precedent of the Nürnberg trials, the principles of which were later adopted unanimously by the General Assembly. 1 U.N. GAOR 1144 (1946). Compare the Report of the International Law Commission, p. 90 n., above.

22. G.A. Res. 285, 3 U.N. GAOR, Resolutions, at 34, U.N. Doc. A/900 (1949).

23. See Part Four, p. 249.

24. The machinery is both political and judicial. Articles 169, 170, and 173 of the Treaty Establishing the European Economic Community (1957), 298 *U.N.T.S.* 3, 75 (1958), permit suits before the Court of Justice of the European Communities to be brought by organs of the Communities, by states, and by individuals. For a discussion of cases instituted under these provisions and under earlier provisions in the treaty establishing the European Coal and Steel Community, see 2 D. Valentine, *The Court of Justice of the European Communities* (1965); also L. Brinkhorst and H. Schermers, *Judicial Remedies in the European Communities* (1969).

25. The significance of "acceptance" of law is stressed by Professor H. L. A. Hart in *The Concept of Law* (1961), particularly 86–88. Compare R. Fisher, "Bringing Law to Bear on Governments," 74 *Harv. L. Rev.* 1130 (1961).

26. § 15, 61 Stat. 3416; T.I.A.S. 1676 § 15 (1947).

27. In early 1967, New York City established a program that included the towing away of illegally parked vehicles belonging to diplomats. *N.Y. Times*, Jan 24, 1967, pp. 1, 24. Within a few days, however, the city retreated in the face of diplomatic protests and instituted exceptions to its "no-exception" tow-away program. *N.Y. Times*, Jan. 26, 1967, pp. 1, 43.

28. In earlier times, it has been suggested, governing classes also shared a

common international morality, now largely destroyed by democracy and nationalism. See H. Morgenthau, "The Twilight of International Morality," 58 *Ethics* 79, 88 (1948).

For a famous comparison of national and individual self-interest and morality, see Hamilton, "Pacificus No. IV, 1793," in 4 *The Works of Alexander Hamilton* 460 (H. Lodge ed., 1904), quoted in part in Conclusion, p. 335.

29. In an earlier day, a well-known observer said of the United States: ". . . although it allows [its statesmen] to say irritating things and advance unreasonable claims, it has not for more than 40 years permitted them to abuse its enormous strength. . . ." 3 J. Bryce, *The American Commonwealth* 354 (1888). Compare the United States reaction in the case of Suez, Chapter 13. See R. Aron, *Peace and War* 474 (1966). Many thought the United States acted immorally in Vietnam; see Chapter 16.

30. The United States has not yet ratified the Genocide Convention of 1949. In 1953, Secretary Dulles reserved the position of the United States in regard to ratifying the human rights conventions. The acceptance by the United States of the "Optional Clause" of the Statute of the International Court of Justice is still subject to the "Connally Reservation." See Chapter 1, n. 7, above.

For more recent U.S. attitudes on ratification of human rights agreements, see Chapter 12.

31. Compare the attitudes of the United States courts in regard to sovereign immunity: *Ex Parte Peru*, 318 U.S. 578 (1943); *Restatement (Second) of the Foreign Relations Law of the United States* § 72 (1965); P. Jessup, "Has the Supreme Court Abdicated One of Its Functions?" 40 *Am. J. Int'l L.* 168 (1946). See Chapter 2, n. 3.

32. See Chapter 16. The United States was, of course, legally responsible for violations like those by Lt. Calley, found guilty of violating the rights of civilians during the Vietnam War, but presumably they did not reflect high-level governmental policy.

33. No doubt this contributed to the failure of the operation. Compare H. Morgenthau, "To Intervene or Not to Intervene," 45 *Foreign Affairs* 425, 431 (1967).

34. For example, on September 3, 1954, President Eisenhower "pocket vetoed" two bills because they were inconsistent with international law and comity. About one, which would have authorized the Court of Claims to determine the amount lost by a U.S. corporation be-

cause of German exchange controls during the Weimar period, he said: "I am informed that this would be contrary to a well-recognized principle of international law and practice." The second bill would have authorized the State of Illinois and the Sanitary District of Chicago to divert water from Lake Michigan. Among the objections which the President listed was the fact that "the Canadian Government . . . has continued its objections to this bill. . . ." 100 Cong. Rec. 15569 (1954).

Of course, Presidential vetoes may be unavailing. On January 29, 1917, President Wilson, vetoing an immigration bill, objected, *inter alia*, to a clause which would have exempted from literacy tests those who could establish that they were fleeing from religious persecution in their native countries. Among Wilson's reasons was that such a provision would probably raise "very serious questions of international justice and comity" between the United States and other governments. 54 Cong. Rec. 2443 (1917). The veto was overridden. 54 Cong. Rec. 2456–57 and 2629 (1917).

35. The executive branch has also been known to respond to congressional and other critics of its policy by saying that the policy was required by international law or treaty.

36. The opposition to U.S. policy in Vietnam has invoked arguments that the United States was violating international law. See *e.g.*, Speech of Senator Wayne Morse, 112 Cong. Rec. No. 7 at 624 (1966). See Chapter 16.

37. *The Paquete Habana*, 175 U.S. 677, 700, 708 (1900); compare *Berizzi Bros. Co. v. S.S. Pesaro*, 271 U.S. 562 (1926). See also Rev. Stat. § 4063 (1875), 22 U.S.C. § 252 (1976). See generally, Henkin, *Foreign Affairs and the Constitution* 221–24 (1972).

38. U.S. Constitution, Article VI; *Foster v. Neilson*, 27 U.S. (2 Pet.) 253, 314 (1829). Henkin, cited n. 37, at 156 *et seq*. Compare the French and German constitutions, cited in n. 60, below.

39. *Asakura v. City of Seattle*, 265 U.S. 332 (1924). Of course, much international law and many treaties cannot make their way into court and be vindicated by the courts. In all cases, moreover, the Congress, and in some cases the President, can decide that the United States will not live up to its obligations and the courts will follow the political decision. *Whitney v. Robertson*, 124 U.S. 190, 194–95. Compare *The Paquete Habana*, cited above, n. 37, at 700, and *id.* at 720 (Fuller C. J., dissenting). See Henkin, cited n. 37, at 163–64, 221–22. But the instances in

which political branches make law for the courts in disregard of international law or an international agreement are few; commonly, the Attorney General or the Legal Adviser of the State Department would be heard on any such proposed action and their objections would prevail.

40. See U.S. Constitution, Amendments V, XIV; *Wong Wing* v. *United States*, 163 U.S. 228 (1896). Compare *Truax* v. *Raich*, 239 U.S. 33 (1915). See Henkin, cited n. 37, at 254.

41. The role of legal advisers has only recently been studied. See *Legal Advisers and Foreign Affairs* (H. Merillat ed., 1964); *Legal Advisers and International Organizations* (H. Merillat ed., 1966); Bilder, "The Office of the Legal Adviser: The State Department Lawyer and Foreign Affairs," 56 *Am. J. Int'l L* 633 (1962).

42. See D. Deener, *United States Attorneys General and International Law* (1957).

43. A. D. McNair, *International Law Opinions* (1956).

44. Compare the statement said to have been made by President Jackson to his Attorney General: "Sir, you must find a law authorizing this action or I will find an Attorney General who will," quoted, *inter alia*, in *Cong. Globe*, 39th Cong., 2d Sess., 439 (1867), and in H. Cummings and C. McFarland, *Federal Justice* 109 (1937).

45. Two United States federal courts have held that Cuban nationalization of American properties violated international law. *Banco Nacional de Cuba* v. *Sabbatino*, 193 F. Supp. 375 (S.D.N.Y. 1961), *aff'd*, 307 F. 2d. 845 (2d. Cir. 1962). See also the same case on remand, *Banco Nacional de Cuba* v. *Farr*, 243 F. Supp. 957 (S.D.N.Y. 1965).

The Supreme Court did not rule on that question, but held that even if the nationalizations were unlawful, American courts had to give them effect under the Act of State Doctrine. *Banco Nacional de Cuba* v. *Sabbatino*, 376 U.S. 398 (1964). For a full discussion, see R. Falk, "The Aftermath of Sabbatino," in Association of the Bar of the City of New York, *Background Papers and Proceedings of the Seventh Hammarskjold Forum* (1965).

46. Compare Acheson, quoted in Conclusion, p. 325 n.

47. But compare the internationalization of human rights, Chapter 12.

48. For the Galindez and Ben Barka affairs in a different context, see Chapter 14, n. 25, below.

49. For a contemporary example, consider Turkey's bombing of Cyprus on August 8, 1964. *N.Y. Times*, Aug. 9, 1964, § 1, pp. 1, 28.

50. Contemporary instances of alleged mistreatment of aliens are collected in A. and A. Thomas, *Non-Intervention, The Law and Its Import in the Americas* 312–26 (1956).
51. Compare the failure of inspection in the Korean Armistice, pp. 77–79, above.
52. Compare the statement of President de Gaulle at his Sixth Press Conference, May 15, 1962, in French Embassy, Press and Information Divison, *Major Addresses, Statements and Press Conferences of General Charles de Gaulle, May 19, 1958–January 31, 1964,* at 180: ". . . new elements of an extraordinary dimension have been introduced into the picture, and France must take them into consideration. First, Soviet Russia also now has an enormous nuclear arsenal which is increasing every day, as, moreover, is that of the United States. Henceforth, America and Soviet Russia will be capable of striking each other directly and, doubtless, of reciprocally destroying each other. It is not certain that they will take this risk. No one can tell today when, how, or why one or the other of these great atomic powers would employ its nuclear arsenal. It is enough to say this in order to understand that, as regards the defense of France, the battle of Europe and even a world war as they were imagined when NATO was born, everything is now in question." See also the statement of General de Gaulle quoted in J. Freymond, "European Views on Arms Control," in *Arms Control, Issues for the Public* 174, 194 (L. Henkin ed., 1961).

Compare the statement of Senator Dandurand of Canada in regard to the League of Nations provisions for collective security, quoted in I. Claude, *Swords into Plowshares* 284 (2nd ed., 1959): "In this association of mutual insurance against fire, the risks assumed by the different states are not equal. We live in a fireproof house, far from flammable material."
53. *E.g.,* Argentina, Chile, Costa Rica, Honduras, and Peru. See M. Sorensen, "The Law of the Sea," *Int'l Conc.* No. 520, 244 (1958). For the U.S. action, see Presidential Proclamation 2667, 10 Fed. Reg. 12303 (1945). See Chapter 11.
54. See, *e.g.,* F. Falk, "Historical Tendencies, Modernizing and Revolutionary Nations, and the International Legal Order," in 2 R. Falk and S. Mendlovitz, *The Strategy of World Order* 172, 184 (1966).
55. See, *e.g.,* Universal Military Training and Service Act, 65 Stat, 75 (1951), 50 U.S.C. app. §§ 454 (a), 456, 467 (a) (1958); *United States* v. *Gredzens,* 125 F. Supp. 867 (D. Minn. 1954).

56. Mr. Justice Brandeis dissenting in *Myers* v. *United States*, 272 U.S. 52, 293 (1926): "The doctrine of the separation of powers was adopted by the Convention of 1787, not to promote efficiency but to preclude the exercise of arbitrary power."

57. In a parliamentary system, too, an act of parliament may later be found to violate international law, and it may not be practical for the government to have the act modified quickly. Compare the statement of Mr. Runciman in the House of Commons of March 4, 1907, on the Norwegian fisheries dispute. 170 Parl. Deb., H.C. (4th ser.) 472 (1907).

58. In the first instance, of course, the President can negotiate treaties only to find that the Senate will not consent to their ratification. The most famous instance is the Treaty of Versailles. A familiar nine-teenth-century example is the rejection by the Senate in 1870 of a proposed treaty providing for the annexation of Santo Domingo by the United States. For the story of the Senate's consideration of that treaty, see C. Tansill, *The United States and Santo Domingo, 1798–1873*, 400–464 (1938). See generally W. Holt, *Treaties Defeated by the Senate* (1933). In 1977–78 there was strong opposition to ratification of the new Panama Canal treaty.

59. In fact, it appears, Congress has never refused to appropriate funds for the execution of a treaty. Nevertheless, the Executive ordinarily re-frains from financial commitment to foreign nations in deference to the congressional power over appropriations. See, *e.g.*, *N.Y. Times*, Feb. 21, 1967, p. 2.

60. Acts of Congress prevail as domestic law over earlier treaty provisions; see the cases cited in this chapter, n. 5, above. But compare Article 55 of the French Constitution of 1958 and Article 25 of the Constitution of the German Federal Republic, which declare that treaties shall have authority superior to that of domestic laws.

61. Compare Justice Black, in *Reid* v. *Covert*, 354 U.S. 1, 17 (1957): "It would be manifestly contrary to the objectives of those who created the Constitution, as well as those who were responsible for the Bill of Rights, . . . to construe Article VI [of the Constitution] as permitting the United States to exercise power under an international agreement without observing constitutional prohibitions." See Henkin, *Foreign Affairs and the Constitution* 137–40 (1972).

62. U.S. Const. Art. VI: *Missouri* v. *Holland*, 252 U.S. 416 (1920); *Asakura* v. *City of Seattle*, 265 U.S. 332 (1924); *The Paquete Habana*, 175 U.S.

677, 700 (1900); *Peters* v. *McKay*, 238 P.2d 225, 231 (dictum) (Ore. 1951). Henkin, cited n. 61, at 222–23, 242.

Some years ago, in order to promote local products, South Carolina required merchants to advertise that they were selling Japanese goods—a requirement that the United States admitted was in violation of a most-favored-nation clause in the Treaty of Friendship, Commerce and Navigation with Japan. See the exchange of notes between Japan and the United States, 34 *Dep't State Bull.* 728 (1956). If a merchant had violated that requirement, and been convicted by state authorities for this violation, the conviction would presumably have been reversed and the treaty given effect. But no merchant challenged the state's requirement, and it appeared that there was no effective way of compelling the state to remove the offending statute from its books and to desist from threats to enforce it. Political persuasion by the State Department was not effective for some time.

It has even been suggested that the various states may decide questions of international law for themselves. See the opinion of Judge Learned Hand in *Bergman* v. *De Sieyes*, 170 F. 2d 360, 361 (2nd cir. 1948). But see *Banco Nacional de Cuba* v. *Sabbatino*, 376 U.S. 398, 425 (1964) and L. Henkin, "The Foreign Affairs Power of the Federal Courts: *Sabbatino*," 64 *Colum. L. Rev.* 805, 819–20, n. 48 (1964); Henkin, cited n. 61, above, at 245–46.

63. See 6 J. B. Moore, *Digest of International Law* § 1026 (1906); compare the case of Italian citizens lynched in New Orleans in 1891, *id.* at 837–41.

64. Compare *Costa* v. *Ente Nazionale per L'Energia Elettrica* (ENEL), 3 *Common Market L. Rep.* 425, 455, 458 (1964).

65. *E.g.*, Iraq announced its withdrawal from the Baghdad Pact eleven months before the initial expiration date and five months before such notification of withdrawal was permitted by the Treaty. *N.Y. Times*, Mar. 25, 1959, pp. 1, 6. It did not participate in the Pact after this announcement.

66. Korean Armistice Agreement, Article II, 8 U.N. SCOR, Supp. July–Sept., at 23, U.N. Doc S/3079 (1953).

67. The Armistice Agreement also "recommended" to the governments concerned a political conference; it was held at Geneva in 1954 and produced nothing. See Report to the United Nations on the Korean Political Conference at Geneva, 9 U.N. GAOR, Annexes, Agenda Item No. 17, at 2, U.N. Doc. A/2786 (1954). It is not clear that either

side had great expectations that something would come of such a conference; for neither side, apparently, was the expectation of some political settlement a condition of its agreement to an armistice.
68. Korean Armistice Agreement, cited above, n. 66, Article III.
69. The United Nations General Assembly affirmed the principle in G.A. Res. 610, 7 U.N. GAOR, Supp. 20, at 3–4, U.N. Doc. A/2361 (1952).
70. Before the agreement went into effect, the government of the Republic of Korea realeased some 27,000 North Korean prisoners of war because, it was asserted, it did not wish these prisoners pressured to return to North Korea. Many observers saw in this step a final effort by the government to frustrate the armistice. The Communists protested but did not refuse to go ahead with the agreement. See Special Report of the Unified Command on the Armistice in Korea, 8 U.N. SCOR, Supp. for July, Aug., Sept., at 17–20, U.N. Doc. S/3079 (1953).
71. See speech by Secretary of State Acheson, 7 U.N. GAOR, First Comm., Agenda Item. No. 16a, at 25, U.N. Doc. A/C. 1/SR. 512 (1952). See also Report of U.N. Commission for Unification and Rehabilitation of Korea, § F, 7 U.N. GAOR, Annexes, Agenda Item No. 16, at 7, U.N. Doc. A/2228 (1952).
72. Korean Armistice Agreement, Article II, A(13)(d), cited above, n. 66, at 24. The Communist negotiators resisted a related provision prohibiting the rehabilitation of airfields, which could readily have been monitored by aerial observation. See Report of U.N. Commission for Unification and Rehabilitation of Korea, cited above, n. 71, at 6.
73. Eventually, in 1956, because the Communists had frustrated the Commission's operations in North Korea, the U.N. Command refused to allow the Neutral Nations Supervisory Commission to continue to operate behind its lines. See Report of Unified Command on Neutral Nations Supervisory Commission in Korea, U.N. Doc. A/3167 (1956).
74. Agreement on the Cessation of Hostilities in Viet Nam, Article 14, 161 *British and Foreign State Papers* 818; Final Declaration of the Geneva Conference, Geneva, 21st July, 1954, § 6, *id.* at 359.
75. The effect of the law of the United Nations Charter outlawing war on peace treaties is uncertain. One may argue tht henceforth an agreement imposed by a victorious aggressor has no legal validity. See 1 L. Oppenheim, *International Law* § 499 (8th ed., Lauterpacht, 1955). If the victim of aggression should prevail, may it impose any agreement

it likes on the defeated aggressor? Compare the position of Israel after its victories in 1948, or in 1967. The General Assembly has adopted resolutions banning the acquisition of territory by force and denying it recognition. See Declaration on Principles of International Law Concerning Friendly Relations and Co-operation Among States in Accordance with the Charter of the United Nations, G.A. Res. 2625, Oct. 24, 1970, 25 GAOR, Supp. 28 (A/3028) at 122–24. Compare the Resolution which approved the Definition of Aggression, G.A. Res. 3314/29, 14 Dec. 1974. It is not wholly clear, however, whether that applies also to a victim of an armed attack which succeeds in conquering territory of the aggressor.

76. There were disarmament and arms control provisions in the Treaty of Versailles, Part V, Articles 159–213. For the text of the Treaty, see 112 *British and Foreign State Papers* 1 (1919), and 13 *Am. J. Int'l L. Supp.* 151 (1919). The end of World War I also saw treaty provisions protecting minorities, *e.g.*, the Minorities Treaty with Poland, June 28, 1919. This Treaty may be found in 1 M. Hudson, *International Legislation* 283 (1931) and 112 *British and Foreign State Papers* 232 (1919). For such clauses in the agreements following the Second World War, see, *e.g.*, the Treaties of Peace with Japan and Italy, respectively, at [1951] 3 U.S.T. & O.I.A. 3169, T.I.A.S. No. 2490, and 61 Stat. 1245, T.I.A.S. No. 1648 (1947).

77. Thirty years ago, Professor Philip Jessup suggested that, for political treaties, the doctrine of *rebus sic stantibus* is pernicious. P. Jessup, *A Modern Law of Nations* 150 (1948).

CHAPTER 4. IS IT LAW OR POLITICS?

1. Compare Holmes, J. (dissenting) in *Compania Gen. de Tabacos v. Coll. Int. Rev.*, 275 U.S. 87,100 (1927).

2. For developments on the law of the territorial sea, see Chapter 11.

CHAPTER 5. LAW AND IDEOLOGICAL CONFLICT IN THE NUCLEAR AGE

1. The "Baruch Plan" was based on the Acheson-Lilienthal report, "A Report on the International Control of Atomic Energy," *Committee on Atomic Energy, Dep't of State, Pub. No. 2498* (1946).

2. Compare, *e.g.*, Declaration of the Soviet Government on General and Complete Disarmament, U.N. Doc. A/4219 (1959), and *United States Arms Control and Disarmament Agency, Pub. No. 4, Blueprint for the Peace Race* (1962). The latest call for "General and Complete Disarmament" seems to have been in G.A. Res. 31/189 of 21 Dec. 1976 to convene a special session devoted to disarmament in New York in May/June 1978. See also the Charter of Economic Rights and Duties of States, G.A. Res. 3281 (XXIX), 12 Dec. 1974, Art. 15. The U.S.S.R. continues to invoke it periodically, for example in Article IV of its proposed "World Treaty on the Non-Use of Force in International Relations," U.N. Doc. A/31/2431 Sept. 28, 1976; compare G.A. Res. 31/9, 8 Nov. 1976.

3. See L. Henkin, "Disarmament—The Lawyer's Interests," in Association of the Bar of the City of New York, *Disarmament: Background Papers and Proceedings of the Fourth Hammarskjold Forum* 22–24 (1964).

4. The Outer-Space Treaty has been ratified by both the United States and the Soviet Union. For the text, see 55 *Dep't State Bull.* 953–55 (1966).

5. G. A. Res. 1653, U.N. GAOR, Supp. 17, at 4, U.N. Doc. A/5100 (1961).

6. *Hearings on the Nuclear Test Ban Treaty (Executive M) Before the Committee on Foreign Relations*, 88th Cong., 1st Sess., at 536–39, 877 (1963). But compare *id.* at 330, 395.

7. The subheading is borrowed from a short, fine monograph by my colleague Professor O. Lissitzyn, *Int'l Conc.* No. 542 (1963), which was revised, expanded, and republished as *International Law Today and Tomorrow* (1965).

8. Even, it has been suggested, by a common international morality. See H. Morgenthau, "The Twilight of International Morality," 58 *Ethics* 79 (1948).

9. See E. Stillman and W. Pfaff, *The New Politics, America and the End of the Postwar World* 43–70 (1961).

10. Q. Wright, *The Role of International Law in the Elimination of War* 21 (1961).

11. See, *e.g.*, P. Corbett, *Law in Diplomacy* 89–109 (1959); T. Taracouzio, *The Soviet Union and International Law* 54–56, 187–89, 237 (1935).

12. The Soviet Union has often been accused, not without some basis, of having violated many of its treaties. See J. Triska and R. Slusser, *The*

Theory, Law, and Policy of Soviet Treaties 394–95 (1962). Little note has been taken of the agreements it has observed. See O. Lissitzyn, *International Law Today and Tomorrow* 57–61 (1965). See also *Hearings on the Nuclear Test Ban Treaty (Executive M) Before the Senate Committee on Foreign Relations*, 88th Cong., 1st Sess., at 967 (Memorandum from the Department of State on Soviet Treaty Violations) (1963).

13. See generally, R. Edwards, "The Attitude of the People's Republic of China Toward International Law and the United Nations," in 17 East Asian Research Center, Harvard University, *Papers on China* 235 (1963); J. C. Hsiung, *Law and Policy in China's Foreign Relations* (1972); J. A. Cohen, *The People's Republic of China and International Law* (1968).

14. Principally, China claimed that India had violated the Chinese border and was preparing a massive invasion of Chinese territory; China also maintained that the MacMahon line, the border which India claims, was drawn illegally. *N.Y. Times*, Oct. 21, 1962, pp. 1, 5.

15. For early attitudes toward alien property, see A. Sack, "Les Réclamations diplomatiques contre les Soviets (1918–38)," 20 *Revue de droit international et de législation comparée* 5, 13 (1939). *Cf.* [1918] (Russia III) *Foreign Rel. U.S.* 33 (1932). Recent attitudes may be garnered from Russian statements and votes in the United Nations. Compare pp. 128–30, above. See K. Katzarov, *The Theory of Nationalization* 34–36, 325–26 (1960).

16. 23 *Dep't State Bull.* 1004 (1950); 43 *Dep't State Bull.* 715 (1960); 49 *Dep't State Bull.* 160 (1963). In 1951, the United States suspended tariff concessions to Communist countries, 25 *Dep't State Bull.* 95, 290, 913 (1951).

17. 19 *Dep't State Bull.* 525 (1948); 26 *Dep't State Bull.* 451 (1952).

18. See Report of the U.N. Command, 7 U.N. GAOR, Annexes 1, Item No. 16, at 7, U.N. Doc. A/2228 (1952); see also G.A. Res. 610, 7 U.N. GAOR, Supp. 20, at 3, U.N. Doc. A/2361 2361 (1952); see p. 77, above.

Perhaps not ideological conflict, but "socialism," brought a major extension of "state trading," which gave impetus to other changes in the law, *e.g.*, a restrictive theory of immunity. In the "Tate Letter" the United States announced that it would deny sovereign immunity from suit in cases arising out of "commercial," as distinguished from "governmental," activities by governments. See 26 *Dep't State Bull.* 984 (1952); *Restatement (Second) of the Foreign Relations Law of the United States*

§ 69 (1965). See also the Foreign Sovereign Immunities Act of 1976, Chapter 2, n. 3, above.

19. The Soviet Union insisted on a "troika," with a built-in veto, for the management of an international disarmament organization. 44 *Dep't State Bull.* 634, 755 (1961); 45 *Dep't State Bull.* 377 (1962). Compare the Soviet Union's proposal for a "troika" to replace the U.N. Secretary General. 15 U.N. GAOR 81 (1960).

20. G.A. Res. 1721, 16 U.N. GAOR, Supp. 17, at 6, U.N. Doc. A/5100 (1961); Multilateral Test Ban Treaty, Aug. 5, 1963, [1963] 2 U.S.T. & O.I.A. 1313, T.I.A.S. No. 5433. More recently also: Treaty on the Prohibition of the Emplacement of Nuclear Weapons and Other Weapons of Mass Destruction on the Seabed and the Ocean floor and in the Subsoil thereof, 11 Feb. 1971; Treaty between the United States of America and the Union of Soviet Socialist Republics on the Limitation of Anti-Ballistic Missile Systems; also The Interim Agreement and the Protocol, May 26, 1972; Protocol to the treaty, July 3, 1974, entered into force May 24, 1976; Agreement between the United States of America and the Union of Soviet Socialist Republics on the Prevention of Nuclear War, June 22, 1973; also the Treaty and Protocol on the Limitation of Underground Nuclear Weapon Tests, July 3, 1973; the Treaty and Protocol on Underground Nuclear Explosions for Peaceful Purposes, May 28, 1976. The texts of the agreements, and some commentary can be found in Arms Control and Disarmament Agency, *Arms Control and Disarmament Agreements: Texts and History of Negotiations* (1977 ed.).

21. The Consular Convention was signed June 1, 1964, entered into force July 13, 1968. 19 U.S.T. 5018, T.I.A.S. 6503, 655 U.N.T.S. 213. See also the Treaty on Principles Governing the Activities of States in the Exploration and Use of Outer Space, including the Moon and Other Celestial Bodies, 1967, 18 U.S.T. 2410, T.I.A.S. 6347, 610 U.N.T.S. 205. Other space agreements followed.

22. T. Taracouzio, *The Soviet Union and International Law* 249–51 (1935).

23. Compare O. Lissitzyn, *International Law Today and Tomorrow* 54, 59–61 (1965) with J. Triska and R. Slusser, *The Theory, Law and Policy of Soviet Treaties* 394–95 (1962).

24. See L. Henkin, "Toward a 'Rule of Law' Community," in *The Promise of World Tensions* 20–27 (H. Cleveland ed., 1961).

25. Instances are collected in A. Thomas and A. Thomas, *Non-Intervention, The Law and Its Import in the Americas* 312–28 (1956).

26. Trade Agreements Extension Act of 1951, ch. 141, §§ 5, 11, 65 Stat. 73, 75.

27. Despite strong pressure, Denmark insisted that delivery of the tanker was required by its agreement with the Soviet Union. The President of the United States decided not to terminate United States aid to Denmark under the so-called Battle Act, because to do so would "clearly be detrimental to the security of the United States." See *United States Mutual Defense Assistance Control Act of 1951, P.L. 213, 82d Congress, First Report to Congress* 53–57 (1952).

28. The controversy led to a decision of the International Court of Justice in favor of the United Kingdom [1974] I.C.J. 3. The parties later settled the dispute by agreement.

29. India sponsored the resolution eventually adopted. See U.N. Doc. A/C. 1/734/Rev. 1 (1952).

30. For example, on March 11, 1967, the Supreme Court of the Russian Republic annulled a three-year sentence imposed on an American tourist by a lower court for a minor infraction in order to "eliminate an irritant in recently improving United States–Soviet relations." *N.Y. Times*, Mar. 12, 1967, § 1, pp. 1, 6.

31. See R. Aron, *Peace and War* 652 (1966).

32. See analysis of the Khrushchev speech on "peaceful coexistence," of January 6, 1961, *Hearings Before the Subcommittee to Investigate the Administration of the Internal Security Act and the Internal Security Law of the Committee on the Judiciary, United States Senate*, 87th Cong., 1st Sess., 52–78 (1961): compare the United Nations G.A. resolution calling for support for anti-colonial forces, G.A. Res. 2908 (XXVII), 2 Nov. 1972.

33. See p. 156, above.

CHAPTER 6. THE THIRD WORLD

1. For an examination of the attitudes of new states toward international law, see, for example, R. P. Anand, *New States and International Law* (1972); also J. Syatauw, *Some Newly Established Asian States and the Development of International Law* (1961).

2. Including prime place in both the International Covenant on Civil and Political Rights and the International Covenant on Economic, Social and Cultural Rights. See also Declaration on the Granting of Independence to Colonial Countries and Peoples, G.A. Res. 1514 (XV), 14 Dec. 1960.

3. K. Katzarov, *The Theory of Nationalization* 34–36, 325–26 (1960).

4. 19 *Dep't State Press Releases* 50–53, 135–39, 165–69, 339–42 (1938).

5. See the debates in the Second Committee of the United Nations General Assembly on the Proposed Resolution on Permanent Sovereignty over Natural Resources. 17 U.N. GAOR, Second Comm. 229, U.N. Doc. A/C.2/SR.834 (1962) and 17 U.N. GAOR, Second Comm. 298, U.N. Doc. A/C.2/SR.846 (1962).

6. See, *e.g.*, S. Roy, "Is the Responsibility of States for Injuries to Aliens a Part of Universal International Law?" 55 *Am. J. Int'l L.* 863 (1961).

   Compare the statement of Mr. Nervo of Mexico in the International Law Commission: "The vast majority of new States had taken no part in the creation of the many institutions of international law which were consolidated and systematized in the nineteenth century. . . . With State responsibility, however, international rules were established, not merely without reference to small States but against them, and were based almost entirely on the unequal relations between great Powers and small States." 1 [1957] *Int'l Law Commission Yearbook* 155.

7. G.A. Res. 1803, 17 U.N. GAOR, Supp. 17, at 15, U.N. Doc. A/5217 (1962).

8. There has also been substantial adherence to the Convention on the Settlement of Investment Disputes Between States and Nationals of Other States, sponsored by the International Bank for Reconstruction and Development. By June 30, 1977, the Convention has been ratified by 67 countries. World Bank, *Annual Report, 1977*, p. 87.

   In regard to expropriation and compensation, it has been suggested that international society might develop and accept a double standard, with rules for the new nations different from those that govern the older powers. See A. Fatouros, "International Law and the Third World," 50 *Va. L. Rev.* 783, 811–17 (1964).

9. G.A. Res. 3281 (XXIX), 12 Dec. 1974, adopted 120 to 6 with 10 absentions. Articles 2(2)(c) declared that each state has the right: "To nationalize, expropriate or transfer ownership of foreign property, in which case appropriate compensation should be paid by the State adopting such measures, taking into account its relevant laws and regulations and all circumstances that the State considers pertinent. In any case where the question of compensation gives rise to a controversy, it shall be settled under the domestic law of the nationalizing State and by its tribunals, unless it is freely and mutually agreed by all

States concerned that other peaceful means be sought on the basis of the sovereign equality of States and in accordance with the principle of free choice of means."

10. For example, in 1964, the newly independent nation of Zambia received about two-thirds of its budget expenditures from copper mines owned by the Anglo-American Corporation and the Rhodesian Selection Trust, Ltd., the latter owned in part by American Metal Climax, Inc. *N.Y. Times*, Oct. 24, 1964, pp. 37, 39.

11. See the statement of newly elected Dudley Senanayake, *N.Y. Times*, Mar. 30, 1965, p. 12. On the effect of the amendment, see the statement of the Acting Legal Adviser, Leonard Meeker, *Claims of U.S. Nationals Against the Government of Cuba, Hearings on H.R. 10327, 10536, 10720, 12259 and 12260 Before the Subcommittee on Inter-American Affairs of the Committee on Foreign Affairs*, 88th Cong., 2d Sess., 145–46 (1964).

12. Egypt's noncompliance with the resolution of the Security Council was, in fact, protected by Soviet veto. See 9 U.N. SCOR, 664th meeting at 12 (1954).

13. The decision (on an interim question) in the Anglo-Iranian Oil Co. case is at [1951] I.C.J. 89. A threat of a Soviet veto led to adjournment of the debate on the issue in the Security Council without a vote. 6 U.N. SCOR, 559th–563rd, 565th meetings (1951).

14. Compare *The Asylum Case* (Colombia v. Peru) [1950] I.C.J. 266, 276.

CHAPTER 7. LAW AND FORCE: THE UNITED NATIONS CHARTER

1. I draw here on L. Henkin, "The United Nations and Its Supporters: A Self-Examination," 78 *Pol. Sci. Q.* 504, 516–19 (1963).

2. Compare C. de Visscher, *Théories et Réalités en Droit International Public* 112–13 (4th ed., 1970): "C'est un droit dont les parties fortes, asurées d'une observation régulière dans la pratique des Etats, ont trait à des questions qui restent sans action réelle sur les problèmes vraiment vitaux; dont les parties faibles, réduites à des prescriptions formelles, concernent l'usage de la force armée, le choix de la paix ou de la guerre entre les peuples." De Visscher quotes 1 Hold-Ferneck, *Lehrbuch des Völkerrechts* 88: "Das Völkerrecht bedeutet Ordnung im Kleinen, die aber stets bedroht ist durch Unordnung im Grossen."

3. U.N. Charter, Article 2(6).

4. For interpretations of the Charter that differ from mine, see the authors cited below. Chapter 13, n. 7, and Chapter 15, n. 29.

5. For this discussion I have drawn on my paper before the American Society of International Law, "Force, Intervention, and Neutrality in Contemporary International Law," in *Proceedings of the American Society of International Law* 147 (1963).

6. The Final Act of the Conference on Security and Cooperation in Europe includes among the Principles Guiding Relations Between Participating States: Sovereign equality, respect for the rights inherent in sovereignty; Refraining from the threat or use of force; Inviolability of frontiers; Territorial integrity of States; and Non-intervention in internal affairs.

7. Declaration on Principles of International Law Concerning Friendly Relations and Co-operation Among States in Accordance with the Charter of the United Nations, G.A. Res. 2625, Oct. 24, 1970, 25 GAOR, Supp. 28 (A/8028), at 122–24.

8. See n. 6, above.

9. See Chapter 3, n. 75.

10. North Atlantic Treaty, Articles 1, 5, and 7, 34 *U.N.T.S.* 243, 244, 246, 248 (1949).

11. See Chapter 13, n. 27; also McDougal, in *57 Proceedings of the American Society of International Law* 163 (1963).

12. J. B. Moore, 2 *Digest of International Law 412* (1906).

13. L. Henkin, "The United Nations and Its Supporters: A Self-Examination," 78 *Pol. Sci. Q.* 504 (1963), at 532–33. The argument in the last-quoted paragraph should not be confused with the one I reject in the Conclusion, p. 333, or with that of Mr. Acheson, pp. 333–34 n.

14. See, for example, *Humanitarian Intervention and The United Nations* (R. Lillich ed., 1973).

15. See G. Kennan, *American Diplomacy, 1900–1950*, 95 (1951), discussed in the Conclusion. Compare, for example, the address by Mr. Acheson, quoted in the Conclusion, p. 333 n.

16. China's taking of Tibet, India's of Goa are, I believe, readily distinguishable. On Goa, see Chapter 8, pp. 169–70.

17. Report of the Special Committee on the Problem of Hungary, 11 U.N GAOR, Supp. 18, at 14–16, U.N. Doc. A/3592 (1957).

18. *N.Y. Times*, Aug. 9, 1964, § 1, pp. 1, 28.

19. *N.Y. Times*, Nov. 24, 1964, § 1, pp. 1, 3.

20. See 19 U.N. SCOR, 1144th meeting (1964); 21 U.N. SCOR, 1320th–1328th meetings (1966).

21. There is dispute as to whether espionage is a violation of international

law. Some have argued that espionage *per se* is not unlawful, although many of the activities through which espionage is carried out may be. *E.g.*, U-2 reconnaissance may be a violation, not because it is a form of espionage, but because it violates the territory of another. See J. Stone, "Legal Problems of Espionage in Conditions of Modern Conflict," in *Essays on Espionage and International Law* 29, 34–35 (R. Stanger ed., 1962). Compare Q. Wright, "Espionage and the Doctrine of Non-Intervention in Internal Affairs," *id.*, 3, at 12–14.

22. See A. Thomas and A. Thomas, *Non-Intervention, The Law and Its Import in the Americas* 74–78 (1956). See also 1 L. Oppenheim, *International Law* § 134 (8th ed., H. Lauterpacht, 1955).

23. *E.g.*, the Charter of the Organization of American States, Article 15, Chapter 15, n. 23; see the Declaration on Principles of Friendly Relations, n. 7, above; and the Helsinki Final Act, n. 6, above.

24. For a discussion of possible lines to be drawn on the basis of motivations, purposes, means, see L. Henkin, "Force, Intervention, and Neutrality in Contemporary International Law," in *Proceedings of the American Society of International Law* 147, 156–57 (1963). Cf. T. Farer, "Intervention in Civil Wars: A Modest Proposal," 67 *Colum. L. Rev.* 266 (1967). Without any definition, nations have continued to invoke general prohibitions against intervention to protest crass forms of meddling in their political affairs.

25. See W. Friedmann, "Intervention, Civil War and the Role of International Law," in *Proceedings of the American Society of International Law* 67, 72 (1965). See generally *The International Law of Civil War* (R. Falk ed. 1971); Compare N. Padelford, "International Law and the Spanish Civil War," 31 *Am. J. Int'l L.* 226, 236–42 (1937).

26. *E.g.*, Peace Through Deeds, G.A. Res. 380, 5 U.N. GAOR, Supp. 20, at 13 U.N. Doc. A/1775 (1950). See Resolution defining aggression, Chapter 3, n. 75; Declaration on Friendly Relations, n. 7, above; Charter on Economic Rights and Duties of States, Chapter 10, n. 6.

27. In a different context, Belgium and the United States invoked the consent of the government of the Congo to justify their "intervention" to save white hostages from massacres by rebel forces. *N.Y. Times*, Nov. 24, 1964, pp. 1, 3.

28. See J. McClaren, "The Dominican Crisis: An Inter-American Dilemma," 4 *Can. Yearbook of Int'l. L.* 178, 181–82 (1966); see also the speech by Senator William Fulbright before the Senate, 111 *Cong. Rec.* 23855, 23859–60 (1965).

29. Compare: "At the present time, international law is a permanent in-
    citement to hypocrisy. It creates an obligation for the superpowers to
    dissimulate what they cannot avoid doing, that is, interfering in the in-
    ternal affairs of member states of the United Nations. No one refrains
    from intervening, but each tries to intervene in such a manner that the
    role [sic] of non-intervention will remain officially unbroken: the chief
    condition of success is for each camp to 'possess' a government which
    is an adherent of its cause. When the two camps attain their goal, the
    third country is either divided, like Germany, or in a state of civil
    war. Occasionally the country is divided and the section not won over
    to communism is in a state of civil war (South Korea, South Viet-
    nam)." R. Aron, *Peace and War* 567 (1966).

30. Even the United States-Belgium airdrop in the Congo in 1965 to save
    white hostages from the rebels (n. 27, above) brought sharp reactions
    although it was minimal, temporary and urgent, hardly ideological,
    and had the consent of the government. Perhaps some saw in this an
    intervention against the rebellion then in progress; perhaps it recalled
    earlier interventions by imperialist powers, allegedly to protect their
    nationals; perhaps the fact that that some of the troops came from
    Belgium, the former colonial power, was particularly resented.

31. See, *e. g.*, J. Stone, "Law, Force and Survival," 39 *Foreign Affairs* 549,
    553–59 (1961). For a criticism, see Q. Wright, *The Role of International
    Law in the Elimination of War* 6, n. 1 (1961).

32. The Hague Conference of 1907 forbade the use of force to collect
    debts if the alleged debtor agreed to arbitrate the claim. See the Con-
    vention Respecting the Limitation of the Employment of Force for the
    Recovery of Contract Debts, October 18, 1907, 36 Stat. 2241, T.S.
    No. 537.

33. L. Henkin, cited above, n. 5, at 165–69. In Anglo-American law, self-
    help is a limited right. See W. Prosser, *Torts* §§ 19–23 (3d ed., 1964).

34. ". . . la paix servira mieux la justice que celle-ci ne servira la paix."
    C. de Visscher, cited above, n. 2, at 384.

CHAPTER 8. THE UNITED NATIONS

1. In this Chapter, too, I draw on my article "The United Nations and
   Its Supporters: A Self-Examination," *78 Pol. Sci. Q.* 504 (1963).

2. *Ibid.* Compare G. Fitzmaurice, "The United Nations and the Rule of
   Law," 38 *The Grotius Society: Transactions for the Year 1952*, 135 (1953).

3. G.A. Res. 500, 5 U.N. GAOR, Supp. 20A, at 2, U.N. Doc.

A/1775/Add. 1 (1951). Sanctions have also been invoked in cases not involving aggression, *i.e.*, in support of "self-determination" and against racism, in Rhodesia and South Africa. See G.A. Res. 2022, 20 U.N. GAOR, Supp. 14, at 54–55, U.N. Doc. A/6014 (1965) and G.A. Res. 2202, 21 U.N. GAOR, Supp. 16, at 20–21, U.N. Doc. A/6316 (1966); more recently, G.A. Res. 3396, 21 Nov. 1975 condemning the continued war of repression in Rhodesia; G.A. Res. 3411, 28 Nov. 1975 condemning the apartheid policies of the government of South Africa; and G.A. Res. 3399, 26 Nov. 1975 condemning South Africa's illegal occupation and use of resources of Namibia.

4. L. Henkin, cited, at 517–18.
5. See 19 U.N. SCOR, 1152d meeting, at 11 (1964).
6. See 16 U.N. SCOR, 987th meeting, at 19–20, 25–30 (1961).
7. Israel expressed similar views to justify its attack on Jordan and Lebanon in retaliation for damage by infiltrators. It emphasized that, despite repeated Arab violations, none was condemned by the Security Council (generally as a result of Soviet veto). *E.g., N.Y. Times*, Nov. 16, 1966, pp. 1, 11. Later, Israel virtually ceased to attend to hostile majorities which the Arabs were able to command.
8. Indonesia had withdrawn on January 7, 1965. U.N. Doc. A/5857; S/6156 (1965); *N.Y. Times*, Jan. 8, 1965, p. 1. It did not return until September 28, 1966. U.N. Doc. A/6419; S/7498 (1966); *N.Y. Times*, Sept. 29, 1966, p. 6.
9. See, *e.g.*, the Resolution of the Security Council of April 21, 1948, calling for a plebiscite in Kashmir. 3 U.N. SCOR, April Supp., at 8–12, U.N. Doc. S/726 (1948). India insisted that the plebiscite could be held only if Pakistan withdrew its troops from Kashmir and discontinued its buildup of *Azad* Kashmir forces. 5 U.N. SCOR, 463rd meeting, at 10–11 (1950).
10. 13 U.N. SCOR, 825th meeting (1958); see also U.N. Doc. S/4113 (1958).
11. The United Nations continues to maintain a force in Cyprus pursuant to the authorizing resolution of the Security Council adopted in 1964. U.N. Doc. S/5575 (1964). There have been numerous Security Council and General Assembly resolutions since.
12. See 18 U.N. SCOR, April–June Supp., at 52–53, U.N. Doc. S/5331 (1963) for the June 11, 1963 resolution calling for disengagement in Yemen. Report of the Security Council to the General Assembly, 16 U.N. GAOR, Supp. 2, at 1–51.

13. U.N. Doc. A/4867 (1961) contains a summary of United Nations actions in the Congo during 1960–61. For a discussion of later U.N. actions in the Congo, see the subsequent reports of the Secretary General: 17 U.N. GAOR, Supp. 1, at 1–36, U.N. Doc. A/5201 (1962); 18 U.N. GAOR, Supp. 1, at 1–16, U.N. Doc. A/5501 (1963); 19 U.N. GAOR, Supp. 1, at 1–6, U.N. Doc. A/5801 (1964); 20 U.N. GAOR, Supp. 1, at 1—6, U.N. Doc. A/6001 (1965).

14. I do not deal here with "internal legislation," with actions by U.N. organs—legally binding—that relate to the organization's affairs and its relations to its members, e.g., budget assessments, voting procedures, elections. See, generally, I. Detter, *Law Making by International Organizations* (1965).

15. Justice Holmes, in *Missouri v. Holland*, 252 U.S. 416, 433 (1920).

16. *E.g.*, Peace Through Deeds, G.A. Res. 380, 5 U.N. GAOR, Supp. 20, at 3, U.N. Doc. A/ 1775 (1950), cited above, Chapter 7, n. 26.

17. If only in a limited context. Compare what "self-determination" has not come to mean, p. 182, above.

18. Compare M. Shukri, *The Concept of Self-Determination in the United Nations* 34–38, 67–76, 335–51 (1965).

19. "Report of the Third Committee," 10 U.N. GAOR, Annexes, Agenda Item 28-I, p. 30 at 39, U.N. Doc. A/3077 (1955). Compare Article 1 of the International Covenant on Civil and Political Rights and Article 1 of the International Covenant on Economic, Social and Cultural Rights.

20. *E.g.*, 17 U.N. GAOR, Second Comm. 332, U.N. Doc. A/C. 2/SR. 851 (1962).

21. *E.g.*, G.A. Res. 1881 and 1978, 18 U.N. GAOR, Annexes 2, Agenda Item No. 30, at 18, U.N. Doc. A/5565 and A/5565/Add. I (1963); see Chapter 12.

22. This includes the programs of the U.N. Specialized Agencies, as well as the Expanded Program of Technical Assistance and the Special Fund, which were combined in the United Nations Development Program by G.A. Res. 2029, 20 U.N. GAOR, Supp. 14, at 20–21, U.N. Doc. A/6014 (1965). See also G.A. Res. 1710, 16 U.N. GAOR, Supp. 17, at 17–18, U.N. Doc. A/5100 (1962) and G.A. Res. 1715, *id.* at 23, which called for the institution of a Development Decade and for increased contributions to the Expanded Program of Technical Assistance and the Special Fund; more recently, the Declaration on the New International Economic Order and the Charter of Economic Rights and Duties of States. See Chapter 10.

23. *E.g.*, the Geneva Conferences on the Law of the Sea, called in 1958 and 1960 in response to G.A. Res. 1105, 11 U.N. GAOR, Supp. 17, at 54, U.N. Doc. A/3572 (1956) and G.A. Res. 1307, 13 U.N. GAOR, Supp. 18, at 54–55, U.N. Doc. A/4090 (1958). For the Third Law of the Sea Conference, see Chapter 11.

24. See the debates on the Draft Convention Relating to the Status of Refugees, 5 U.N. GAOR 669–74 (1950). See also the debates on the Draft Convention on Consent to Marriage, Minimum Age for Marriage and Registration of Marriages, 17 U.S. GAOR 691–712 (1962).

25. *E.g.*, in regard to rights of women. See G.A. Res. 843, 9 U.N. GAOR, Supp. 21, at 23, U.N. Doc. A/2890 (1954).

26. *E.g.*, the Declaration of Legal Principles Governing the Activities of States in the Exploration and Use of Outer Space, G.A. Res. 1962, 18 U.N. GAOR, Supp. 15, at 15–16 U.N. Doc. A/5515 (1963). In regard to nuclear weapons, see G.A. Res. 1653, 16 U.N. GAOR, Supp. 17, at 4–5, U.N. Doc. A/5100 (1961).

27. See, *e.g.*, L. Gross, "The United Nations and the Role of Law," 19 *Int'l Organization* 537, 555–58 (1965); R. Falk, "On the Quasi-Legislative Competence of the General Assembly," 60 *Am. J. Int'l L.* 782, 784–86 (1966). See also O. Asamoah, *The Legal Significance of the Declarations of the General Assembly of the United Nations* (1966).

28. G.A. Res. 1962, 18 U.N. GAOR, Supp. 15, at 15–16, U.N. Doc. A/5515 (1963).

29. See Chapter 5, n. 21.

30. G.A. Res. 217, 3 U.N. GAOR 71–79, U.N. Doc. A/810 (1948).

31. G.A. Res. 1653, 16 U.N. GAOR, Supp. 17, at 4–5, U.N. Doc. A/5100 (1962). The resolution was adopted by a vote of 55 to 20, 26 states abstaining. 16 U.N. GAOR 808 (1961).

32. For a discussion of Russian views on the legality of the military use of nuclear weapons, see P. Maggs, "The Soviet Viewpoint on Nuclear Weapons in International Law," in *The Soviet Impact on International Law* 112, 113–16 (H. Baade ed., 1965).

33. *E.g.*, G.A. Res. 1663, 16 U.N. GAOR, Supp. 17, at 10–11, U.N. Doc. A/5100 (1962). The vote in the Assembly was 97 to 2 in favor of adoption, with one abstention. 16 U.N. GAOR 889 (1961). Many resolutions to the same effect followed.

34. G.A. Res. 95, 1 U.N. GAOR 188, U.N. Doc. A/64/Add. 1 (1947).

35. See, *e.g.*, G.A. Res. 2031, 20 U.N. GAOR, Supp. 14, at 8, U.N. Doc. A/6014 (1965); G.A. Res. 1908, 18 U.N. GAOR, Supp. 15 at 13–14, U.N. Doc. A/5515 (1963).

36. Compare the history of efforts to establish a major U.N. Development Fund. See W. Friedmann, G. Kalmanoff, and R. Meagher, *International Financial Aid* 450–56 (1966); see also n. 22 above.

37. 17 U.N. GAOR 22 (1962). See also, U.N. GAOR, Fifth Comm. (4th Special Sess.), 12–13, U.N. Doc. A/C.5/SR. 986 (1963); R. Gardner, "The 18th General Assembly: A Testing Ground of Hopes and Opportunities," 49 *Dep't State Bull.* 501, 504 (1963).

38. Disarmament and arms control are not primarily designed to release national budgets from the burden of armaments so that more can be contributed to international welfare programs. But compare G.A. Res. 1252, 13 U.N. GAOR, Supp. 18, at 3–4, U.N. Doc. A/4090 (1958).

39. L. Henkin, "Disarmament—The Lawyer's Interests," Association of the Bar of the City of New York, *Disarmament: Background Papers and Proceedings of the Fourth Hammarskjold Forum* 22–26 (1964).

40. 4 U.N. GAOR, Spec. Sess., Fifth Comm., 9–12, 79–81, U.N. Doc. A/C. 5/SR. 986 and A/C. 5/SR. 998. See also R. Gardner, cited above, n. 37.

41. G.A. Res. 2022, 20 U.N. GAOR, Supp. 14, at 54–55, U.N. Doc. A/6014 (1965); G.A. Res. 2107, *id.* at 62–63. See also G.A. Res. 1899, 18 U.N. GAOR, Supp. 15, at 46–47, U.N. Doc. A/5515 (1963). See also Security Council Res. 418, 4 Nov. 1977 calling for a mandatory arms embargo against South Africa over racial violence.

42. See the case of the Concorde airplane, Part IV, p. 249.

43. With infrequent exceptions. Compare Chapter 1, n. 9, above.

44. *E.g.*, C. Jenks, *The Prospects of International Adjudication* (1964). See, generally, *The Future of the International Court of Justice* (L. Gross ed., 1976); also, L. Bloomfield, "Law, Politics and International Disputes," *Int'l Conc.* 516 (1958).

45. Advisory opinions on legal questions may be requested by the Security Council or the General Assembly of the United Nations or by those specialized agencies of the organization authorized to make such requests by the General Assembly. U.N. Charter, Article 96(2). The General Assembly during its first session also authorized the Economic and Social Council to do so. G.A. Res. 89, 1 U.N. GAOR 178, U.N. Doc. A/64/Add. 1 (1946).

46. Compare, in the case of the United States, the so-called Connally Reservation, discussed above, Chapter 1, n. 7.

CHAPTER 9.   COMPETING AGENDAS FOR NEW LAW

1. See Chapter 5, n. 20.
2. Treaty on the Non-Proliferation of Nuclear Weapons, July 1, 1958, entered into force March 5, 1970, 729 U.N.T.S. 161.
3. See Henkin, "Disarmament—The Lawyer's Interests," Chapter 1, n. 6, above.
4. See Chapter 8 n. 3, above. In 1977 the U.N. Security Council called for an arms embargo against South Africa on account of its race policies and accompanying violence, S.C. Res. 418, 4 Nov. 1977.
5. See articles by Abramovsky "Multilateral Conventions for the Suppression of Unlawful Seizure and Interference with Aircraft," 13 *Col. J. Transnational L.* 381 (1974); 14 *id.* 268, 451 (1975).
6. But compare the terrorist attack at Larnaca, Cyprus, *New York Times,* Feb. 17, 1978, p. 1.
7. See, *e.g.*, Abramovsky, n. 5, above.
8. Convention on the Prevention and Punishment of Crimes Against Internationally Protected Persons, Including Diplomatic Agents, 14 Dec. 1973, in force 20 Feb. 1977.
9. See the initiative for a convention outlawing the taking of hostages, G.A. Res. 31/103, 21 Jan. 1977; also Drafting of an International Convention Against the Taking of Hostages, Report of the Sixth Committee, A/31/430, 14 Dec. 1976.
10. See, *e.g.*, the Stockholm Conference on the Environment, Stockholm 5–16 June 1972 (A/Conf. 48/14/Rev. 1).
11. See, *e.g.*, "The Control of Program Content in International Telecommunications," 13 *Col. J. Transnational L.* 1 (1974).
12. See Friedmann, Lissitzyn and Pugh, *International Law, Cases and Materials* (1969) 439.
13. See Chapter 7, n. 23, above.
14. Notably in the Charter of Economic Rights and Duties of States. See Chapter 10.

CHAPTER 10.   THE POLITICS OF ECONOMICS:
THE NEW INTERNATIONAL ECONOMIC ORDER

1. Compare Chapter 7, and the discussion of peace treaties, p. 80, above. Under the Vienna Convention on the Law of Treaties, a treaty is void if it is obtained by coercion of a state's representative, or by force or threat of force against a state in violation of the U.N. Charter, Articles 51, 52. Presumably, then, a treaty would be valid and binding

if imposed by force which was not in violation of the Charter, for example, by a state that emerged victorious after being victim of an armed attack under Article 51. See Chapter 7. Economic or political pressures apparently do not vitiate the agreement, but the Vienna Conference adopted a Declaration condemning such pressure. See Final Act of the U.N. Conference on the Law of Treaties, U.N. Doc. A/Conf. 39/26, 23 May 1969, Annex. Fraud and some errors render a treaty voidable. Articles 48, 49.

2. See, *e.g.*, Wilson, "Postwar Commercial Treaties of the United States," 43 *A.J.I.L.* 262 (1949).

3. See the International Covenant on Civil and Political Rights, Article 1; the International Covenant on Economic, Social and Cultural Rights, Article 1. See Report of the Secretary General, Permanent Sovereignty over Natural Resources; Policies of Selected Countries, U.N. Doc. E/5425, 3 Oct. 1973. See also the Charter of Economic Rights and Duties of States, G.A. Res. 3281 (XXIX), 12 Dec. 1974, Chapter I.

4. See Chapter 6.

5. For some of many writings, see R. Vernon, *Sovereignty at Bay: The Multinational Spread of U.S. Enterprises* (1971); R. J. Barnet, *Global Reach: the Power of the Multinational Corporation* (1974); R. Gilpin, *U.S. Power and the Multinational Corporation: The Political Economy of Foreign Direct Investment* (1975); also papers by Gardner, Hellawell and Schachter at the Conference on the Regulation of Transnational Corporations, 15 *Col. J. Transnational L.* 367 *et seq.* (1976); Rubin, "Transnational Corporations: Supervision, Regulation, or What?" 1 *Int'l Trade L.J.* 1 (1975).

6. Declaration on the Establishment of a New International Economic Order, G.A. Res. 3201 (5-VI), 1 May 1974; Programme of Action on the Establishment of a New International Economic Order, G.A. Res. §202 (5-VI), 1 May 1974; Charter of Economic Rights and Duties of States, G.A. Res. 3281, 12 Dec. 1974.

7. On 8 December 1962 the U.N. General Assembly endorsed the decision of the Economic and Social Council to convene a U.N. Conference on Trade and Development. G.A. Res. 1785 (XVII). See also the Joint Declaration of the Developing Countries annexed to G.A. Res. 1897 (XVII), 11 Nov. 1963. The Conference met in 1964 and its findings and recommendations were set forth in the Final Act of the Conference. In Res. 1995 (XIX), 30 Dec. 1964, the General Assembly established UNCTAD as an organ of the General Assembly.

CHAPTER 11. REMAKING THE LAW OF THE SEA

1. See Henkin, "Changing Law for the Changing Seas," in *Uses of the Seas* (E. Gullion ed., 1968); also Henkin, *Law for the Sea's Mineral Resources* (1968). The classic history is T. W. Fulton, *The Sovereignty of the Sea* (1911); on the territorial sea, see generally P. C. Jessup, *The Law of Territorial Waters and Maritime Jurisdiction* (1927).

 I draw here on my article "Politics and the Changing Law of the Sea," 89 *Pol. Sci. Q.* 46 (1974).

2. Presidential Proclamation 2667, Sept. 28, 1945, Natural Resources of the Subsoil and Sea Bed of the Continental Shelf, 10 *Fed. Reg.* 12303 (1945), 59 Stat. 884.

3. The 1958 Conference produced four conventions: Convention on the High Seas, 450 U.N.T.S. 82, T.I.A.S. No. 5200; Convention on the Territorial Seas and the Contiguous Zone, 516 U.N.T.S. 205, T.I.A.S. No. 5639; Convention on the Continental Shelf, 499 U.N.T.S. 311, T.I.A.S. No. 5578; Convention on Fishing and Conservation of the Living Resources of the High Seas, 559 U.N.T.S. 285, T.I.A.S. No. 5969.

4. U.N. G.A. Res. 2749 (XXV), 17 Dec. 1970.

5. See the Principles of Mexico on the Judicial Regime of the Sea, adopted at the 1956 Meeting of the Inter-American Council of Jurists at Mexico City. Compare the Declaration of Montevideo, U.N. Doc. A/AC. 138/34, 9 *Int'l Leg. Materials* 1081 (1971); Declaration of Lima, U.N. Doc. A/AC. 138/28 (1970), 10 *Int'l Leg. Materials* 207 (1971); Declaration of Santo Domingo, U.N. Doc. A/AC. 138/80 (1972), 11 *Int'l Leg. Materials* 892 (1972); also *id.* at 894. Compare the African Seminar held at Yaoundé June 1972, U.N. Doc. A/AC. 138/79, 21 July 1972. That coastal states could decide their jurisdiction for themselves had been denied earlier by the International Court of Justice. *Fisheries Case* (United Kingdom v. Norway), [1951] I.C.J. Rep. 116, 132; compare Report of the International Law Commission, 8th session, 23 April-4 July 1956, GAOR 11th Sess. Supp. No. 9 (A/3159), p. 12, comment on draft article 3.

6. For a classification of states by such geographical criteria, see Alexander, "Indices of National Interest in the Oceans," 1 *Ocean Development and International Law Journal* 21, 37 *et seq.* (1973).

7. Fishery Conservation and Management Act of 1976, P.L. 94-265, 90 Stat. 331 (1976), 16 U.S.C.A. §1801 *et seq.* (Supp. 1977).

 Later Congress also extended U.S. jurisdiction to control pollution in that zone, in effect undercutting further the effort of the Executive

Branch to limit coastal state jurisdiction in the emerging Economic Zone. See the Clean Water Act of 1977, P.L. 95–217, 27 Dec., 1977, section 58, amending the Federal Water Pollution Control Act, 33 U.S.C.A. 1501 (Supp. 1977).

8. As of early 1979 the extent of agreement was largely reflected in the Informal Composite Negotiating Text, U.N. Third Conference on the Law of the Sea A/Conf. 62/WP 10, 15 July 1977, as amended in particular documents of later sessions. For the story of the negotiations until 1978, see the articles by Stevenson and Oxman, 68 *Am. J. Int'l L.* 1 (1974); 69 *id.* 1, 763 (1975), and by Oxman 71 *id.* 247 (1977), 72 *id.* 57 (1978), and 73 *id.* 1 (1979).

9. See, *e.g.*, Convention on the Prevention of Marine Pollution by Dumping of Wastes and Other Matter, 11 *Int'l Leg. Materials* 1294 (1972); Convention for the Prevention of Pollution from Ships, 12 *id.* at 1319 (1973). There have also been regional conventions.

10. U.N. G.A. Res. 2574 D (XXIV), 15 Dec. 1969. For the U.S. position in dissent see 9 *Int'l Leg. Materials* 831 (1970).

11. See "The Nixon plan," U.N. Doc. A/AC. 138/22 (1970); 62 *Dept. State Bull.* 737 (1970); U.N. GAOR 25th Sess. Supp. No. 21, A/8021, Annex V, 9 *Int'l Leg. Materials* 1046 (1970).

12. See, *e.g.*, H.R. 3350, 95th Cong. 1st sess., H.R. Rep. 95–588, Aug. 9, 1977.

CHAPTER 12.   IDEALISM AND IDEOLOGY:
THE LAW OF HUMAN RIGHTS

1. I draw here on my book *The Rights of Man Today* (1978), and on the following articles: "The Internationalization of Human Rights," in *Human Rights, A Symposium*, Part 1, Fall 1977, University Committee on General Education, Columbia University; "Human Rights and 'Domestic Jurisdiction,' " in *Human Rights, International Law and the Helsinki Accord* (T. Buergenthal ed., 1977); "Human Rights: Reappraisal and Readjustment," in *Essays on Human Rights: Contemporary Issues and Jewish Perspectives* (D. Sidorsky ed., 1979).

2. See, generally, H. Lauterpacht, *International Law and Human Rights* (1973).

3. Constitutions are collected in Blaustein and Flanz, *Constitutions of the Countries of the World* (1971–); also in Peaslee, *Constitutions of Nations* (rev. 3d ed. 1970, rev. 4th ed. 1974). See Henkin, *The Rights of Man Today* Chapter 2.

4. See Chapter 2 above.
5. Lemkin, "Genocide as a Crime Under International Law," 41 *Am. J. Int'l L.* 145 (1947), and works there cited, especially R. Lemkin, *Axis Rule in Occupied Europe* (1944) Chapter IX.
6. See Sohn in *The U.N. and Human Rights*, Eighteenth Report of the Commission to Study the Organization of Peace.
7. See Chapter 10.
8. Some have argued—erroneously in my view—that one party cannot complain to another that it has committed a violation, unless the a-greement clearly provides that it may do so. Compare articles by Henkin, Bastide and Frohwein in *Human Rights, International Law and the Helsinki Accord* (Buergenthal ed.) n. 1, above.
9. International Covenant on Civil and Political Rights, Article 41.
10. Protocol to International Covenant on Civil and Political Rights.
11. As of Jan. 1, 1979 only 21 had adhered to the Protocol, only 10 had made the Declaration under Article 41.
12. As of Jan. 1, 1979, 102 states had adhered to the Convention.
13. See Articles 11, 14.
14. See A. H. Robertson, *Human Rights in Europe* (2d ed., 1976); Morrisson, *The Developing European Law of Human Rights* (1967); Jacobs, *The European Convention on Human Rights* (1975).
15. The American Convention came into force in 1978. See, generally, A. Schreiber, *The Inter-American Commission on Human Rights* (1970); L. J. LeBlanc, *The OAS and the Promotion and Protection of Human Rights* (1977).
16. In October 1977 President Carter signed the principal International Covenants, but not the Protocol. In February 1978 the Covenants, the Convention on the Elimination of All Forms of Racial Discrimination, and the American Convention were sent to the U.S. Senate for consent to ratification, with elaborate reservations. See Henkin, "Constitutional Rights and Human Rights," 13 Harv. C.R.-C.L. L. Rev. 593 (1978).
17. Compare the Report of the International Law Commission on the work of its 28th session 3 May-23 July 1976, GAOR, Supp. No. 10 (A/31/10) pp. 226 *et seq.*
18. Compare the development of the procedure for receiving private complaints, which began with apartheid and expanded to include any other "consistent pattern of gross violations." ECOSOC Res. 1503 (XLVIII), 27 May 1970. See L. Sohn and T. Burgenthal, *International Protection of Human Rights* (1973) Chapter VI, especially pp. 722–856.

19. See Security Council Resolution 418, 4 Nov. 1977, Chapter 8 note 41 above.
20. See Weissbrodt, "Human Rights Legislation and United States Foreign Policy," 7 *Ga. J. Int'l & Comp. L.* 231 (1977).
21. For a preliminary report, see Statement of Arthur J. Goldberg before the Commission on Security and Cooperation in Europe, U.S. Congress, March 21, 1978.
22. See Weissbrodt, n. 20, above, and materials cited.
23. See n. 16, above.

PART FOUR: THE LAW IN OPERATION

1. The Cuban crisis, as well as the others, may have had important influence also on the United Nations and the Organization of American States, and on the law of these organizations. I do not deal with these.
2. *Hearings on the Nuclear Test Ban Treaty (Executive M) Before the Senate Committee on Foreign Relations*, 88th Cong., 1st Sess., at 274, 427, 434, 479, 551, 615, 672–95, 963 (1963).
3. *Id.* at 13, 25, 43, 101–5, 159, 212, 291.
4. *Hearings on the Southeast Asia Collective Defense Treaty (Executive K) Before the Senate Committee on Foreign Relations*, 83d Cong., 2d Sess., at 16–17 (1954).
5. *N.Y. Times*, Jan. 21, 1965, § 1, p. 2.

CHAPTER 13. SUEZ: THE LAW WORKS, THEN FAILS BUT IS VINDICATED

1. For one story of the events, see T. Robertson, *Crisis: The Inside Story of the Suez Conspiracy* (1965) [hereinafter cited as Robertson].
2. Tripartite statement of August 2, 1956, 35 *Dep't State Bull.* 262 (1956).
3. 11 U.N. SCOR, Oct.–Dec. Supp., at 47–48, U.N. Doc. S/3675 (1956). For the Egyptian acceptance see U.N. GAOR, Annexes, Agenda Item No. 5 (Emer. Sess. I), at 13–14, U.N. Doc. A/3287 (1956).
4. *Dept. of State, Pub. No. 6392, The Suez Canal Problem* 35 (1956).
5. But see R. Delson, "Nationalization of the suez Canal Company: Issues of Public and Private International Law," 57 *Colum. L. Rev.* 755, 772–75 (1957).
6. Q. Wright, "Intervention, 1956," 51 *Am. J. Int'l L.* 257, 261 (1957). There were, in addition, subsidiary arguments suggesting that the na-

tionalization was impermissible under international law because it did not have a public purpose but was solely an act of retaliation against the United States, which had withdrawn an offer of aid to build the Aswan Dam. For a discussion of motives see S. Strange, "Suez and After," 11 *Yearbook of World Affairs* 76, 77 (1957). Compare Robertson, p. 65.

7. Republic of Egypt, Ministry for Foreign Affairs, *White Paper on the Nationalization of the Suez Maritime Canal Company* 9, 15–35 (1956).

8. To paraphrase Ezekiel 29:3.

9. Compare R. Delson, cited 762–75, with T. Huang, "Some International and Legal Aspects of the Suez Canal Question," 51 *Am. J. Int'l L.* 277, 278–86 (1957).

10. A. Eden, *Full Circle: The Memoirs of Anthony Eden* 474 (1960) [hereinafter cited as Eden].

11. The treaty between Egypt and the United Kingdom was signed Oct. 19, 1954. 210 U.N.T.S. 3, 24. The Egyptian government terminated it by a decree of Jan. 1, 1957, effective retroactively to Oct. 31, 1956. 269 U.N.T.S. 366.

12. Eden, pp. 474–75.

13. Eden, pp. 478–79. In fact, lawyers told him that force would be illegal even as a last resort. In the House of Lords, on September 12, 1956, Lord McNair, one of Great Britain's leading international lawyers, said that he was "puzzled by the massing and display of armed force in the Eastern Mediterranean." He went on to remind the government that the law was no longer what it had been fifty years earlier, and concluded that "so far as the events in the present controversy up to date are known to us, I am unable to see the legal justification of the threat or use of armed force by Great Britain against Egypt in order to impose a solution of this dispute." 199 Parl. Deb., H.L. (5th ser.) 659–62 (1956).

14. See n. 3, above.

15. This, it is said, was President Nasser's expectation too. See *N.Y. Times*, Oct. 9, 1966 § 1, p. 21.

16. Robertson, pp. 10–11, 19–21.

17. *Id.* at 171–72.

18. *Id.* at 238.

19. G.A. Res. 997 and 1000 (Emer. Sess. I), U.N. GAOR, Supp. 1, at 2, U.N. Doc. A/3354 (1956).

20. For opposing views compare those of A. Goodhart and Q. Wright,

"Some Legal Aspects of the Suez Situation," in *Tensions in the Middle East* 243 (C. Thayer ed., 1958).

21. Article I of the Treaty of Constantinople provides: "The Suez Maritime Canal shall always be free and open, in time of war as in time of peace, to every vessel of commerce or of war, without distinction of flag." For the Security Council resolution calling on Egypt to remove its restriction, see 6 U.N. SCOR, 558th meeting, 2–3 (1951). A brief statement of the Israeli position appears in Israel Office of Information, *The Gulf of Akaba* (1957).

22. Roberston, p. 159.

23. See Chapter 8, pp. 141 *et seq.*

24. Robertson discusses the Anglo-French commitment of aid to Israel at 157–74. This has been confirmed in a book by one close to the events and decisions, Anthony Nutting, *No End of a Lesson, the Story of Suez* (1967).

25. Compare Robertson, pp. 85 and 127, for differing attitudes toward Egypt.

26. Compare Lord McNair's admonitions in the House of Lords, n. 13, above, though these were not addressed to the use of force in the context of an Israeli attack. See also, *e.g.*, Q. Wright, "Intervention, 1956," cited above, 272–74.

27. Later, indeed, especially after and in the light of Suez, some British and Commonwealth writers did argue that self-defense against armed attack was not the only unilateral force permitted by the Charter, that the Charter does not bar necessary force to protect vital interests against injustice or against violations of international law. See, *e.g.*, J. Stone, cited above, Chapter 7, n. 31; J. Stone, *Aggression and World Order* (1958); D. Bowett, *Self-Defense in International Law* (1958) 182–99; J. Brierly, *The Law of Nations* (6th ed., H. Waldock, 1963) 413–32. But in 1956 the British and French Foreign Offices must have known this was not the accepted view, or the view that would probably prevail in this case. And indeed this was not the view espoused by these governments.

28. *Restatement (Second) of the Law of Torts* §§ 116, 119(c) (1965).

29. See the sharply critical speech delivered on September 12, 1956, by the British Leader of the Opposition, Hugh Gaitskell, 558 Parl. Deb., H.C. (5th ser.) 15–32 (1956). On November 3, Gaitskell demanded the resignation of the government because it had flouted the call for a cease-fire by the United Nations General Assembly. *Id.* at 1858–62.

30. 11 U.N. SCOR, 749th meeting, 31 (1956).
31. For a critical discussion of United States policy at Suez see essays by A. Wolfers, E. Hula, and H. Morgenthau in *Alliance Policy in the Cold War* (A. Wolfers ed., 1959).
32. See, *e.g.*, 35 *Dep't State Bull.* 745 (1956).
33. See L. Henkin, "The United Nations and Its Supporters: A Self-Examination," 78 *Pol. Sci. Q.* 504, 519–20 (1963). See also B. Cohen, *The United Nations; Constitutional Developments, Growth, and Possibilities* 43–66 (1961).
34. See *Hearings*, cited above, Chapter 5, n. 32.

CHAPTER 14.   THE LAW FAILS:
THE CASE OF ADOLF EICHMANN

1. C. Clarke, *Eichmann, The Man and His Crimes* 145–49 (1960) [hereinafter cited as Clarke]. See, generally, M. Pearlman, *The Capture and Trial of Adolf Eichmann* 79 (1963).
2. 15 U.N. SCOR, Supp. April–June 1960, at 27–28, U.N. Doc. S/4336 (1960).
3. 15 U.N. SCOR, Supp. April–June 1960, at 35, U.N. Doc. S/4349 (1960).
4. *N.Y. Times*, Aug. 4, 1960, pp. 1, 3.
5. For the text of the statute, see United Nations, *Yearbook on Human Rights for 1950*, 163 (1952).
6. H. Baade, "The Eichmann Trial: Some Legal Aspects," *Duke L. J.* 400 (1961), [hereinafter cited as Baade].
7. Clarke, pp. 147–48.
8. Baade, p. 411.
9. See *The Nürnberg Trial, 1946*, 6 F.R.D. 69, 107–10 (1946).
10. The majority opinion in the principal case, *The Lotus*, [1927] *P.C.I.J.*, Ser. A, No. 10, at 18–19, 31, places the burden on those who challenge the jurisdiction of a state to show that there is a principle of international law depriving the acting state of jurisdiction. Israel, then, might have drawn some support from this "burden" on its critics. It is now commonly assumed, however, that a state's jurisdiction must be based on one of several accepted principles.
11. Compare *Restatement (Second) of the Foreign Relations Law of the United States* §§ 17, 30 (1965); 1 L. Oppenheim, *International Law* §§ 144, 145 (7th ed., H. Lauterpacht, 1948).

12. See "Harvard Research in International Law, Jurisdiction with Respect to Crime," Article 8, 29 *Am. J. Int'l L. Supp.* 435, 561–63 (1935).
13. *Restatement (Second) of the Foreign Relations Law of the United States* § 33 (1965).
14. See 1 L. Oppenheim, *International Law* §§ 146, 340h, and Appendix 983–84, n. 2 (8th ed., H. Lauterpacht, 1955). Compare Article 6 of the Genocide Convention, 78 U.N.T.S. 277, 280–82, which came into effect on January 12, 1951. The Convention does not purport to apply to acts antedating its adoption. See also the Report of the International Law Commission, Chapter 12, n. 17.
15. Compare "Harvard Research in International Law, Jurisdiction with Respect to Crime," cited above, n. 12, Article 10, at pp. 573–85.
16. But compare L. Green, "The Eichmann Case," 23 *Modern L. Rev.* 507, 512 (1960).
17. *Ibid.* The Federal Republic of Germany made no effort to have Eichmann extradited; indeed, it perhaps hoped to take advantage of the Eichmann trial to gain evidence to support prosecution of other Nazis in Germany. See *N.Y. Times*, May 28, 1960, p. 9; *N.Y. Times*, May 29, 1960, §4, p. 2.
18. See 15 U.N. SCOR, 866th meeting, at 11–12 (1960); 867th meeting, at 3–4 (1960).
19. Compare 15 U.N. SCOR, Supp. April–June 1960, at 30, 31–33, U.N. Doc. S/4342 (1960).
20. See *N.Y. Times*, May 28, 1960, p. 9.
21. On September 26, 1944, the Argentine Ambassador in London delivered to the Foreign Office a note stating that in no case would those accused of war crimes receive refuge in Argentina. *N.Y. Times*, Feb. 10, 1945, p. 3.
22. The Genocide Convention, cited above, n. 14 at 282, expressly provides in Article 7 that genocide should be extraditable, and not considered a "political offense."
23. The debates in the Security Council are to be found at 15 U.N. SCOR, 865th–868th meetings (1960).
24. If Argentina had insisted on Eichmann's return, Israel might have been hard pressed, although it probably would have risked much to retain Eichmann and hold the trial. If Israel had insisted on keeping him, it might have been held to have violated the Security Council resolution; the consequent trial might not have been illegal under traditional principles. *Male captus, bene detentus.* But see "Harvard Research

in International Law, Jurisdiction with Respect to Crime," cited above, n. 12, Article 16, p. 623.

25. In addition to known European cases like the abduction of the Moroccan Mehdi Ben Barka in France in 1965, *N.Y. Times*, Nov. 2, 1965, p. 13, there is the case of Professor Galindez, who—it is generally accepted—was kidnapped from the United States in 1956, and murdered at the behest of the Dominican authorities. *N.Y. Times*, July 5, 1962, pp. 1, 8. See also the seizure of the former Congo Premier Moise Tshombe, *N.Y. Times*, July 1, 1967, p. 1; also the alleged kidnapping by Korean agents of Korean citizens in Germany, *N.Y. Times*, July 5, 1967, p. 8. More recently there have been charges of official involvement in murder and other crimes against individuals in foreign countries, in various parts of the world.

CHAPTER 15.   THE LAW'S OTHER
INFLUENCES: THE CUBAN QUARANTINE

1. For example, a detailed review of the events and disclussions by high officials, which led to the quarantine, appeared soon afterward in the *N.Y. Times*, Nov. 3, 1962, § 1, pp. 1, 6. Other reports, including some by participants (or witnesses) in the processes of making decisions, appeared later; *e.g.*, T. Sorensen, *Kennedy* (1965) [hereinafter cited as Sorensen], E. Abel, *The Missile Crisis* (1966) [hereinafter cited as Abel], R. Hilsman, *To Move a Nation* (1967) [hereinafter cited as Hilsman], and A. Schlesinger, *A Thousand Days: John F. Kennedy in the White House* (1965) [hereinafter cited as Schlesinger].

2. These, and other lawyers among those consulted, did not, of course, all agree in their recommendations. See Abel, pp. 72–73.

3. For the text of President Kennedy's address, see 47 *Dep't State Bull.* 715 (1962).

4. 15 U.N. SCOR, Supp. Oct.–Dec., 1962, at 146, U.N. Doc. S/5181 (1962).

5. 17 U.N. SCOR, 1022d meeting (1962).

6. The OAS resolution is set forth in 47 *Dep't State Bull.* 722, 723 (1962).

7. Proclamation N. 3504, 27 Fed. Reg. 10401, reprinted in 47 *Dep't State Bull.* 717 (1962).

8. Later, the United States established procedures whereby shippers might get advance clearance to take their cargoes through the quarantine area. *N.Y. Times*, Oct. 28, 1962, § 1, p. 32.

   In addition to the naval blockade, some nations were asked to deny air transit privileges to assure that weapons were not flown to Cuba. Abel, pp. 136–37; Schlesinger, p. 815.

9. Sorensen, pp. 715–16; M. Travis, "John F. Kennedy: Experiments with Power," in *Powers of the President in Foreign Affairs* 133, 188–89 (E. Robinson ed., 1966) [hereinafter cited as Travis].

10. Sorensen, p. 720.

11. The United States has apparently continued such surveillance since that time to assure against recurrence of the threat. Dep't of State Press Release No. 644, 47 *Dep't State Bull.* 747 (1962); *N.Y. Times,* Nov. 17, 1978, p. A-11.

12. See, *e.g.*, Sorensen, pp. 676–78, 683. In his address, President Kennedy said that the Soviet move "cannot be accepted by this country if our courage and our commitments are ever to be trusted again by friend or foe." See also Schlesinger, pp. 796–97: "Every country in the world, watching so audacious an action ninety miles from the United States, would wonder whether it could ever thereafter trust Washington's resolution and protection."

13. Schlesinger, pp. 797, 811.

14. Compare the discussion of the game of "chicken" in global terms. T. Schelling, *Arms and Influence* 116–25 (1966).

15. Compare Sorensen, pp. 676–78. The Soviet Union may also have sought to secure Cuba against possible invasion, and thus confirm its place in the Soviet satellite system.

16. Hilsman, p. 195.

17. Sorensen, p. 685; Abel, p. 63.

18. When, in 1954, the United States sought to persuade other nations to embargo arms to Guatemala, its efforts were unsuccessful. R. Stebbins, *The United States in World Affairs, 1954,* 381 (1956).

19. Compare Abel, pp. 72–73. And see *N.Y. Times,* Nov. 3, 1962, § 1, pp. 1, 6.

20. Abel, pp. 63–64.

21. A. Chayes, "The Legal Case for U.S. Action on Cuba," 47 *Dep't State Bull.* 763 (1962); A. Chayes, "Law and the Quarantine of Cuba," 41 *Foreign Affairs* 550 (1963); L. Meeker, "Defensive Quarantine and the Law," 57 *Am. J. Int'l L.* 515 (1963) [hereinafter cited as Meeker, "Defensive Quarantine"].

For a later exposition of the U.S. case, see A. Chayes, *The Cuban Missile Crisis* (1974), p. xiv n., above.

22. The history at San Francisco shows that the members were aware of,

and acquiesced in, the Act of Chapultepec providing for collective action in defense of the hemisphere. See Meeker, "Defensive Quarantine," pp. 518–19.

23. See the Charter of the Organization of American States, Chapter V, [1951] 2 U.S.T. & O.I.A. 2394, T.I.A.S. No. 2361; Inter-American Treaty of Reciprocal Assistance (Rio Pact), Article 6, 62 Stat. 1681 (1948) T.I.A.S. No. 1838.

24. A. Chayes, "The Legal Case for U.S. Action in Cuba," cited above, n. 21, at 765.

25. Meeker, "Defensive Quarantine," p. 522.

26. *Id.* at 523.

27. See my statement in *Proceedings of the American Society of International Law, 57th Annual Meeting* 165–67 (1963). See Chapter 7.

28. Meeker, "Defensive Quarantine," pp. 515, 524.

29. See, for example, D. Bowett, cited above, Chapter 13, n. 27, 182–99; articles by C. Fenwick and M. McDougal in the symposium on this subject in 57 *Am. J. Int'l L.* 588, 597 (1963). See also Professor McDougal's statement in *Proceedings of the American Society of International Law* 162 (1963). Compare J. Stone, cited above, Chapter 13, n. 27.

30. See, *e.g.*, the British position in the case of "The Caroline," n. 37 below.

31. *E.g.*, Q. Wright, "Intervention, 1956," cited above, Chapter 13, n. 6.

32. Meeker, "Defensive Quarantine," p. 523.

33. Compare Abel, p. 115.

34. See Chapter 7, p. 142, drawing on L. Henkin, "The United Nations and Its Supporters: A Self-Examination," 78 *Pol. Sci. Q.* 504 (1963), and my statement in *Proceedings of the American Society of International Law*, 165 (1963).

35. L. Henkin, cited, at 532–33.

36. L. Henkin, cited at 532.

37. Note by Secretary of State Daniel Webster to Lord Ashburton, in "Destruction of the 'Caroline,' " 2 J. Moore, *Digest of International Law* § 217, at 412 (1906). For the reaffirmation of this principle at the Nürnberg Trials, see 22 *Proceedings in the Trial of the Major War Criminals Before the International Military Tribunal* 411, 448 (1948).

38. Meeker, "Defensive Quarantine," p. 523.

39. Compare the right of an individual in domestic law to threaten the use in defense of his property of greater force than he would actually be entitled to use. 1 *Restatement (Second) of the Law of Torts* § 81 (2) (1965).

40. Compare C. Christol and C. Davis, "Maritime Quarantine: The Naval Interdiction of Offensive Weapons and Associated Material to Cuba, 1962," 57 *Am. J. Int'l L.* 525, 537–39 (1963).
41. Compare Treaty on the Non-proliferation of Nuclear Weapons, July 1, 1968, 21 U.S.T. 483, T.I.A.S. 6839, 729 U.N.T.S. 161.
42. *N.Y. Times*, Jan. 9, 1954, § 1, p. 1; Mar. 2, 1954, § 1, p. 1. Compare M. McDougal and N. Schlei, "Hydrogen Bomb Tests in Perspective: Lawful Measures for Security," 64 *Yale L. J.* 648 (1965).
43. Convention on Fishing and Conservation of the Living Resources of the High Seas, adopted by the United Nations Conference on the Law of the Sea, Geneva, April 28, 1958, U.N. Doc. A/CONF. 13/L.54 (1958); Convention on the Continental Shelf, adopted by the United Nations Conference on the Law of the Sea, Geneva, April 28, 1958, U.N. Doc. A/CONF. 13/L.55 (1958). Even if these are viewed as "codifications" of customary law, the customary law itself was a limitation on freedom of the seas. And see the more radical changes negotiated at the Third Law of the Sea Conference, Chapter 11.
44. See, generally, J. Murchison, *The Contiguous Air Space Zone in International Law* (1956).
45. Abel, p. 196.
46. See n. 11, above.
47. Compare 72 Stat. 798 (1958), 49 U.S.C. § 1508 (1976): "The United States of America is hereby declared to possess and exercise complete and exclusive national sovereignty in the airspace of the United States. . . ."
48. In his televised speech, President Kennedy said: "I have directed the continued and increased close surveillance of Cuba and its military buildup. The Foreign Ministers of the OAS in their communiqué of October 3 rejected secrecy on such matters in this hemisphere." 47 *Dep't State Bull.* 715, 718 (1962). See also Q. Wright, "The Cuban Quarantine," 57 *Am. J. Int'l L.* 546, 548 (1963).
49. For a discussion of sovereignty over airspace, see 1 L. Oppenheim, *International Law* § 197c (8th ed., H. Lauterpacht, 1955).

CHAPTER 16.   VIETNAM: THE UNCERTAIN TRUMPET OF
UNCERTAIN LAW

1. For a brief history of U.S. involvement in Vietnam, see G. M. Kahin and J. W. Lewis, *The United States in Vietnam* (1967). See also J. Buttinger, *Vietnam: The Unforgettable Tragedy* (1977). A convenient compen-

dium of documents and articles is contained in *The Vietnam War and International Law* (R. Falk ed., 1968–74).

2. South-East Asia Collective Defense Treaty, and Protocols, Sept. 8, 1954, 6 U.S.T. 81, T.I.A.S. 3170, 209 U.N.T.S. 28.

3. P.L. 88–408, 78 Stat. 384 (1964). The resolution was later terminated, PL 91–672, 84 State. 2055 (1971). On the legal significance of the termination see Henkin, *Foreign Affairs and the Constitution* 108 (1972).

4. Agreement on Ending the War and Restoring Peace in Viet-Nam and Protocols, Jan. 27, 1973, 12 *Int. Leg. Mat.* 48 (1973); see also the International Conference on Vietnam, Act Concerning the Paris Agreement on Ending the War and Restoring the Peace in Vietnam, March 2, 1973, 12 *Int. Leg. Mat.* 392.

5. Compare Falk, "International Law and the United States Role in the Vietnam War," 75 *Yale L. J.* 1122 (1966); Moore, "The Lawfulness of Military Assistance to the Republic of Viet-Nam," 61 *Am. J. Int'l L.* 1 (1967); Falk's response at 76 *Yale L. J.* 1095 (1967); see also Falk, *The Six Legal Dimensions of the Vietnam War* (1968). Compare also their contributions to "Symposium on the United States Military Action in Cambodia, 1970, in the Light of International and Constitutional Law," 65 *Am. J. Int'l L.* 1 (1971). See also generally, J. N. Moore, *Law and the Indo-China War* (1972). Some of these, and other relevant articles, are to be found in the Falk compendium, n. 1, above.

6. Compare Chapter 7, above.

7. See, *e.g.*, Meeker, "Viet-Nam and the International Law of Self-Defense," 46 *Dep't State Bull.* 54 (1967), reprinted in Falk compendium, n. 1, above, at 318; also Moore, n. 5, above.

8. "Hammarskjold Forum: Expansion of the Vietnam War into Cambodia—The Legal Issues." 45 *N.Y.U.L. Rev.* 625 (1970); see also the Symposium, n. 5, above.

CONCLUSION

1. The new nations have themselves taken a step in this direction by establishing the Asian-African Legal Consultative Committee. Its activities are described in annual reports published by the Secretariat of the Committee in New Delhi. See also K. Takayangi and H. Tanaka, "The First Session of the Asian Legal Consultative Committee," 2 *Japanese Annual of International Law* 110–24 (1958). See also R. Wilson, "A Decade of Legal Consultation: Asian-African Collaboration," 61 *Am. J. Int'l L.* 1011 (1967).

2. Compare D. Acheson, "Foreign Policy of the United States," 18 *Ark. L. Rev.* 225, 232 (1964); D. Acheson, "The President and the Secretary of State," *The Secretary of State* 27, 35 (D. Price ed., 1960).

3. G. Kennan, *American Diplomacy, 1900–1950*, 95–99 (1951) [hereinafter cited as Kennan, *American Diplomacy*]. For perceptive contemporaneous criticism of Mr. Kennan's views, see C. Oliver, "Reflections on Two Recent Developments Affecting the Function of Law in the International Community," 30 *Texas L. Rev.* 815 (1952); M. McDougal, "Law and Power," 46 *Am. J. Int'l L.* 102 (1952).

4. Kennan, *American Diplomacy*, p. 102.

In later lectures, in fact, Mr. Kennan said: "No one who has spent many years of his life in practical contact with the workings of international affairs can fail to appreciate the immense and vital value of international law in assuring the smooth functioning of that part of international life that is not concerned with such things as vital interest and military security. . . . In general, I think, you will find that foreign offices and professional diplomatists are very much attached to international law as an institution, and cling to it as one of the few solid substances in their world of shifting, unstable values.

"But it is important to the efficacy of international law itself that we should not overstrain its capabilities by attempting to apply it to those changes in international life that are clearly beyond its scope of relevance. I am thinking here of those elementary upheavals that involve the security of great political systems or reflect the emotional aspirations and fears of entire nations. The mark of a genuine concern for the observation of the legal principle in the affairs of nations is a recognition of the realistic limits beyond which the principle cannot be pressed." G. Kennan, *Realities of American Foreign Policy* 38–39 (1954, 1966) [hereinafter cited as Kennan, *Realities*]. See also his statements about the United Nations organization, pp. 45–46, and morality and international life, pp. 47–50. Compare his letter on Vietnam, *N.Y. Times*, Sept. 25, 1966, § 4, p. E 11.

5. His later lectures make it clear that he was not objecting to arbitration, but to the attitude that made major policy of the proliferation of arbitration agreements which in fact were hardly invoked or used. Kennan, *Realities*, pp. 18–19.

6. His list of examples reflecting the legalistic approach includes the Kellogg-Briand Pact, the League of Nations, the United Nations, "Article 51," as well as "World Law and World Government." Kennan,

American Diplomacy, p. 95. His later lectures focus on this theme. Even his encomium to international law, quoted in n. 4 above, includes in its proper domain only "that part of international life that is not concerned with such things as vital interest and military security."

7. These views do not appear radically modified in Kennan's later lectures, published in 1954, and reissued in 1966 with a preface stating: "I am unregenerate and unrepentant." Kennan, *Realities*, p. viii (1966).

8. Others agree with him. See, *e.g.*, R. Aron, *Peace and War* 730–36 (1966).

9. Compare: "I do not think that we need trouble ourselves with the thought that my view depends upon differences of degree. The whole law does so as soon as it is civilized. . . . [A]nd between the variations . . . that I suppose to exist and the simple universality of the rules in the Twelve Tables or the Leges Barbarorum, there lies the culture of two thousand years." Mr. Justice Holmes concurring in *LeRoy Fibre Co. v. Chicago, M. & St. P. Ry.*, 232 U.S. 340, 352, 354 (1914).

Enlightened domestic law has long had flexibility in civil matters, through standards like "reasonableness." Such flexibility is less desirable in criminal law, where the norm or standard ought to be as clear and precise as possible to give fair warning and effectively to deter violation. The law also has to threaten that violations will be dealt with, and some certainty as to how the law will respond to violations will increase its deterrent influence. On the other hand, the law of a developed society usually has substantial flexibility about consequences of violation. In the United States, for example, flexibility is supplied, among other ways, through the independence of juries (which can acquit, regardless of law and evidence), through relief for "mitigating" circumstances, and through flexibility and discretion in sentencing. The last have recently come under attack.

10. Compare Mr. Justic Harlan in *Banco Nacional de Cuba v. Sabbatino*, 376 U.S. 398, 423 (1964): ". . . the public law of nations can hardly dictate to a country which is in theory wronged how to treat that wrong within its domestic borders."

The League of Nations did indeed prescribe responses as, for example, in Article 16, providing that, in the event of aggression, the members were to sever relations with the offending state. The League's experience with that Article persuaded the drafters of the U.N. Charter to leave the response for determination by organs of the United Nations, principally the Security Council.

In some kinds of treaties it is important to prescribe how the parties will respond to the actions of others. The North Atlantic Treaty, for example, sought to make the obligation of all to fight in the common defense as unambiguous and automatic as possible, in order to enhance security and to increase the treaty's deterrent influence upon an aggressor.

11. Kennan, *American Diplomacy*, pp. 100–101. Compare H. Morgenthau, *In Defense of the National Interest* 101–02 (1951) [hereinafter cited as Morgenthau, *National Interest*].

12. This emerges more clearly in Mr. Kennan's later lectures, *e.g.*, in his discussion of the arbitration treaties. Kennan, *Realities*, pp. 18–19. See also D. Acheson, *Morning and Noon* 121–22 (1965).

13. H. Morgenthau, "Diplomacy," 55 *Yale L. J.* 1067, 1078 (1946) [hereinafter cited as "Diplomacy"].

14. *Id.*; see also Morgenthau, *National Interest*, pp. 101–02.

15. "Diplomacy," p. 1080.

16. H. Morgenthau, *Dilemmas of Politics* 73 (1958) [hereinafter cited as Morgenthau, *Dilemmas*].

17. In different contexts Professor Morgenthau has looked at the law more broadly. For example, in the jurisprudential article, he rejects the "positivist" in favor of a "functional" approach to international law. Morgenthau, *Dilemmas*, pp. 210–35.

18. Morgenthau, *National Interest*, p. 144. Compare "Diplomacy," p. 1080. Professor Morgenthau has written perceptively in defense of the national interest and one should not quarrel with his basic principle that nations do—and must—act in the "national interest." The question remains, how does one see the national interest? Morgenthau would define it in terms of "power politics." One need not wholly disagree; power and politics, their purposes and uses, may be conceived differently. Whatever may be said about other countries or about the United States at other times, the question is whether considerations of "power politics" really afford a meaningful guide to determine the national interest in most issues that face the United States as it moves into the last decades of the twentieth century.

19. Professor Morgenthau suggests that the Soviet Union correctly so calculated in regard to Hungary in 1956; he may be interpreted as suggesting that the United States might well have so calculated and acted more forcefully at the Bay of Pigs. H. Morgenthau, "To Intervene or Not to Intervene," 45 *Foreign Affairs* 425, 431 (1967).

Compare my suggestion that the *fait accompli* is a tempting form of violation, Chapter 3, p. 71.

20. Jurisprudentially, the result might be justified in various ways. One might suggest that, as a matter of interpretation of relevant principles or provisions, those called upon to determine the law should adopt an interpretation that avoids an absurd result. One might suggest that an amendment in the law was being achieved by a new informal consensus of nations. Or one might say that the law, always dynamic, is, in fact, or has become other than had previously been thought, with the action in this instance and the reaction of the community both contributing to the process that achieved the change.

21. In his later lectures, Mr. Kennan suggests a distinction which is not fully explained: "In particular, let us not assume that the *purposes* of states, as distinct from the methods, are fit subjects for measurement in moral terms." Kennan, *Realities*, p. 47.

22. A. Hamilton, "Pacificus No. IV," in 4 *The Works of Alexander Hamilton* 460, 464 (H. Lodge ed., 1904).

23. *Id.* at 461.

24. I do *not* dismiss dedicated, imaginative efforts like G. Clark and L. Sohn's *World Peace Through World Law* (1958), which were not pressed as immediate programs, but which served important educative functions.

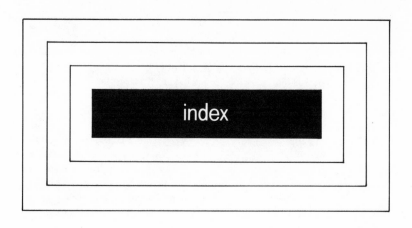

index

Intervention, 18, 80, 146, 287; African, 152, 157, 159–60, 162; by Communist states, 150–51, 161; and "counterintervention," 158; and ideological conflict, 157–59; indirect aggression, 156, 177; law against, 154; law as deterrent to, 162–64; and new nations, 147, 151, 153, 157, 162, 198; "preemptive," 158; and U.N. Charter, 155–56, 160, 174–76; in Vietnam, 146, 157, 160, 304–309
Iran, 133, 153, 167
Iraq, 153, 182
Israel, 16, 53, 145, 151, 184; and Eichmann case, 44, 58, 269–78, 378; Sinai war, 258–62; special reasons for law observance by, 260–61, 274; and Suez Canal, 260, 261

Jessup, Philip, 342
Johnson, Lyndon, 305
Joint ventures, 130
Jordan, 259
Jurisdiction, compulsory, 124n; prescriptive, 271

Kaplan, M., x, 341–42
Kashmir, 16, 17, 46, 122, 146, 147, 148, 167, 170–71
Katzenbach, N., x, 341–42
Kellogg-Briand Pact, 136, 137
Kennan, George, 322; on diplomacy vs. law, 326–27; and law against force, 324–26; and "legalistic-moralistic" approach, 3, 323–24, 327–28, 387; quoted, 322–33, 384–85

Kennedy, John F., 111, 279, 280, 281, 285, 292–93
Kennedy, Robert F., 280, 286n
Khrushchev, Nikita, 111, 115, 283
Korea, 16, 43, 110, 309; North, 71, 168
Korean Armistice Agreement, lessons of, 77–79, 81–82
Korean War, 43, 57, 73, 114, 138, 150–51, 167, 242n, 326, 328

Laos, 305, 308
Latin America, nuclear free zone, 104
Law, international: of "abstention," 20n, 21; acceptance of, 29–32, 88–98, 122; agendas for, 189–91, 194–98; attitudes toward, 2–4, 9–11; benefits of, 29; change in, 5, 100–101, 106–107, 122–25; and common policy, 90n; compliance with, 5, 23 (see also Law observance, Violation); consensus and, 23, 89–90; of cooperation, 20–21; criminal, 90n; criticisms of, 24–27, 88–89, 322–33; customary, 23, 29, 33–35, 123–24, 179; depreciation of, 88–97, 322–33; deterrent effect of, 94–95; diplomat's view of, 3; economic, traditional, 200–202, 203, 209–10, 226–27; enforcement of, 24; European origins, 121–22; failures to make, 37–38; against force, see Internal war, Law against the use of force; and foreign policy, 6, 39–45, 49–53, 245–49; laissez-faire vs. welfare, 199, 206, 209–10,

Date Due

MAR 2 3 1981			
JAN 2 8 '93			
FEB 1 5 '93			
FEB 27 '93			
MAR 16 '93			
APR 5 '93			
APR 1 9 '93			
MAY 05 '93			